PLEASURES IN SOCIALISM

PLEASURES IN

SOCIALISM

Leisure and Luxury

in the Eastern Bloc

Edited and with an introduction by

David Crowley and Susan E. Reid

NORTHWESTERN UNIVERSITY PRESS

EVANSTON, ILLINOIS

Northwestern University Press
www.nupress.northwestern.edu

Copyright © 2010 by Northwestern University Press. Published 2010. All rights reserved.

Printed in the United States of America

10 9 8 7 6 5 4 3 2 1

ISBN 978-0-8101-2871-2

The Library of Congress has cataloged the original, hardcover edition as follows:

Pleasures in socialism : leisure and luxury in the Eastern Bloc / edited and with an introduction by David Crowley and Susan E. Reid.
    p. cm.
Includes bibliographical references.
ISBN 978-0-8101-2690-9 (cloth : alk. paper)
1. Leisure—Social aspects—Europe, Eastern—History—20th century.
2. Luxuries—Social aspects—Europe, Eastern—History—20th century.
3. Consumption (Economics)—Europe, Eastern—History—20th century.
4. Europe, Eastern—Social life and customs—20th century. 5. Socialism and culture—Europe, Eastern—History—20th century. I. Crowley, David, 1966–
II. Reid, Susan Emily.
GV118.E852P58 2010
306.481'2094—dc22

2010012860

CONTENTS

ACKNOWLEDGMENTS

The editors would like to express their thanks to the Program on East European Cultures and Societies and the Faculty of Humanities of the Norwegian University of Science and Technology for supporting the cost of illustrations in this volume. Anne Gorsuch offered advice, for which the editors are grateful. We also thank Cornell University Press for allowing revised chapters from Paulina Bren's forthcoming book, *The Greengrocer and His TV: The Culture of Communism After the 1968 Prague Spring*, and Kristin Roth-Ey's new study, *Soviet Culture in the Media Age*, to appear in this volume. Susan Reid would like to acknowledge the AHRC for a Research Leave award.

PLEASURES IN SOCIALISM

Exercises at miners' sanatorium in the Black Sea resort of Sochi, Soviet Union, 1963

Introduction: Pleasures in Socialism?

David Crowley and Susan E. Reid

Command Happiness and Pleasures Taken

What is the place of pleasure in socialism? More precisely, what can a study of pleasure contribute to our historical understanding of "real existing socialism" as experienced in the countries of Central and Eastern Europe between the end of the Second World War and the crumbling of the Soviet Bloc? After all, these are best known as societies of shortage in which the state exercised "dictatorship over needs."[1] To make pleasure and, specifically, leisure and luxury the focus of a study of state socialist society and culture might seem a perverse or, at best, trivial undertaking.

This was not, however, a world without pleasure. Nor was it one in which authority eschewed interest in its production and modes of consumption. Pleasure was integral to the utopian promise of communism, based as it was on notions of future abundance and fulfillment. But to speak of "socialist pleasures," as if such pleasures as were taken reproduced the state's ideology or were the direct and intended product of planning, is problematic. Soviet musicals of the Stalin era such as Grigorii Aleksandrov's *Spring* (*Vesna*, 1947) were, of course, intentionally amusing, complete with song and dance routines, glamour, and spectacle, even as they projected messages about "politically correct" behavior or the moral superiority of socialism over capitalism. Later, in the 1960s and 1970s, such cinematic pleasures were supplemented by televisual ones. Soap operas set in supermarkets and panel-housing estates, as well as spy thrillers and detective series, engaged the free time and fantasy of citizens of the Bloc. Although ethical, social, and ideological messages of enlightenment continued to be woven into popular entertainment, it is debatable to what extent the pleasure it gave was "socialist" in the sense that the viewer derived his or her pleasure from the ideological content.[2]

Pleasure is an elusive phenomenon. As an emotional state, it is seemingly immaterial and ahistorical. For the purpose of analysis in the specific conditions of Eastern European state socialism, we may draw a provisional distinction between happiness and joy, on the one hand, and pleasure and enjoyment, on the other. The citizens of the Soviet Union and its allied states were represented in official ideology as the most joyful people on Earth. Optimism was a statutory requirement of socialist realist aesthetics, as numerous novels, films, and paintings of the Stalin era exemplified.[3] Conversely, pessimism became a crime against progress. Advancing toward utopia, Eastern Bloc states claimed to be fulfilling the Enlightenment pursuit of happiness through the exercise of reason. In the name of achieving the greatest happiness for the greatest number in the radiant future, the official value system generally emphasized asceticism and self-denial in the present, along with industrial production, international security, and the rule of rationality and planning. Joy was, in this context, a kind of abstracted, disembodied higher goal. Meanwhile, the satisfaction of everyday, individual, and ephemeral needs associated with bodily gratification was often inadequately provided for by the party-state, which perpetuated—and imposed on the masses—the revolutionary intelligentsia's traditional disdain for "petit bourgeois" material comfort and suspicion of sensuality.

The image of compulsory happiness, official optimism, and highly regulated leisure—which was both part of the authorized self-representation of these regimes and often taken at face value by outside observers—cannot tell us what people actually did or how they experienced such places and events. The time off work granted by the state was used not—or not solely—for demonstrations of loyalty to the regime and accession to its definition of joy, or for purposeful recreation of body and mind. It was also spent in less edifying pleasures, such as feasting and drinking with friends and family, for indulgence, play, relaxation, and enjoyment. The spaces given by the state for the people's constructive recreation were also used in ways that were not necessarily coterminous with their intended purpose. Take the Parks of Culture and Rest, for example, an institution laced with lofty, civilizing ideals introduced in Moscow in the 1920s and brought to the new People's Republics of Central Europe in the course of their Sovietization as evidence of progress in the late 1940s.[4] In the more remote regions of Moscow's Gorky Park couples would roam for illicit sex, or a group of men

Young people partying in the woods, Soviet Union, 1963

might share a bottle of vodka. Meanwhile, Black Sea sanatoriums, intended for healthy rest, were associated in popular mythology in the Soviet Union with sexual adventure.[5]

While happiness and pleasure were different, they were not necessarily mutually exclusive. After all, participation in highly valorized activities such as a May Day parade or labor competition did not necessarily preclude pleasure, even if the pleasures taken did not coincide with the official intention.[6] Pleasure, whether sanctioned or not, cannot be compelled, planned, or even fully regulated. Whatever the conditions and the resources at hand, it is always produced in and by the subject. It can even be found in the most desperate of circumstances and in the smallest of things. Ethnography provides examples of the small pleasures that may be found in hard times. Nancy Ries, in her study of Russian conversation during the period of perestroika, describes the perverse pleasures to be found in shopping even in conditions of shortage. She cites one Muscovite who loved "the peacefulness of standing in line, and the thrill of maybe getting something at the end."[7] However exceptional voices of this kind might be, they remind us that attitudes toward such matters as poverty or income distribution are subjective.[8]

Pleasure, understood in these terms, also has the potential to cast light on one of the much-discussed and most problematic conceptual frameworks used in many analyses of Eastern European life under communist rule: the public-private dichotomy.[9] Control over one's environment and its boundaries, access to secluded space or mobility—a separate apartment, a dacha, a car—which allowed one to choose the pleasure of one's own company, were not, in themselves, guarantees of pleasure.[10] But their denial could cause distress. Moreover, pleasurable withdrawal might take place within the most public of settings—in the Parks of Culture and Rest or Black Sea sanatoriums as suggested above—or in the darkened space of the cinema while the newsreels played.

To prioritize the concept of pleasure is to insist on some degree of agency on the part of the subject. Pleasure—as a concept that encapsulates voluntary and sometimes irrational and unregulated behavior and attitudes—emphasizes subjective experience. Understood in these terms, pleasure could be a wayward aspect of everyday life in an environment that claimed to be governed by collective reason and consciousness rather than spontaneity. The fantastic, psychological, and physiological aspects of pleasure have been emphasized by many writers in terms of the "pleasure principle" or "*jouissance*."[11] Typically, such psychosexual interpretive schemata represent seemingly universal experiences taking place within abstracted, even ahistorical bodies. There may be merits in stressing the common dimensions of pleasure across geography and time. But history requires historicity. Accordingly, the contributors to this volume were invited to explore two fields in which pleasure was both materialized and subject to wide public scrutiny: leisure and luxury. Our focus is on the concrete historical conditions in which pleasure was produced and taken, and on the specific historical practices and experiences of pleasure in postwar Eastern European state socialism.

How to historicize pleasure? And to what sources should the historian turn in order to write its histories? It need hardly be said that fleeting pleasures such as a summer night in a park orchestrated around a bottle of vodka leave little immediate material or textual trace beyond, perhaps, a few glass shards upon whose ritual significance some future archaeologist might ponder. Thus they mark a cognitive limit for the historian. From the outset it is important to stress that the ways, places, and times in which pleasure could be taken during the historical period of state socialism in Europe were delimited or structured, if not determined, by material, spatial, ideological, and legislative frameworks. Production priorities, the economic plan, allocation of space, pricing policies, the length of the working day, the pensionable retirement age, all set limits on what pleasures could or could not be taken, where and when, and, ultimately, on who could enjoy them. How citizens

chose to spend their leisure time or consume luxury commodities were matters of considerable state interest, not least in terms of how to manage these
activities. If pleasures could not be dictated, they were nonetheless subject
to regulation and constraint. Legislation, pricing structures and tax regimes,
authorized discourses, infrastructure, and access to material equipment or
space—whether in the form of sports facilities, cinemas, or countryside for
camping, rambling, and hunting—all combined to define what were (or
were not) "legitimate" or "normal" forms of pleasure. Other pleasures had
to be taken against the grain or gleaned in the interstices of the working
day, involving significant resourcefulness and sometimes the transgression
of limits that were set in law.

To acquire the material resources of pleasure frequently entailed activity in the second economy, since this was in many cases the only source of
commodities and services that were in short supply or disregarded by the
central planning agencies.[12] It also required the careful cultivation and de-
ployment of social networks, as well as the appropriation of time from the
workplace or from sanctioned forms of leisure.[13] The pleasures which official discourses defined as "legitimate" or "illegitimate" were not constant sets
of artifacts and activities; the content of these categories varied significantly
in different parts of the Bloc and changed over the course of its forty-year
history. The interests and desires of ordinary citizens were also subject to
change. Although not necessarily directly determined by official sanctions
and policies, they varied in response to evolving material and social conditions and shifting horizons of knowledge and expectation.

How, then, to gauge the effects of this fugitive phenomenon, pleasure?
The categories of leisure and luxury can serve, we propose, as two such
indices. Leisure and luxury constituted key contexts in which pleasure was
apprehended. Moreover, leisure and luxury have left traces that can be written into history, in the form of artifacts, spaces, discourses, and legislation.
Viewed abstractly, luxury and leisure seem like distinct analytical categories.
But considered in terms of experience and material traces, they often over-
lap. Tobacco, alcohol, pornography, and television—the subjects of some
of the essays in this book—are all commodities that have been resources
for leisure, consumed at moments of rest. At the same time, they have, in
different times and places, all been classed as luxuries in the sense that they
serve *wants* rather than meeting *needs*—concepts which are inevitably understood in terms of, and are contingent upon, the sumptuary, moral, and
ideological frameworks of the societies in which they have been produced
and consumed. This corresponds to a classical definition of luxury advanced
in many analyses from Plato onward, according to which distinctions can be
drawn between necessary and unnecessary desires.[14] Moreover, such com-

modities point to a further feature of luxury that has been described by Colin Campbell as the capacity to promote "sensuous or pleasurable experience." As he points out, mundane things can become luxuries in particular conditions: "One may contrast a 'luxury item' with a 'basic necessity,' but to 'luxuriate,' for example in a hot bath, is to contrast a rich sensuous and pleasuring experience with an ordinary, unstimulating or unpleasant one."[15] In other words, ostensibly ordinary things, consumed in moments of leisure or in conditions that render them special, *can* produce a heightened sense of pleasure.

In this volume, the authors reflect on the ways in which leisure and luxury were produced in the conditions of Soviet-style socialism between the late 1940s and the end of communist rule. They do so in terms of the dynamic relations between ideology, policy, and the material environment, on one hand, and the range of practices that characterized the consumption of leisure and luxury, on the other. Each essay approaches a particular national setting, for it is necessary to be attentive to ways in which the historical experience of leisure and luxury was shaped by varying historical and cultural experience, as well as by diverse material conditions across the Bloc that was formed after the Second World War. Only by bringing together scholarship that considers the historical experience of the different societies are we able to grasp both the differences and the similarities between these contexts. The contributions also represent different academic traditions, including anthropology, social history, and cultural studies. These fields, while distinguished by their preferred sources, concerns, and methods, share a common interest in the ways that the broad forces of ideology as well as economic and technical change are registered in everyday life. They also share a concern with the relation between social, economic, and ideological structures and the agency of the individual or social group in the production of their own pleasures. In so doing, many of our contributors have developed approaches to their subject matter that engage with subjectivity. Thus, György Péteri, a historian, has turned to an unorthodox body of materials to document a largely unrecorded history: that of elite hunting practices in Hungary in the 1960s. His sources include snapshots from his own family albums, that is, from a "private" resource that provides evidence that cannot be found in the official, public record of Kádár's Hungary. Narcis Tulbure and Anna Tikhomirova, in their chapters, combine anthropological approaches to their historical subject matter—the production and consumption of alcohol in Ceauşescu's Romania, and the meanings attached to fur garments in Russia since the 1960s. Through oral history and ethnographic interviews, they reveal how people engaged in consumption practices that were disparaged or proscribed. Writing history through testimonials of this kind is not without its oft-noted limitations, which are magnified by the continuing controversy attached to the memory of and, in particular, nostalgia for socialism in the region.[16] This notwithstanding, it is important to gather and reflect on such unrecorded sources while the people involved are still alive and their memories can be recorded.

To historicize pleasure the authors were also encouraged to treat things— or what is sometimes called "material culture"—as an important category of historical evidence in its own right. Objects are far from mute. They are capable of embodying values in their forms and signifying meanings in their usage.[17] Things can "speak" even when the people who use, inhabit, or even destroy them are silenced. This book is thus, in part, a contribution to the writing of what anthropologist Victor Buchli has called "the archaeology of socialism."[18] In this regard, perhaps a lesson can be learned from Slavoj Žižek. Power is inscribed with contradictions, which he describes as "imps of perversity."[19] That which is ostensibly repressed by an "ideological edifice" returns, not as political rhetoric nor even in the parapraxes of speech, but in the form of things; it is articulated, that is, in "the externality of its material existence."[20] The artifacts and spaces of leisure and luxury in the Bloc were just such "imps of perversity" that materialize repressed contradictions. In the historical and concrete manifestations of leisure and luxury, many of the paradoxes of state socialism are revealed. In this book, these include state-published pornography in East Germany, a society which trumpeted the liberation of women; "people's cars" which could only be acquired with extraordinary investment of time and money; and tiers of Soviet shops which served different classes of consumers in a "classless society." Such materializations of socialist leisure and socialist luxury can be read to reveal the particular form of modern civilization that constituted the Bloc.

State Socialism Found Wanting: Shortage and Consumption

The dominant paradigm for the analysis of ordinary people's everyday experience—both material and subjective—of state socialism has not been luxury, leisure, and pleasure, but on the contrary, *need, command,* and *shortage.* Reports of life in the Eastern Bloc have conventionally been framed in terms of uniformity, grayness, and the ubiquitous queue.[21] These themes were not the unique property of right-wing Cold War hawks. They have been core preoccupations of most writing on the Bloc, including the analyses produced by commentators on the left from the 1970s and, in recent years, by social historians writing after the collapse of Soviet socialism. We need only glance at the titles of some of the most important studies to confirm this:

Ferenc Fehér, Ágnes Heller, and György Márkus's *Dictatorship over Needs* (1983); János Kornai's *Economics of Shortage* (1980); Julie Hessler's innovative dissertation, "Culture of Shortages: A Social History of Soviet Trade, 1917–1953" (1996); Ina Merkel's *Utopia and Need* (*Utopie und Bedürfnis*) (1999); and Mariusz Jastrząb's *Empty Shelves: The Problem in the Provision of Everyday Goods in Poland, 1949–1956* (*Puste półki: Problem zaopatrzenia ludności w artykuły powszechnego użytku w Polsce w latach 1949–1956*) (2004).[22] It is axiomatic in much of this scholarship that consumption in state socialism was subordinated to the requirements of heavy industry and defense. Shortage and need have been deployed to explain a remarkable range of phenomena, thus becoming a governing paradigm of analyses of Soviet-style socialism and its collapse. In their controversial 1983 intervention, Fehér, Heller, and Márkus presented short supply and high demand not merely as incidental effects of state planning and its inefficiencies but as systemic instruments of control that maintained the hierarchies and structures of power.[23] Others have claimed shortage as a determinant of Eastern Bloc aesthetics, arguing, for example, that the modernist *Existenzminumum* apartments of the Khrushchev era owe their "efficient" forms and proportions to attempts to manage deficits.[24] Shortage has been considered by some as the source of social anomie and by others as a key ingredient in the social glue which bound the people together in opposition to the state.[25]

Our purpose is not to replace the gray-tinted glasses of Cold War observers or indigenous dissidents by rosy retro-spectacles. The persistence or—in the case of the more industrialized Central and Eastern European states, which before World War II had enjoyed a high standard of living—the *return* of shortage cannot be denied or ignored. The problem of "deficit" goods (those in inadequate supply) was encountered by the majority of citizens living in the Bloc in the course of everyday life. The indignity of having to buy toilet paper on the black market in Poland in the 1980s or the disappearance of meat from Soviet shops was amplified by the increasingly surreal claims of progress made by the state.[26] Ordinary citizens coped as best they could through various tactics: by always going out armed with a "just in case" bag (*avoska* in Russian) for chance purchases;[27] by hoarding and home-preserving; by hand-making and adapting; and by exchanging goods or services and exercising *blat* (pull) in the shadow economy.[28] Consumers also expressed their daily frustrations in various ways, ranging from carefully phrased petitions addressed to official institutions to explosive outbursts of rage.[29] Dissatisfaction with the low purchasing power of wages as well as with the uncertain supply of the most basic staple goods occasionally erupted into angry demonstrations, notably in East Germany and in Plzeň,

Czechoslovakia, in 1953, Novocherkassk in southern Russia in 1962, or the Hunger Marches in Łódź in 1981.[30] Regarding a world where people took to the streets to protest the unavailability of bread or price increases for staples such as meat or milk, and where such protests were brutally repressed, leisure and luxury may seem a misguided and historically irresponsible focus for analysis.

Yet there is no shortage of evidence that luxury goods and modern forms of leisure *were* produced and enjoyed in the Soviet Bloc. Sometimes luxuries were even produced in excess of demand and at the expense of necessities, creating the paradox of a glut of luxuries in what is often referred to as a shortage economy.[31] The consumption and gradual redefinition of luxury, along with access to particular forms of leisure, not only by a privileged few but increasingly by the masses, together mark one of the most fundamental yet still widely overlooked historical changes that took place in the period studied in this volume: beginning in the late 1950s and 1960s, the countries of socialist Eastern Europe became mass consumer societies. The process was not inexorable, nor was the pace uniform across the Bloc; by the end of the 1960s, the East Germans, Hungarians, and Czechs, as well as citizens in nonaligned Yugoslavia, were coming to enjoy the reputation of being the most affluent citizens of state socialism (particularly in comparison with their comrades in the central Asian Soviet republics).

By the late 1970s the transition had taken place even in Soviet Russia. For wide and growing sections of the population, having a dacha or *chata,* having the leisure time to enjoy a holiday there, and possessing a car to drive there, became "reasonable" expectations.[32] Likewise, wearing fashionable clothes or perfume, dining out in restaurants under gilded chandeliers, and celebrating with champagne—once the preserve of the rich and privileged few—came to seem normal aspirations for the many by the 1970s, that is, "common" or "democratic luxuries" for special occasions, if not for every day. Moreover, entirely new categories of goods and experiences—televisions, private automobiles, refrigerators, foreign holidays—began to be acquired and enjoyed by ordinary citizens.[33]

Can the existence, indeed, the centrally planned production of such commodities and services simply be dismissed as tokens of a Potemkin modernity, that is, as ideological facades that obscured the "true" nature of socialist rule dominated by austerity and work? Such characterizations have had the effect of maintaining unassailed a constitutive Cold War distinction, according to which Soviet-type societies continue to function as the antithesis of Western modernity. If mass consumerism is a—or perhaps *the*—defining aspect of modernity in the capitalist West, as many scholars

Window-shopping in Warsaw in 1960

concur, the socialist Other in the East was excluded a priori from this experience: it was tacitly assumed that communist countries could not, by definition, be consumer societies.[34] Leisure and luxury have thus been at once accommodated and marginalized within a conceptual apparatus that excludes state socialism from modernity. For the purpose of analysis, in the following section we will distinguish two chief characterizations of leisure and luxury which have effectively underpinned Western Cold War paradigms for understanding life in Eastern Bloc societies: first, as a privilege reserved for an elite which, as a correspondent of shortage, maintained social hierarchies and relationships of domination; and second, as a safety valve or palliative that served to maintain the status quo.

Privileges and Palliatives

Luxury, insofar as its existence in state socialism has been addressed at all, has primarily been characterized in terms of privilege enjoyed by the ruling elite at the expense of the majority. Such representations have often been sharply polemical, written by the enemies of communism or by left-wing critics of the existing socialist regimes. Writing in 1936, Leon Trotsky in *The Revolution Betrayed* identified the formation of an elite class in Stalin's Russia marked by privileged access to consumer goods:

> One of the very clear, not to say defiant, manifestations of inequality is the opening in Moscow and other big cities of special stores with high-quality articles under the very expressive, although not very Russian, designation of "Luxe." At the same time ceaseless complaints of mass robbery in the food shops of Moscow and the provinces, mean that foodstuffs are adequate only for the minority . . .
> Granted that margarine and *makhorka* [cheap tobacco] are today unhappy necessities. Still it is useless to boast and ornament reality. Limousines for the "activists," fine perfumes for "our women," margarine for the workers, stores "de luxe" for the gentry, a look at delicacies through the store windows for the plebs—such socialism cannot but seem to the masses a new re-facing of capitalism, and they are not far wrong. On a basis of "generalized want," the struggle for the means of subsistence threatens to resurrect "all the old crap," and is partially resurrecting it at every step.[35]

The most strident accusations of communist avarice often came from revisionist Marxists. Identifying what he called "the new class," in 1959 former high-ranking Yugoslav communist Milovan Djilas wrote that "in Communism, power or politics is the ideal of those who have the desire or the prospect of living as parasites at the expense of others."[36] Similarly, a former Polish United Workers' Party member and latterly a strong critic of the regime, Kazimierz Brandys, writing in 1980, the year of Solidarity's sharp rise in Poland, identified the spread of what he ironically dubbed "classless luxury."[37] The private villas, hunting grounds, swimming pools, and exquisite kitchens acquired by the ruling cadres at the expense of the majority were material evidence of acute social distinctions in what was supposed to be a classless society.

Privilege has also been a key analytical tool of historical analyses of social stratification in Soviet-type societies. Vera Dunham, in her pioneering study of Soviet literature in the late Stalin period, coined the term "Big Deal" to describe the tacit contract between the regime and technical specialists and senior managers in the hungry years after 1945. Under the unspoken terms of the Big Deal, the regime agreed to provide this vital group with material comforts in return for supporting its efforts to build socialism, for "loyalty to the leader, unequivocal nationalism, reliable hard work, and professionalism."[38] Thus a narrow tier came to enjoy concessions unavailable to the broad masses, such as spacious single-family apartments, housemaids, access to a chauffeur-driven car, and free trips to Black Sea sanatoriums. The Big Deal was a symptom of a larger cultural turn in the Soviet Union that had begun in the mid-1930s but which was consolidated after the war, whereby social stability was valued over the Leninist project of social transformation, and the private interests of a few were indulged at the expense of the living standards of the many.[39]

One of the important contrasts between the Stalin years and the Khrushchev period, both in the Soviet Union and in its Eastern European satellites, is the way in which the needs of the majority began to be addressed. A crisis of legitimacy followed Stalin's death and Khrushchev's 1956 denunciation of his "excesses," manifested as a wave of anger and criticism that climaxed in the Hungarian Uprising. In response, the post-Stalinist regimes throughout the Bloc extended what are conventionally described as "concessions" to their populations, seeing improvements in living conditions as a means to shore up support and reclaim legitimacy. Khrushchev and his allies in the Kremlin interpreted the causes of the Polish and Hungarian uprisings not primarily as political demands for greater personal freedom but as protests against poor living standards, and feared that mass disorder could erupt in the Soviet Union, too, for the same reasons.[40] The events of 1956 in the satellites thus lent added urgency to the reorientation of Soviet economic priorities toward raising the material well-being of Soviet workers, which had begun already in 1953. Soviet living standards had to be improved to forestall political conflict, to reclaim the legitimacy of state socialism, and to inject credibility into claims—intensified in the conditions of Cold War "peaceful competition"—that central state planning would provide a better life than either free market capitalism or the mixed economies of social democratic states.

To make these claims a reality—and not only for the few but for the many—a significant reorientation of the command economy toward the mass production and distribution of consumer goods took place in the Soviet Union and its satellites. Post-Stalinist regimes built the material and

ideological conditions for a relatively rapid growth in consumption and
the production of socialist consumer culture. Improved social security and
a reduced working week set new conditions for life. The cornerstone of attempts to improve the conditions of life was the massive housing programs
initiated throughout Eastern Europe. These stimulated, in turn, the demand
for consumer goods such as domestic furniture and appliances.

What was the deal now, after the watershed years of the mid-1950s? If,
in the late Stalin period, a degree of "private" life and material benefits had
been afforded to a narrow sector of the population in exchange for loyalty,
what was demanded in return for the extended range of goods and services,
now that these were supposed to be accessible to all? It must be stressed that
during the Khrushchev period, the extension of mass consumption in the
Soviet Union coexisted with concerted efforts to reinvigorate mass political activism; the promise of Soviet socialism demanded *both* the political
mobilization of the masses *and* full refrigerators.[41] Mass consumption was
a socialist project alongside other large-scale Khrushchevist visions including the Virgin Lands program, the reform of Party organizational structures, and the voluntary espousal of "communist morality." Above all, the
post-Stalinist leadership sought to increase the production levels of Soviet
industry to raise living standards. Elsewhere in the Bloc, post-Stalinist regimes launched major projects to demonstrate their command of modern
technology in prestigious fields like nuclear power generation and high-
rise housing, alongside political reforms such as the initiation of (short-
lived) worker councils.[42] In the course of the 1960s and 1970s, however,
the two-pronged approach—predicated both on mass consumption *and* on
socialist construction and political mobilization—was replaced by a new
kind of contract based on political passivity, acquiescence, and a ritualized
semblance of support.[43] This was perhaps most evident in the period of
"normalization" in Czechoslovakia following the suppression of the political reforms of the Prague Spring.[44] Václav Havel, writing in 1978, described
this uneasy contract in succinct terms when he wrote, "The post-totalitarian
system has been built on foundations laid by the historical encounter between dictatorship and the consumer society."[45]

The ordinary consumer—and no longer the outstanding individual
Stakhanovite worker, or technical specialist favored by the Big Deal—came,
after the Stalin years, to occupy the hallowed place in consumption politics
and representation. As Khrushchev would brag to Richard Nixon in 1959,
when faced with the American dream home implanted on Soviet soil as an
advertisement for "people's capitalism": "In Russia all you have to do to get a
house is to be born in the Soviet Union. You are entitled to housing."[46] Bluff
aside, such claims indicated a legitimate horizon of expectations. Moreover,

in constantly trumpeting production statistics in fields such as housing and consumer goods to underpin the slogan that the Soviet Union would imminently "catch up and overtake America," the party-state set suburban, white American living standards as the ambitious benchmark against which Soviet success was to be measured.

Such rhetoric was inflationary. Goods and services that had once seemed like luxuries came, within a decade, to be considered normal or commonplace, particularly by those without memory of the grinding poverty of the 1930s and the war years. As early as 1959 Edward Crankshaw, writing about the attitudes of young people in Khrushchev's Russia, detected a shift in their horizon of expectations:

> They are taking for granted certain material improvements which still fill their elders with delight—though with less delight than one might expect: memories are short, and the appetite grows with feeding ... Ten years ago they would have given their eyes to see in the shops what can now be seen every day. Now they grumble because all these undreamt-of things are so dear that they cannot all be bought simultaneously.[47]

Much the same point was made by Paul Neuburg in his 1973 survey of youth attitudes in the People's Republics.[48] The post-Stalinist regimes which took power in these states in the mid-1950s also addressed the appalling living conditions that still prevailed a decade after the end of the Second World War. During the late 1950s and 1960s commentators first pointed to "goulash socialism" and then to its "refrigerator," "car," and even "weekend cottage" variants, such was the inflationary push and pull of provision and expectation.[49] Such possessions, hitherto "undreamt-of" even by the elite, slipped down the hierarchy of things to become necessities of modern urban life.

By the late 1980s, these same citizens had come to understand themselves as frustrated consumers unable to command goods and services to which they had a right. That state socialism had engendered expectations it could not satisfy may well have had a critical, even decisive effect on the fate of the common project of the Bloc. It is fast becoming orthodoxy in analyses of the failure of Soviet-type socialism in Europe that it was caused by the late socialist regimes' inability to match goods to promises and reality to the aspirations they raised through their own pronouncements, and by the failure to balance consumer interests with those of the military-industrial complex.[50] Yet if the system was as fraught with contradictions as is widely charged, would it not be more illuminating to ask: how did it survive as long as it did? Any analysis of the Eastern Bloc that is built on shortage or command alone is ill-equipped to explain its endurance—and indeed much else about the experience of living under state socialism.

To understand socialist modernity better we need to investigate the specificity of socialist consumerism. This requires a more dynamic understanding of the relations of shortage to entitlement, of need to want, and of necessity to luxury. Except in the most abject circumstances, "shortage" is a relative, culturally ascribed, historically contingent term. We must, then, be historically specific. Against what norm or horizon of expectations were shortages, as experienced in Eastern Bloc societies, defined? Where, when, and how did people acquire their sense of what constituted "normal" entitlements to leisure and consumer goods? What role was played by the awareness of lifestyles in the West or, for that matter, other parts of the Bloc? What impact did travel and tourism, both within the Bloc and through the "Iron Curtain," have on ordinary expectations of life? What were the social and political effects of periodic attempts to introduce "market socialism" and make the economy more responsive to consumer demand?[51] And what new needs and entitlements were produced by attempts to manage social expectations through the introduction of rational consumption norms at different times in different places in the history of the Bloc?[52] These questions cannot be dealt with exhaustively here. All require further research in the diverse national contexts of the Bloc. In what follows we shall examine the dynamic relationship between luxury and modern consumer goods in state socialism before turning to the effects of leisure in socialist societies.

Modern Luxuries in Socialist Lives

Luxury is neither a static category whose content is fixed nor an essential quality inhering in particular objects. Rather, it is dynamic and historically contingent. It is determined by changes in technology and the mode of production, shaped by ideological preoccupations and discourses, and managed through resource allocation, pricing policies, or tax regimes, all of which in turn reflect state priorities. It is also defined through popular attitudes and horizons of information and comparison.[53] It can operate in many different keys, conjured up in bacchanalian displays of abundance as well as in subtle, even highly coded, measures of refinement and assertions of taste. The practices which have shaped luxury have historically contained strong, if sometimes suppressed, moral imperatives. In her contribution to this volume, Ina Merkel explores the paradoxes of luxury in the German Democratic Republic (GDR). Luxury was written into socialist economics in the form of differentiated pricing categories and classes of shops, thereby contradicting claims to an egalitarian, classless society. Tapping the savings of East German citizens, relatively expensive, up-market stores selling branded goods and high-quality foodstuffs were presented and justified as a mechanism for ensuring general prosperity.[54] The revenue they drew from wealthy pockets would be reinvested for the benefit of all. Such explanations could not, however, explain away the social distinctions the availability of such luxuries exaggerated. Although these high-end stores were presented as a short-term measure, they became a permanent feature of the retail environment of East Germany. Over the years such structured distinctions, as Merkel demonstrates, came to seem normal.

The systemic and long-term failure of Soviet Bloc economies made the production of "luxury" goods like cigarettes, "exclusive" foodstuffs such as caviar, and, of course, distilled liquor a necessity of a particular kind: the export of such products was one of the few ways in which hard currency income could be ensured. Export goods were another face of socialist luxury. As Mary Neuburger notes in her discussion of the manufacture and consumption of cigarettes in Bulgaria, tobacco was made into a vital national product that could be exchanged on international markets for tractors, machinery, and other capital goods, which would ensure that socialism could be built. At the same time, Georgi Dimitrov, Bulgaria's first communist leader, encouraged abstention at home: tobacco smoking was represented, in the early years of socialist rule, as a Western affliction. However, over the course of the 1950s and 1960s, as Neuburger shows, the consumption of cigarettes came to be seen as the birthright of socialist workers. The ordinariness of this product was written into policy when, in the early 1960s, tobacco was regarded by state economists as a staple feature of Bulgarian household budgets. Like the structural distinctions in East German retailing described by Merkel, cigarettes—with their bright packaging and showy brand names—came to be regarded as everyday pleasures.[55]

The processes by which erstwhile luxury was "normalized" comprise a key motor of modernity. Progress is often measured in the invention and distribution of things, not least in the "standard of living," a gauge by which material things are interpreted in ontological terms. In the Cold War contest of images of modernity and the good life, representations of socialist abundance were accompanied by another trope to argue the superiority of state socialism over capitalism: that of redistribution.[56] Furs, champagne, palaces, and hunting were persistent motifs in communist discourse throughout the history of Eastern European socialism for precisely this reason. For the Bolsheviks in revolutionary Russia, the presence of such things in the real and imagined lives of the tsarist aristocracy and as markers of foreign capitalist decadence had provided a rich reservoir of images of selfish luxury

against which their own asceticism could be positively judged. But such
things acquired a different valence in the 1930s; at that time, the Stalin
regime turned the accession of the people to forms of luxury that had once
been the preserve of the upper classes into a measure of progress. According
to Jukka Gronow in his groundbreaking book on Soviet luxury, *Caviar with
Champagne,* the presence of such traditional luxuries in the Soviet Union
in the 1930s can be explained by the rhetoric of democratization: their
consumption by Soviet citizens was to symbolize the redistributive power
of socialist economics.[57] The order of "aristocratic luxuries"—goods with
long and symbolic genealogies—required careful management by the state
and its ideologues to re-present these as "democratic" or "common luxuries."
Such negotiations continued throughout the history of the Soviet Union.
In her essay in this volume, Anna Tikhomirova addresses the networks and
semiotics of fur consumption in Brezhnev-era Russia. She establishes the
complex and subtly structured hierarchies in which fur coats, an expensive
and rare commodity, were ranked according to their material and their place
of origin. Her work is based on a large number of interviews with educated
women living in provincial cities. Most expressed their support for the core
principle of Soviet economics, the equitable distribution of common resources. Yet, at the same time, her informants viewed without bitterness the
privileged access to fur enjoyed by the *nomenklatura.* Reproducing in their
discourse the hierarchies and class differences that operated in late Soviet
society, they demonstrate the extent to which such benefits had come to be
seen as "natural" returns for talent or effort. Moreover, Tikhomirova's interviewees indicate that even as they coveted the elite lifestyles of actresses and
wives of leading Party members, unspoken "sumptuary codes" operated in
Soviet society, which ensured that some luxuries remained exclusive, limited
to elite social groups.

   While some traditional notions of luxury persisted in Eastern Europe
throughout the life of the communist system, new material distinctions
emerged. One category of luxury goods that gained new meaning in Eastern Europe consisted of commodities from the West. Crossing national
borders, they found new meanings in translation. Particular significance
was attached by ordinary citizens of the Bloc to everyday Western things,
including clothes, toiletries, foodstuffs, and long-playing records. The biographies of such things were diverse and included forms of aid such as the
United Nations Relief and Rehabilitation Administration parcels which
were distributed in Eastern Europe in the wake of the Second World War,[58]
contraband and other smuggled goods, and the goods on sale in special
hard currency shops.[59] Objects that were mundane in their original, capitalist context came to carry heightened significance not only because of

their rarity: the unfamiliar materials and seductive forms of Western consumer goods could trigger fantasies about capitalist civilization. Fantasy
came to play an important role in ordinary people's relations with things.
This was particularly acute in East Germany. By imagining life in the West
as more beautiful, satisfying, and substantial—a vision stimulated by the
ready access to West German media—citizens of the GDR could imagine
that the world in which they lived was somehow illusory and unreal. As
Milena Veenis has described, "All answers to, all alternatives for, and all
flights out of a daily life characterized by tensions between what is and
what appears to be, and what is supposed to be, could be transported to the
other side of the wall. There, they were attached to the material goods that
were such identificatory tropes for their countrymen but were at the same
time so elusive."[60]

Western goods also provided actual models for the socialist states to
adopt and adapt, in their attempts to demonstrate their hold on modernity.
The Khrushchev regime recognized as a legitimate social aspiration the
desire to have up-to-date and attractive clothes and to acquire new ones
not only when the old ones were worn out but in accordance with changing
fashion. To fill this need, Soviet experts turned to Western luxury fashion
for models of the best clothing production. Soviet fashion designers—as
Larissa Zakharova describes in her essay in this volume—went to Paris
in 1957, 1960, and 1965 to study the working methods of French haute
couture houses producing custom-made garments for the very rich. While
evidently fascinated by what they saw, these Soviet experts were unable
to transpose their findings onto the reality of Soviet garment production.
Fashion was a luxury which the Soviet clothing industry, oriented to mass
production and long production cycles, was ill-equipped to deliver. Moreover, the five-year succession of the state economic plan was hardly com-
mensurate with the seasonal cycles of haute couture. The achievements of
Soviet fashion were largely impressionistic, appearing as prototypes in fashion shows and as images on the pages of the embryonic fashion press in the
Soviet Union. The designs of Yves Saint-Laurent for Christian Dior did,
however, have a material impact on Soviet fashion, albeit in narrow social
circles. Zakharova traces the influence of his designs shown on a catwalk
in Moscow in 1959 on elite Soviet women who commissioned workshops
with suggestive names such as Liuks (Luxe) to make up garments in the
Dior style, sometimes in fabrics smuggled into the U.S.S.R. from the West.
In what appears to be a classic "trickle-down" pattern, Dior style was reproduced on the pages of the Soviet press, simulated by designers employed in
the official fashion institutes, popularized in films such as *Carnival Night*
(*Karnaval'naia noch'*, 1956, dir. El'dar Riazanov), copied by seamstresses

working in commercial ateliers, and ultimately imitated by home dress-makers. Emulation required adjustment to Soviet conditions; Dior's luxury fabrics were unavailable, and highly structured tailoring was not easy to reproduce by amateurs. It also required some negotiation of meaning. The final product of such cycles of style and taste was not a symbol of socialism; yet it resulted, albeit indirectly, from the tacit recognition by a socialist state that the desire to possess fashionable clothes was legitimate.

Fashionable clothes were not the only category of modern goods in which matters of style carried powerful symbolic associations. With indus-trial production and the increasing use of synthetic materials, entirely new categories of luxury unimagined by Marx, Lenin, or Trotsky (or even by the class enemy whose tastes they repudiated) emerged in the course of the Soviet experiment. Such modern luxuries, we suggest, have different origins, material characteristics, and social effects from their glittering forebears. The symbolic value of automobiles, refrigerators, televisions, tape recorders, and other modern consumer goods when they first appeared lay not only in their potential for democratization; their very forms and the materials from which they were made were crucially important too. Electronic components and synthetic materials like plastics, nylon, and synthetic fur, as well as their employment in novel designs or their status as representatives of modern technology in domestic everyday life, all staked a claim for the advanced na-ture of state socialism and its ability to benefit ordinary people, a claim that was particularly urgent in the context of Cold War "peaceful competition."[61] In science fiction films and novels of the period—a thriving Eastern Bloc genre—synthetics and electronics were projected into the zones of unfet-tered fantasy, thereby serving popular utopian dreams as well as ideology.[62]

Regimes of Socialist Consumption

The engagement with the material culture of capitalist modernity during the late 1950s and 1960s did not necessarily amount to an unequivocal surrender of socialist principles, contrary to the hopes and expectations of cold warriors that the popular appetite for consumer goods, once un-leashed, would destabilize the socialist order. Rather, the socialist regimes were engaged in a careful, if ultimately unsuccessful, balancing act. They sought ideologically legitimate ways to raise living standards and satisfy demand without triggering the unending process of demand generation and insatiable desire that was the original sin of consumerism in the capitalist West. As George Breslauer noted with reference to the Soviet Union, the regime needed simultaneously to meet and depress consumer expectations of current consumption.[63] The management of consumption played a par-

ticularly important role in the maintenance of power after Stalin's death.
New economic priorities were put in place in Kádár's Hungary after the
violent trauma of the events of October 1956, while in East Germany, the
movement of people, things, and (especially after the erection of what Ulbricht called his "antifascist protection wall" in August 1961) images of the
West German *Wirtschaftswunder* put socialism under pressure.[64] Regimes
across the region struggled to reconcile rising consumer expectations with
Marxist doctrine. The new, socialist person was supposed to possess a rational consciousness of the relation between his or her individual needs and
the greater good of the collective, to better serve the challenge of building communism.

Excess and extravagance became the object of a good deal of hostile
attention in the U.S.S.R. after Stalin's death. They were repudiated ex ca-
thedra by Khrushchev as early as December 1954, in relation to the elaborate architectural ornament and the use of artisanal, labor-intensive construction methods in late Stalinist architecture.[65] This was an early shot
in what was to become a new campaign for socialist modernity. Attacks
on overrefined luxury goods and superfluous ornament became widespread
in the Khrushchev-era Soviet Union. This was, in effect, a moral as well
as aesthetic discourse, which associated the Stalin years with "excess" and
waste. Overproduction of unwanted or poor-quality goods which failed to
meet demand and, as a consequence, sat gathering dust in warehouses or on
store shelves was also singled out as a symptom of Stalinist profligacy. In
the new climate, modern needs were now to be satisfied by applying rational
principles of economy and utility. The rational socialist consumer would
find pleasure in the beauty of utility. Armed with historical consciousness
and distinguished by civil self-discipline, she would limit her own potential
desires voluntarily within "rational consumption norms."[66]

Plain, simple, "functional" designs were valorized in post-Stalinist discussions of consumer goods, not least because they facilitated mass production.[67] A crucial distinction drawn by Khrushchev-era modernizers was
whether or not items could be made available en masse, in terms of their
design, mode of production, and materials. Synthetics such as man-made
fibers, plastics, and building materials were claimed as a new field of socialist achievement, capable of making the promise of abundance for all a
reality.[68] New types of scent that made use of the latest advances such as
synthetic oils, presented in vials with plastic stoppers and encased in synthetic velvet, were a modern, socialist solution to the "problem" of luxury.
Recuperated as both socialist and modern, they were reconstructed as a
democratic luxury that was a gift to all women from the solicitous state
in exchange for their labor and loyalty, while at the same time serving as

compensation for putting up with daily privations. The democratization of this luxury was made possible by modern science and industry: chemistry had freed the art of perfumery from reliance on precious oils and essences by synthesizing natural aromas. Modern synthetic scents such as "Sputnik" might not be as potent or enduring as those of the past, but they were affordable and available to the masses. And their production would, it was hoped, curb desire for—and black market trade in—French perfume.[69] As modern demonstrations of democratic luxury, industrially produced Soviet perfumes testified to the redistributive capacity of the command economy.[70] Such commodities, which had once been the prerogative of social elites, could now become the herald of future abundance for all. At the same time, they seemed to corroborate the party-state's claims that socialist science was uniquely positioned to benefit everyday life. That perfume—the most immaterial and inessential of commodities—had been allotted a place in the state economic plan at all may be less the product of policy than a consequence of unexamined assumptions on the part of planners and economists about what was needed for a modern, urbane lifestyle.

Certain "democratic luxuries," made widely available after the Thaw, never quite shook off their associations with individualism and acquisitiveness, however.[71] In 1960 the Soviet ideologue Georgii Shakhnazarov defined communist consumption morality precisely in these terms: "Communism excludes those narrow-minded people for whom the highest goal is to acquire every possible luxurious object."[72] In similar fashion, Marx's writings on the fetishistic relations that were characteristic of commodities under capitalism were invoked by Hungarian critics of "goulash socialism."[73] One Hungarian commentator, writing in 1961, outlined the threat to socialism in blunt terms:

> The desire to own personal goods is on the rise ... And, if the person achieves his desires, doesn't the fact that he locks himself up in his apartment with his television, that he is isolated from pedestrians when sitting in his car, blunt him into a petty bourgeois and a Philistine? Isn't the mentality of the petty bourgeois being reproduced in this television-automobile-weekend house-motorcycle lifestyle? ... Some would put it sharply: on one side there is television, automobile, foreign trips, hoop skirts, and on the other, declining interest in politics, languishing attention to the products of socialist culture, the revival of bourgeois morality, individuation.[74]

Discussing camping in East Germany in the 1960s and 1970s, Scott Moranda's essay in this volume examines the anxieties concerning com-

modity fetishism held by the authorities there. Camping equipment threatened to disturb the egalitarianism and ascetic idealism associated with this
leisure activity. With nature highly valorized in the official culture of the
German Democratic Republic, the comforts of modern life were to be kept
in check to ensure that "noble," and as such, properly socialist, relations to
nature could be experienced by East German citizens on holiday. Camping
enthusiasts, however, took a very different view, as Moranda shows, imagining the natural world as a type of outdoor "parlor" complete with modern
amenities and small luxuries. Camping in East Germany in the 1970s was
pulled two ways, between the earnest asceticism advocated by loyalists as a
distinctly socialist form of leisure, and the standards of comfort that others
demanded as a modern right for socialist citizens.

The "problem" of acquisitiveness was addressed during the Thaw in
other ways, too. In the Soviet Union, Khrushchev and his allies set great
ideological store by collective consumption and socialized services. These
were supposed to represent a specifically socialist route to higher living
standards. Thus, writing in 1960, a Soviet journalist presented the official
line on car ownership:

> The U.S. still enjoys a higher standard of transport facilities due to the
> large number of private cars. N. S. Khrushchev has indicated that the
> Soviet Union does not intend to vie with the U.S.A. in this respect. In
> very many cases air transport is much more convenient and economi-
> cal. There will also be much wider use of taxis, hired cars, motorcycles
> and scooters, with charges progressively reduced, as they are being al-
> ready . . . The socialist method is a comprehensive solution by develop-
> ing all types of transport facilities. Where necessary and convenient,
> some of these facilities will remain in individual use, but the bulk will
> be operated as a public service.[75]

But as Gronow and Zhuravlev show here in their examination of the
car as one of the key markers of luxury and its transformation in the Soviet
Union, alternative forms of collective ownership foundered in the face of
growing demand for private cars, not least from influential quarters, including the Kremlin under Khrushchev's successor, Brezhnev.[76] Their work joins
a growing body of studies that see the automobile as a revealing artifact in
the archaeology of late socialist consumer society.[77] By the mid-1960s the
highly automated AvtoVAZ factory was being built in Togliatti in conjunction with Fiat. Its declared aim was to provide the average Soviet citizen
with access to a car of European quality, the Zhiguli, to be produced in
three models, "standard," "luxury," and "family." Production of the new car

began, after delays, in 1970 and capacity was reached in 1974. This pattern of trumpeting collective consumption and communal services while delivering commodities for individual or private possession was repeated in other fields. Shared services like public canteens and public laundries were also much vaunted. Yet at the same time, great emphasis was placed on the image of labor-saving devices such as vacuum cleaners and washing machines designed for the private home. Such symbols were required to demonstrate the advances of socialist modernity in the Cold War competition with the West.

Rational norms, collective consumption, and other instruments through which to curb the destabilizing effects of consumer modernity may perhaps be seen, with hindsight, to have come to little.[78] But to assume that this was inevitable is to commit the mistake of teleology. How, when, and why this happened, and indeed whether the legacy of state socialism is, rather, a particular hybrid consumer culture, requires further research and analysis.[79] Nevertheless, it is not premature to assert that in the course of the 1960s and 1970s the range of modern luxuries and leisure experiences that were licensed and, indeed, provided by the state expanded greatly. Advertising, packaging, and commodity aesthetics articulated a clear claim that Eastern Bloc states had become "consumer societies" in the Western mold. Life— at least as illustrated in the pages of color "lifestyle" magazines and in the windows of hard currency shops—appears to have been lived increasingly in a "brandscape" which took its cues from the West and spoke in a kind of international consumer Esperanto: in Poland a man could dab on "Konsul woda kolońska" ("Consul" eau de cologne) while a woman might apply "Być może" ("Maybe") perfume with the fictional legend "Paris" on the label. A Budapest apartment might be furnished with Ikon furniture, made locally in the Kanizsa factory to foreign designs, and a Videotron stereo made in Hungary in partnership with the Japanese manufacturer Akai.[80] Or consider the Polski Fiat 126P, a car which was designed in Turin but made with low-grade recycled Soviet steel, the base matter of socialist alchemy. It was prone to premature rust and, consequently, had a shorter life expectancy than its Italian progenitor. Nevertheless, despite its material limitations and poor performance on the potholed roads of Poland, it was a luxury to the extent that it took years on a waiting list to acquire one and because of the attention that had to be lavished on it by its owner to keep it running.[81]

This latter case confronts us with one of the many paradoxes of late socialism. Objects in short supply such as cars could simultaneously represent norms—in the sense that citizens came to understand them as a requisite of a normal, modern, civilized life—while, at the same time, their scarcity, along with the constant investment of time and precious resources they demanded and their sometimes questionable usefulness (in the conditions of the Bloc), aligned them with luxury.[82]

The Scales of Luxury

Reflecting on the long life of artifacts—or what is sometimes called the "biography of things"—in Eastern Bloc societies offers ways to understand shifts in the hierarchies of value against which things have been judged, as well as the kind of emotional and practical investments they have attracted from their owners and users.[83] Take, as an item that at one time enjoyed the status of a modern luxury, the refrigerator. What can its vertiginous slide down the career ladder of things during the postwar period tell us?[84] What is the relationship of images of such commodities to their availability (or lack thereof)? Might ordinary consumer goods such as this serve as a barometer of socialist modernity, of changing modes of governance and regime-society relations, and of the development of the socialist countries of Central and Eastern Europe into mass consumer societies?

The refrigerator was a key image of prosperity in the context of the Cold War, combining in one symbol the promise of abundance with technological modernity. In the German Democratic Republic, as Katherine Pence writes, "the politics of iceboxes became a central aspect of how the Cold War came home to German kitchens."[85] In West Germany, 1953 was designated the year of the consumer, focused on the production of household appliances to "help the housewife." In the same year the GDR also embarked on its consumer-oriented New Course following the June 17 uprising over shortages and low wages.[86] There too, "the push for modernization and rising living standards in the mid-1950s featured a greater state effort to offer women labor-saving appliances which were rational, scientific and modern." New apartments on East Berlin's Stalinallee—the model of socialist housing in East Germany built in the mid-1950s—allocated a space for a refrigerator in their small, efficient "working kitchens."[87] Distinct, socialist meanings were attached to such consumer durables; they were claimed as a means to alleviate the domestic labor of *working* women; as such, these socialist objects were to be distinct from capitalism's chrome-plated frame for a full-time "professional housewife."

Refrigerators first began to enter ordinary people's lives on a significant scale during the 1960s, serving as a marker of rising prosperity, convenience, and modernity. Until the postwar period only the highest *nomenklatura* in the Soviet Union had had domestic refrigerators.[88] Mass production of domestic refrigerators began there in 1949 with a single model. Although

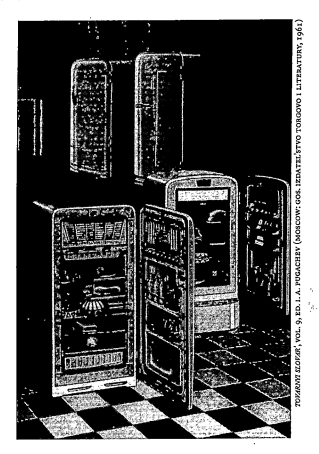

TOVARNI SLOVAR', VOL. 9, ED. I. A. PUGACHEV (MOSCOW: GOS. IZDATEL'STVO TORGOVO I LITERATURY, 1961)

Soviet refrigerators, 1961

refrigerator production rose from 49,000 in 1953 to 910,000 in 1963, they remained expensive and hard to come by. It was not until the Brezhnev era that refrigerators became truly mass items, "standard" home equipment accessible to ordinary Soviet households.[89] There and in other parts of the Bloc the relative cost, measured in terms of the work hours required to earn the money for the purchase, remained, however, much higher than in the West.[90]

If refrigerators were given symbolic status in the West as emblematic items of individualistic consumption, they were capable of carrying rather different meanings in the context of state socialism.[91] They could be co-opted for collective consumption; one refrigerator might serve numerous neighbors. The satirical magazine *Krokodil* told of how one man became popular overnight when he acquired a refrigerator, which all his neighbors immediately claimed a natural right to use.[92] Meanwhile, any claim to be a marker of a rational, scientific, and modern lifestyle might be equivocated by the refrigerator's contents. A glance into any Soviet refrigerator from the 1960s to the 1990s would reveal that it was filled not with the products of an advanced food-processing industry but with jars of home-preserved fruits grown at the dacha or gathered in the forest, holdovers of a pre-industrial subsistence economy.

In assessing the impact of refrigerated domesticity on Soviet society, it is important to stress that it began to exercise social effects in advance of actually entering mass consumption. As the subject of jokes, feuilletons, and cartoons, the refrigerator had already become part of the common culture by the late 1950s.[93] The domestication and "demotion" of such erstwhile luxuries was due not only to their mass production but also to their *repro-*duction as images in Soviet public culture. By the mid-1960s authoritative statements in the Soviet press would routinely include refrigerators among "normal" needs for the modern Soviet home.[94] Thus in terms of discourse, if not of everyday life, they were already a "necessity" before they arrived in ordinary homes. In this regard, the history of the appearance of the refrig-erator in the Bloc conforms to one of the key aspects of modern consumer-ism: consumer societies are systems of representation in which it is not only the thing itself that is acquired but also its image.[95]

Even if refrigerators were only available in a limited range of models inscribed in the official economic plan or by international trade within the Bloc, this does not exhaust their significance as consumer goods. While Eastern Bloc consumers enjoyed relatively limited choices in the shops, they nevertheless exercised other kinds of choices in their consumption practices. The fact that the penetration of "time-using" devices like radios and, be-ginning in the 1950s, televisions into homes was faster than that of "time-saving" kitchen appliances can tell us something about the priorities set by the state; while the Soviet regime raised prices on certain luxury consumer items in 1959, not only were television sets excluded, but their price was even reduced.[96] But it also has the potential to tell us about the choices be-ing exercised by ordinary people in their consuming practices, about social attitudes toward the home and to women's work, about decision-making in relation to household budgets, and about the significance of leisure in late socialism.[97]

High levels of what Western economists call "market penetration" were achieved in the Soviet Union in the late 1970s (a few years after the more affluent People's Republics). Despite this, the refrigerator was never fully naturalized into its domestic landscape. It remained a conspicuous feature, not least because the tiny kitchen of the standard apartments designed in the mid- to late 1950s, into which people began to move en masse by 1960, offered insufficient space for this new item of household equipment (unlike those in the earlier Stalinist design of Stalinallee apartments in East Berlin). Soviet planners had not seen far enough ahead into the mass technological future to allocate adequate space for these modern necessities. At the same time, they also deprived apartment dwellers of the traditional, pre-industrial method of keeping food chilled—a cold cupboard beneath the kitchen window—by installing a radiator there.[98]

Even when highly coveted and difficult to obtain, modern luxuries such as refrigerators or private cars cannot be conceived as discrete, autonomous things in the way that the objects of desire of earlier eras might be. They function as nodes in spatial, servicing, and energy networks and, as such, depend either on the market or on the state's capacities to provide not only the commodities but also the conditions that allow their operation.[99] Practices of repair played a key role in people's relations with their possessions. It appears that householders viewed their refrigerators as utilities to be repaired more than as alienable commodities to be replaced. The cycles of acquisition and disposal that came to operate in the West—particularly in the United States—did not, or not yet, shape the consumption patterns of such goods in the Soviet Union. Despite the pronounced difficulties of securing spare parts, repair was widely conducted in official workshops or, more frequently, by enterprising householders themselves. Moreover, high cost (relative to wages) and the difficulty of securing the appliance from the Soviet distribution system in the first place ensured that while the refrigerator was a common feature of the Soviet home, it remained an object of solicitous care.[100] Even as commodity fetishism was condemned as a bourgeois capitalist relation with things, the shortcomings of socialist production and distribution produced a particular emotional relationship with material things, which, according to Ekaterina Degot', came to be treated as friends who should be cared for when they hit hard times.[101] Soviet appliances, like the Soviet cars described by Jukka Gronow and Sergei Zhuravlev in their essay in this book, required considerable maintenance to offset the risk of failure.[102] A sparkling, new refrigerator might be presented as evidence of the distributive capacities of socialism; standing unplugged and dysfunctional, positioned in the crowded hallway of a communal apartment, or dominating the tiny Khrushchev-era flat, it testified, rather, to the disconnected and uneven experience of socialist modernity.

Socialist Leisure

Leisure—the "right to rest"—was an essential aspect of the promise of communism. Citizens were warned not to envisage the radiant future as a life of untrammeled ease, however. Leisure without labor was like dessert without savory; a fully human, rounded life consisted of both, not least because unalienated labor, quite unlike alienated drudgery under capitalism, was a path to self-realization. In an oft-cited passage in *Das Kapital,* Marx described communism as a realm of freedom and fully human existence in which both leisure and work would satisfy the intellectual, social, and material needs of the individual.[103]

The utopia of full communism was only loosely sketched in Soviet futurology, despite its hallowed position as the target of history's arrow. Nevertheless, progress was calibrated in a number of ways, among which the increased provision of leisure featured as an important measure.[104] The Third Program of the Communist Party of the Soviet Union, promulgated in 1961 as a modern-day *Communist Manifesto,* announced that incremental reductions in the working week would take place over the next two decades, made possible by increased labor productivity. As a result, "the Soviet Union will thus have the world's shortest and, concurrently, the most productive and highest paid working day. Working people will have much more leisure time, and this will add to their opportunities for improving their cultural and technical level."[105]

As the 1961 pronouncement made clear, virtuous socialist leisure was understood in communist morality as productive or reproductive activity. It was distinguished from the alienated forms of "amusement" that prevailed under capitalism in that it was to contribute to the integration of the individual, to allow her full self-possession and realization of her human essence as well as restoring her for the next day's labor.[106] A visit to the house of culture or the cinema, or a Sunday spent listening to Tchaikovsky in the local Park of Culture and Rest would reinvigorate the worker in readiness for the great challenges in the workplace and for building socialism. Socialist leisure was charged with realizing the untapped potential of the working classes for self-development. The emphasis on cultural enlightenment (with roots in nineteenth-century socialist movements) was put into practice immediately after the Bolshevik Revolution by the Proletarian Culture organization, which sought to accompany political and economic revolution with a cultural one.[107] Some of the major achievements of experimental revolutionary architecture resulted from the need to invent a new building type, the workers' club.[108] The collectivization of agriculture was accompanied by an infrastructure of new houses of culture, staffed by professional cultural

workers who sought to shape the political consciousness of the working
people through education and the arts. Houses of culture and workplace
clubs not only promoted high culture (understood in the canonical terms
associated with the official aesthetic doctrine of socialist realism), but also
sought to inculcate positive attitudes toward the socialist order, to shape
the New Person, and to cement the collective. Czesław Miłosz, in his early
Cold War critique of Sovietization, *The Captive Mind*, wrote about the new
program of cultural enlightenment introduced into the People's Republics
in the late 1940s in the darkest terms:

> People who attend a "club" submit to a collective rhythm, and so come
> to feel that it is absurd to think differently from the collective ...
> as these individuals pronounce the ritual phrases and sing the ritual
> songs, they create a collective aura to which they in turn surrender.[109]

For Miłosz writing in 1953, the emphasis on active, participatory, *collective*
enjoyment in the form of mass songs or group tourism was a suppression
of the individual.[110]

The emphasis on collective forms of leisure was gradually supplemented
after Stalin by a number of innovations that may be identified in general
terms with modernization and—with caveats—with privatization. These
included the provision of separate apartments beginning in the late 1950s—
accompanied by the growth in TV set ownership and airtime—as well as a
more positive revaluation (or at least sanctioning) of individual or family-
oriented interests such as car maintenance and dacha ownership.[111]

Nevertheless, the idea that properly socialist leisure should have improving effects, whether for the collective or the individual, did not disappear
with the redrawing of leisure and its spaces. How people spent their leisure
time was presented as a measure of rising living standards. At the same
time, the way *young* people, in particular, spent—or misspent—their leisure
was the cause of no little anxiety to Party and Komsomol and on the part
of official sociology.[112] Gender differences in access to leisure time were
recognized as an issue; when Soviet sociology revived, beginning in the
Khrushchev era, time budget surveys provided worrying evidence of gender
inequalities in access to time for self-improvement and sleep, which resulted
from women's "double burden." Inequalities in this regard were recognized
as inhibiting women's self-actualization and ability to participate in political and social activity.[113] Even in the 1980s, by which time the concept of
a comfortable private life had become accepted, de facto, as a legitimate
social aspiration—and even a *need*—across most of the Bloc, the party-state
continued to direct the free time of its citizens in structured occupations.

Amateur film and photography clubs continued to operate in factories, theater productions were mounted in local houses of culture, and housing committees undertook to improve the environment by collective gardening and
house painting schemes, often by mounting "actions" on symbolic days on
the calendar such as May Day.[114] Houses of culture hosted discos, ten-pin
bowling, and other fashionable pursuits in an effort to attract the young
through their doors and demonstrate relevance.[115]

By the late socialist period two pictures of the socialist citizen at leisure emerge: in one, she was engaged in the production of socialist identities through increasingly banal collective activities; in the other, she had
withdrawn from public culture into a privatized realm of individual and
home-oriented interests. Their differences notwithstanding, both characterizations accord with the dominant paradigms for understanding the ways
in which the state influenced the behavior of its citizens. In a discussion of
the "etatization of time" in Romania in the late 1980s, Katherine Verdery
has, for instance, identified attempts by the communist state to "seize time"
by compelling individuals into particular activities which, in addition to
work, included parades and queues and organized leisure such as group
tours.[116] According to this model, the choices facing individuals were either
to acquiesce (or simulate acquiescence) or to withdraw from the temporal
economy of state socialism. Collective and privatized forms of leisure represent the polar extremes of the same phenomenon, that is, state control over
its citizens' time outside work.

But are control and compliance the only, or even the most productive,
paradigms with which to approach the practices of leisure—even state-
provided and sanctioned leisure? What did people get out of it? And what
did they put into it? How did they use state leisure facilities and the time
spent in sanatoriums or on "cultural" tourist trips, to form relationships,
have sex and indulge the body, establish little dominions of power, go shopping, indulge in fantasy and dream ... in short, enjoy themselves? What
emotional investment did ordinary people of different social groups have in
certain forms of leisure? What role did such experiences as "wild tourism" or
the deluxe camping holidays with full home comforts discussed here by Scott
Moranda, or air travel to sun-and-sand holidays in Black Sea resorts play in
"real existing socialism"? And what were the effects of these transformations
on the lifestyle and expectations of ordinary citizens back home in the daily
grind? Answers to such questions are beginning to emerge as scholars turn
their attention to the phenomenon of tourism by Eastern European citizens
both within the Bloc and further afield. Essays in Anne Gorsuch and Diane
Koenker's recent edited volume, *Turizm,* explore not only the mechanisms
of control which sought to align the Eastern European tourist experience

with socialist principles of collectivity and cultural enlightenment, but also the "private" interests driving tourism, which sometimes included shopping and sexual adventure.[117] Alongside tourism, it is important to acknowledge here that some spheres of popular culture closely connected with leisure, such as rock music, have also enjoyed the attention of scholars. Writers like Timothy Ryback and Uta Poiger have both explored the aesthetic qualities of Soviet-style rock 'n' roll music and attended to its social effects.[118] From the mid-1950s youth cultures that made Western musical and sartorial fashions their own upset the conventionalized cultural and class categories on which state socialism was predicated.[119] Initially socialist regimes (and many elements of society) responded with censure, often equating affection for these styles with ideological wavering, treachery, and thralldom to the capitalist West. But with time they became more tolerant and pragmatic, seeking to compete with the seductions of Western products and media by fostering the production of homegrown socialist equivalents and licensing youthful experimentation, if only as a safety valve, through an infrastructure of radio programs, record companies, and rock festivals.

Katherine Lebow explores the early tensions between the Polish state and young people over the "correct" forms of leisure. Focusing on the new city of Nowa Huta, a flagship project designed to demonstrate the vitality of socialist industry and planning, she explores the attitudes of young men and women drawn to work in constructing the city in the early 1950s. By organizing their labor and directing their leisure time, the state imagined that it was not only building a new city but also new citizens. As Lebow shows, the young builders of Nowa Huta were at times indifferent and even antagonistic to improving activities organized for their edification in the *świetlice*—or "red corners"—of the cramped hostels in which they lodged. Surveying the official reports sent from the city to the Polish capital, she records the growing sense of disappointment and frustration among cultural activists who expected socialist realist novels and lectures on politics to prevail over the pleasures of alcohol, jazz, and sex. Unsurprisingly, the preference of Nowa Huta's young builders for such pleasures led to conflict. In Lebow's analysis, the battle lines being drawn over leisure were as much generational as ideological, with young people rejecting the stifling cultural elitism of the older generation.

New cultural forms came to occupy the leisure hours of the citizens of the Eastern Bloc in the 1960s and 1970s, with television claiming the prominent role. In this volume Paulina Bren and Kristin Roth-Ey offer novel ways of investigating this key instrument of modern leisure. Eschewing the narrow hermeneutic analysis characteristic of many film and television studies, Bren focuses on the interplay between televisual images and

political events in Czechoslovakia during the years which saw the emergence of the Charter 77 dissident movement. In her analysis, the highly
popular television series *The Woman Behind the Counter*, set in the unmistakably symbolic location of a well-stocked supermarket, was not simply a
spectacular distraction from real events, as critics of television on both sides
of the East-West divide have characterized the medium.[120] On the contrary, the Czechoslovak state, recognizing the magnetic appeal of television
characters for ordinary Czechoslovak viewers, employed the serial to frame
women's roles and their relationship to consumer desires and pleasures.

Josie McLellan, in her contribution to this volume, explores another
leisure product co-opted by the state as a political instrument. Framed as
a luxury in terms of the pricing and distributive mechanisms of the East
German economy, various forms of erotica were licensed there as legitimate
pleasures in socialism. In her essay, McLellan examines the publication of
erotica in the GDR from the 1960s to German reunification. Focusing on
the most popular magazine in the country, *Das Magazin*, she explores the
reasons why this publication included nude "pinups" in its pages, alongside
other seemingly bourgeois themes such as home and family, the "art of seduction," tourism, and fashion. *Das Magazin* was published largely to satisfy
East German demands for erotica (and, in particular, to dent the demand
for material smuggled from the West). This inexpensive, extremely popular
but hard-to-obtain luxury functioned as a palliative and is an example of
how leisure and luxury are overlapping categories. As McLellan argues,
the editors of this magazine and other erotic material produced with official imprimatur in the GDR were uncertain about the extent to which
their products were to emulate those published in the West or were to offer
an alternative. Liberal attitudes to sexuality were supposed to support the
projection of East Germany as a young, healthy socialist society, yet what
prevailed on *Das Magazin*'s pages was hardly liberating. Its editors conflated
emancipated sexuality with pornography.

Leisure as Production

Marxist futurology, as we noted above, predicted that the differences between work and leisure would disappear in the conditions of full communism. In a world without alienation, the individual would take complete
pleasure in her work, and her leisure would be oriented to productive tasks
like self-education. It is a nice irony that, as several essays in this volume
demonstrate, "free time" in the Bloc societies was often productive, just as
official ideology prescribed. But neither the practices nor the products nor
the types of pleasures taken in the process were ones the party-state had

in mind. Narcis Tulbure, in his study of alcohol consumption in Romania in the 1980s, shows how it was associated with the exchange of goods and services appropriated from state enterprises and circulating in the sphere of the second economy. Drinking on the job was also a way of pocketing control back from the state and expropriating work time that "belonged" to the commonwealth. Despite the official campaigns promoting restraint, this form of leisure was not only tolerated but actually facilitated by the state; for the government held a near monopoly over alcohol production and distribution, as well as over the spaces in which it could legitimately be consumed. Moreover, the monopoly over production ensured the flow of tax revenues to state coffers. Alcohol was, nevertheless, widely produced at home during leisure hours or in the workplace, while the foreman or the manager turned a blind eye. Like many other products that circulated in the second economy, moonshine was manufactured in the interstices of work and leisure. Ostensibly distinct spheres of economic life were blurred in such illegal though tolerated practices. Leisure time was, in other words, a time of industry, while the time spent at work often constituted an interval of relative leisure.

The productive effects of leisure in the form of hunting, as practiced by communist elites on publicly owned estates in Hungary in the 1960s, are described here by György Péteri. Hunting, one of the elite's preferred forms of leisure, not only put cheap and high-quality meat on the tables of those who enjoyed this chain of privileges, but also enabled the social reproduction of elite networks. The right to extend the invitation to hunt to those of higher or lower rank, or the opportunity to shoot on the richest hunting grounds, represented a kind of power within Party circles. Hospitality produced indebtedness. And distinctions of rank within the Hungarian Communist Party could, as Péteri shows, be measured by the number and quality of invitations received by a hunter, often in excess of the skills he possessed. Thus this leisure activity could play as important a role in the social reproduction of elite groups as education and work.[121] Accordingly, leisure and luxury should not simply be viewed as the privatization of common resources by the powerful; they were also the means by which that power reproduced itself.

Kristin Roth-Ey, in her essay exploring the early years of Soviet television broadcasting in the late 1950s and subsequent developments in the Brezhnev era, approaches the question of the creative uses of leisure from a different perspective. The mass media in the Bloc has conventionally been analyzed in terms of its propaganda effects or its capacity to distract.[122] Roth-Ey concentrates here on the agency and interests of the people who made Soviet television in the early years of its development. The first gen-

eration of television makers was drafted into this embryonic but very rapidly developing industry with little consideration for their expertise or their
political credentials. Genuine enthusiasts for the medium, they imagined it
in terms of its capacity to capture the spontaneity and truth of everyday life.
In a particularly vivid episode, Roth-Ey describes the live, interactive program *VVV* (*Vecher veselykh voprosov; Evening of Merry Questions*) broadcast
in 1957, which invited its viewers to participate in the shows as themselves
and not as the stereotypical characters of Soviet socialism (the "leading
worker," the "prize-winning athlete," the "model plant manager," and so
on). When the studio was swamped with brawling contestants dressed in
homemade costumes competing for its modest prizes, the broadcast had to
be suspended. The carnivalization of the ideal of collective leisure had backfired. Though short-lived, this approach to live broadcasting was shaped
by the conviction among television's pioneers that the medium by its very
nature revealed "truth," "reality," and the contemporary *lichnost'* (individual
or personality) to its viewers. In the intellectual setting of the Thaw, these
values would help Soviet society remake itself after the corruption of Stalinism. Spectatorship was to become participation, akin, as Roth-Ey argues, to
a civic act. This brief experiment was not, however, shaped by a democratic
or participatory conception of cultural production: Soviet TV pioneers saw
their efforts in terms of moral education, as well as providing an opportunity
for political mobilization. In this regard, they assumed a position close to
that occupied by the artistic avant-garde of the 1920s.

The differences between Péteri's Hungarian hunters and a Romanian
peasant manufacturing hooch with a homemade still in the 1980s or even,
for that matter, the viewers of early Russian TV programs, whose enthusiasm for the medium roused them to invade the production studios, are
evident. Yet the free-time activities of each can only be understood by in-
terpreting them as creative and productive actions in which individuals produced things, identities, and forms of sociality. Moreover, in attending to
the ways in which individuals and groups asserted control over their own
pleasures, we have to come to terms with the fact that social identities are
neither fixed nor necessarily consistent. This is not to say that they are
incoherent from the perspective of those concerned, however. As Lebow's
essay on the builders of Nowa Huta shows, young people in Poland in the
1950s could be both active constructors of the new world as the much-
feted pedocracy of socialism, and rock 'n' roll–loving hedonists, disparaged
in the press as *bikiniarze* (bikini boys). In conventional political discourse,
their love of American music and Hollywood fashion positioned them as
enemies of socialism.[123] Their leisure-time interests were, it seems, diamet-

rically opposed to their productive role in the socialist economy. The coin-
cidence of two apparently conflicting signifying systems in one social being,
the "socialist *bikiniarz*," testifies to the elective aspects of identity even in
what are still sometimes described as "totalitarian" conditions, and to the
importance of consumption in self-fashioning even under state socialism.
Similarly, Alexei Yurchak has recently noted the ways Russian Komsomol
youth in the 1980s participated in the official sphere while at the same time
adopting the signifiers of Western style such as rock music and fashionable clothes. He argues that the apparently dichotomous ordering of social
identities in Soviet society was not necessarily in contradiction. "Without
the hegemony of the authoritative rhetoric," he writes, "the Imaginary West
would not exist, and vice versa, without such imaginary worlds, the hyper-
normalized authoritative discourse could not be reproduced."[124]

Feelings and emotion—along with Yurchak's preoccupation in this passage, fantasy—are among the most challenging realms of investigation for
the historian. Here the potential of leisure and luxury comes to the fore as
an analytical tool through which to understand the experience of socialism
in the Bloc. Recently some scholars have steered what has been dubbed an
"emotional turn" in historical studies, identifying negative feelings of fear
and disgust as important drivers of action and social attitudes in contexts
like the Gulag or war.[125] But, as the essays in this book demonstrate, investigation of more positive emotions such as pleasure may also help us grasp the
ways Soviet-style socialism was experienced in less extraordinary settings,
and the diverse and manifold ways in which life in the Bloc was imagined
beyond the terms set by ideology. Fantasy and emotion are constitutive of
the self in ways that, in the context of the Bloc, may well have exceeded the
narrow social frames of class, ethnicity, and occupation into which individuals were inscribed by the state. Imagining "otherness" may well have constituted an attempt to escape from the alienating effects of modern life. But,
as the sociologists Phil Cohen and Laurie Taylor have argued, fantasy is not
only a flight from reality; it is produced in relation to the actual conditions
of life, often employing the resources at hand.[126] Moreover, the relation of
fantasy to "paramount reality" is never static or ahistorical. The development and spread of imaginary worlds within the fabric of socialist societies
changed them. In turn, the fantasies of everyday life were transformed by
socialism. It seems likely that the repertoire of fantasies of leisure and luxury
were more richly textured and diverse at the end of the communist system
than at the outset. This was in part because the borders between the East
and West (and those within the Bloc) were far more permeable than conventional accounts allow. But the resources for fantasy, as of pleasure, were

not exclusively alien, originating outside the Bloc; as we have argued here, official policy attempted to allow cultural and material innovations, and then struggled to contain their unwanted results.[127]

Leisure and luxury, as this essay has set out to map and as the chapters that follow will demonstrate, present rich seams of material deeply ingrained with diverse, changing, and sometimes conflicting meanings. These materials and their meanings can be explored to expose the persistence not only of need and scarcity in Soviet Bloc societies but also of desire and excess. Analysis of their forms and discourses can reveal both the uneven processes of socialist modernity and the persistence of older attitudes and traditional practices. The presence of social distinctions in these "classless" societies comes into sharp focus when viewed through these prisms, as do the ambiguous relations of socialist modernity to capitalism. Above all, research into leisure and luxury demands that we pay attention to the relations between provision—usually, though not invariably, managed by the state—and appropriation, that is, the practices of individuals and groups. The pleasures that could be found in socialism were the products of this dialectic.

Notes

1. Ferenc Fehér, Ágnes Heller, and György Márkus, *Dictatorship over Needs* (New York: St. Martin's, 1983).

2. Denise J. Youngblood, "Entertainment or Enlightenment? Popular Cinema in Soviet Society, 1921–1931," in *New Directions in Soviet History*, ed. Stephen White (Cambridge, Eng.: Cambridge University Press, 1992), 41–61; Richard Stites, *Russian Popular Culture: Entertainment and Society Since 1900* (Cambridge, Eng.: Cambridge University Press, 1992).

3. Katerina Clark, "Socialist Realism with Shores: Conventions for a Positive Hero," and Leonid Heller, "A World of Prettiness: Socialist Realism and Its Aesthetic Categories," both in *Socialist Realism Without Shores*, ed. T. Lahusen and E. Dobrenko (Durham, N.C.: Duke University Press, 1997), 27–50 and 51–75, respectively; Marina Balina and Evgeny Dobrenko, eds., *Petrified Utopia: Happiness Soviet Style* (London: Anthem, 2009).

4. Katharina Kucher, "Raum(ge)schichten: Der Gorkij-Park im frühen Stalinismus," *Osteuropa*, no. 3 (2005) (special issue on space: "Der Raum als Wille und Vorstellung: Erkundungen über den Osten Europas," guest edited by Karl Schlögel): 154–67; Karl Schlögel, "Der 'Zentrale Gorkij-Kultur und Erholungspark' (CPKIO) in Moskau: Zur Frage des öffentlichen Raums im Stalinismus," in *Stalinismus vor dem Zweiten Weltkrieg: Neue Wege der Forschung*, ed. Manfred Hildermeier, Schriften des Historischen Kollegs, Kolloquien 43 (Munich, 1998), 255–74; Stephen Bittner, "Green Cities and Orderly Streets: Space and Culture in Moscow, 1928–1933," *Journal of Urban History* 25, no. 1 (1998): 40.

5. Anna Rotkirch, "Traveling Maidens and Men with Parallel Lives—Journeys as Private Space During Late Socialism," in *Beyond the Limits: The Concept of Space in Russian History and Culture*, ed. Jeremy Smith (Helsinki: Suomen Historiallinen

Seura, 1999), 131–65. Similarly, group tourist trips abroad, with the official purpose of acquiring knowledge and culture, often served for the acquisition of other experiences, and not least for shopping, real and virtual. See especially Anne Gorsuch, "Time Travelers: Soviet Tourists to Eastern Europe," and Wendy Bracewell, "Adventures in the Marketplace: Yugoslav Travel Writing and Tourism in the 1950s–1960s," in *Turizm: The Russian and East European Tourist Under Capitalism and Socialism*, ed. Anne Gorsuch and Diane Koenker (Ithaca, N.Y., and London: Cornell University Press, 2006), 205–26 and 248–65, respectively. See also the following essays for Yugoslav and Hungarian perspectives on this theme: A. Wessely, "Travelling People, Travelling Objects," *Cultural Studies* 16, no. 1 (2002): 3–15; T. Dessewffy, "Speculators and Travelers: The Political Construction of the Tourist in the Kádár Regime," *Cultural Studies* 16, no. 1 (2002): 44–62; Alenka Švab, "Consuming Western Image of Well-Being: Shopping Tourism in Socialist Slovenia," *Cultural Studies* 16, no. 1 (2002): 63–79; Breda Luthar, "Remembering Socialism: On Desire, Consumption and Surveillance," *Journal of Consumer Culture* 6, no. 2 (2006): 229–59.

6. See Karen Petrone, *Life Has Become More Joyous, Comrades: Celebrations in the Time of Stalin* (Bloomington: Indiana University Press, 2000); David Crowley, "People's Warsaw/Popular Warsaw," *Journal of Design History* 10, no. 2 (1997): 203–24; Carol S. Lilly, *Power and Persuasion: Ideology and Rhetoric in Communist Yugoslavia, 1944–1953* (Boulder, Colo.: Westview, 2001); Paweł Sowiński, *Komunistyczne święto: Obchody 1 maja w latach 1948–1954* (Warsaw: Trio, 2000). A recent essay on GDR town planning asserts, by contrast: "What kind of happiness can exist outside the official framework of 'really existing socialist society'? Clearly none." Ed Taverne, "Henselmann, a Socialist Superstar," in *Happy: Cities and Public Happiness in Post-War Europe*, ed. Cor Wagenaar (Rotterdam: NAI, 2004), 129–49, esp. 129.

7. Nancy Ries, *Russian Talk: Culture and Conversation During Perestroika* (Ithaca, N.Y., and London: Cornell University Press, 1997), 59–60. The pleasure of the chase could be a luxury, however. Ries distinguishes between the shopping of mothers and grandmothers under pressure to procure the necessities for the family and forced to endure daily lengthy waits in queues to feed them; and that of "browsers" who because of age, gender, or marital status were "free to fail at their shopping attempts, or to wander freely, reaping the thrill of serendipity."

8. See Jeni Klugman, ed., *Poverty in Russia: Public Policy and Private Responses* (Washington, D.C.: Economic Development Institute, World Bank, 1997), 249.

9. V. Shlapentokh, *Public and Private Life of the Soviet People: Changing Values in Post-Stalin Russia* (Oxford: Oxford University Press, 1989); M. Garcelon, "Public and Private in Communist and Post-Communist Society," and O. Kharkhordin, "Reveal and Dissimulate: A Genealogy of Private Life in Soviet Russia," both in *Public and Private in Thought and Practice: Perspectives on a Grand Dichotomy*, ed. Jeff Weintraub and Krishan Kumar (Chicago and London: University of Chicago Press, 1997), 303–32 and 333–64, respectively; Lewis Siegelbaum, ed., *Borders of Socialism: Private Spheres of Soviet Russia* (Houndmills, Eng.: Palgrave Macmillan, 2006).

10. See Katerina Gerasimova, "Public Privacy in the Soviet Communal Apartment," and David Crowley, "Warsaw Interiors: The Public Life of Private Spaces," in *Socialist Spaces: Sites of Everyday Life in the Eastern Bloc*, ed. David Crowley and Susan E. Reid (Oxford and New York: Berg, 2002), 181–206 and 207–30.

11. Roland Barthes, *Le plaisir du texte* (Paris: Éditions du Seuil, 1973).

12. Alena Ledeneva, *Russia's Economy of Favours: Blat, Networking and Informal*

Exchanges (Cambridge, Eng.: Cambridge University Press, 1998); Stephen Lovell, Alena V. Ledeneva, and Andrei Rogachevskii, eds., *Bribery and Blat in Russia: Negotiating Reciprocity from the Middle Ages to the 1990s* (Houndmills, Eng.: Macmillan, 2000); Dennis O'Hearn, "The Consumer Second Economy: Size and Effects," *Soviet Studies* 32, no. 2 (April 1980): 218–34; G. Grossman, "The 'Second Economy' of the USSR," *Problems of Communism* 26, no. 5 (1977): 25–40.

13. See Elżbieta Firlit and Jerzy Chłopecki, "When Theft Is Not Theft," in *The Unplanned Society: Poland During and After Communism*, ed. J. Wedel (New York: Columbia University Press, 1992), 95–109. On kinship ties in socialist and post-socialist society, see Katherine Verdery, *What Was Socialism, and What Comes Next?* (Princeton, N.J.: Princeton University Press, 1996); and M. Burawoy, P. Krotov, and T. Lytikina, "Involution and Destitution in Capitalist Russia," *Ethnography* 1, no. 1 (2000): 43–65.

14. For a survey of different concepts of luxury, including what he describes as classical definitions, see Christopher Berry, *The Idea of Luxury: A Conceptual and Historical Investigation* (Cambridge, Eng.: Cambridge University Press, 1994).

15. Colin Campbell, *The Romantic Ethic and the Spirit of Modern Consumerism* (Oxford: Basil Blackwell, 1987), 59. See also Werner Sombart, *Luxury and Capitalism* (Ann Arbor: University of Michigan Press, 1967), 59.

16. See Svetlana Boym, *The Future of Nostalgia* (New York: Basic Books, 1991); Paul Betts, "The Twilight of the Idols: East German Memory and Material Culture," *Journal of Modern History* 72 (2000): 731–65; D. Berdhal "(N)ostalgie for the Present: Memory, Longing, and East German Things," *Ethnos,* 64, no. 2 (1999): 192–211; Martin Blum, "Remaking the East German Past: Ostalgie, Identity, and Material Culture," *Journal of Popular Culture* 34, no. 3 (2000): 229–53; Zala Volcic, "Yugo-Nostalgia: Cultural Memory and Media in the Former Yugoslavia," *Critical Studies in Media Communication* 24, no. 1 (March 2007): 21–38; Filip Modrzewski and Monika Sznajderman, eds., *Nostalgia: Eseje o tęsknocie za komunizmem* (Wołowiec, Pol.: Wyd. Czarna, 2002). Recent work on the Soviet experience making use of oral testimony includes Ries, *Russian Talk;* Donald Raleigh, *Russia's Sputnik Generation: Soviet Baby Boomers Talk About Their Lives* (Bloomington: Indiana University Press, 2006); and Alexei Yurchak, *Everything Was Forever, Until It Was No More: The Last Soviet Generation* (Princeton, N.J.: Princeton University Press, 2005). Susan Reid is currently completing a project on "Everyday Aesthetics in the Modern Soviet Flat," funded by the Leverhulme Trust, which makes extensive use of oral testimony.

17. See various essays in Ian Hodder, ed., *The Meaning of Things: Material Culture and Symbolic Expression* (London: Routledge, 1991); Judy Attfield, *Wild Things: The Material Culture of Everyday Life* (Oxford: Berg, 2000); and Steven Lubar and W. David Kingery, eds., *History from Things: Essays on Material Culture* (Washington, D.C.: Smithsonian, 1993).

18. Victor Buchli, *The Archaeology of Socialism* (Oxford and New York: Berg, 1999).

19. Slavoj Žižek, "When the Party Commits Suicide," *New Left Review* (November–December 1999): 46.

20. Slavoj Žižek, "Design as an Ideological State-Apparatus," lecture presented at ERA05, the World Design Congress held in Copenhagen in 2005. See www.icograda .org (accessed November 2006).

21. For example, Vladimir Sorokin, *The Queue* (London: Readers International, 1988); V. O. Rukavishnikov, "Ochered'," *Sotsiologicheskie issledovaniia* 16, no. 4 (1989): 3–12; Joseph Hraba, "Consumer Shortages in Poland: Looking Beyond the Queue in

a World of Making Do," *Sociological Quarterly* 26, no. 3 (1985): 387–404; Małgorzata Mazurek and Matthew Hilton, "Consumerism, Solidarity and Communism: Consumer Protection and the Consumer Movement in Poland," *Journal of Contemporary History* 42, no. 2 (2007): 315–43; Elena Osokina, "Proshchal'naia oda sovetskoi ocheredi," and Vladimir Nikolaev, "Sovetskaia ochered': Proshloe kak nastoiashchee," both in *Neprikosnovennyi zapas* 5, no. 43 (2005): 48–54 and 55–61.

22. Fehér, Heller, and Márkus, *Dictatorship over Needs;* János Kornai, *Economics of Shortage,* 2 vols. (Amsterdam and Oxford: North-Holland, 1980); Julie Hessler, "Culture of Shortages: A Social History of Soviet Trade, 1917–1953" (Ph.D. diss., University of Chicago, 1996) (the first part of the title is dropped from her book based on this research, *A Social History of Soviet Trade: Trade Policy, Retail Practice, and Consumption, 1917–1953* [Princeton, N.J.: Princeton University Press, 2004]); Ina Merkel, *Utopie und Bedürfnis: Die Geschichte der Konsumkultur in der DDR* (Cologne: Böhlau, 1999); Mariusz Jastrząb, *Empty Shelves: The Problem in the Provision of Everyday Goods in Poland, 1949–1956 (Puste półki: Problem zaopatrzenia ludności w artykuły powszechnego użytku w Polsce w latach 1949–1956)* (Warsaw: Trio, 2004); David M. Kemme, "The Chronic Shortage Model of Centrally Planned Economies," *Soviet Studies* 41, no. 3 (1989): 345–64.

23. Fehér, Heller, and Márkus, *Dictatorship over Needs,* 84. See also Elena Osokina, *Ierarkhiia potrebleniia: O zhizni liudei v usloviiakh stalinskogo snabzheniia 1928–1935 gg.* (Moscow: MGU, 1993); Mark G. Meerovich, *Kak vlast' narod k trudu priuchala: Zhilishche v SSSR—sredstvo upravleniia liud'mi: 1917–1941 gg.* (Stuttgart: Ibidem-Verlag, 2005).

24. Stephen E. Harris, "In Search of 'Ordinary' Russia: Everyday Life in the NEP, the Thaw, and the Communal Apartment," *Kritika: Explorations in Russian and Eurasian History* 6, no. 3 (2005): 583–614.

25. Verdery, *What Was Socialism?* 55; Kathy Burrell, "The Political and Social Life of Food in Socialist Poland," *Anthropology of East Europe Review* 21, no. 1 (2003): 189–94; Charlotte Chase, "Symbolism of Food Shortage in Current Polish Politics," *Anthropological Quarterly* 56, no. 2 (April 1983): 76–82; and Wojciech Pawlik, "Intimate Commerce," in Wedel, *The Unplanned Society,* 78–94.

26. In a perverse gesture of international solidarity, in the mid-1980s the Polish government spokesman Jerzy Urban organized a campaign to collect donations of blankets from Polish households for the homeless of New York. See Associated Press, "Sourly, the Poles Offer Blankets to New York," *New York Times,* May 14, 1986.

27. The *avoska* was a key piece of equipment for chance purchases. It came synecdochically to represent consumer anxiety. During perestroika, Raisa Gorbacheva was reputed to have declared that the *avoska* "must disappear from the Soviet home." Irina H. Corten, *Vocabulary of Soviet Society and Culture* (London: Adamantine, 1992), 19; Ries, *Russian Talk,* 54.

28. Reet Piiri, "This Storing Habit: About Food Culture in Soviet Estonia," and Reet Ruusmann, "Deficit as Part of Soviet-Time Everyday Life in the Estonian SSSR," both in *Yearbook of the Estonian National Museum* 49 (Tartu: Eesti Rahva Muuseum, 2006), 49–90 and 125–56; Sheila Fitzpatrick, "Blat in Stalin's Time"; Alena Ledeneva, "Continuity and Change of Blat Practices in Soviet and Post-Soviet Russia"; and Caroline Humphrey, "Rethinking Bribery in Contemporary Russia," all in *Bribery and Blat,* ed. Lovell, Ledeneva, and Rogachevskii, 166–82, 183–205, 216–41.

29. Elena Bogdanova, "Gazetnye zhaloby kak strategii zashchity potrebitel'skikh

interesov: Pozdnesovetskii period," *Teleskop: Nabliudeniia za povsednevnoi zhizn'iu pe-terburzhtsev,* no. 6 (2002): 44–48; *Księga listów PRL-u. part I, 1951–1956* (Warsaw: Baobab, 2004); *Księga listów PRL-u. part II, 1956–1970* (Warsaw: Baobab, 2004); *Księga listów PRL-u. part III, 1971–1989* (Warsaw: Baobab, 2005).

30. Katherine Pence, "'You as a Woman Will Understand': Consumption, Gender and the Relationship Between State and Citizenry in the GDR's Crisis of 17 June 1953," *German History* 19, no. 2 (2001): 218–52; Matthew Stibbe, "The SED, German Communism and the June 1953 Uprising: New Trends and New Research," in *Revolution and Resistance in Eastern Europe: Challenges to Communist Rule,* ed. Kevin McDermott and Matthew Stibbe (Oxford: Berg, 2006), 37–55; V. A. Kozlov, *Mass-ovye besporiadki v SSSR pri Khrushcheve i Brezhneve* (Novosibirsk: Sibirskii khronograf, 1999). On Plzeň, see Kevin McDermott, "Popular Resistance in Czechoslovakia: The Plzeň Uprising: June 1953," forthcoming; and Samuel H. Barron, *Bloody Saturday in the Soviet Union: Novocherkassk, 1962* (Stanford, Calif.: Stanford University Press, 2001). On Łódź, see Padraic Kenney, "The Gender of Resistance in Communist Poland," *American Historical Review* 104, no. 2 (April 1999): 399–425.

31. The paradoxical overproduction of luxuries at the expense of necessities was identified as a key problem of the Soviet planned economy under Khrushchev. Stock-piles of unwanted goods allegedly accumulating in the early 1960s included silk dresses, and jam and jelly. See, for example, K. Skovoroda, "Zadachi dal'neishego uluchsheniia torgovogo obsluzhivaniia naseleniia," *Planovoe khoziaistvo,* no. 2 (1960): 43–53.

32. On organized leisure and tourism in the Bloc, see the essays in Gorsuch and Koenker, *Turizm;* and Paweł Sowiński, *Wakacje w Polsce Ludowej: Polityka władz i ruch turystyczny (1945–1989)* (Warsaw: Trio, 2005). On the dacha, see Paulina Bren, "Weekend Getaways: The *Chata,* the Tramp and the Politics of Private Life in Post-1968 Czechoslovakia," and Stephen Lovell, "Soviet Exurbia: Dachas in Postwar Russia," both in Crowley and Reid, *Socialist Spaces,* 123–40 and 105–22; Stephen Lovell, *Summerfolk: A History of the Dacha, 1710–2000* (Ithaca, N.Y., and London: Cornell University Press, 2003); and Diane P. Koenker, "Whose Right to Rest? Contesting the Family Vacation in the Postwar Soviet Union," *Comparative Studies in Society and History* 51 (2009): 401–25.

33. Jennifer A. Loehlin, *From Rugs to Riches: Housework, Consumption and Moder-nity in Germany* (Oxford and New York: Berg, 1999); Karin Zachmann, "A Socialist Consumption Junction: Debating the Mechanization of Housework in East Germany, 1956–1957," *Technology and Culture* 43, no. 1 (2002): 73–99; Susan E. Reid, "The Khrushchev Kitchen: Domesticating the Scientific-Technological Revolution," *Journal of Contemporary History* 40, no. 2 (2005): 289–316; Jane Zavisca, "Consumer Inequalities and Regime Legitimacy in Late Soviet and Post-Soviet Russia" (Ph.D. diss., University of California, Berkeley, 2004).

34. Similar reasons for the neglect of consumption in GDR are offered by Pence, "'You as a Woman Will Understand,'" 218–52. In recent years a tide of studies have demonstrated the emergence of mass consumer societies in the countries of socialist Eastern Europe, and especially in regard to the GDR. Examples include Konrad H. Jarausch, ed., *Dictatorship as Experience: Towards a Socio-Cultural History of the GDR,* trans. Eve Duffy (Oxford: Berghahn, 1999); Stephan Merl, "Sowjetisierung in der Welt des Konsums," in *Amerikanisierung und Sowjetisierung in Deutschland 1945–1970,* ed. Konrad Jarausch and Hannes Siegrist (Frankfurt am Main: Campus, 1997), 167–94; Stephan Merl, "Staat und Konsum in der Zentralverwaltungswirtschaft:

Russland und die ostmitteleuropäischen Länder," in *Europäische Konsumgeschichte: Zur Gesellschafts-und Kulturgeschichte des Konsums, 18–20. Jahrhundert,* ed. Hannes Siegrist, Harmut Kalble, and Jürgen Kocka (Frankfurt am Main: Campus, 1997), 205–41; André Steiner, "Dissolution of the 'Dictatorship of Needs'? Consumer Behaviour and Economic Reform in East Germany in the 1960s," and Ina Merkel, "Consumer Culture in the GDR," both in *Getting and Spending: European and American Consumer Societies in the Twentieth Century,* ed. S. Strasser, C. McGovern, and M. Judt (Cambridge, Eng.: Cambridge University Press, 1998), 167–85 and 281–99, respectively; Merkel, *Utopie und Bedürfnis;* Uta G. Poiger, *Jazz, Rock, and Rebels: Cold War Politics and American Culture in a Divided Germany* (Berkeley: University of California Press, 2000); Milena Veenis, "Fantastic Things," in *Experiencing Material Culture in the Western World,* ed. Susan M. Pearce (New York: Leicester University Press, 1997), 154–74; Judd Stitziel, *Fashioning Socialism: Clothing, Politics and Consumer Culture in the GDR* (Oxford and New York: Berg, 2005). Regarding Soviet Russia, see Jukka Gronow, *Caviar with Champagne: Common Luxury and the Ideals of the Good Life in Stalin's Russia* (Oxford and New York: Berg, 2003); Susan E. Reid, "Cold War in the Kitchen: Gender and the De-Stalinization of Consumer Taste in the Soviet Union Under Khrushchev," *Slavic Review* 61, no. 2 (Summer 2002): 211–52; and Zavisca, "Consumer Inequalities." For the way the concept of consumption—and by extension, modernity—has tended to be monopolized by the anglophone West, leaving China, for example, on the margins of its discourses, see Craig Clunas, "Modernity Global and Local: Consumption and the Rise of the West," *American Historical Review* 104, no. 5 (1999): 1497–511.

35. Leon Trotsky, *The Revolution Betrayed* (New York: Pathfinder, 1970), 119–20.

36. Milovan Djilas, *The New Class: An Analysis of the Communist System* (San Diego: Harcourt Brace Jovanovich, 1959), 46.

37. Kazimierz Brandys, *A Warsaw Diary 1978–1981* (London: Chatto, 1984), 105.

38. Vera Dunham, *In Stalin's Time: Middleclass Values in Soviet Fiction,* 2nd ed. (Durham, N.C.: Duke University Press, 1990), 17.

39. The classic account is Nicholas Timasheff, *The Great Retreat: The Growth and Decline of Communism in Russia* (New York: E. P. Dutton, 1946). For counterargument see David L. Hoffmann, *Stalinist Values: The Cultural Norms of Soviet Modernity, 1917–1941* (Ithaca, N.Y.: Cornell University Press, 2003).

40. Aleksandr Fursenko and Timothy Naftali, *Khrushchev's Cold War* (New York: Norton, 2006), 140–41. For the Soviet regime, the 1953 crisis in East Germany had already reinforced the need to attend to matters of consumption.

41. Theodore Friedgut, *Political Participation in the USSR* (Princeton, N.J.: Princeton University Press, 1979); Jeffrey W. Hahn, *Soviet Grassroots: Citizen Participation in Local Soviet Government* (London: I. B. Tauris, 1988).

42. Francois Fejtö, *A History of the People's Democracies* (Harmondsworth, Eng.: Pelican, 1974), 362–412.

43. James Millar, with reference to Vera Dunham, calls this phenomenon in the Brezhnev-era Soviet Union the "little deal." James R. Millar, "The Little Deal: Brezhnev's Contribution to Acquisitive Socialism," *Slavic Review* 44, no. 4 (1985): 694–706.

44. M. Simecka, *The Restoration of Order: The Normalization of Czechoslovakia, 1969–1976* (London: Verso, 1984), esp. chap. 15, "Corruption."

45. Václav Havel, *The Power of the Powerless* (1978; London: Hutchinson 1985),

37–40. For Havel's views on consumerism, see Robert B. Pynsent, *Questions of Identity: Czech and Slovak Ideas of Nationality and Personality* (Budapest: Central European University Press, 1994), 23–26.

46. For a transcription of the "kitchen debate" in English, see http://www.cnn .com/SPECIALS/cold.war/episodes/14/documents/debate/ (accessed November 2006).

47. Edward Crankshaw, *Khrushchev's Russia,* rev. ed. (Harmondsworth, Eng.: Penguin Books, 1962; 1st ed. 1959), 136. Compare the results of surveys of youth attitudes conducted in the early 1960s under the auspices of *Komsomol'skaia pravda.* B. A. Grushin, *Chetyre zhizni Rossii v zerkale oprosov obshchestvennogo mneniia: Epokha Khrushcheva* (Moscow: Progress-Traditsiia, 2001), esp. chap. 2, "Dinamika i problemy urovnia zhizni naseleniia."

48. Paul Neuburg, *The Hero's Children: The Post-War Generation in Eastern Europe* (New York: William Morrow, 1973), 273–74.

49. William Shawcross, *Crime and Compromise: János Kádár and the Politics of Hungary Since Revolution* (London: Weidenfeld and Nicolson, 1974), 176; Heino Nyyssönen, "Salami Reconstructed: 'Goulash Communism' and Political Culture in Hungary," *Cahiers du Monde russe* 47, nos. 1–2 (2006): 153–72.

50. The most influential articulation of this argument in recent years has been Verdery, *What Was Socialism, and What Comes Next?* It was already a premise of David Riesman's 1951 essay "The Nylon War," in Riesman's *Abundance for What?* (New York: Doubleday, 1964), 65–77.

51. See Zsusanna Varga, "Questioning the Soviet Economic Model," in *Muddling Through in the Long 1960s: Ideas and Everyday Life in High Politics and the Lower Classes of Communist Hungary,* ed. János M. Rainer and György Péteri (Trondheim: PEECS, 2005), 109–34; H. G. Skilling, *Czechoslovakia's Interrupted Revolution* (Princeton, N.J.: Princeton University Press, 1976), 119–25; Abraham Katz, *The Politics of Economic Reform in the Soviet Union* (New York: Praeger, 1973); Philip Hanson, *The Rise and Fall of the Soviet Economy* (London: Longman, 2003). For some preliminary discussion of the cultural implications, see Susan E. Reid, "Khrushchev Modern: Agency and Modernization in the Soviet Home," *Cahiers du Monde russe* 47, nos. 1–2 (2006): 227–68.

52. Jane Shapiro, "Soviet Consumer Policy in the 1970s: Plan and Performance," in *Soviet Politics in the Brezhnev Era,* ed. Donald R. Kelley (New York: Praeger, 1980), 104–28.

53. Berry, *Idea of Luxury;* Matthew Hilton, "The Legacy of Luxury: Moralities of Consumption Since the Eighteenth Century," *Journal of Consumer Culture* 4, no. 1 (2004): 101–23.

54. A similar approach was adopted in Lenin's Russia under the New Economic Policy. See Alan M. Ball, *Russia's Last Capitalists: The Nepmen 1921–29* (Berkeley: University of California Press, 1987).

55. Of course, cigarettes might be considered necessities when used to stifle hunger during periods when food was in short supply.

56. On the relations of luxury to abundance, see Werner Sombart, *Luxury and Capitalism* (1913; Ann Arbor: University of Michigan Press, 1967). Tamas Aczel and Tibor Meray describe Budapest's shops during the Second Festival of Youth held in the city in 1949 with these words: "The shops abounded in goods. The bread shone

white as snow. Red meat filled the windows of the butcher shops, and, on the market stands, the apples smiled, the pears, juicy in their golden-yellow skins, offered themselves, and multi-coloured grapes stood in mountains. The war was far away ... The standard of living rose steeply, and it seemed as though the road to socialism were running straight and sunny toward the not-so-distant pinnacles." Tamas Aczel and Tibor Meray, *The Revolt of the Mind* (London: Thames and Hudson: 1960), 70.

57. Gronow, *Caviar with Champagne.*

58. Rodger P. Potocki Jr., "The Life and Times of Poland's 'Bikini Boys,'" *Polish Review* 39, no. 3 (1994): 259–90.

59. Torgsin shops were first introduced to the Soviet Union in 1936, according to Elena Osokina, *Za fasadom stalinskogo izobiliia* (Moscow: Rosspen, 1998). For a report on Czechoslovakia's Tuzex hard currency stores, Polish Pewex shops, and the Bulgarian Corecom, see J. L. Kerr, *Hard Currency Shops in Eastern Europe,* Radio Free Europe/Research RAD Background Report 211 (October 27, 1977); Jonathan R. Zatlin, *The Currency of Socialism: Money and Political Culture in East Germany* (Cambridge, Eng.: Cambridge University Press, 2007), esp. chap. 6, "Consuming Ideology."

60. Veenis, "Fantastic Things," 170.

61. Raymond Stokes, *Constructing Socialism: Technology and Change in East Germany, 1945–1990* (Baltimore and London: Johns Hopkins University Press, 2000); Ina Merkel and Felix Mühlberg, *Wunderwirtschaft: DDR-Konsumkultur in den 60er Jahren,* ed. Neue Gesellschaft für Bildende Kunst (Cologne: Böhlau, 1996). See also Alfred Zauberman, *Industrial Progress in Poland, Czechoslovakia and East Germany, 1937–62* (Oxford: Oxford University Press, 1964).

62. Eli Rubin, *Synthetic Socialism: Plastics and Dictatorship in the German Democratic Republic* (Chapel Hill: University of North Carolina Press, 2009), 109–10.

63. George Breslauer, *Khrushchev and Brezhnev as Leaders* (London: Allen and Unwin, 1982), 139–40; Marshall Goldman, "More for the Common Man: Living Standards and Consumer Goods," *Problems of Communism* 9, no. 5 (1960): 33; M. E. Ruban, "Private Consumption in the USSR: Changes in the Assortment of Goods, 1940–1959," *Soviet Studies* 13, no. 3 (1962): 37–54. For fuller argumentation, see Reid, "Cold War in the Kitchen"; Reid, "Khrushchev Modern," 244–55.

64. Although Hungarians enjoyed a rapid rise in living conditions under Kádár (prompting one commentator to conclude that "consumerism was the principal means by which the State built its bridges with the people" [Fejtö, *History of the People's Democracies,* 166–67]), there was considerable discussion within Party circles about what were perceived to be the malign effects of "refrigerator socialism" on society and the individual. See Tibor Iván Berend, *The Hungarian Economic Reforms, 1953–1988* (Cambridge: CUP Archive, 1990), 147–67; Steiner, "Dissolution of the 'Dictatorship of Needs'?," 170–71.

65. N. S. Khrushchev, *O shirokom vnedrenii industrial'nykh metodov, uluchshenii kachestva i snizhenii stoimosti stroitel'stva: Rech' na Vsesoiuznom soveshchanii stroitelei, arkhitektorov i rabotnikov promyshlennosti stroitel'nykh materialov, stroitel'nogo i dorozhnogo mashinostroeniia, proektnykh i nauchno-issledovatel'skikh organizatsii, 7 dekabria 1954 g.* (Moscow: Politizdat, 1955); N. Khrushchev, "Remove Shortcomings in Design, Improve the Work of Architects," *Pravda* and *Izvestia,* December 28, 1954, trans. in *Architecture Culture 1943–1968,* ed. Joan Ockman (New York: Rizzoli, 1993), 184–88.

66. Grey Hodnett, ed., *Resolutions and Decisions of the Communist Party of the Soviet Union*, vol. 4: *The Khrushchev Years 1953–1964* (Toronto: University of Toronto Press, 1974), 209–10, 247.

67. Susan E. Reid, "Destalinization and Taste, 1953–1963," *Journal of Design History* 10, no. 2 (1997): 177–201; Reid, " Khrushchev Modern," 227–68; V. Buchli, "Khrushchev, Modernism, and the Fight Against Petit-Bourgeois Consciousness," *Journal of Design History* 10, no. 2 (1997): 161–76; A. Minta, "The Authority of the Ordinary: Building Socialism and the Ideology of Domestic Space in East Germany's Furniture Industry," in *Constructed Happiness: Domestic Environment in the Cold War Era,* ed. M. Kalm and Ingrid Ruudi (Tallinn: Estonian Academy of Arts, 2005), 102–17; Eli Rubin, "The Form of Socialism Without Ornament: Consumption, Ideology, and the Fall and Rise of Modernist Design in the German Democratic Republic," *Journal of Design History* 19, no. 2 (2006): 155–68.

68. Stokes, *Constructing Socialism*. In 1958 a conference on synthetic plastics opened in East Germany under the motto "Chemicals Provide Bread, Prosperity, and Beauty." See Betts, "Twilight of the Idols," 756.

69. T. Trotskaia, "Kompozitory aramatov," *Ogonek,* no. 10 (March 6, 1960): 25. The insufficient supply of suitable oils and fats had presented the main obstacle to the development of the Soviet cosmetics and perfume industry on a mass scale in the 1930s. Anastas Mikoian, *Tak bylo: Razmyshleniia o minuvshem* (Moscow: Vagrius, 1999), 297–99.

70. This was an extension of a pattern identified by Jukka Gronow in the industrialized production of caviar and "Sovetskoe" champagne in the 1930s. Gronow, *Caviar with Champagne.*

71. Cars in private ownership, for instance, remained particularly problematic in the 1960s. See Lewis Siegelbaum, *Cars for Comrades: The Life of the Soviet Automobile* (Ithaca, N.Y.: Cornell University Press, 2008), 235–38.

72. Cited by Jerome M. Gilison, *The Soviet Image of Utopia* (Baltimore: Johns Hopkins University Press, 1975), 173, from G. Shakhnazarov, *Kommunizm i svoboda lichnosti* (Moscow, 1960), 48.

73. *Társadalmi szemle* (October 1959): 2, cited by G. Gömöri, "'Consumerism' in Hungary," *Problems of Communism* 12, no. 1 (1963): 64.

74. Cited by Akos Rona-Tas, *The Great Surprise of the Small Transformation: The Demise of Communism and the Rise of the Private Sector in Hungary* (Ann Arbor: University of Michigan Press), 92, from *Új írás* 8 (1961): 737.

75. P. Mstislavsky, "The Standard of Consumption," *New Times,* no. 22 (May 1960): 11.

76. Lewis H. Siegelbaum, "Cars, Cars, and More Cars: The Faustian Bargain of the Brezhnev Era," in *Borders of Socialism,* ed. Siegelbaum, 83–106; Siegelbaum, *Cars for Comrades;* Larissa Zakharova, "Fabriquer le bon goût: La Maison des modèles de Leningrad a l'époque de Hruščev," and Nordica Nettleton, "Driving Towards Communist Consumerism," both in *Cahiers du Monde russe* 47, nos. 1–2 (2006): 195–226 and 131–52; Zatlin, *Currency of Socialism,* 203–42. The most "chic" Soviet car of the 1960s–80s was the Chaika, produced at the Gorky car factory starting in 1959 and based on the American Picard. The ordinary person could only admire this car, according to Nataliia Lebina, for it was never put on sale, being intended only for official use by the highest bureaucrats and as a gift to such notables as cosmonauts Iurii Gagarin and Valentina Tereshkova. Even by the end of the 1980s it still represented

untold luxury for the Soviet person, and was even mythologized in the rock music of the perestroika period, for example, in a song by Zh. Aguzarov; "And you once again are on foot, while I fly past in a Chaika." Nataliia Lebina, "XX vek: Slovar' povsednevnosti," *Rodina*, no. 5 (2006): 107.

77. Siegelbaum, *Cars for Comrades;* Zatlin, *Currency of Socialism*, 203–24; Karol Jerzy Mórawski, *Syrena: Samochód PRL* (Warsaw: Trio, 2005).

78. We should be careful not to make premature judgments about the effects of Soviet consumer policy. There are indications that official policies and experience continue to shape attitudes to consumption in the former territories of the Bloc. Evidence thrown up by oral histories of life in the Soviet Union suggests that there was considerable popular support for the moral framework of Khrushchev- and Brezhnev-era policies that accentuated thrift, and that patterns of behavior and moral economies established thirty or forty years ago continue to influence actions in the present. Susan Reid, interviews conducted with the support of the Leverhulme Trust, "Khrushchev Modern: Making Home and Becoming a Consumer in the Soviet Sixties," 2004–07.

79. Studies of post-socialist consumption include Olga Shevchenko, *Crisis and the Everyday in Postsocialist Moscow* (Bloomington: Indiana University Press, 2008); Jennifer Patico, *Consumption and Social Change in a Post-Soviet Middle Class* (Palo Alto, Calif.: Stanford University Press, 2008); Zavisca, "Consumer Inequalities."

80. See *Örökség: Tárgy- és környeszetkultúra Magyarországon, 1945–1985* (Budapest: Műcsarnok, 1985), 88.

81. For reflections on the woes of Moscow car owners, see Vladimir Polupanov, "Krutaia tachka—i roskosh', i golovnaia bol'," *Aif-Moskva*, no. 17 (2001).

82. The ethnographer Krisztina Fehérváry has observed that in post-communist societies, "people regularly describe as 'normal' high-quality commodities and living environments otherwise considered extraordinary in their local context." This was no less true before the fall of the Wall. Krisztina Fehérváry, "American Kitchens, Luxury Bathrooms, and the Search for a 'Normal' Life in Postsocialist Hungary," *Ethnos* 67, no. 3 (2002): 369–400.

83. Igor Kopytoff, "The Cultural Biography of Things: Commoditization as Cultural Process," in *The Social Life of Things*, ed. Arjun Appadurai (Cambridge, Eng.: Cambridge University Press, 1986), 64–94.

84. Compare, on the refrigerator's shift from luxury to necessity in West Germany in the 1950s and 1960s, Loehlin, *From Rugs to Riches*, 61–66, here 64; and on the status of appliances in interwar France, Robert Frost, "Machine Liberation: Inventing Housewives and Home Appliances in Interwar France," *French Historical Studies* 18 (1993): 109–30.

85. Katherine Pence, "Cold War Iceboxes: Competing Visions of Kitchen Politics in 1950s Divided Germany," unpublished paper for the workshop "Kitchen Politics in the Cold War," Deutsches Museum, Munich, July 1–3, 2005.

86. Stibbe, "The SED."

87. Pence, "Cold War Iceboxes."

88. Over the same period the manufacture of vacuum cleaners rose from 45,000 to 720,000 units, and washing machines from 4,000 to 23,000,000. By the mid-1960s, there were three models of refrigerators available, and in 1965, 1.5 million refrigerators were to be produced. Lebina, "XX vek," 106; "Novye tovary (Tsifry i fakty)," *Sovetskaia torgovlia*, no. 10 (1961): 61–62. The latter source gives 1951 as the start of

mass production of refrigerators. By 1968 there were 27 million TV sets, 25 million washing machines, 13.7 million refrigerators, and 5.9 million vacuum cleaners for some 60–70 million homes, but as Matthews notes, we do not know how many of these appliances were working. Mervyn Matthews, *Class and Society in Soviet Russia* (London: Allen Lane, 1972), 84. See also Zavisca, "Consumer Inequalities"; Shapiro, "Soviet Consumer Policy."

89. According to official statistics, the number of refrigerators produced (or "guaranteed to") per 1,000 population rose from 29 in 1965 to 210 in 1977. Equivalent figures for washing machines were 59 and 200, and for television sets 68 and 229. Shapiro, "Soviet Consumer Policy," 116, table 5.2, based on Tsentral'noe statisticheskoe upravlenie, *Narodnoe khoziaistvo SSSR v 1975 g.* (Moscow: Statistika, 1976), 595; Tsentral'noe statisticheskoe upravleniia, *SSSR v tsifrakh v 1977 g.* (Moscow: Statistika, 1978), 204.

90. Bogdan Mieczkowski, *Personal and Social Consumption in Eastern Europe* (New York: Praeger, 1975), 287.

91. Sandy Isenstadt, "Visions of Plenty: Refrigerators in America Around 1950," *Journal of Design History* (Winter 1998): 311–21.

92. Parsadan, "Istoriia s kholodil'nikom," *Krokodil,* no. 7 (March 10, 1958): 3.

93. What to do when the notoriously unreliable refrigerator breaks down became a common subject of humor, for example, a cartoon by S. Kuz'min, "Kogda kholodil'nik 'Oka' ne rabotaet," *Krokodil,* no. 35 (December 20, 1959).

94. For example, Russian State Archive of the Economy (RGAE), f. 4372, op. 65, d. 177 (Initsiativnye predlozheniia po proizvodstvu predmetov potrebleniia, 28.12.1962–27.12.1963), l. 10; Skovoroda, "Zadachi," 43–53; and see the luxury edition of *Tovarnyi slovar'* for articles on dishwashers (vol. 9, 1961) and "universal domestic electric machines" (vol. 8, 1960), 1135–44.

95. Jean Baudrillard characterizes the refrigerator as an emblematic object of capitalism in these terms. He argues that the function of this piece of domestic equipment is less important than its capacity to symbolize modern consumer lifestyles. See Jean Baudrillard, "The System of Things," in *Design After Modernism: Beyond the Objects,* ed. J. Thackara (London: Thames and Hudson, 1988); Daniel Miller, ed., *Acknowledging Consumption* (London: Routledge, 1995).

96. Kristin Roth-Ey, "Mass Media and the Remaking of Soviet Culture, 1950s–1960s" (Ph.D. diss., Princeton University, 2003), chap. 4, "Finding a Soviet Home for Television," 247–313; Kristin Roth-Ey, "Finding a Home for Television in the USSR, 1950–1970," *Slavic Review* 66, no. 2 (2007): 278–306.

97. The faster take-up of television sets than other appliances is corroborated repeatedly in many of the more than seventy interviews conducted for Susan Reid's project "Everyday Aesthetics in the Modern Soviet Flat," supported by the Leverhulme Trust.

98. N. I. Andreeva, "Gigienicheskaia otsenka novogo zhilishchnogo stroitel'stva v Moskve (period 1947–1951 gg.)," *Gigiena i sanitariia,* no. 6 (1956): 22. In this survey of Moscow residents in 1955, some expressed the desire for a refrigerator in the kitchen or, if too expensive, to be provided with a space to install one in the future.

99. See, for example, Siegelbaum, *Cars for Comrades.*

100. Appliances that took more labor to make them work than they saved were a common comic theme in the popular Soviet press in the Khrushchev era, for example, in the illustrated magazines *Ogonek* and *Krokodil.* See also Matthews, *Class and Society,*

84. For problems of washing machines that stood useless, see A. Holt, "Domestic Labour and Soviet Society," in *Home, School and Leisure in the Soviet Union,* ed. J. Brine, M. Perrie, and A. Sutton (London: Allen and Unwin, 1980), 26–54. Khrushchev, during the notorious kitchen debate at the outset of the drive to modernize the home with white goods in the late 1950s, had challenged America's endorsement of product obsolescence by asserting the long durability of Soviet products. This feature, he argued, was valued by Soviet civilization and designed into its products. Today, many old Soviet-era refrigerators continue to work, not because of the quality of their manufacture, but because of the care and repairs of their owners. On the labor demanded by Soviet durables and on their longevity, see Ol'ga Gurova, "Prodolzhitel'nost' zhizni veshchei v sovetskom obshchestve: Zametki po sotsiologii nizhnego bel'ia," *Neprikosnovennyi zapas* (2004), no. 2. http://magazines.russ.ru/n2/2004/34/gurov9 .html; Galina Orlova, "Apologiia strannoi veshchi: 'Malen'kie khitrosti' sovetskogo cheloveka," *Neprikosnovennyi zapas* (2004), no. 2. http://magazines.russ.ru/nz/2004/ 34/ovl10.html; and Olga Shevchenko, "In Case of Fire Emergency: Consumption, Security, and the Meaning of Durables in a Transforming Society," in *Journal of Consumer Culture* 2, no. 2 (2002): 147–70. The Russian sociologists Ekaterina Gerasimova and Sofia Chuikina designate the Soviet Union a "mending society": see Ekaterina Gerasimova and Sofia Chuikina, "Obshchestvo remonta," *Neprikosnovennyi zapas,* no. 34 (2004), available at http://www.magazines.russ.ru/nz/2004/34/ger85 .html (accessed November 1, 2004).

101. Ekaterina Degot', "Ot tovara k tovarishchu: K estetike nerynochnogo predmeta," *Logos,* no. 5–6 (2000), http://www.ruthenia.ru/logos/number/2000_5_6/ 2000_5-6_04.htm (accessed December 8, 2003).

102. On luxury American cars from the 1950s still in use and lovingly maintained in Cuba today, see Viviana Narotzky, "Our Cars in Havana," in *Autopia: Cars and Culture,* ed. Peter Wollen and Joe Kerr (London: Reaktion, 2002).

103. "The realm of freedom actually begins only where labour which is determined by necessity and mundane considerations ceases." Karl Marx, *Capital,* vol. 3 (London: Lawrence and Wishart, 1997), 820. Increased leisure was promised as part of the transition to communism, for example, in the Third Party Program in 1961. Hodnett, *Resolutions and Decisions,* 229–30.

104. See, for example, S. Strumilin, "Mysli o griadushchem," *Oktiabr',* no. 3 (1960): 140–46; Gilison, *Soviet Image.*

105. Hodnett, *Resolutions and Decisions,* 231.

106. For a Western Marxist critique by Frankfurt School philosophers on the relation between leisure and work under capitalism, see Theodor Adorno and Max Horkheimer, *Dialectic of Enlightenment* (1947; London: Verso, 1979). See also Rudy Koshar, *Histories of Leisure* (Oxford: Berg, 2002), 1–26.

107. Lynn Mally, *Amateur Theater and the Soviet State, 1917–1938* (Ithaca, N.Y.: Cornell University Press, 2000). See also Richard Stites, *Revolutionary Dreams: Utopian Vision and Experimental Life in the Russian Revolution* (New York: Oxford University Press, 1989).

108. See, for example, the Rusakov Workers' Club, Moscow (1929), designed by Konstantin Melnikov, and discussed in Vigdariia Khazanova, *Klubnaia zhizn' i arkhitektura kluba 1917–1941* (Moscow: Zhiraf, 2000). See also Anne White, *De-Stalinization and the House of Culture: Declining State Control over Leisure in the USSR, Poland and Hungary, 1953–89* (London: Routledge, 1990), 35; and Simone Hain

and Stephan Stroux, *Die Salons der Sozialisten: Kulturhäuser in der DDR* (Berlin: Ch. Links, 1996).

109. C. Miłosz, *The Captive Mind* (1953; Harmondsworth, Eng.: Penguin, 1980), 197–98.

110. The received view that only collective leisure was valorized is nuanced, however, by Diane Koenker's findings regarding Soviet proletarian tourism in the 1930s. Diane P. Koenker, "The Proletarian Tourist in the 1930s: Between Mass Excursion and Mass Escape," in Gorsuch and Koenker, *Turizm*, 119–40.

111. Vladimir Shlapentokh, *The Public and Private Life of the Soviet People* (New York: Oxford University Press, 1989); Siegelbaum, *Borders of Socialism;* White, *De-Stalinization;* Lovell, *Summerfolk.*

112. Concern with youth leisure was frequently expressed in the Soviet Komsomol press already in the early 1950s; for example, "Zabota o byte i dosuge molodezhi," *Komsomol'skaia pravda,* August 2, 1952. The Komsomol Central Committee decreed in 1956 that a number of periodicals should carry materials on young people's leisure activities. Catriona Kelly, *Refining Russia: Advice Literature, Polite Culture, and Gender from Catherine to Yeltsin* (Oxford: Oxford University Press, 2001), 353. The reborn discipline of sociology in the late 1950s and early 1960s in the Soviet Union paid particular attention to problems of youth leisure and consumption, undertaking surveys of youth attitudes under the auspices of *Komsomol'skaia pravda.* B. A. Grushin, *Chetyre zhizni Rossii: V zerkale oprosov obshchestvennogo mneniia: Epokha Khrushcheva* (Moscow: Progress-Traditsiia, 2001); Boris Grushin, *USSR: The Problem of Leizure* [*sic*] (Moscow: Novosti, 1968). See also M. Edele, "Strange Young Men in Stalin's Moscow: The Birth and Life of the Stiliagi, 1945–1953," *Jahrbücher für Geschichte Osteuropas,* vol. 50 (2002): 37–61; Juliane Fürst, "The Arrival of Spring? Changes and Continuities in Soviet Youth Culture and Policy Between Stalin and Khrushchev," in *The Dilemmas of De-Stalinization,* ed. Polly Jones (London: Routledge, 2006), 135–53; Allen Kassof, "The New Soviet Generation: Youth vs. the Regime: Conflict in Values," *Problems of Communism* 6, no. 3 (May–June 1957): 15–23; S. Strumilin, "Rabochii byt i kommunizm," *Novyi mir,* no. 7 (1960): 208; Gilison, *Soviet Image,* 119–22, 146–47; Erich Goldhagen, "The Glorious Future—Realities and Chimeras," *Problems of Communism* 11, no. 6 (1960): 17–18.

113. L. A. Gordon and E. V. Klopov, *Chelovek posle raboty* (Moscow: Nauka, 1972). See Matthews, *Class and Society* (97–98), for some examples of time budget studies; and, with a focus on gender, Gail Warshofsky Lapidus, *Women in Soviet Society: Equality, Development, and Social Change* (Berkeley: University of California Press, 1978), 269–78.

114. White, *De-Stalinization,* 74–75; Alfred DiMaio Jr., *Soviet Urban Housing: Problems and Policies* (New York: Praeger, 1974).

115. Krzysztof Kosiński, "Prywatki młodzieże w czasach PRL," in *PRL Trwanie i Zmiana,* ed. Dariusz Stol and Marcin Zaremba (Warsaw: Trio, 2003), 324–26.

116. Verdery, *What Was Socialism?* 29–57.

117. Rudy Koshar, "Seeing, Travelling, and Consuming: An Introduction," in Koshar, *Histories of Leisure;* Anne E. Gorsuch, "'There's No Place Like Home': Soviet Tourism in Late Stalinism," *Slavic Review* 62, no. 4 (Winter 2003): 760–85; Christian Noack, "Coping with the Tourist: Planned and 'Wild' Mass Tourism on the Soviet Black Sea Coast," and Scott Moranda, "East German Nature Tourism 1945–1961: In

Search of a Common Destination," both in Gorsuch and Koenker, *Turizm*, 281–304 and 266–80.

118. Key works in what is now a significant field of scholarship include Sabrina Ramet, *Rocking the State: Rock Music and Politics in Eastern Europe and Russia* (Boulder, Colo.: Westview, 1994); Timothy Ryback, *Rock Around the Bloc: A History of Rock Music in Eastern Europe and the Soviet Union* (New York and Oxford: Oxford University Press, 1990); Artem Troitsky, *Back in the USSR* (London: Faber and Faber, 1987); Hilary Pilkington, *Russia's Youth and Its Culture: A Nation's Constuctors and Constructed* (London: Routledge, 1994); Uta G. Poiger, *Jazz, Rock, and Rebels: Cold War Politics and American Culture in a Divided Germany* (Berkeley: University of California Press, 2000); Przemysław Zieliński, *Scena rockowa w PRL* (Warsaw: Trio, 2005).

119. Edele, "Strange Young Men."

120. See, for instance, Ellen Propper Mickiewicz, *Split Signals: Television and Politics in the Soviet Union* (Oxford: Oxford University Press, 1988); Neil Postman, *Amusing Ourselves to Death: Public Discourse in the Age of Show Business* (New York: Viking, 1985).

121. For a recent discussion of the operation of different social and professional networks in Eastern Bloc societies, see various essays in György Péteri, ed., *Patronage, Personal Networks and the Party-State: Everyday Life in the Cultural Sphere in Communist Russia and East Central Europe*, Trondheim Studies on East Europe Cultures and Societies 13 (Trondheim: PEECS, 2004).

122. See David Wedgwood Benn, *Persuasion and Soviet Politics* (Oxford: Blackwell, 1989).

123. See Potocki, "Life and Times of Poland's 'Bikini Boys,'" 259–90.

124. Yurchak, *Everything Was Forever*, 204.

125. See various essays in *Slavic Review* 68, no. 2 (2009), a special issue under the title "Emotional Turn? Feelings in Russian History and Culture," edited by Jan Plamper; J. Plamper and B. Lazier, eds., *Fear: Across the Disciplines* (Pittsburgh: University of Pittsburgh Press, forthcoming 2010); Jan Plamper, S. Schahadat, and M. Elie, eds., *Rossiiskaia imperiia chuvstv: Podkhody k kul'turnoi istorii emostsii* [In the Realm of Russian Feelings: Approaches to the Cultural History of Emotions] (Moscow: Novoe literaturnoe obozrenie, forthcoming 2010).

126. Phil Cohen and Laurie Taylor, *Escape Attempts* (London: Routledge, 1992), 85.

127. Yurchak, *Everything Was Forever*, 213.

CHAPTER ONE

Luxury in Socialism: An Absurd Proposition?

Ina Merkel

This classic essay on the subject of luxury in the German Democratic Republic, by a scholar who is able to combine theoretical analysis with personal experience, appears here in English translation for the first time. Historian Ina Merkel has been one of the leading figures researching the rhetoric, policies, and effects of consumption in Eastern European societies under communist rule, a growing sphere of investigation in recent years. Scholarship on the GDR has led the field. The reasons for this may be found, in part, in the close proximity of the two Germanies. Border crossings by citizens from the West and the capacity to tune in to broadcasting signals from the Federal Republic, as well as the economic priorities of the East German state, created a sharp awareness of the politics of consumption.[1]

Consumption in the German Democratic Republic became an emotive issue long before German reunification. Shortages of particular consumer goods—from bananas to cars—had been a common explanation for the exodus to the West known as "voting with your feet." According to such arguments, East Germans "chose the Deutschmark" in order to gain access to the world of goods in the West, which had been presented by the media for decades. In discussions of this process, the central problems of socialist consumption have frequently been reduced to the shortage of particular consumer goods; the aesthetic impoverishment and lack of variety of products; wage and price policies that were not based on achievement and which resulted in a widespread leveling of cultural and social differences; the Socialist Unity Party's (SED's) paternalistic claims to provide for all through subsidy and distribution policies; and, finally, the privileging of certain strata of society (Party leaders, Stasi officers, captains of industry, artists, etc.).[2]

The socialist "way of life" appears, in this model, as highly homogenized: a lack of choice between products created a certain uniformity, while consumption was overdetermined by social expectations and state constraints, leaving only very limited "niches" for individual action and decision-making. These circumstances have been represented through opposing concepts such as collectivism and individualism, or homogenization and pluralism, and interpreted primarily in terms of the contradiction between norms and needs. Most analyses of this kind take as their starting point the end of the GDR, which they frequently attribute to shortage in the consumer sphere and restricted freedom to travel abroad.

A classic example of this reductivist argument is provided by the Bundestag Enquiry Commission (Enquete-Kommission des Bundestages) in the closing statements of a report entitled "Overcoming the Consequences of the SED Dictatorship in the Process of German Unity":

> The experience of shortage was an inalienable aspect of everyday reality in the GDR. To live in the GDR was, in many respects, to live in shortage and to live with shortage. Shortage was a defining and characteristic quality of everyday life in the GDR, quite consciously experienced by all, regardless of their political views. These experiences are not bound to particular historical periods, specific regions, or to certain social circles; rather, they were present all the time and everywhere.

Shortage was supposed in many respects to have been politically significant and characteristic, and therefore it was "justified to speak of the GDR as a 'society of shortage.'"[3] Material shortages as well as spiritual impoverishment were not, of course, political aims, but they were nevertheless system specific.

Shortage was put down, on the one hand, to the central command economy with its plan that had the force of law, and on the other, to the primacy of politics to which economic necessity was always subordinated. The underlying assumption here was that shortages could have been avoided in other political and economic conditions, specifically those in which private property and market competition prevail. According to this hypothesis, a discussion of luxury under state socialism would appear paradoxical: first, because the unsophisticated and inadequate supply of consumer goods left little scope for luxurious fantasies; and second, because the socialist ideal was oriented toward the abolition of social differences. Conspicuous consumption was, if not impossible, certainly taboo. Nevertheless, people lived extravagantly (the groaning tables at private celebrations became proverbial);

luxury goods were produced (and sold in a chain of specially designated shops with brand names like Exquisit and Delikat); and particular social circles cultivated exclusive lifestyles, purchasing antique furniture, chrome-plated bathroom fittings from the Intershop stores [a chain of shops selling rare items and Western goods in exchange for hard currency], and Western cars. My own childhood memories, for instance, include an incident at the beginning of the 1970s. I recall a sports convertible pulling up outside the high school in Königs Wusterhausen, a small town near Berlin. Two long-haired guys in stolen jeans with books in their arms got out. It was Maxim Dessau, son of the famous composer, and his friend arriving at school in the way that was, for them, quite normal. With their simple ability to have fun, to enjoy driving fast and the pleasure of being stared at in amazement, they seemed to me the embodiment of pure luxury, not only in the sense of conspicuous consumption, but also in their individualism and independence from prevailing norms and values.

The question of the specific socialist relationship to luxury and con-sumption was also important for another reason. Luxury and shortage or need do not exist in themselves: they are relative terms that must first be filled with concrete historical content. That which, in specific historical con-ditions, is perceived as necessity, shortage, or luxury is determined by what is perceived, in those particular circumstances, to be normal. The concrete meaning of shortage or luxury is not only subject to enormous historical processes of transformation but also differs greatly according to class or other social distinctions.

Transformation from Luxury into Necessity

We must, then, always seek out the specific historical patterns of consump-tion. It is here that a society expresses what it deems legitimate need and what it considers luxury and thus rejects as excess. These historically specific relations reflect the norm and value structure of society; as Mary Douglas and Baron Isherwood note, "the patterns of consumption show up the pat-terns of society."[4]

Historical development is marked by a tendency for objects to "sink" from the category "luxury" to that of "normal." "That which formerly seemed luxury is now necessity," as Marx described this process in his *Grundrisse* (*Foundations of the Critique of Political Economy*) of 1857–58, analyzing "the transformation of that which seemed superfluous into necessity, historically generated need."[5] Luxury is thus continuously reinterpreted in opposition to necessity, which is itself in a constant process of transformation. This was problematic for the GDR, for by the end of the 1960s, living standards in West Germany had come to stand as a benchmark for those in the East too, and this called into question the value structure of socialist society. Televisions, refrigerators, washing machines, and cars all sank from being luxuries into the condition of general "necessity." The desire for such goods was no longer considered exaggerated or absurd but normal for an urban industrial society. Yet this normalization was contradicted by GDR price policies which continued to mark them out as luxury goods.

Luxury as "Irrational Consumption"

Luxury had a second meaning in the GDR: as the opposite of shortage. As such, it served as the starting point for a critique of relations in a system of distribution in which certain social strata were unable to satisfy their human needs while others consumed goods in excess. Marx called the latter "overconsumption and irrational consumption, that turns out to be monstrous and bizarre."[6] Here the concept of luxury is connected with a cultural critique of exaggeration, of the unnecessary, of extravagance. Luxury came to mean anything that exceeds "normal" living standards in terms of expenditure and splendor and which is not only unnecessary, but also consumed at the expense of others who have to do without even bare necessities.

Shortage and luxury function here as terms defined in relation to each other. Both stand in critical relation to the principles of distribution based on the equitable redistribution of resources which were supposed to prevail in the GDR. The ideological explanation of luxury is founded in precisely this discourse. The relations of consumption in a socialist society are perfectly clear: no one should enrich themselves at the expense of others. That forms of privilege did exist nevertheless (enjoyed, for example, by important specialists or high-ranking politicians) was hard to reconcile with this principle. But far more problematic than these concessions to achievement was the growing influence of a second currency, the "Westmark," on consumer relations in the GDR. Relations with the West made possible a form of symbolic distinction that was actually forbidden under socialist conditions. The Intershop became an extraterritorial space, an enclave of luxury in the midst of a product culture based on necessity. Exquisit shops (selling high fashion) and Delikat shops (for luxury food products) were also opened, in which Western goods were sold for GDR currency, albeit at extremely inflated prices.

Longing for Luxury

The yearning for luxury had a third dimension. It signified not only a demand for distinction and extravagance, but also for pleasure. A pleasure-oriented consumer yearns for objects that are not only beautiful and costly, but also comfortable and elegant. Even leisure is a form of luxury when it is spent—or squandered—as free time with no other purpose but enjoyment. In other words, luxury also means to live pleasurably.

Thus the question of luxury brings us to the theme of hedonism, and to the ability to enjoy oneself as an active consumer. Here we come up against a paradox: shortage does not necessarily imply an inability to enjoy oneself, nor is luxury synonymous with hedonism. Rather, in some circumstances exactly the opposite is true. Consider, for example, consumption in the immediate postwar period in Germany. It is clear that in these years only the most immediate needs could be satisfied and even then not always adequately. Many consumer desires were put on hold. The overriding principle of distribution according to need ensured by the system of rationing had strongly equalizing effects. Nevertheless, one cannot underestimate the significance of objects that were freely traded and acquired on the black market. It was precisely the rarity of certain things that made them desirable and which rendered their consumption particularly satisfying. Shortage did not automatically lead to ascetic patterns of consumption; life was enjoyed to the full in hedonistic feasts, among other things. Limited resources provoked creativity and innovation.

The temptation to spend one's resources immediately on satisfying one's needs instead of saving them up for "rational" use is designated in the literature as a basic characteristic of proletarian consumer relations: "consumption defined by frugal and irregular pleasures fosters an elementary hedonism," writes Dietrich Mühlberg. In his view, such practices "made the proletariat the descendants of feudalism."[7] Proletarian consumer practices have two aspects: thrift, in which needs are met by making goods last and by using them up completely; and rapid, spontaneous consumption to compensate for inescapable misery. Food, clothing, and accommodation have to be cheap and "practical," thereby exacerbating the need occasionally to break free of such restrictions.

In these forms of consumer relations, to replace one good by a more fashionable version or to discard an object prematurely before it is completely exhausted appears luxurious. The pinnacle of luxury is the acquisition of "senseless" objects that do not even demonstrate economic and cultural potency but simply represent a waste of time and money, that is, from a bourgeois intellectual perspective, kitsch: a saltshaker in the shape of a piglet, a porcelain figurine of a dancer, a painted plate, an indoor fountain, and the cheap, fleeting pleasures offered by the circus, dance hall, cinema, fairground, and so on. The proletariat treat themselves to this order of luxury perhaps precisely because it stands in complete contradiction to the unremitting exploitation of the workforce in capitalism.

This behavior reveals the contradiction between ideals and daydreams. Popular fantasies of Schlaraffenland—unlike the great social and state utopias of Rousseau, Owen, Fourier, and Marx—are not concerned with the abolition of luxury but with its democratization.[8] They are not concerned with the provision of work for all but with enrichment through idleness. They do not seek the equal distribution of money but its abolition. Whereas the communist vision of utopia had an ideal image of productive, working, creative citizens at its heart, popular utopias tended to hark back to a feudal *habitus* in which each individual was an aristocrat.

Why is it important to examine the issue of luxury in the context of the GDR? This was a society whose social structures were shaped largely by the lower middle [*unterbürgerlichen*] classes. There, ideological and idealized images of the proletariat engaged in class struggle were propagated. The real—and much vaunted—needs of the workforce stood, however, in contrast to this image. The ideals set in consumer politics reproduced the *habitus* of the parsimonious petit bourgeois, but the requirements of the lower classes and of the young, a new consumer group emerging in the postwar period, were more hedonistically oriented.

Contradictions of Consumer Politics

There are GDR-specific dimensions to all three registers of luxury discussed above. The first is the competition presented by the object-world of the West, both in the form of images presented by the media and also in tangible things: this influenced consumer culture in the East. The second is that the utopian ideals of justice could count on a broad consensus in the "workers' society" (Wolfgang Engler). Finally, the traditional consumption practices of predominantly lower-class strata have to be acknowledged. Out of this combination of factors, exacerbated by a tense industrial and political situation, ever-new tensions continued to arise between utopia and need, and between social ideals and individual subjectivity. These tensions may be discerned in the contradictions of GDR consumer politics. In what follows we shall discuss one of these contradictions as an illustration: pricing policies were supposed to equalize lifestyles through the mechanism of fixed prices, yet they promoted social distinctions through the operation of two price classes. Price policies thus came into systematic contradiction with the state's guiding political ideals. Moreover, these policies operated in conditions of pressure from the population. The ensuing compromise was, in the end, not only economically contradictory but also robbed the pricing policies of their own logic.

Redistribution of Wealth

In order to understand the conflicts which the consumer politics of the
GDR had to negotiate, it is necessary to review briefly the communist conception of utopia in regard to wealth and consumption, against which background the system and policies were constructed. The alpha and omega of
socialist consumer politics after 1945, with roots in socialist thought of the
1920s, was the ideal of the satisfaction of need. However, in the conditions
of real existing socialism this could only be met in a partial and fragmented
way. The utopian substance of the socialist ideal of society was defined essentially by antithesis to and in distinction from the capitalist model of state
and economy. It was to represent an alternative to the Western model of
affluence by creating a "counter-modernity" [*Gegenmoderne*].[9] This impera-
tive remained even when, in the course of postwar development, enormous
and widespread transformations took place in the living standards of the
working classes.

Integral to this vision of society was a particular idea of what mankind
needed for its well-being, how people should live, what they should consume, and how they should spend their time. The communist ideal—to
provide "to each according to his needs"—aimed to abolish serious differences between rich and poor and was based on the assumption that, when
these differences were overcome, private property (although not individual
possessions) would become meaningless. Such notions are deeply rooted in
the Western Christian tradition and also have always played a large part in
the political ideals of the workers' movement.

Under the conditions of classless society, it was thought, consumption
would no longer have any significance as symbolic capital. Objects would be
reduced, even in their aesthetic form, to their use value. Cultural differences
would not be expressed through objects acquired, but through diversity of
forms and rich individuality. Curiously, such utopias are also familiar in the
Western world, to be found in nearly every science fiction film.[10] What appears problematic now is that real existing socialism was concerned mainly
with leveling social differences and opposed the projection of personality,
treating it with skepticism, rejection, and indeed anxiety. This confuses the
picture, but it is important to remember that the commitment to the all-
round development of the individual was central to the original utopian
project.

A simple formula for the communist conception of utopia is the aim of
winning free time for the development of the individual and of accumulating a wealth of relationships rather than a wealth of objects. The communist

utopia also emphasizes utility value rather than cultural-symbolic distinction. This only holds good under the conditions of developed need, in which the acquisition of objects is governed by their necessity for use rather than for ownership.

In contrast to Christian concepts of equality, the communist ideal was founded on a concept of need that not only distinguished between necessity and luxury, but also between consumptive and productive needs. Work was to become the salient sphere of human self-development and even the primary requirement of life. This presupposed the abolition of alienating working conditions, and the dissolution of the differences between mental and physical labor and between country and city. The reorganization of property relations was understood to be a necessary premise for this, although it was not a sufficient condition in itself.

The socialist ideal of equality seemed to be attainable in that the relations of production and consumption were not to be regulated by the market—as a system of supply and demand that regulated itself by means of price—but instead by the central plan, through fixed prices that were determined by social criteria, and by subsidizing basic needs. Faith in the possibility of planning social processes was one of the most important components of the communist utopia. If societal and human needs could be calculated, then, it was hoped, resources would not be wasted unnecessarily, work time could be reduced to the minimum, and people would only desire what they truly needed to secure their existence or free development. Such a concept did not automatically require abnegation on the part of the consumer, nor did it imply dictatorship over needs. Rather, it focused on the culturally critical distinctions between genuine and false, excessive demands. Consumption over and above these real needs was interpreted as compensation for an unsatisfying life. True satisfaction lay in being productive and creative.

Such thinking, which may also be found in the Western bourgeois critique of consumption, displayed a paternalistic attitude toward the population. It required of them rational consumption:

> The class enemy also wants to harm us by orienting the population's needs towards the so-called "American way of life." The American way of life is in truth nothing other than a life of luxury for a small minority at the expense of the majority and a waste of material value that the working classes have created.[11]

Luxury here not only connoted uneven relations of distribution, but also included a moral appeal to all to be economical with the resources available. The problem lay in the attitude of some consumers in whom a multitude of habits and vestigial attitudes from capitalist society are still present. This is why it is necessary to exert a constant active influence over the development of the needs of man ... This will only succeed in struggle against various forms of prestige consumption and the fight against manifestations of egoism or the privileging of personal interests over the interests of society.[12]

The education of consumers to become rational users was formulated as a long-term task not only because they were resistant and continued to insist on their habits, but also because the improvement of living standards and the welfare of the majority had been inscribed on socialism's banners. The goal and claim of socialist production was, as every Party meeting emphasized, the constant improvement in the satisfaction of the population's needs. The legitimacy of the socialist system depended fundamentally on success in the sphere of consumption.

This was not so easy to achieve, however. The party-state leadership found itself under pressure to succeed—an effect of constant comparison with the West—if it wanted to avoid exposing its economic strategy to open discussion. Nevertheless, the debate continued to be marked by an irrepressible rhetoric of superiority, for under socialism, everyone was guaranteed the basic requirements of life (work, clothing, food, accommodation) and there was no division of society between the prosperous, who could afford any bauble and deliberate wastefulness (bathing in champagne), and the poor, living in wretched penury, who had to sleep under bridges and go hungry.

The socialist ideal of the satisfaction of needs rested on a consensus behind a number of assumptions, such as the just distribution of goods and the elimination of unnecessary wastage. But conflict ensued from other assumptions at the heart of the ideology, such as the view of work as a necessity, or the ideal of rational consumption norms and collective ownership of property as against individual requirements and expectations. To be sure, official consumption policies attempted to serve both interests, but ultimately all decisions were made according to the priorities of economic policy. These were often in opposition to communist ideals and tacitly promoted something that should actually have been a matter of contention: the individual striving for possessions and for distinction. Pricing policy was a key example of this dilemma of socialist consumption politics.

The Dilemma of Price Policies

Alongside the abolition of private, capitalist property relations, important features of GDR consumer politics included the policy of fixed prices and the subsidization of basic needs. Price was the next most important instrument after the plan for shaping the national economy. In the GDR the gradual abolition of rationing was combined with the creation of a complicated administrative system of fixed prices that applied to the same wares throughout the republic, regardless of the time and place of purchase. Since prices were not determined by the relations of supply and demand but were set in advance, they could not, as in other societies, be modified to regulate the market. Indeed, this was not seen as their role. Their fundamental purpose was to create and maintain social justice and equality.

But since the necessary net income could only be accumulated through prices, and the socialist state had an insatiable need to accumulate capital for its investment, prices still reflected the relations between the needs of society and those of individuals. While particular groups of commodities were heavily subsidized, the prices of others were artificially inflated in order to provide the capital needed for state investment in industry. This was potentially a source of enormous social conflict. For prices signaled what could and could not be deemed legitimate wants of the individual.

Pricing policy in the GDR was exercised through various strategies that in part contradicted one another. On the one hand, it was focused on the demands of population groups with the lowest income. Thus the prices of basic goods and services—accommodation, nutrition, transport, culture, education—were maintained at artificially low rates subsidized by the state. On the other hand, since the net income required by the state had to be raised, all other goods were distinguished either according to the principle of differential pricing (reflecting "standard" and "high" demand) or were classified as luxury goods and were sold for sometimes extremely high prices. Although these price policies protected a minimal standard of living, they also created precisely what they sought to avoid, namely social differentiation.[13] Over the years this proved problematic for two reasons. First, the structure of demands underwent fundamental transformation. New consumer goods appeared for the first time on the market, and what had once been exclusive commodities systematically sank to become basic needs (for example, refrigerators, washing machines, and even cars). The fixed price system, however, resisted this dynamic. Second, it became increasingly evident that two different levels or classes of goods were emerging: there were ever fewer standard goods, and those no longer represented a genuine alternative to those at the higher price level. This development resulted in stealthy price increases. Although the goal set by ideology was to end social differentiation, the actual effect of state price policies was to exacerbate it. Moreover, paternalistic subsidies resulted in the abuse and waste of resources—starting with bread and extending to water, heating, and even to living space.

When price policy, as outlined in general terms here, was discussed by the Party leadership, East-West comparisons invariably lurked in the background. However, throughout the years the same conclusions were drawn from this comparison: the prices of staple goods, rent, transport, and culture were decisively lower in the GDR, while those for textiles, shoes, and industrially manufactured consumer goods were lower in the Federal Republic. Such differences between very different kinds of goods hardly compensated for each other. On the contrary, the perception of price advantages shifted in favor of West Germany as the structure of needs changed. And because the value of an object or service was not adequately expressed in its price, consumers also lost the sense of its cultural and social value. Rent and travel were no longer really perceived as costs, a fact that changed quickly after the "Wende" (the transition from state socialism and the planned economy to democracy and the market economy in East Germany after 1989).

Wage increases and price reductions were the most important propaganda tools in the 1950s and 1960s to make palpable the German Democratic Republic's prosperity and progress, and the growing well-being of each individual. The superiority of the socialist system had to be proven through price stability at low levels. In this respect, price policy had a profound symbolic significance which was very well understood by the population. However, it also raised expectations that the existing prices were the highest they would ever be, and—in accordance with the logic of growth in work productivity—would therefore systematically fall until, one day, no price would be set and no money would be needed. This utopian ideal was not so much the measure of reality as of the government's legitimacy. It restricted enormously the political and economic room for maneuver and came increasingly into contradiction with the changing requirements of the population. The Party leadership found itself in a dilemma of its own making resulting from its propaganda. Fixed prices emerged ever more clearly as the Achilles' heel of economic policy the longer the GDR survived.

Compromises: Enclaves of Capitalism

As early as 1948, economic functionaries (especially from the Ministry of Trade and Supply, as well as the Plan Commission) attempted to create a market economy alongside the fixed-price principle. During the rationing period a chain of "HO" shops (Staatliche Handelsorganisation: State Trade Organization) opened up a market niche in which goods that were in short supply were put on sale at very high prices.[14] Although even these prices were not negotiable, they were nevertheless much more susceptible to the dynamics of supply and demand. Just three years after the abolition, in 1961, of rationing of goods essential for survival (including butter, bread, vegetables, clothing, footwear, and coal), this institution was complemented by the chain of Exquisit stores and, in 1966, by Delikat stores. All three institutions offered select goods at high, and sometimes extremely inflated, prices. They represented another important face of GDR consumption politics.

There were, of course, differences between the HO, where goods in short supply still dominated, and Exquisit and Delikat, which, as the names suggest, were founded explicitly on high-end demand. The products on offer were not only scarce commodities but superior goods such as high-fashion clothing and quality foodstuffs at absurd prices. In these shops you could find something special, exquisite indeed: that is, luxuries. The introduction of these stores was intended to siphon off the buying power of the elevated social strata. They were also intended, from a political point of view, to motivate and secure the loyalty of well-paid, highly qualified specialists such as engineers, doctors, and artists. Their privileges were legitimized by arguing that their labors supported the common weal.

Although intended for the higher strata, these expensive shops attracted an unexpectedly large flow of customers from a broad range of the population. When in 1958, as an experiment, the first "Sybille" fashion store was opened in Berlin, journalists fell over themselves with enthusiasm. Euphoric newspaper articles recounted the unrestrained pleasure that was to be found in such fantastic offerings as "the pure silk afternoon dress from Poland next to the sea-green linen dress by the Art and Fashion VEB [Volkseigener Betrieb—"publicly owned enterprise"]. A Dutch mohair jacket hung in the window next to the fashionable afternoon jacket with large fur trimming by VEB Elegant Berlin . . . leather waistcoats and cherry-red underclothing, golden evening slippers and petticoats of batiste and Perlon."[15] Pure silk, linen, mohair, leather, good-quality and precious materials were on offer here. Journalists reveled in descriptions of "shopophilia" [*Kauflust*], i.e., to be able at last to rummage again among the paraphernalia and to choose among abundance. Money was a secondary issue, not in a practical but in a symbolic sense. As an aside, it was noted with regret that "most things in the shop are unfortunately still too expensive. The custom-made and high-quality imports are simply very costly."[16] Only a few sentences later, however, attention was drawn to the great influx of consumers that the boutique experienced in its first days.

Although very expensive designer clothing was for sale here, it did not lead to a fundamental debate about the price structure among either the Party leadership or the population. The latter—already primed by the HO—were prepared to accept higher prices for particular goods.

In order to make it clear that such shops should remain the exception and that cheap, standard goods would continue to exist, it was decreed in 1961 that only a limited number of clearly identified shops could sell select items of clothing: "top-quality, custom-made" products that met the most exacting criteria. The highest possible prices were set.[17] These shops were explicitly branded for the public as "Exquisit" stores. Individual shops additionally had their own names, such as Yvonne, Jeannette, Madeleine, Kavalier, Pinguin, Piccolo, or Charmant; almost all borrowed from French and evidently chosen to evoke Parisian haute couture.

Such branded stores were carefully selected and ostentatiously fitted out. The personnel were selected from the best salespersons and were extensively trained. Exquisit shops offered individual service, countering the tendency toward self-service. The tone of sales staff was civil and attentive: "allow us to show you everything in our salon without obligation," proclaimed the ladies' fashion salon Honetta on its visitors' cards.[18] Items in shopwindows were not allowed to display their prices.[19] In 1969 the Exquisit store chain developed its own brand identity, a little cursive "e" with "Modesalon" inscribed beneath it, which thereafter not only distinguished the shops but also decorated its labels, bills, and letterhead.[20] All this lifted the Exquisit shops above ordinary retail traders. The government placed particular emphasis on this exclusive sales culture. Beginning with the external appearance and continuing in the interior design of the shop, they were to create a quality shopping atmosphere. Objects presented in this way, in comparison with the stockpiling of cheap standard goods, produced the particular aura that seemed to justify the steep prices. The Exquisit shops exuded an air of bourgeois elegance that raised them above the coarse, pragmatic way of dealing with things in the normal HO shops, an experience which was either satisfying or nerve-wracking, depending on your generation and class background.

This highlights a double anachronism in the institution of the Exquisit shops: the step into modernity to meet world standards was carried out in a bourgeois and exclusive realm. Meanwhile, in the area that represented the real appeal of Western consumer society—the overwhelming availability of cheap goods—the GDR set itself the task to provide serviceable, practical things justified by need.

Boutiques and Exquisit and Delikat shops were a great success, a fact that indicates their high level of public acceptance. Reports spoke again and again of the great popularity that the Exquisit shops enjoyed with GDR citizens.[21] In the vernacular they came to be known by the abbreviation

"Ex," and the Delikat stores even became "Freß-Ex" (Posh Nosh). This is surprising given their high prices, and can only be explained by the status value of their goods. Exquisit shops functioned, in an otherwise thoroughly standardized consumer culture, as a hallmark of the exceptional. They attained the status of a brand. The effect of a brand is based on the connection that is established between it and the commodity. In the case of Exquisit, the brand name testified to a particular provenance, the West, and to a particular quality, luxury.

Despite the high acceptance of such shops, the state and Party leadership still faced problems legitimizing them. This is evident in their refusal to engage in public debate or argumentation about their existence. Only in 1965 would an article first appear in *Young World* (*Junge Welt*) under the provocative title: "Do You Think It Is Right That We Have Exquisit Shops Here?" The problem addressed was that the young did not have enough money to shop there:

> Fritz: What don't you like about select goods being sold in particular shops? After all, that's what Exquisit means in German: select.
>
> Horst: The prices. Only a few people can afford to shop there.[22]

The specific object of their discussion was nylon shirts, for which one had to pay 80 marks in Exquisit, while in the West they only cost 15 to 20 Deutschmarks (DM). Thus, imports from the West were the issue, but *Young World* carefully sidestepped this:

> Fritz: . . . Because they are the latest thing, there aren't many of them at first. Usually just one designer or design group created them, and only a single manufacturer has picked them up. As long as there is only a relatively small number of them, they count as high fashion.
>
> Horst: I see. You mean that as long as there are only a few, they should have a high price.
>
> Fritz: Yes, don't you think so? If someone wants to be the first to wear a high-fashion coat, or pullover, or a scarf like this or to wear a newly launched shoe style, why shouldn't they pay more for them? And they do so too.[23]

The article went on to explain why the GDR was not yet able to afford, in economic terms, to produce more goods of this sort and thus lower the prices correspondingly:

Horst: So Exquisit shoppers contribute, to some extent, to higher-quality goods being produced for everyone. I like that.[24]

Those with higher income levels were to pay for general prosperity. Justice was thus restored. While under Walter Ulbricht, Exquisit and Delikat shops were conceived as a necessary evil because they generated income, under Honecker they became the chief instrument of consumption politics. He developed them into regular alternatives for GDR citizens without access to Western money. They became a kind of equivalent to the Intershops. Such explanations as the discussion presented on the pages of *Young World* did not, however, remove the basic problem that the two classes of prices or products indirectly promoted the formation of level-specific differences; they only made them more acceptable.

From the start all strata of society shopped at the HO, and at Exquisit and Delikat. For those who earned little, these were rare excursions into a fascinating world of goods, while for higher income groups shopping in these stores became the norm, a habit they could not do without. The policy of having two classes of products was at first targeted at the distinctive needs of the elevated levels, in order systematically to siphon off their buying power. In the end, it led to a deeper social inequality that not only expressed itself in income differences but also consolidated cultural distinctions. If the Exquisit and Delikat shops were originally only aimed at elevated, exclusive demands, over the years, they came to be seen as normal. This shift also reflected transformations in GDR consumption patterns, which became increasingly oriented toward enjoyment and pleasure in shopping.

Subsistence Versus Life Building

In cultural terms, GDR consumption politics were concerned with the structure, manner, and extent of the needs of the socialist society's inhabitants. These needs were assessed, influenced, and, in varying degrees, also satisfied. Socialist ideals of equality aimed at the abolition of differences between the living conditions of the rich—a squandering, profit-oriented, parasitical exploiting class—and of the poverty-ridden, exploited working classes. These ideals were elevated to a cultural value. So too was the idea of social security, enshrined as dogma in the trinity Work, Bread, Housing. Socialism always proclaimed its superiority with regard to the satisfaction of basic needs: in low rent, inexpensive groceries, cheap fares, health care, and childcare, and in the absence of unemployment and homelessness. This represented a foretaste of the communist vision of consumption. However, in regard to the higher demands of life building (*Lebensgestaltung*), the state and Party leadership were confronted with an enormous social transformation. European postwar development had unexpectedly produced ever-increasing prosperity for the masses. Despite, or perhaps even because of, the development of a broad middle class both in the East and in the West and the social assimilation of their living standards, the desire for a refined lifestyle and cultural distinction grew. The socialist system of values and the very criteria used for East-West comparison came into conflict. But not because these desires for refined lifestyles and the values they expressed contradicted communist ideals (which were focused not on the accumulation of material wealth but rather on the development of productive needs, that is, the need to produce rather than to consume). Rather, it was because their needs could only be partially afforded. Ultimately, it was the needs of the cherished working class that were granted legitimacy.

"Prosperity for all" (*Wohlstand für alle*) was the declared goal of socialist consumption policy, whereby the authorities and the population shared the same expectations of prosperity and satisfaction. However, these equalizing tendencies, on the one hand, and the urge for distinction and individualization on the other, collided again and again. The historic relations between legitimate and unacceptable, excessive needs were not fixed once and for all, but had to be constantly renegotiated. The conservatism of the Party leadership—a product of their age and life experiences—rendered the state ill-suited to deal with this reality.

Notes

1. This essay is a translation of Ina Merkel, "Luxus im Sozialismus: Eine widersinnige Fragestellung?" in *"Luxus und Konsum": Eine historische Annäherung,* ed. Reinhold Reith and Torsten Meyer (Münster: Waxmann, 2003), 221–36. Translated by Nadine Stares with Susan E. Reid.

2. See Ina Merkel, *Utopie und Bedürfnis: Die Geschichte der Konsumkultur in der DDR* (Cologne: Böhlau, 1999).

3. Final report of the Bundestag Enquiry Commission, "Überwindung der Folgen der SED-Diktatur im Prozeß der deutschen Einheit," item 13/11000 (June 10, 1998), 197.

4. Mary Douglas and Baron Isherwood, *World of Goods: Towards an Anthropology of Consumption* (London: Routledge, 1996), n.p.

5. Karl Marx, *Grundrisse der Kritik der politischen Ökonomie,* Marx-Engels-Werke 42 (Berlin: Dietz, 1973), 434. For an English translation, see Karl Marx, *Grundrisse: Foundations for the Critique of Political Economy (Rough Draft),* trans. Martin Nicolaus (Harmondsworth, Eng.: Penguin and New Left Books, 1973).

6. Ibid., 347.

7. Dietrich Mühlberg et al., "Zeit im Kapitalismus und proletarische Freizeit-kultur: Zur historischen Ausbildung sozialistischen Freizeitkultur: Thesen 1986," in

Freizeit als Lebensraum arbeitender Menschen im Sozialismus—Ihr Platz in der Freizeit-kultur des 20. Jahrhunderts (Berlin: Humboldt-Universitat, 1987), 12.

8. See Dieter Richter, *Schlaraffenland: Geschichte einer populären Phantasie* (Frankfurt am Main: Fischer, 1989).

9. Rainer Land, "Unvereinbar: Avantgardismus und Modernismus. Discussion: Waren die Reformsozialisten verhinderte Sozialdemokraten? Teil 1" ("Incompatible: Avant-Gardism and Modernism. Discussion: Were the Reform Socialists Would-Be Social Democrats? Part 1"), *Neues Deutschland,* April 23–24, 1994, 10.

10. Two forms of consumer utopia can be distinguished. On the one hand, there is the simple vision of superfluity, as in Schlaraffenland. The constant availability of every desired thing, however, quickly leads to boredom. On the other hand, we have images of uniformity and asceticism, coupled with productivity and creativity. Twentieth-century science fiction films frequently include scenes of unbelievable monotony. All rooms are identically furnished. They are very functionally organized. The various accessories that might reveal the status of the occupant are all absent. People are all identically dressed, indeed in costumes that, serving purely practical functions, are similar to uniforms. Against this background their individuality, which we have no doubt that they possess, is expressed only through gesture, facial expression, posture, voice, and through what they say and do. Thereby, this individuality is all the more striking. The people of the future no longer need to be distinguished through clothing and ornament. This new lifestyle is premised on the idea that money no longer exists and no one wants to have more than he absolutely needs for life. It is quite incredible that such an anti-consumption concept fills audiences with such enthusiasm today. Perhaps this is because the renunciation of consumption is not the focus, but rather a concrete and wholeheartedly enjoyed pleasure in social relationships. And because these new people are given something in exchange: endless time free of external pressures for survival in which to devote themselves entirely to developing their personalities.

11. Stiftung Archive of Party and Mass Organization in the GDR in the Bundesarchiv (SAPMO BA), Dy 30/IV 2/610/14, unpaginated, commissioned for the Politburo (September 16, 1961).

12. Ibid.

13. Social differentiation through the consumption of goods available for purchase requires different levels of expendable income. Income policy in the GDR comes into play here. There were social strata with significantly higher-than-average incomes, including small-scale entrepreneurs, engineers in important economic fields, academics in economically relevant positions (such as inventors and researchers), and artists of national significance.

14. The HO stores were established in 1948 in response to black market trading. In the years that followed, reductions in the prices of goods for sale in the HO stores were much vaunted in propaganda as a defining feature of socialist economics. A gradual convergence of market prices and those charged in HO stores occurred until 1958, when rationing was officially lifted and fixed prices introduced (which were to remain in place until the end of the GDR). However, here yet another principle was at play. Creeping price increases took place either through changes in the goods (such as the use of more valuable materials) or because new goods appeared on the market (innovations) and replaced cheaper ones that had once fulfilled the same function.

15. Inge Kerzcher in *Neues Deutschland,* August 16, 1958.

16. Ibid.

17. Dresses cost between 250 and 900 DM, ladies' jackets and coats from 45 to 1,200 DM, shoes from 110 to 185 DM, knitwear from 120 to 290 DM. SAPMO BA, Dy 30/IV A2/2021/720, Bl.27, report delivered to the Politburo (September 28, 1962).

18. SAPMO BA, Dy 30/IV 2/610/130, B1. 156. Siegfried Spann: Interview with representative of the GDR Ministry for Trade and Supply Fritz Recknagel on the meaning of the Exquisit shops (April 18, 1962).

19. SAPMO BA, DL 1–11613 (unpaginated draft), directive for the establishment of Exquisit outlets (July 1, 1962).

20. "Zeichensatzung für das Verbandzeichen 'Modesalon,'" *Verfügungen und Mitteilungen des Ministeriums für Handel und Versorgung (Decrees and Announcements of the Ministry for Trade and Supply),* vol. 8 (1969): 89.

21. SAPMO BA, Dy 30/IV 2/610/130, Bl. 156, Siegfried Spann: Interview (as in note 18).

22. Emil Dusiska, "Exquisite Waren—Exquisite Preise? Ein Gespräch um die Frage: Findest du es richtig, daß es bei uns Exquisit-Läden gibt?" ("Exquisite Goods—Exquisite Prices? A Conversation About the Question: Do You Think It Is Right That We Have Exquisit Shops Here?"), *Junge Welt,* February 2, 1965.

23. Ibid.

24. Ibid.

CHAPTER TWO

Kontra Kultura: Leisure and Youthful Rebellion

in Stalinist Poland

Katherine Lebow

For generations of East European intelligentsia, the "idiocy of rural life" proclaimed in the *Communist Manifesto* meant, above all, the cultural aridity of the village landscape. In this view, rural leisure was merely the cessation of work—a respite from toil, during which one sought temporary oblivion in drink, religion, or sleep. Like the Russian *narodniki* (nineteenth-century populists), Polish reformers had sought since the nineteenth century to awaken a desire for moral and intellectual improvement among rural common folk. Thus, when Poland's twentieth-century communist leaders planned their flagship city, Nowa Huta, it was a given that its inhabitants would have a full range of worthwhile recreational activities. Leisure in the new town would be the very antithesis of its pre-communist form; it would educate and uplift, infusing its participants with *kultura.*

Nowa Huta—like Stalinstadt in East Germany, Sztálinváros in Hungary, Nová Ostrava in Czechoslovakia, or Dimitrovgrad in Bulgaria—was designed as a model town or "socialist city," following a pattern established by Magnitogorsk in the Soviet Union in the 1930s. Like Magnitogorsk, each was centered on a large, new metallurgical plant and was to serve as a flagship not only for the new socialist economy but also for the "construction of socialism" as a whole. Nowa Huta was the biggest and arguably the most significant of the East European "socialist cities"; the gargantuan scale of the steelworks planned in Nowa Huta resulted in a projected population of one hundred thousand, and its location a stone's throw from the medieval Polish capital of Kraków heightened its symbolic importance in complex and controversial ways.

Of those who migrated to Nowa Huta in its early years, a vast majority were under the age of thirty and many were younger still, although reliable statistics are hard to come by; according to one source, in 1954, 68 percent of the workers engaged in building the steelworks were classified as "youth."[1] For the writer Marian Brandys, Nowa Huta's youthful population was to be considered "the most precious raw material of the Six-Year Plan," one which the Party would "purify . . . of all friable alloys and process into refined, stainless human steel."[2] In particular, by directing how Nowa Huta's young workers spent their leisure time, the Stalinist regime hoped to hasten their rapid transformation into "new men." Party, planners, and cultural activists hoped that the appropriate structuring of space and time devoted to leisure would equip the inhabitants for their leading role in the new order. In fact, while many newcomers to Nowa Huta aspired to put their peasant pasts behind them, many also started exhibiting a set of difficult-to-understand behaviors that were neither particularly countrified nor especially "cultured." Youth, in particular, were behaving in ways that appeared nothing short of philistine to their would-be "civilizers." Unexpectedly, the campaign for culture turned out to involve an active struggle against an autonomous sub-culture flourishing outside the bounds of formal cultural life and supervised leisure in Nowa Huta. In parallel with contemporary Western concern over "nonconformist," "work-shy," and "narcissistic" youth, authorities drew on the Soviet discourse of "hooliganism" and invented a new term, *bikiniarstwo,* to address these phenomena, which, while not unique to Nowa Huta, were particularly troubling to find in the new town.

The encounter between youth and the architects of socialist leisure in Nowa Huta is particularly revealing of the tensions that beset the Stalin-ist enterprise in post–World War II east-central Europe. Over the longer term, it raises important questions about the bases of support for and op-position to communism, and suggests that in some cases, generational and cultural divisions may have been as important as ideological ones in de-termining one's stance toward the new regime.[3] For example, while some commentators have portrayed young East European rebels of the 1950s as anticommunist heroes championing American culture and Western-style individualism, I will argue that the youth dubbed "hooligans" and *bikiniarze* in Polish communist discourse can hardly be seen as "resisting" or reject-ing communism.[4] To be sure, they flouted the stodginess, repression, and hyper-conformism of official Stalinism, with its emphasis on austerity and self-sacrifice. But this by no means translated automatically into opposition to the new government's agenda. Indeed, contemporary sources noted the apparent paradox that many of the same youth who spent their leisure time in ways entirely unacceptable to the Party were enthusiastic "builders of socialism" during the working day.[5] Moreover, Nowa Huta's hooligans and *bikiniarze* were just as much in conflict with traditional cultural elites—some of them critics of the regime—over their choice of identities based in transatlantic sartorial and musical styles. This is clear from the way that reformist intelligentsia of the Thaw era—standard-bearers of a nineteenth-century conception of *kultura*—felt just as puzzled by the irreverent, hedonistic hooligans and *bikiniarze* as did the Stalinists themselves.

In the end, for Nowa Huta's youth as well as Britain's teddy boys, Italy's *teppisti,* or Germany's *Halbstarken,* the adoption of transatlantic cultural styles represented above all a rejection of hierarchical understandings of cultural value bound to caste, class, or *Volk.* This helps explain some of the enthusiasm for "building socialism" (which on the face of it similarly opposed elitism, nationalism, etc.) among young workers who, after hours, were listening to jazz or hand-painting the Bikini atoll on their silk ties. But perhaps more important, both forms of activity unleashed a creative urge—on the one hand, the creation of a new world, on the other, of a new self. This is why it seems appropriate that Nowa Huta, where Polish socialism achieved its most utopian expression, became especially notorious for its anarchic hooligans and bikini boys. For tens of thousands of Poles, the modern promise of self-fashioning—forging an identity of one's own choosing, rather than being defined by one's accidental place in an organic social order—was sought, and sometimes fulfilled, in a city created from scratch. In this way, the story of Nowa Huta's hooligans and *bikiniarze* can help us reimagine the nature of social relations in postwar Eastern Europe.

Cultural Enlightenment

The *bikiniarze* are particularly interesting not only because they emerged within a regime that placed special emphasis on youth—based, of course, on Lenin's concept of youth as the natural ally of revolution—but because the emergence of a youth counterculture challenged, by definition, the regime's project of socialized leisure. In Leninist eyes, leisure was to be much more than the cessation of work. Apart from being time for sleep—or "passive rest"[6]—leisure hours would allow the good socialist time for purposeful self-improvement (under the tutelage, of course, of the Party). The Leninist model of "cultural enlightenment" was undeniably an element of the regime's project of political indoctrination. And yet cultural enlightenment was also an end in itself—"socialization 'through culture' but also 'for culture.'"[7]

As Anne White points out, communist leaders' understanding of "cultural enlightenment" grew out of deeply rooted Central and East European
traditions about the role of the intelligentsia and the nature of "culture"
itself.[8] Norbert Elias's comments about German *"Kultur"* are equally applicable to a Slavic context: the Polish word *kultura* designates both what
would be termed "high culture" in English as well as something more abstract and ineffable, often rendered through the untranslatable Russian word
kul'turnost'—the personal attributes of a "cultured" person. *Kul'turnost'* was
reflected in the way one spoke, ate, dressed, made love, and went to the
bathroom. It was also reflected, of course, in one's taste in music, literature, and theater.[9] East European intellectuals placed a high premium on
kul'turnost' and since the nineteenth century had considered it part of what
they believed was their mission to educate and uplift the downtrodden
peasant masses.[10] To do so was considered an essential step toward national
revitalization. The communists who came to power first in Russia and then
throughout Eastern Europe bore the strong imprint of this tradition; as
Sheila Fitzpatrick has suggested in her analysis of power struggles between
the Bolsheviks and the Russian intelligentsia, the two may have "had more
in common than either cared to admit," among other things the fact that
both "shared an idea of culture as something that (like revolution) an enlightened minority brought to the masses in order to uplift them."[11]

The actors in this chapter therefore form a triangle of communists, intelligentsia, and workers. Many members of the Polish intelligentsia were
attracted to the communist cultural platform of 1943, which stressed goals
broadly shared with other groupings: rebuilding schools and cultural institutions, mandatory schooling to age sixteen, free high school and university
study, and general support by the state for the development of knowledge,
literature, and the arts.[12] It was not until 1949 that cultural affairs were
"Stalinized" by resolutions of the fifth plenums of the Polish United Workers' Party Central Committee and Central Council of Trade Unions, respectively, and the aims of cultural work were explicitly politicized, with the
goals of cultural enlightenment defined as "indoctrination and encouraging
the fulfillment of productivity quotas."[13] But by then, many non-Stalinists
were already committed to working with the new order.

Although Nowa Huta's architects and planners had made plans for an
impressive range of cultural facilities in the new town—theaters, houses of
culture, libraries, cinemas, and more—funding for these institutions trickled
down slowly from Warsaw, which was more intent on devoting scarce resources to Nowa Huta's productive enterprises. As a result, by the mid-1950s
many of these plans had been scaled back or scratched. By default, then, the
burden of cultural enlightenment work fell to those institutions that were

cheapest to build and operate, but the demands that were placed on them were far from modest. The very conditions that made their work difficult—namely, the chaos and disarray of daily life in a "frontier" town—also generated pressure upon the network of cultural activists and facilities to compensate for these problems by providing appropriate leisure-time activities for workers.

The fundamental institutions of cultural enlightenment work in Nowa Huta were thus the *świetlice*—or, as they were often called, "red corners"—in effect, common rooms in the workers' hostels. The intimacy of these spaces was envisioned as a key factor in promoting culture among Nowa Huta's masses: "Without much fatigue and even in house slippers, the worker can go down to the Red Corner and join in cultural and educational life," noted one cultural worker.[14] Importantly, *świetlice* were spaces for both planned and unplanned leisure. They were intended as places where a worker could find quiet relaxation after hours—picking up a book or newspaper, or enjoying a board game like "The Oder and the Vistula" or "Don't Get Irritated, Man!" with friends—as well as sites for literacy classes, lectures on current events, slide shows, reading aloud of books and news, instruction in the latest anthems and mass songs, "Radio University" circles, Russian-language courses, book clubs, editorial clubs for the "wall newspaper," amateur music, dance or drama troupes, and arts and crafts.[15] The larger *świetlice* could also serve as performance spaces for visiting artists; in short, red corners were to serve as the antechambers to the high culture represented by the People's Theater and House of Culture, as well as the gateways to further education.

And of course, as one official put it, the "fundamental assignment" of red corners was "to mold the Marxist-Leninist world view of residents, awaken in them sacrifice and initiative, ... [and] socialize them in the spirit of common responsibility for the nation's future and the realization ... of socialism in our country." But they should also expose workers to "the achievements of national and general human culture."[16] Sometimes these two goals overlapped. Thus, we learn that in 1950 a group of Francophone African performers came to the *świetlica* in Czyżyny. According to the local newspaper *We Are Building Socialism*, the show "raised among the spectators great enthusiasm and long, loud bravos. [The workers'] interest in original African art [and] culture was great ... The cry given in Polish by the leader of the Black group Keit Fodeb—'LONG LIVE PEACE'—repeated three times by the members of the group, generated unprecedented enthusiasm among the audience." The performance closed, according to the report, with Africans and Poles chanting in unison, "STALIN-PEACE."[17]

The first three *świetlice* in Nowa Huta were organized by the Union of Construction Workers in 1949; by 1952, there were a total of 56 red corners in the workers' hostels. At the time, however, only 15 of these were deemed by authorities to be properly furnished; 23 were without radios, 10 without games, and 5 without libraries. Staff were overstretched, underqualified, and underpaid. In 1954 a *świetlica* director earned a mere 600 to 805 złotys, roughly half of what a qualified worker could hope to make—no surprise, then, that in a single week in September 1954, seven *świetlica* directorships changed hands.[18] A 1954 inspection determined that the *świetlice* in Nowa Huta were "dirty, cold, and unaesthetic."[19] Several were hardly ever used; some were used as storerooms.[20]

For all these reasons, the occasional successes of cultural programming in Nowa Huta's *świetlice* seemed all the more remarkable. One of the more robust institutions seems to have been the Inter-Union Worker's Club (MKR), which opened its doors in 1951 with an impressive three-day-long New Year's party for the children of Nowa Huta, complete with an orchestra, storytelling, movies, colored hats, and gifts. The event, which featured "Grandfather Frost" (a Soviet stand-in for Father Christmas), was designed to be educational as well as entertaining: when children were greeted under the tree by Grandfather Frost, he "emphasized that we can play carefree because the Soviet Union looks after us [while] . . . at this moment children in Korea are being slaughtered and killed"; meanwhile, the walls were hung with slogans like "When the whole nation to Nowa Huta says 'yea,' they [the class enemy] with asinine resistance bray" (accompanied by "appropriate decoration").[21] According to organizers, the party was a big success: "The kids were enchanted with the party, so much so that when Grandfather Frost said it was time to go home, they made such a racket that they didn't want to go . . . The parents were very pleased, and in conversations they expressed surprise that we could do all this for the children." Organizers noted that the party, which was attended by 1,545 children, had served as excellent propaganda for the center, and generated high demand in following months from children wishing to participate in activities, use the reading room, and so on.[22] Activists further measured their success by the fact that the clergy of nearby Mogiła had agitated against the work of the MKR: the priests allegedly forbade congregants from attending the MKR, and threatened to expel parents who took their children to events there on Sunday.[23]

Even the local *świetlice,* with far fewer resources, could boast successes. Zofia Kulinowska—who began her career in Nowa Huta as a bricklayer before being "socially advanced" to the job of director of the Czyżyny *świetlica*— noted that the charismatic author and Sejm deputy from Kraków, Adam Polewka, was a popular speaker; likewise, Maria Rokoszkowa's "living word" presentations gained a certain following. In a radio interview in 1979, cultural worker Rokoszkowa remembered how, in 1951, "they sent me ten boys ... and said I should do something for May Day" with them. Thus began Rokoszkowa's locally famous career as the director of Nowa Huta's Living Word Ensemble, whose performers used a combination of word and song to dramatize Polish literary classics or to illustrate a theme of contemporary relevance. As in her creation "The Marriage of Nowa Huta with Old Kraków," Rokoszkowa often addressed the subject of Nowa Huta itself. In it, Nowa Huta professes her love for Old Kraków ("for your proud walls, and because every one of your monuments is a lesson in culture"), who in turn replies:

> I love you, Nowa Huta, because you teach work and raise your walls
> ever higher while teaching socialist culture; because you are as Polish
> as an ode of Mickiewicz; because you take your example from Komso-
> molsk and set an example for all youth; because Bierut's words inspired
> your youth, dearest Nowa Huta.[24]

Following these appearances, Kulinowska observed an increased demand for classics of Polish literature dramatized by Rokoszkowa. According to Kulinowska, the availability of cheap editions under the "Czytelnik" imprint and the wide circulation of the press also, little by little, started to shape reading habits.

But these sorts of incremental changes were difficult to convey to superiors, who looked for quantifiable results and evidence that the *świetlice* had fulfilled their weekly, monthly, or yearly plans. Cultural workers were caught between the competing and often incompatible demands of their users, on the one hand, and the inspectors, supervisors, and administrators from the cultural wings of unions, the Party, or the hostel administration, on the other. Kulinowska and other cultural workers often ended up resorting to subterfuge to ensure attendance at, for example, lectures on unpopular subjects like Alexandra Kollontai or the constitution, by scheduling them right before a film was shown or pay handed out.[25] Those who provided innovative cultural programming were sometimes punished for their initiative. Even Kulinowska—an authentic "worker-intellectual" if ever there was one—was ultimately criticized by a supervisor for being "too individualistic" and was removed from her position.[26]

The Idiocy of Urban Life

Problems involving oversight and management of the *świetlice*—not to mention their funding—resulted in a gradual shift away from programming in the *świetlice* and toward a more centralized approach to leisure and culture.[27] Starting in the mid-1950s, authorities concentrated on developing larger and more visible institutions in Nowa Huta such as the District House of Culture, the International Press and Books Club, and the People's Theater—which in the late 1950s received international attention for its stylish and politically unorthodox productions.[28] The People's Theater's highbrow aesthetics were a far cry from those of Nowa Huta's original amateur theater, "Nurt," located in a leaky barracks, at which (according to actress Aleksandra Mianowska) audience members unaccustomed to theatrical conventions attended performances in their muddy work clothes and shouted out advice to the characters onstage.[29]

Not surprisingly, the increased professionalism of cultural offerings affected the day-to-day leisure patterns of Nowa Huta's inhabitants unevenly. Research by the Institute for Residential Building in 1954 ascertained that, broadly speaking, skilled workers made the most use of Nowa Huta's cultural facilities. Unskilled workers, on the other hand, tended to spend their free time at home, while white-collar workers preferred to entertain themselves in Kraków.[30] If anything, the declining emphasis on cultural programming in *świetlice* diminished the potential impact of such activities on that sector of the population that was, by official estimates, most in need of them: the unskilled, young, and mostly single workers inhabiting the hostels. From their own point of view, hostel dwellers still needed a comfortable, welcoming space where they could socialize and be entertained on a day-to-day basis, and the *świetlice* were not serving this purpose.[31]

One reason for this had less to do with poor programming than with a fundamental planning error; hostel residents wanted to socialize with members of the opposite sex, while the hostels—including the *świetlice*—officially maintained a strict single-sex policy. Of course, this does not mean that the rules were always upheld, as men were occasionally found in women's *świetlice* and vice versa.[32] More often during the colder months, however, hostel residents sought out indoor spaces that were cozier and more intimate—and less supervised—than the *świetlice*.[33] Hostel inspectors found it particularly irksome that residents seemed to prefer spending their afternoons and evenings in the crowded shared bedrooms—spaces designated for "passive" (i.e., sleep) rather than "active" repose, as an educational lecture on the "hygiene of communal living" explained. It was particularly uncultured, the talk went on, to lie on the bed while still clothed—especially with one's shoes on;[34] yet, inspectors regularly encountered groups of workers lounging in their bedrooms, still dressed in their muddy work clothes, at times even in mixed groups—an expressly forbidden practice.[35] Occasional raids on the women's hostels by groups of youth brigade volunteers (activists) challenged this gender segregation even more overtly. In warmer months, improvised outdoor spaces provided alternatives to the crowded hostel rooms; one of the most popular hangouts for mixed crowds of young, single workers, for example, was the paved area outside the post office in Settlement D.[36]

Many of Nowa Huta's workers also availed themselves of commercial establishments rather misleadingly called "restaurants." These state-run venues—sporting names like "Lotus" or "The Little Fish"—acquired a reputation for dissipated, "Dantesque scenes"[37] such as the one described by writer and town resident Bohdan Drozdowski:

> Some [customers] are submerged in drunkenness . . . some in sadness, still others in homesickness, while naturally the merry ones call the tune. They sing their village songs [as] swearwords rise above the din every few seconds. They are carefully dressed, in suede shoes, expensive suits, watches, long hair, and whiskers. The great paws of these boys betray their workingman's strength . . . Not one of the half-pints of vodka is full. The bills often don't add up, but who checks the sums? In Nowa Huta they earn well, and don't have anything to do with their money.

An orchestra, a Czech dancer with great legs dubiously named Stella Vesela (Happy Stella), the *czardasz*, and the tango all enlivened the scene.[38] As Drozdowski's description indicates, such venues catered primarily to single men; women might attend, but their very presence would tend to cast their virtue in doubt. The dark, unlit terrain surrounding the restaurant "Giant," where some couples retreated after leaving the bar, moreover, was also the haunt of petty thieves. Those who fell asleep in the open air after a night out would most likely awake to find themselves stripped to their socks and relieved of their valuables.[39]

But if "Giant" was the lowest circle of Nowa Huta's leisure purgatory, there were plenty of other causes for concern, in local authorities' view, regarding a cultural crisis in the new town. Among the local *apparat*—and increasingly in Warsaw, as news from Nowa Huta trickled up through Party and organizational channels—there was a growing perception that the cultural enlightenment project in Nowa Huta was a failure, particularly among the majority of young, unskilled workers still living in the hostels. An eighteen-page Union of Polish Youth (ZMP) central office report, entitled "An Evaluation of Socialization Work Among the Youth of Nowa Huta," argued that the cultural interests of youth were "often narrow and primitive," citing lack of success in attracting audiences to theater performances, in spite of active efforts by ZMP leaders and others. It was equally difficult to involve young people in literature, museums, or exhibits, the report went on: "it suffices, however, to have a jazz orchestra for a moment, for a tremendous gathering of youth to form instantly."[40] Although libraries reported that Polish and foreign classics were among the most borrowed books, inspectors also found sentimental and pulp fiction circulating through the hostels—books with titles like *Leper, Gehenna,* and *I Was an Ugly Girl.* (Their presence indicated possible contamination by "decadent" Kraków, since they had allegedly been "brought from Kraków by intellectual workers and young intelligentsia.")[41] Girls had even been found using pages from the socialist realist classic, *How the Steel Was Tempered,* as curl papers.[42] Such incidents were indications, the report explained, of widespread

> cultural passivity among individuals for whom thoughts of tomorrow have still not been awakened, those who live from one day to the next, shut themselves off from collective life, and limit themselves solely to attending to the bare necessities of life. Our research on the attitude of youth who have been under the strong influence of the church shows that the old clerical principle of education, "pray and work," has been transformed into the principle, "pray and work, but work only as much as is necessary to maintain a livelihood."

In other words, old mentalities—the "primitive" and "passive" attitude of the peasant—had combined with new, urban desires (e.g., a "lust" for dancing), forming a particular kind of youthful alienation.[43] Cultural activists therefore found themselves engaged on a new front, combating not only the ignorance and superstition that newcomers brought with them from the village, but the habits that they quickly picked up, unprotected by the influences of family or tradition, in the new town. These ranged from widespread drunkenness, swearing, and fighting, on the one hand, to tastes for "American" fashion, music, and dance, on the other—what authorities called "hooliganism" and "dandyism" (*bikiniarstwo*), respectively.

The terms *chuligan* and *bikiniarz* were, at least initially, labels chosen by the regime rather than by the young men to which they were applied. The discourse of "hooliganism" dated back to late imperial Russian public debates about youthful deviance, whence they had passed into the Soviet lexicon. Under Stalin, hooliganism became a prosecutable offense, and thus a legal category as well.[44] Authorities in Nowa Huta used the term loosely, applying it to any kind of rowdy behavior by young men perpetrated while under the influence; miscreants were also sometimes called *awanturzyści* (brawlers), but this colloquialism lacked the same overtones of deviance and delinquency and, further, political suspicion. Thus one Party official in Nowa Huta defined hooliganism as speaking vulgarly to someone in authority, having a "penchant for alcohol," or a combination of the two, such as being drunk at an official function.[45] Alcohol and defiance toward authority, in other words, were linked in some obscure but definite way in the person of the hooligan.

What is most remarkable in contemporary reports is just how little cowed by authority the so-called hooligans seemed to be. As director of the Czyżyny *świetlica*, for instance, Zofia Kulinowska was instructed by her superiors to institute a mock court punishing misdemeanors like drinking and swearing. Because these practices were so widespread, she later recalled, Kulinowska tried to focus on only the most egregious violations. However, if the "trials" were intended as a kind of educational theater, the defendants seemed to enjoy playing their roles. Kulinowska describes how one resident, charged with having ten bottles of vodka under his bed, replied in a tone of "complete amazement": "Your Excellency, if you lived in a barracks like this and held office in the mud and the cold, then your Excellency herself would drink with me." Another had used vulgar language in an altercation with a (female) bus driver:

> I said, how can you speak that way to women, in those words? And he said to me, "On the contrary, I told her twice that I didn't have any money, that I had drunk a quarter-liter. Whatever, it wasn't any of her business, so in the end I called her by name—and after all, I couldn't speak to her in French, because she wouldn't have understood me."

Kulinowska noted that, far from having a deterrent effect, the "punishments" the court meted out, weeklong "imprisonment" in the hostel, "were greeted as a kind of holiday—[the accused] played cards, drank, slept."[46]

With tongue only somewhat in cheek, author-*bikiniarz* Leopold Tyrmand once argued that "drunkenness is . . . a sign of humanism" under the perversions of communism—a rejection of the Party's puritan ideals of discipline and self-denial and of its demands over the innermost self.[47] But in Nowa Huta, the connections between drinking and Party control could be much less subtle, although ambiguous nonetheless. Take, for example, Stefan B., a twenty-year-old bricklayer who, following involvement in a knifing at "Giant," allegedly hit a ZMP member while drunk at the Fourth Electoral Congress of the ZMP and "wanted to throw himself at the leader of the ZMP District Office Szparniak." Clearly, being drunk provided license for the expression of emotions that could have spelled serious trouble if the perpetrator were sober. When hauled before a committee of district Party officials, Stefan B. promised to stop drinking, upon which Party officials agreed to reinstate his Party candidacy.[48] Conversely, in the case of another worker—Tadeusz G., a Party member since 1948 and a "notorious drunk"—a lack of contrition was deemed grounds for rescinding Party membership. Tadeusz G. "accepted the charges laid against him, explaining that he couldn't stop himself from drinking vodka and that he would go right on drinking."[49] It seems the Party could tolerate physical attack more readily than alcoholism and the repudiation of self-discipline implied in Tadeusz G.'s reply. In this case, perhaps Tyrmand was right.

Perhaps even more striking were manifestations of hooliganism among members of the Stalinist youth work brigades Service to Poland (Służba Polsce, or SP). A sort of cross between the ROTC and the Civilian Conservation Corps that operated in the years after World War II, SP was a volunteer organization that provided mostly unskilled, underemployed rural youth with a uniform, a bed, and a hot meal in exchange for backbreaking labor on Nowa Huta's building site, as well as on other work sites associated with the Six-Year Plan. While brigade commanders in Nowa Huta were generally pleased with brigade members' performance during work hours, many complained that after hours the young men ran wild: they went about with their belts undone, unshaven, and dirty. They could be found drinking in restaurants and creating a ruckus on the streets of Kraków. Despite strict orders to the contrary, they were frequently discovered in women workers' quarters in Nowa Huta, "behaving immorally" or getting into fights, often while drunk.[50] There are also reports of brigade members' attacking militia officers (i.e., the police)—sometimes in response to attempted interventions or arrests, but on occasion, too, apparently in unprovoked attacks on the uniformed representatives of the state's monopoly of violence. On one occasion a youth volunteer was shot and killed by police during such a melee; generally, however, gendarmes seem to have felt constrained from using firearms, so that when large groups of brigade members gathered, even the police could not easily disperse or manage them.[51] "Allegedly it's impossible to control [the volunteers], as they constitute a force in themselves," reported one Party commission in 1956. "An informant explained to us: 'What can five militia officers do, when 200 youth volunteers gather in front of a women's hostel?'"[52]

We also find reports of SP members launching assaults on non-SP workers' hostels or roaming about in small gangs that randomly terrorized passersby. According to one eyewitness, meeting such a group on Nowa Huta's unfinished terrain could spell misfortune, especially if the brigade members "didn't like the look of someone." Then they would challenge the person with a kind of riddle:

> "What don't you like, the system or SP?" It was dangerous to answer "the system," but worse still "SP." Then you'd have to reckon

with returning home via a detour through the hospital with a dozen broken ribs.[53]

The remarkable ambiguity of this question, coupled with such shockingly random violence, can only complicate our view of the young hooligans' understanding of themselves and their relations to authority. They presented themselves as defenders of "the system" and were willing to fight in its name (fighting that was, paradoxically, condemned by "the system"), but group allegiance (to SP) was evidently even more important. Their behavior was that of a classic gang: capricious, territorial, and fiercely loyal. And yet, unlike most Western delinquents, they explicitly situated themselves within a context coded in political terms—although what they imagined these terms to be is far from clear.

Bikiniarstwo, an exaggerated form of youthful fashion mimicking imagined American styles, was another sticky issue for authorities in Nowa Huta. Fashionable clothes were a must-have for a night on the town, and if one did not have one's own finery, one borrowed from a friend—as electrician Szczepan Brzeziński remembered, it was important not just to look smart, but that one's friends did so, too.[54] A suit, shirt, and shoes were highly prized possessions, and were often a worker's first big purchases; a wristwatch, superfluous in the rural settings whence most of the young men came, would be considered the crowning touch.[55] As the sociologist Renata Siemieńska notes, clothes became the marker of assimilation into the new environment and of difference from those who remained in the village[56]—not for nothing did youth brigade recruits often burn their civvies upon issuance of their uniforms.[57]

Bikiniarze—loosely, "bikini boys"—took such fashion consciousness one step further. On the one hand, they exaggerated the dandified tendencies of many youth, their preference for rich, bright colors, and so on.[58] On the other hand, like the jitterbugging youth of the Third Reich or the *Halbstarken* of East Germany, *bikiniarze* looked to an imagined American popular culture for their tastes in clothes, music, and dance, consciously flouting official disapproval of these styles.[59] Jacek Kuroń, who first encountered *bikiniarze* as a ZMP activist in high school, describes the *bikiniarz's* uniform as follows: "Narrow, short trousers, under which showed striped socks [known as *sing–singi*],[60] shoes with crepe rubber or other thick soles. Add to this a very colorful, hand-painted silk tie—best of all with a view of the Bikini atoll," and of course the essential long, combed-back hair, or "swallow." According to Kuroń, *bikiniarstwo* was already "a significant counterculture" in Warsaw in the late 1940s, to the point where American music was often played on the loudspeaker system at his school until some

ZMP activists intervened. The leadership of the Warsaw ZMP encouraged members to beat and intimidate *bikiniarze;* at times they were expelled from school or criminally prosecuted.[61]

Despite their popularization by writers like Tyrmand, whose novels were peopled with members of Warsaw's shadowy netherworlds and who was himself fancied something of a *bikiniarz,* much about the *bikiniarze* remains shrouded in mystery. They are said to have originated in the 1940s, but while some sources claim the original *bikiniarz* subculture was working class, others argue that the first *bikiniarze* were well-off youth with access to Western goods, who were then imitated by their peers in Warsaw's tougher districts.[62] Where did their impressions of American culture come from? Certainly, in the 1940s (and even in the 1950s) it was easy enough to hear jazz on "Voice of America"; nor was Hollywood completely cut off from distribution (in 1948, 33 of 99 films being shown in Poland were American, versus 23 from the Soviet Union).[63] Gift parcels from the West—the contents of which often ended up on the black market—supplied *bikiniarze* with many of the necessary props, including the slightly outdated jazz-age styles found in used clothes or *ciuchy.*[64] The decision to paint a mushroom cloud (the first atomic tests in the Bikini atoll occurred in 1946) or scantily clad bathing beauty on one's tie seems to need no explanation—the images were American, exotic, erotic, and explosive, all in one.

Tadeusz Binek, an engineer, described the impression created by one *bikiniarz* in Nowa Huta in 1953. While working on an upper floor of one of the buildings under construction, Binek heard a commotion and looked down to the street:

> A single youth walked along between the tracks of the crane—a *bi-kiniarz.* Hair combed to the top of his head, a light-colored jacket with wide, quilted sleeves, narrow trousers halfway down his calves, and garishly colored socks with horizontal stripes and loafers on thick pigskin soles. The classic dress of a classic *bikiniarz,* as if taken from *Szpilki* [a satirical journal].

Binek goes on to add that the noise he had initially heard was "booming, lively, honest laughter" from the other workers on the construction site.[65] Binek's reference to anti-*bikiniarz* propaganda seems significant, as the way in which he frames the anecdote echoes the official line on *bikiniarze.* In other words, the "classic" *bikiniarz* was an isolated figure, an object of derision among healthy (note the "booming" laughter) people.

This, indeed, is what local activists liked to claim in their reports on fighting *bikiniarstwo* in Nowa Huta. After a series of social evenings organized by the ZMP, for example—at which criticism of "inappropriate behavior" and the "public unmasking of individuals steeped in *bikiniarstwo*" accompanied ping-pong and instruction in folk dancing—organizers claimed that such measures had been effective "in creating a uniform opinion among the majority of youth against mannered elements, who left the party or holed themselves up in corners without the usual disputes and arguments." In particular, they noted, there was an increasing tendency, especially among girls, to oppose "bikini-ist" dances and to turn down drunken dance partners.[66] Similarly, after an education campaign against "widespread" *bikiniarstwo* discovered among members of the elite song-and-dance troupe of the Lenin Steelworks, the troupe's director was "satisfied that our work was to considerable effect, both among the troupe and the individuals involved . . . The least manifestation of such behavior today offends all members, all of whom have taken up the slogans declaring self-government and the struggle against dandyism and hooliganism."[67]

Beyond giving rise to the suspicion that the report writers seriously exaggerated the efficacy of their anti–bikini-ist campaigns, the language of these reports reveals an important truth: namely, that the construct "*bikiniarstwo*" was an artificial designation for what authorities, in fact, recognized as a widespread "tendency" not limited to a few outlandishly dressed individuals. It was not just the intense popularity of jazz, as noted above, that made *bikiniarze* representative of a much broader phenomenon. For cultural organizers in Nowa Huta, the *bikiniarz* typified the general lack of interest in high culture among the majority of Nowa Huta's residents: "The ideology of boycotting books, theater, events, is represented by the leading active *bikiniarze* in Nowa Huta. We have determined through discussions with them that they show a complete cultural abnegation," theorized the report giver, "even though on the other hand they aren't short of a certain mental shrewdness."[68]

Conclusion

> I believe in rebellion as the highest value of youth. I believe in rebellion
> as the highest form of hatred of terror, oppression, and injustice and
> I believe, moreover, that there is no rebellion without a cause—even
> if it is in the world's interest, [despite the fact that it] loves its rebels,
> to kill them.[69]

By their very nature, youthful rebels tend to provide us with little evidence of their thoughts, views, or perceptions of themselves, yet they are extensively reported upon and interpreted by others. As Dick Hebdige argues, "the politics of youth culture is a politics of metaphor: it deals in the currency of signs and is, thus, always ambiguous":

> For the subcultural *milieu* has been constructed underneath the authorised discourses, in the face of the multiple disciplines of the family, the school, and the workplace. Subculture forms up in the space between surveillance and the evasion of surveillance, it translates the fact of being under scrutiny into the pleasure of being watched. It is a hiding in the light.[70]

Of course, there is surveillance and there is surveillance. Can we compare the experiences, motivations, and logic of youthful nonconformists on either side of the Wall? Did the *bikiniarze* and hooligans resemble their Western counterparts—the teddy boys, *zazous, teppisti, Halbstarken,* and other national variants—merely in appearance? Were they, in fact, unsung heroes of anticommunism? What do we make of the fact that, as Hebdige argues, while youth in liberal democratic societies are invisible (and, one might add, officially outside the polity until they reach voting age) until they rebel, youth under communism were explicitly mobilized and politicized as youth?[71] Did this fundamentally alter the political equation of youthful rebellion in the East?

Observing the crowds at "Lotus," Bohdan Drozdowski and others like him tended to interpret their behavior as apolitical: it was the by-product of a bumpy transition from a rural to an urban way of life—if not inevitable, then at least part of an intelligible social process, one that members of the Polish intelligentsia had been concerned with since long before the advent of communism. As Zofia Kulinowska put it some years later, "culture and civilization are two different things"—in other words, urban consumption habits, including fashionable clothes and heavy drinking, are far easier to acquire than the putative inner qualities of a cultured person.[72]

For those more directly implicated in the Stalinist social revolution, the apparent failure of the cultural enlightenment project in Nowa Huta posed a different problem. As one union activist wrote following a hostel inspection,

> It pains us to see how these workers, who work hard 12 hours a day, go about drunk on the building site in their free time after work. It pains us to see that the newly built *świetlica* gleams with emptiness; it pains us to see, walking through workers' quarters, how drunken workers lie in bed fully clothed, in dirty, muddy shoes ... Who is at fault here ... ? We know, comrades, that the capitalist system came to an end here,

that in the new system, work should proceed along completely different tracks, but it must with regret be said that in very many parts
of [Nowa Huta] the style and form of work remain just as they were
under capitalism.[73]

In a Stalinist frame of reference, the problem of leisure was a political one.
By extension, the failure of the regime's leisure policies—above all in Nowa
Huta—was a political failure, and its repercussions would be felt after 1953
when, following Stalin's death, the "thaw" in Polish public discourse would
unleash torrential criticism of the prevailing regime, ultimately contributing
to its overthrow in 1956.

In particular, the crisis of culture in Nowa Huta gave an opening to
people like Drozdowski or Kulinowska, intellectuals who had initially supported what they saw as the communist regime's "civilizing mission" but who
would increasingly come to criticize its flawed and perverted execution.[74]
In their eyes, the greatest philistines were no longer the backward peasants
but the Party leaders; the Stalinists themselves were the enemies of culture.
Lost in this discussion, however, were the dreams and desires—indeed, the
cultural values—of young people themselves (grudging comments on their
"shrewdness" aside). The idea that boogie-woogie might have had some
intrinsic value was just as inconceivable to Drozdowski or Kulinowska as it
was to any Party hack. They differed only inasmuch as one group perceived
the problem as pedagogical, the other as political. Was it, then, totalitari-
anism that young people rejected, or stifling cultural elitism? Was theirs a
principled stand against a particular political system, or an expression of
what Alf Lüdtke calls *Eigensinn*—a sense of their difference and distance
from parents, priests, cultural activists, and Party bosses alike—of which
their hybridized transatlantic cultural style was a badge and a symbol?[75]

The latter explanation seems more persuasive, especially if we presume
that youth subcultures in the East and West did not occur in complete
mutual isolation. Kaspar Maase, for example, suggests that West Germany's working-class *Halbstarken*—and the middle-class youth who co-opted
their style—rejected hierarchical understandings of cultural value based
in a rigid prewar class system.[76] Meanwhile, Uta Poiger argues that the
Halbstarken's taste for African-American music tapped a deep undercur-
rent of German racism, showing how the rhetoric that adult commentators
used to attack *Halbstarken* in the 1950s echoed Nazi propaganda against
entartete jazz, boogie-woogie, and swing of two decades earlier.[77] In both
accounts, then, young rebels stood against the continuing stranglehold of
prewar cultural elites and their values on the postwar present. In particular, they implicitly opposed a rigid view of the classes, races, and sexes,

according to which these were meant to stay strictly in their own respective and stratified spheres; for when the *Halbstarken* took to the dance halls and movie theaters, these distinctions were blurred, upended, and transgressed.

So, too, Nowa Huta's hooligans and *bikiniarze*—like their analogues elsewhere in Eastern Europe—vehemently rejected the organizing principles of their parents' and grandparents' worlds.[78] In a sense, this helps us understand why they could at the same time be cultural rebels and enthusiastic "builders of socialism" or champions of "the system," since Stalinist rhetoric and, to a certain degree, practice also rejected the rigid sociocultural hierarchies of Europe's distant and recent past. In particular, as Stalinism broke up semifeudalism in the rural hinterland and young people flocked to the cities and factories, many sought to forge new identities based not on birth or caste, but on voluntary affiliation and choice. Nowa Huta—a town with no memory—provided ideal terrain for reinventing the self along such lines.

Whereas most settlers in Nowa Huta built their new lives around family and friends, a minority did so through a hyper-visible allegiance to their SP troupe or to a social milieu that shared their tastes in music, dance, and fashion. More generally, however, young workers in Nowa Huta rejected the idea that they should bow to the superior cultural judgment of their betters. In opting for a transatlantic cultural beat, moreover, they challenged one of the most dearly held assumptions of the intelligentsia and Stalinists alike: namely, the superiority of "national" culture. Thus, rather than somehow revealing a desire for American-style capitalism, the taste for jazz among Nowa Huta's youth can be seen as displaying an acute awareness, shared with their Western peers, of two central values of late (or incipient post-) modernity: cultural hybridity and transnationalism. Were these values "political"? Perhaps not yet—but they would become so, as successive generations throughout the Eastern Bloc demanded, ultimately successfully, that their isolation from the rest of the world come to an end.

Notes

1. Czesław Bąbiński, "O Budowie Huty im. Lenina," *Budownictwo Przemysłowe* 3, nos. 7/8 (1954): 4.

2. Quoted in Anna Bikont and Joanna Szczęsna, "O Nowej to Hucie poemat," *Gazeta Wyborcza*, February 26–27, 2000, 24.

3. On the significance of generational factors in the support for communism in Eastern Europe after World War II, see Bradley F. Abrams, "The Second World War and the East European Revolution," *East European Politics and Societies* 16, no. 3 (2003): 658.

4. Rodger P. Potocki Jr., "The Life and Times of Poland's 'Bikini Boys,'" *Polish Review* 39, no. 3 (1994): 259–90.

5. See my "Public Works, Private Lives: Youth Brigades in Nowa Huta in the 1950s," *Contemporary European History* 10, no. 2 (2001): 199–219.

6. Archiwum Urzędu Miasta Krakowa (hereafter AUMKr), Prezydium Dzielnicowej Rady Narodowej—Nowa Huta, Komisja Zdrowia 185/9, n.p.

7. Anne White, *De-Stalinization and the House of Culture: Declining State Control over Leisure in the USSR, Poland and Hungary, 1953–89* (London: Routledge, 1990), 1–3.

8. Ibid., 6.

9. Norbert Elias, *The Civilizing Process: The History of Manners* (New York: Urizen Books, 1978), 5.

10. On the evolution of the concept in nineteenth-century Russia, see Vadim Volkov, "The Concept of *Kul'turnost'*: Notes on the Stalinist Civilizing Process," in *Stalinism: A Reader*, ed. Sheila Fitzpatrick (London: Routledge, 2000), 210–30.

11. Sheila Fitzpatrick, *The Cultural Front: Power and Culture in Revolutionary Russia* (Ithaca, N.Y.: Cornell University Press, 1992), 5.

12. Jerzy Kossak, *Rozwój kultury w Polsce Ludowej* (Warsaw: Iskry, 1974), 28.

13. Party Secretary Edward Ochab quoted in White, *De-Stalinization*, 48.

14. Archiwum Państwowe w Krakowie (hereafter APKr), Komitet Powiatowy Polskiej Zjednoczonej Partii Robotniczej—Nowa Huta 60/IV/5, k. 425. The tradition of the *świetlica* in Poland dated back at least to the end of World War I. The term "red corner," on the other hand, was of Bolshevik coinage, originally referring to a shrinelike area in a Soviet household that should be dedicated to the revolution. White, *De-Stalinization*, 46.

15. APKr Okręgowa Rada Związków Zawodowych Województwa Krakowa (hereafter APKr ORZZWK) p. 593, t. 6443, n.p.

16. Ibid.

17. *Budujemy Socjalizm*, September 26, 1950, 3.

18. APKr ORZZWK p. 593, t. 6443, n.p.; APKr Komitet Dzielnicowej Polskiej Zjednoczonej Partii Robotniczej—Nowa Huta (hereafter KD PZPR) 60/IV/12, k. 596.

19. APKr ORZZWK p. 594, t. 6453, n.p.

20. AUMKr PDRN (Polska Dzielnicowa Rada Narodowa), różne komisji Rady, Og. I-3, 1/9, n.p.

21. "Gdy cały naród budować Nową Hutę chce, oni z oślim uporem mówią nie."

22. APKr ORZZWK p. 594, t. 6477, n.p.

23. APKr ORZZWK p. 594, t. 6475, n.p.

24. "Jubileusz o Marii Rokoszkwej," nr aud. 2890, Radio Kraków.

25. "Bez patosu," nr aud. 2782, Radio Kraków; APKr ORZZWK p. 594, syg. 6466, n.p.

26. "Bez patosu."

27. For example, it was decreed that since educational lectures (*odczyzty*) at the hostels were so "boring," all further such events should be conducted centrally. *Świetlica* instructors, meanwhile, were charged with "ensuring attendance" at these events. APKr KD PZPR 60/IV/19, k. 637.

28. Joanna Woźniak, *Trzydzieści lat Teatru Ludowego w Krakowie—Nowej Hucie* (Kraków: Krajowa Agencja Wydawnicza, 1988), 6.

29. Aleksandra Mianowska, *Teatr "Nurt,"* Nowa Huta: Kartki ze wspomnień (Kraków: Towarzystwo Przyjaciół Książki, n.d.), 22.

30. Instytut Budownictwa Mieszkaniowego, "Wyniki wstępnego badania war-

unków bytu ludności w Nowej Hucie," *Materiały i dokumentacja* Seria B, no. 4/26/1954 (1954), 34–35.

31. "Generally speaking, young people rather occupy themselves outside the *świetlica*," as one ZMP activist put it in 1955. APKr ORZZWK p. 262, t. 2654, n.p.

32. APKr ORZZWK p. 594, t. 6468, n.p.

33. "Elf" writes that while stationed with the youth brigade in Czyżyny, he and his fellow volunteers used to spend their afternoons after work in the bathrooms, both because it was warmer there than the sleeping hall and because it was out of eyeshot of brigade supervisors. "Elf," "Najgorszy był jednak początek," in *Krajobraz ogni: Antologia reportaży o Nowej Hucie*, ed. Stefan Kozicki and Zbigniew Stolarek (Warsaw: Iskry, 1971), 49–50.

34. AUMKr PDRN Komisja Zdrowia 185/9, n.p.

35. APKr ORZZWK p. 594, t. 6468, n.p.

36. Jerzy Mikułowski Pomorski, *Kraków w naszej pamięci* (Kraków: Secesja, 1991), 261.

37. "Elf," 62.

38. Bohdan Drozdowski, *Tylko pamięć: Reportaże 1955–63* (Kraków: Wydawnictwo Literackie, 1964), 30.

39. Edmund Chmieliński, "Tu chciałem żyć i pracować," in *Robotnicze losy: Życiorysy własne robotników*, ed. Aurelia Szafran-Bartoszek et al. (Poznań: Wydawnictwo Naukowe UAM, 1996), 480–82.

40. Archiwum Akt Nowych (hereafter AAN) Związek Młodzieży Polskiej Zarząd Główny 451/VI-40, k. 244–45.

41. AAN ZMP Zarząd Główny 451/VI-40, k. 48.

42. AAN Komitet Centralny Polskiej Zjednoczonej Partii Robotniczej 237/V-72, k. 48.

43. AAN ZMP 451/VI-40, k. 246.

44. On "hooliganism" in late imperial Russia, see Joan Neuberger, *Hooliganism: Crime, Culture, and Power in St. Petersburg, 1900–1914* (Berkeley: University of California Press, 1993). For the Soviet Union, see Anne E. Gorsuch, *Youth in Revolutionary Russia: Enthusiasts, Bohemians, Delinquents* (Bloomington: Indiana University Press, 2000); and Gabor T. Rittersporn, "Extra-Judicial Repression and the Courts: Their Relationship in the 1930s," in *Reforming Justice in Russia, 1864–1996*, ed. Peter H. Solomon Jr. (Armonk, N.Y.: M. E. Sharpe, 1997), 207–27.

45. APKr KD PZPR 60/IV/14, k. 275.

46. "Bez patosu." After 1955, a citizens' court in Nowa Huta also adjudicated over instances of "brawling and drunkenness"—which constituted the vast majority of its cases—but with little more success. Most of the defendants in these cases were between the ages of nineteen and twenty-six and lived in the workers' hostels or the village of Mogiła, and almost all were manual workers. Recidivism was common, as in the case of Kazimierz K., who reportedly was punished more than ten times with no improvement in his behavior. APKr KD PZPR 60/IV/18, kk. 363–66.

47. Leopold Tyrmand, *The Rosa Luxemburg Contraceptives Cooperative: A Primer on Communist Civilization* (New York: Macmillan, 1972), 13.

48. APKr KD PZPR 60/IV/10, k. 183.

49. APKr KD PZPR 60/IV/10, k. 81.

50. APKr Powszechna Organizacja "Służba Polsce" 100, n.p.

51. Instytut Pamięci Narodowej—Oddział w Krakowie III/1734, kk. 31, 34; see also AAN Komenda Główna Powszechna Organizacja 'Służba Polsce' 316, k. 30. Jacek Kuroń, writing of hooligans in Warsaw during the 1950s, notes that in those days, officers had little means to protect themselves, having neither sticks nor dogs—"only guns." Jacek Kuroń and Jacek Żakowski, *PRL dla początkujących* (Wrocław: Wydawnictwo Dolnośląskie, 1997), 64. According to "Elf," when alerted to SP exploits, militia officers "simply avoided encountering them" to the best of their ability. "Elf," 62.

52. Jarosz Dariusz, "Jak słowo stawało się ciałem," *Mówią Wieki*, vol. 38, no. 10 (1996): 19–23.

53. "Elf," 62.

54. Szczepan Brzeziński, "Polubiłem ten fach," *Polityka* 14, no. 27 (1970): 7.

55. "Bez patosu."

56. Renata Siemieńska, *Nowe życie w nowym mieście* (Warsaw: Wiedza Powszechna, 1969), 106–7.

57. Chmieliński, "Tu chciatem żyć i pracować," 448, 450. See also "Relacja Anny Siatkowskiej," nr aud. 2661, Radio Kraków.

58. "Bez patosu." For a general discussion of *bikiniarstwo*, see Maciej Chłopek, *Bikiniarze: Pierwsza polska subkultura* (Warsaw: Wydawnictwo Akademickie "Żak," 2005).

59. Uta G. Poiger, "Rebels with a Cause? American Popular Culture, the 1956 Youth Riots, and New Conceptions of Masculinity in East and West Germany," in *The American Impact on Postwar Germany*, ed. Rainer Pommerin (Oxford: Oxford University Press, 1995), 93–124.

60. Potocki, "Life and Times of Poland's 'Bikini Boys,'" 262.

61. "One day in 1952, the district secretary of the Party called in a rather broad contingent of activists. 'When the father speaks to the son and the son doesn't listen, sometimes it's necessary to give him a licking,' he said. 'The time has perhaps come to apply pressure to the *bikiniarze* who dance boogie-woogie.'" The violence against *bikiniarze* was directed from above. At dances, suitable music would be played, then squads of young workers would pull *bikiniarze* off to the side, one by one, and beat them up. Kuroń and Żakowski, *PRL dla początkujących*, 63–64.

62. Ibid., 63–64, and Potocki, "Life and Times of Poland's 'Bikini Boys,'" 263.

63. See PolishJazz.com, http://www.polishjazz.com/pjn/101/4050.htm; Marek Haltof, *Polish National Cinema* (New York: Berghahn Books, 2002), 39.

64. Potocki, "Life and Times of Poland's 'Bikini Boys,'" 265–67.

65. Tadeusz Binek, *Śląsk—Wojna—Kresy—Wrocław—Nowa Huta: Wspomnienia 1930–1960* (Kraków: Oficyna Cracovia, 1997), 124.

66. AAN ZMP 451/VI-40, k. 245.

67. APKr KD PZPR 60/IV/14, kk. 275–76.

68. AAN ZMP 451/VI-40, k. 246.

69. From an open letter by Marek Hłasko to *Trybuna Ludu*, cited in Wolna Encyclopedia Wikipedia, http://pl.wikipedia.org/wiki/Marek_H%C5%82asko.

70. Dick Hebdige, *Hiding in the Light: On Images and Things* (London: Routledge, 1988), 35.

71. Ibid., 17.

72. The journal *Po prostu*, closely associated with Thaw intellectuals, diagnosed

hooliganism as a symptom of general social frustration caused by the absence of cultural opportunities; discussed in Kuroń and Żakowski, *PRL dla początkujących,* 63.

73. APKr ORZZWK p. 594, t. 6453, n.p.

74. The most famous of these was Adam Ważyk—a onetime hard-line Stalinist whose explosive "Poem for Adults," credited with initiating the Thaw in Polish cultural life, dwelt extensively on the alleged failures of Nowa Huta. See Marci Shore, "Some Words for Grown-Up Marxists: 'A Poem for Adults' and the Revolt from Within," *Polish Review* 42, no. 2 (1997): 131–54.

75. Alf Lüdtke, "Organizational Order or *Eigensinn?* Workers' Privacy and Workers' Politics in Imperial Germany," in *Rites of Power: Symbolism, Ritual, and Politics Since the Middle Ages,* ed. Sean Wilentz (Philadelphia: University of Pennsylvania Press, 1985), 303–33.

76. Kaspar Maase, "Establishing Cultural Democracy: Youth, 'Americanization,' and the Irresistible Rise of Popular Culture," in *The Miracle Years: A Cultural History of West Germany, 1949–1968,* ed. Hanna Schissler (Princeton, N.J.: Princeton University Press, 2001), 428–50.

77. Uta G. Poiger, "Rock 'n' Roll, Female Sexuality, and the Cold War Battle over German Identities," *Journal of Modern History* 68, no. 3 (1996): 577–616.

78. These were, among others, the Hungarian *jampec,* Romanian *malagambista,* and Soviet *stiliag.* See Chłopek, *Bikiniarze,* 65–76. On Hungary, see Karl Brown, "Dance Hall Days: Jazz and Hooliganism in Communist Hungary, 1948–1956," *Trondheim Studies on East European Cultures and Societies* 26 (October 2008); and Sándor Horváth, "Hooligans, Spivs and Gangs: Youth Subcultures in the 1960s," in *Muddling Through in the Long 1960s: Ideas and Everyday Life in High Politics and the Lower Classes of Communist Hungary,* ed. János M. Rainer and György Péteri (Trondheim and Budapest: Institute for the History of the 1956 Hungarian Revolution and Program on East European Cultures and Societies, 2005), 199–223.

1. Вечернее платье из тафты. Лиф удлиненный, прилегающий. Рукава втачные, узкие, длиной 3/4. Юбка состоит из семи присобранных волнов. Ширина ворота и низ юбки обшиты отделкой строчкой. Рекомендуемые размеры 44—50.
Автор М. Осипова (Ателье художественного фонда).

ВЕЧЕРНИЕ

Evening gown designed by M. Osipova of the Art Fund's dressmaking workshop

Chapter Three

Dior in Moscow: A Taste for Luxury

in Soviet Fashion Under Khrushchev

Larissa Zakharova

In El'dar Riazanov's comedy *Carnival Night*, filmed in 1956, the Palace of Culture administrator Lena Krylova (Liudmila Gurchenko) opens a New Year ball with the song "Five Minutes," wearing a white shining dress with a fitted top, and an ample lined skirt fitted tightly at the waist. She then performs a second song in a black dress of the same silhouette matched with a white fur muff. Throughout the film she appears in six different dresses, five of which have this silhouette, very similar to Christian Dior's "new look," albeit in its slightly modified form of the "lily of the valley" line launched in 1954. Other "unpretentious but talented Soviet employees" who take part in this festive concert are also dressed in fashionable clothes. For example, the librarian Adelaida Kuzminichna Romashkina (O. Vlasova) sings on stage in a long evening brocade dress touching the ground, matched with a light *kapron* scarf. The presence of such luxurious clothes in a film which was meant to reflect the realities of Soviet life is crucial for our understanding of the ideals and the practices of socialist consumption. How could it be that attributes of luxury were ascribed to mass consumption in a socialist society?

Soviet clothing designers were not very original when they took over the common idea according to which luxury in fashion was symbolized by collections from the Christian Dior house. Public discourses did not approve of Dior's luxurious dresses, as they were thought to be unsuitable for Soviet living conditions. L. K. Efremova, one of the most famous Soviet clothing designers of the 1950s and 1960s, declared in one of her many articles in fashion magazines that the appearance of the French haute couture fashion in Soviet reality would seem inappropriate.[1] In another publication, French haute couture dresses were described as "refined models of uselessness."[2] But an unpublished report after a mission to France by a delegation of Soviet clothing designers (including Efremova) did not criticize haute couture. On the contrary, it claimed that the "house of Christian Dior holds great interest for the study of design . . . It is a firm of the highest level which has absorbed the best French secular traditions in this field . . . There is nothing [in its collections] which could be reproached, or that would be seen as unacceptable for us."[3]

What does this double language mean? What was Soviet clothing designers' real attitude toward luxury? Did luxury have a place in Soviet fashion during the Khrushchev era? What kinds of artifacts were considered luxurious? And what was the symbolic significance of luxury? To answer these questions, we will first look at various discursive definitions of luxury in clothing practices. We will then analyze the creative activities of Soviet clothing designers, and finally we will study clothing consumption practices in the U.S.S.R.

Discursive Stigmatization of Luxury in Clothing Practices

Soviet Economists Define Luxury

The Khrushchev regime's declared aim to satisfy the material needs of Soviet people was the starting point of many reflections by Soviet economists about the limits of these needs and the role of fashion in clothing consumption. The Party leader himself was not very explicit about his views when he spoke of the need "to give more beautiful and good-quality clothes to the Soviet people" as part of his commitment to raise standards of living. While condemning excesses in the arts, and particularly in architecture, he never took it upon himself to judge the aesthetics of clothing. Yet there are indications that he approved the existence of fashion and its influence on consumer demand. In his report to the Fourth Session of the Supreme Council of the U.S.S.R. in 1964, "On Measures for Realizing the Communist Party Program in the Field of Raising the People's Prosperity," he declared, "Working people want to acquire clothes and shoes that have an up-to-date style and beautiful color and that correspond to the season and to fashion. This is a good thing."[4] But the Third Party Program to which he referred (adopted at the Twenty-second Party Congress in 1961), which promised the arrival of full communism in the 1980s, made no mention of the notion of fashion. As for clothing consumption, it was only meant to satisfy the "rational needs of reasonable people."

Soviet economists had to evaluate these needs in order to quantify norms for the production of clothes and shoes in the central plan. They elaborated norms of clothing consumption for citizens of different regions of the U.S.S.R.; that is, the number of suits, coats, dresses, shoes, and so on which were necessary for a reasonable person, such as members of communist society were supposed to be.[5] A sort of basic necessity pack of goods was calculated in the same way as, for instance, the numbers of calories needed daily. These norms varied according to region, age, climate conditions, and physiological specificities. But no cultural, social, aesthetic, or other qualitative characteristics were taken into account. Moreover, all the clothes were to be used until worn out. Thus, fashion was stigmatized as a phenomenon of "luxury" because it prevented people from using up their "out-of-date" but functional and even "rational" clothes.[6]

The Soviet economist A. Braverman defined the borderline between reasonable and luxurious consumption in terms of the material value of the work done to produce a good. According to him, the level of individual consumption should be determined by the amount of work done by the person; the former might be less but never more than the latter. So if a person worked five hours, he or she could consume a product that required the same or a smaller amount of time to be made.[7] Luxury was associated with the satisfaction of passing fancies and the "secondary needs" of some, while another person's basic needs were not entirely satisfied. Such an egalitarian approach to consumption corresponded perfectly to the idea of the opposition of two political blocs in the Cold War climate. Economists condemned luxury as a trait of upper-class consumption practices in socially differentiated capitalist society. Although "the theory of the leisure class," formulated by the American sociologist Thorstein Veblen at the end of the nineteenth century, was not mentioned, Soviet economists seemed to update his definition of luxury as conspicuous consumption by prosperous classes who follow fashion to demonstrate their distinctiveness.[8] Thus, from the point of view of Soviet economists, luxury was inappropriate because it serves the purpose of accentuating social distinctions (and was, as such, unneeded in a society where class distinctions were supposed to be erased).

At the same time, efforts to persuade the Soviet people that they would live a better life than people in capitalist countries increased the political significance of conspicuous consumption. Luxury in clothing practices could be seen from abroad as evidence of the advantages of socialism. But to avoid the phenomenon of distinction between social groups, prosperity and luxury had to become accessible to all members of the society of equals. Soviet clothing designers worked within conditions set by this paradox.

Luxury According to Soviet Clothing Designers

Soviet clothing designers were civil servants employed in Houses of Clothing Design, which formed part of the system of industrial production of clothes. The first institution of this type was founded in Moscow in 1934 on Kuznetskii Most, a central street of the capital. In 1949 it became the All-Union House of Clothing Design, the most important part of a network of similar institutions in the capitals of the Soviet republics and in some other big cities. They had to create patterns for factories that specialized in garments, hats, furs, and knitwear. These establishments had a dual profile, both artistic and industrial, because their work was subordinate to the interests of the garment industry. The concept of "industrial art" (*proziskusstvo*)—based on the idea both of the embellishment of everyday life and of the creation of a new socialist lifestyle (as a result of art becoming accessible to the masses)—facilitated the union of these two profiles.

These ideas were largely developed by Nadezhda Lamanova (1861–1941) after the Bolshevik Revolution. As a graduate of the well-known dressmaking school of O. A. Suvorova, she had created dresses for the imperial court before 1917. Her talent was also recognized abroad, as she regularly went to Paris in order to practice. Paul Poiret, one of the most celebrated French designers of the time, wanted her to work with him. She nonetheless preferred to stay in Russia, where she became the first theoretician of socialist fashion. Lamanova's contribution to the theory of garment design was substantial. She wrote the program for the Workshops of Contemporary Dress and the curricula of the first Soviet schools for clothing design and of the Central Institute of the Garment Industry founded in 1919, presented reports at various conferences, and wrote a number of articles.[9] Her theory was based on the ideas of functional and rational clothes classified according to the purposes for which they were created. She also drew up rules for combining the right elements in dress which became the criteria for "good taste." Lamanova believed that art had to penetrate all spheres of life and develop the artistic taste of the masses. Clothes were, according to her, the simplest way to achieve this goal.

The social function of designers, as a vanguard called upon to educate the taste of consumers by imposing their creative ideas upon them, was strengthened by the campaign for *kul'turnost'* (literally, "culturedness") in the second half of the 1930s. Designers who graduated from the

Institute of the Garment Industry, where they absorbed Lamanova's ideas, became employees of the Moscow House of Clothing Design, which was also founded on the wave of the *kul'turnost'* campaign. The House's first director, Nadezhda Markova (1898–1969), was a student and disciple of Lamanova. They remained open-minded toward artistic experimentation and evolution, especially during the Thaw of the 1950s and 1960s, when nonconformist and abstract artists contributed to the training of clothing designers. For example, Elii Beliutin, the initiator of a studio of nonconformist artists in his house in Abramtsevo, near Moscow, taught at the Textile Institute and at the All-Russian House of Clothing Design until 1963. After the "Manege Affair" at the end of 1962 (when Khrushchev condemned a major art exhibition for including semiabstract work), he was dismissed from these posts for "formalism," but he continued to give further education lectures at some textile and garment factories such as the Trekhgornaia Manufaktura and at the All-Union Institute of the Culture of Clothes (VIALEGPROM).[10] This institute edited the *Fashion Journal* (*Zhurnal mod*), the U.S.S.R.'s premier fashion magazine. In its pages designers were able to express their ideas on fashion. The magazine was also a tool used to educate consumer taste. According to the magazine, "good taste" was incompatible with "extravagance" and "eccentricity." Both these characteristics were associated with luxury and were exemplified by "dresses in gold brocade" or "long evening dresses with collars of ostrich plumes," garments that were supposed to typify Western fashion.[11] The distinction between "socialist" and "bourgeois" fashion was summed up by the terms "rationality" and "functionality." The designers had to conceive models for the real everyday activities of all Soviet consumers:

> In order to create clothes in harmony with the image of people of the socialist era, clothing designers must attentively analyze and observe their contemporaries and their life in all its various dimensions, understanding the ideals, aspirations, and interests by which the whole society lives, and finally they must absorb the spirit of our time, of our era.[12]

Soviet designers contrasted the "good taste" of socialist clothing practices with "exaggerated," luxurious clothing consumption in capitalist countries. They defined "good taste" as a "sense of measure," "the skill to select clothes according to different conditions and to individual peculiarities of the body," and finally as the "skill not to set oneself apart by overly smart or extravagant dress."[13] They engaged in a "struggle" against the glaring lack of taste of certain luxurious artifacts, such as a brooch produced by a Soviet factory in the shape of the word "Moscow" made from large diamonds set in platinum.[14]

This definition of Soviet fashion did not mean that the example of international fashion was rejected outright. The political context of the competition between the two systems made Soviet designers refer to the best models of Western clothing production, first to critique them and then to outperform them. The Soviet government and Party commanded designers to extract "useful benefit" from Western clothing design in order to improve the Soviet system of clothing production.[15] The paradigm of "peaceful coexistence" with the West made it possible for designers to establish contacts with Western creators. Soviet clothing designers who were thus able to choose "partners" in Western Europe turned to French haute couture houses (to Christian Dior, for instance, who had a reputation of being the best French designer). The decision to turn to Paris was another sign of Lamanova's continuing influence on Soviet clothing design. Soviet designers visited the Dior company in France in 1957, 1960, and 1965.[16] During a mission to the United States in the context of the Soviet Exhibition in New York in 1959, a group of Soviet designers was invited by a representative of the Christian Dior house in the city to visit the workshops of the company and to see its new collection.[17] Close observation of their French colleagues' work aroused Soviet specialists' genuine fascination; this is evident when reading their internal reports. Enthusiastic remarks on French haute couture could never be publicized, however, because of ideological pressures. Soviet designers had, therefore, to adopt a double language. Their professional culture demanded that they refer to haute couture, but at the same time they were responsible for the competitiveness of Soviet fashion. In public discourse they expressed the politically correct clichés regarding "bourgeois fashion exaggerations," but in internal reports they justified the need for regular visits to France by referring to the positive aspects of French haute couture that could nourish Soviet clothing design.

These public discourses also justified the limitations of the Soviet industry. The garment industry, reluctant to innovate, could not accept complicated "luxurious" models for mass production because it lacked the necessary equipment. Factories preferred to produce clothes using the same designs for five years running in order to accomplish the plan successfully. New patterns would have disrupted this process. Thus, the artistic preoccupations of Soviet clothing designers found little practical application in this situation. They could only use their professional skill in so-called luxury examples intended for fashion shows and magazines. The creation

Christian Dior fashion show in Moscow, June 18, 1959

of luxurious garments transformed their profession into an art form free from industrial constraints.[18] Let us now examine what these luxury models were and how their existence was inscribed in the concept of rational and functional socialist fashion.

"Materialized" Luxury in Soviet Clothing Design

Integration of Elements of Haute Couture into Soviet Design

The organization of work in the Houses of Clothing Design gave artists a degree of freedom. They were divided into two groups: the first group created models for the garment industry; the second specialized in "prospective design." The designs conceived by this second group were "experimental."[19] They incarnated new trends in fashion, being intended for exhibitions and fashion shows without having the constraint of immediate industrial reproduction. Thus the vanguard function of Soviet "prospective design" was similar to the role played by haute couture in Western fashion in the 1950s and the 1960s. The most beautiful examples were published in fashion magazines.

In consulting Soviet fashion magazines, one is puzzled by the mixture of principles behind the classification of clothes. First there is the industrial principle, which reproduced the division of the Houses of Clothing Design into workshops that mapped onto Soviet clothing factories. Next there is the "functional" principle, which distinguished clothes to wear at home, at work, and for different types of leisure. Finally there is the "elite" principle, which corresponds to luxurious lifestyle clothing practices: morning dress, afternoon dress, cocktail dress, and evening dress.[20] The functional and the "elite" principles conform to the classification of clothing in press reports in France identified by Roland Barthes as being either "popular" or "aristocratic." The "popular" press proposed functional dress organized around the question of "what to do," while the "aristocratic" magazines operated with the distinction of dressing according to the time of day.[21] At the same time, Soviet fashion magazines reflected the subordination of artistic creativity to industry, the weight of the theory of rational socialist fashion, and the aspiration to integrate the traditions of French haute couture into Soviet clothing design. The evolution of fashion shows at the International Congresses of Fashion is revealing in this regard. Organized from 1950, these annual meetings of clothing designers from socialist countries were supposed to develop a concept of socialist fashion that was differentiated from capitalist fashion by its accessibility to all consumers and by its adaptation to their everyday practices.[22] The dresses presented during the first congresses were classified into functional groups. But from the beginning of the 1960s, designers started distinguishing "morning," "afternoon," "cocktail," and "evening" dresses.[23] Thus the climate of competition with the capitalist world stimulated the desire among socialist designers to be recognized by Western creators and to become part of the international community of fashion designers. A professional culture based on an imported system of clothing classification displaced the observation of daily practices. The results may also be seen in the ways Soviet designers set about "educating consumers' tastes" in fashion magazines and fashion shows.

All Soviet fashion and women's magazines (such as *Woman Worker* [*Rabotnitsa*]) contained many articles written in a didactic tone which explained how to combine clothes with accessories in order to be in "good taste." Soviet designers blamed Soviet women for having "bad taste": combining clothes of the same color but of different tones; mixing a checkered piece of clothing with a spotted one; or wearing a summer dress with heavy shoes. They also disapproved of wearing dresses in "winter" fabrics such as velvet or brocade (!) in summer, or wearing high-heeled shoes with socks. Designers presented Soviet consumers with new norms borrowed from

Western fashion magazines and haute couture collections, such as, for example, the wearing of a dress with matching gloves, shoes, and bag.[24]

According to Thorstein Veblen, luxury is at its most obvious in clothes worn for leisure in which style is more important than functionality.[25] Soviet clothes designers paid special attention to the creation of clothes for different types of leisure and for celebrations, which they classified as "smart dresses" (*nariadnye plat'ia*). They thus tried to embellish the monotony of daily clothing practices by means of style. This approach was diametrically opposed to the economists' idea of the basic necessity pack. Designers also taught Soviet consumers to distinguish day and evening "smart dresses." This distinction was subject to further, more detailed classification that included dresses for home celebrations, for theater, concerts, exhibitions and museums outings, dance parties, public festivities, national and official celebrations, receptions and visits, New Year parties, balls, and, finally, weddings. These different types of dresses could be more or less luxurious: "Dresses for home celebrations do not have a luxurious appearance; dresses to attend opera and ballet performances are more solemn; exhibitions and museums should be visited in dresses of sharpened form and elegant simplicity," and so on.[26] Luxurious dresses could exist under cover of this concept of functionality; they had a function in Soviet reality, but were strictly reserved for precise types of leisure activities: "Concerning evening dresses it is necessary to remember that long dresses touching the ground are only fit for solemn occasions—receptions, banquets, jubilee performances, great New Year balls and music-hall presentations."[27]

Rather than stratify wearers in terms of class, style in socialist fashion distinguished social activities and, as such, offered no threat to the idea of social equality. Since the materials from which the clothes were made differed in value, they could also determine the luxurious look of clothes. According to designers' advice, there was no restriction with regard to the use of luxurious materials to make clothes for Soviet consumers. Furs, for instance, traditionally associated with luxury in Western clothing practices, were omnipresent in the creations of Soviet designers:

> Coats in inexpensive natural fur are often cut in a sports style, with short collars and fastenings. Coats in more valuable furs are to be fashioned as smart, solemn dresses with ornamentation in another fur for contrast. The smartest and most fashionable silhouettes are used for these coats but in a very tactful, reticent manner. Coats in artificial furs have two silhouettes—straight or flared. Artists offer very laconic treatments of these coats without superfluous details, with the result that they look smarter and more expensive.[28]

If brocade was stigmatized as a fabric for "eccentric" Western dresses, its equivalent in Soviet production appeared as suitable for "luxurious" evening dresses. Thus *Woman Worker* could suggest that "for a solemn evening event, a play or a concert, it is appropriate to sew a dress in silk fabric of jacquard binding similar to brocade."[29] In another issue of the magazine we learn that "evening dresses can be smartened up not only thanks to expensive fabrics but also by being decorated with some fringe, fur, and embroidery."[30] Embroidered fabrics were used in Western haute couture as a means of symbolically distinguishing exclusive, luxurious, handmade dresses from industrially produced clothes for mass consumption. Despite Soviet fashion's claims to be for mass consumption, the designers were fascinated with embroidery. As the Soviet garment industry could not embroider clothes, the designers published albums of embroidery to help Soviet women make dresses more "luxurious" according to the taste of the time.

Clothing designers, then, invented a luxury of a Soviet type, superimposing elements of French haute couture onto their vision of Soviet reality. At first glance, such propositions of luxurious evening dresses in fashion magazines intended for all Soviet women (in accordance with the concept of mass and egalitarian socialist fashion) would seem to suggest that Soviet fashion contributed to the creation of a specific form of socialism where the attributes of luxury could be introduced into mass consumption. Thus luxury examples by Soviet designers could become a sort of material demonstration of the advantages of socialism (after being visual "proof" on the pages of fashion magazines).

In reality, however, those "evening dresses" could not be produced by the Soviet clothing industry. In the face of shortage and central planning, designers were powerless to realize their visions. The photographs of models published in fashion magazines were intended for personal commissions in dressmaking establishments. This strategy of consumption was more expensive than the purchase of ready-made clothes in state shops. Therefore, the luxury models were destined for privileged Soviet social categories and marked a symbolic distinction in Soviet society. How, then, did people react to these contradictions between the egalitarian, rational, and functional theory of Soviet fashion and the luxurious models created by Soviet designers?

Public Reception of Luxury Designs Created by Soviet Clothing Designers

If we compare the silhouettes in vogue in Western and Soviet fashion, we notice that Soviet fashion always tried to catch up with Western haute

Dresses designed by N. Shal'nova (*left*) and E. Nikol'skaia (*right*) for
the House of Clothing Design, Soviet Union

couture trends. Dior's "lily of the valley" line could be found in every Soviet
fashion magazine in the second half of the 1950s as a "proposition for young
women, for evening dresses and for ball gowns." Contemporaries noticed
this obvious parallel. An article in *Decorative Art of the USSR* devoted to
the annual meeting of Soviet clothes designers in 1964 in Moscow (whose
purpose was to define Soviet fashion trends for the year ahead) criticized
the lack of realism of most of the designs. Stating that the Soviet garment
industry could never reproduce such models for the masses, the author ex-

plained that this was because Soviet designers tried to adapt French haute couture to Soviet living conditions and economy, but that they did not want to "get rid of Christian Dior completely."[31] The rhetorical justification of these tendencies in Soviet fashion by designers does not seem very convincing:

> Contemporary Soviet fashion, contrary to that in the West, is based upon the most practical and beautiful silhouettes of international fashion. Eschewing artificial, far-fetched, exaggerated forms and silhouettes in women's clothes—sensational novelties of the West—our actual fashion aspires to the natural and laconic decoration of a woman's body—to the smooth line of the shoulder, to the natural line of the waist. That is why two silhouettes in women's summer dresses became very popular during the last few years. These are a fitted top with a straight narrow skirt and a fitted top with a wide ample skirt. Both of these silhouettes are elegant and feminine.[32]

At the IX International Fashion Congress, socialist designers presented the "trapeze" line which had been introduced by Yves Saint-Laurent in 1958. What was the difference, specialists asked in response, between socialist and "bourgeois" fashion? Soviet designers tried to square this circle by insisting on the trapezoidal form of the Russian traditional dress, the *sarafan*.[33] As they argued, the inspiration was totally legitimate, because it had been derived from national sources and was independent of international trends in fashion. Thus, their creativity satisfied the requirement that art should be "national in form and socialist in content."

However, such folkloric inspiration was not obvious to people attending fashion shows in the Houses of Clothing Design. Besides the didactic role to educate taste, these shows had to illustrate the concept of Soviet fashion's accessibility for the masses and to demonstrate the achievements of the clothing production system. They were also meant to prove that the state took care of its citizens. Stenographic records were kept at some of these shows, which were open to the public. These give us valuable insight into the public perception of Soviet designers' creations.

During the presentation of the autumn-winter 1954–55 collection of the Leningrad House of Clothing Design, spectators saw a "smart" velvet coat decorated with silvered fox fur that cost 2,415 rubles. The initial response was unanimous: "How beautiful it is!"[34] But then some less enthusiastic remarks followed: "It is necessary to produce designs for mass production. But is it possible to produce such luxurious goods on a mass scale?"[35] A Communist Party member answered the question, pointing out the gap between publicized theoretical principles of Soviet fashion and the models shown:

> Everything that you have shown here is accessible mainly to fashion victims who do not work and who have great means. What we would like to see are clothes accessible to working women who would also like to be dressed well and elegantly. It is therefore necessary to make more goods accessible for the majority.[36]

This remark on the inaccessibility of this design for ordinary people is fair. According to materials on budgets produced by the state Statistics Authority, the average monthly income per person in a worker's family in the first quarter of 1956 was 519 rubles, 647 rubles in an engineer's family, 550 in an employee's family, 627 in a teacher's family, 845 in a doctor's family and 572 rubles in a nurse's family.[37] With such incomes it was very hard to buy a 600-ruble man's summer suit, a 230-ruble artificial silk dress for a young girl, a 227-ruble short evening dress, a 460-ruble New Year's Eve smart dress, or a 550-ruble "smart" suit composed of a black coat and a white dress, all created by Leningrad designers in December 1955.[38]

People attending fashion shows in the Houses of Clothing Design perceived them as a staging of fashionable trends in luxurious examples in the manner of French haute couture. The main function of these institutions ascribed to them by the state—to provide factories with models—was invisible to spectators in such presentations:

> Today we have seen a lot of designs. They give a very pleasant impression by their shapes, colors, sewing, and purpose. But we would have liked better to see examples of dresses in which to go to work, because we all wish to be dressed nicely and elegantly ... Maybe most of us when going to the theater or a concert will put on these smart coats which look so beautiful, rich, and elegant. Everybody and especially young people wish to be dressed smartly for a celebration, as it has been shown here. Everything is beautiful. But all of us work, and we need various dresses for office and industrial work. Sarafans with blouses are very good for work. We would like to see here models of *sarafan* for office work, of work and office dresses, and of blouses, of jackets. It seems to me that such dresses would be very successful with our population.[39]

Thus the discourse conceptualizing socialist fashion, as formulated and publicized by designers, was partly neglected in their output. Nevertheless, functionality and rationality when demanded by Soviet consumers (like those expressing their views of the House of Clothing Design shows) acted as a constraint on design. Even when the principles of socialist fashion were thrown out by its creators, they returned, like a boomerang, in the preferences of Soviet citizens. When designers emphasized the rich and expensive face of Soviet fashion under the influence of haute couture, they were nevertheless reminded of the ascetic aspect of socialist fashion when the public only accepted luxurious dresses as leisure wear.

But presentations of such designs also had the opposite effect. Privileged Soviet consumers with higher incomes developed a taste for luxury in clothes. Soviet designers offered them a classic means of social and status distinction. A presentation organized by Leningrad designers for Communist Party bureaucrats on January 14, 1955, proves this point. This fashion show (which was also recorded by a stenographer) was formally structured according to the concept of functionality. The models demonstrated clothes for all types of private and public activities. Thus, the way fashion trends were shown represented a genuine adaptation of Western haute couture. But in the Soviet context, this form of presentation exaggerated the regulating role of fashion (sometimes to the point of caricature). The audience could see models dressed in chic dressing gowns as well as nightdresses on the stage:

> Model No. 8003—a silk dressing gown for a woman ...
>
> A voice from the hall: It's remarkable!
>
> Model No. 8002—a woman's smart silk dressing gown "Moroccan crepe" decorated with a silk cord ...
>
> A voice from the hall: How much does this dressing gown cost?
>
> Answer: 338 rubles.[40]

The latter garment echoes luxurious clothing practices presented on the pages of French fashion magazines in the 1950s and 1960s. Such examples were very enthusiastically received by the Leningrad Party bureaucrats: "It is a very good dress!" "This is a delightful dress," "It is not a dress, it is a dream!"[41] These consumers looked for symbols of luxury in clothes: "Will these models be for sale, especially those decorated with mink fur?"[42]

The indirect initiation of Soviet consumers into the traditional luxury of Western fashion by Soviet designers prepared Muscovites for the reception of the true haute couture.

The Symbolic Significance of Luxury in Soviet Clothing Practices

Success of Western Fashion

The climate of the Thaw and the partial opening of Soviet society in the 1950s and 1960s made regular contacts between the U.S.S.R. and other countries possible. The number of foreign exhibitions in the U.S.S.R. is very significant in this sense: forty-two foreign exhibitions took place from 1946 to 1958, and ninety foreign exhibitions were organized from 1959 to 1961.[43] The Soviet authorities' interest in inviting Western firms to show their products in the U.S.S.R. was linked to the idea of using foreign experience to improve Soviet production. But the cultural dimension was hardly separable from economic motivation. Almost every foreign exhibition in the U.S.S.R. (some of which were entirely devoted to consumer goods) was accompanied by fashion shows. Since such events were largely publicized by the Soviet mass media, the number of visitors was very important (although this depended on the country that organized the exhibition, as is obvious from table 3.1), and the shows certainly had an impact on the taste of the Soviet consumer.

The exhibitions from capitalist countries were accompanied by "ideological work and counter-propaganda" which maintained that eccentric and exaggerated tendencies in Western fashion were incompatible with the Soviet way of life.[44] Paradoxically, the clothing presented by socialist countries was distinguished by its accentuated luxurious aspect. The comparison of Japanese and Hungarian exhibitions by French Ambassador Maurice Dejean testifies to this phenomenon:

> It is the Hungarian exhibition and not the Japanese one which brings a luxurious note. According to the impression formed among the Soviet public, we can no longer say that the capitalist countries have a monopoly on prosperity today. A considerable confusion must reign in the minds of visitors in this field ... Both exhibitions give great importance to textiles ... While Japanese goods are of a very ordinary quality without luxurious fabrics, the Hungarian presentation of clothes for the city, for winter sports, and for children distinguishes itself by its aesthetic look and quality.[45]

The emphasis on luxury in the exhibitions from socialist countries could be considered a form of counter-propaganda wherein luxurious clothing became a pawn in the competition between the two world camps. Luxury was

Table 3.1 Attendance at foreign exhibitions presenting
consumer goods in Moscow (1949–1963)

Country organizing the exhibition	Dates	Consumer and fashionable goods presented at the exhibition	Number of visitors (thousands)
Hungary	May 21–June 9, 1949	Furs, fabrics, shoes, leather goods. Fashion show	170
German Democratic Republic	June 5–July 5, 1954	Mass consumption section with textiles and goods of garment industry	500
Austria	May 13–24, 1959	Textiles, leather and garment industry goods	300
German Democratic Republic	October 7–25, 1959	70 models of clothes	300
United States	July 24–September 5, 1959	Presentation of American way of life	2,100
Poland	September 4–30, 1959	Various consumer goods	1,000
Finland	May 10–22, 1960	Various consumer goods	400
Yugoslavia	May 25–June 19, 1960	Exposition devoted to goods of mass consumption	400
Hungary	August 12–September 4, 1960	Fashion shows	500/16*
Great Britain	May 19–June 4, 1961	Fabrics, clothes, shoes	1,100
German Democratic Republic	June 3–25, 1961	Exposition devoted to goods for mass consumption followed by fashion shows	520
France	August 15–September 15, 1961	Various consumer goods	1,800
Bulgaria	September 1963	Various consumer goods and fashion shows	353

*500,000 visitors to the exhibition; 16,000 spectators of the fashion shows

Source: Russian State Archive of the Economy, f. 635 (U.S.S.R. Chamber of Commerce), op. 1, d. 566, l. 22–23, 26–31, 33–36

thus officially legitimated for Soviet society. And in this situation it made sense that the Soviet public's reception of Western haute couture was very enthusiastic. The Christian Dior show in Moscow in June 1959 proves that the Soviet population had a great interest in French haute couture. From 10,000 to 12,000 people attended ten shows of the new collection created by Yves Saint-Laurent for the Christian Dior house; and the unsatisfied demand for tickets was estimated at a further 30,000. If we trust the opinion of the commercial attaché to the French embassy in Moscow, Jean Bernard, most tickets were given to Soviet designers, indicating that the need for Soviet experts to learn from such events was still paramount. At one of the shows, however, the audience was composed of journalists and of actors from the Bolshoi Theater.[46]

Members of this social elite associated with the theater developed a taste for French fashion and luxurious clothes. They chose models from Western fashion magazines and commissioned them from dressmaking establishments.[47] The system of Soviet dressmaking establishments was well adapted to this differentiated consumer taste: the most expensive workshops were named "luxury" (*liuks*) and were intended for these pretentious consumers.[48] The elites also used illegal means, such as contraband, to get hold of goods made abroad. For example, in December 1955 in Odessa, judicial bodies uncovered a smuggling ring that bought goods made in the United States from Bulgarian sailors and then sold them in major cities around the U.S.S.R. The investigation showed that a part of the merchandise was sold to the composer Nikita Bogoslovskii (a French-speaking dandy who personally knew Yves Montand), and also to Muscovite actors including Lidiia Atmanaki, Aleksandr Menaker, Mariia Mironova, Nikolai Rykunin, and Efim Berezin during their stay in Odessa.[49]

When Soviet actors were on tour abroad, they took the opportunity to purchase Western goods. In one case a Russian Federation National Laureate actress ordered several dresses at a Paris workshop while on a tour. According to the report of the Central Committee's Commission for Foreign Travel, some "white emigrants" covered the fee for the dresses in Paris, while the actress repaid her debt to their relatives in Moscow.[50]

Even if the Central Committee of the Communist Party condemned this passion for French fashion for "shaming the honor of Soviet man," the wife and daughters of the First Secretary of the Communist Party, N. S. Khrushchev, shared the same sin. In 1960, during an official visit to France by the Soviet head of state, they attended a fashion show in the Christian Dior house on April 1.[51] This indicates once again that Khrushchev had nothing against "exaggerations" in clothes. The paradox of the Soviet leader's personal support for luxury has its roots in the contradiction between the dream of social justice and the system of material privileges that was created in the 1930s and which lasted until the end of the regime. Without abandoning the communist project, Party officials ensured that the "valuable" social strata were better supplied, for many reasons: to get their loyalty;[52] to present them as an example for other social groups in order to stimulate their effort in the workplace and social mobility (as in the case of Stakhanovites); or to ensure that these individuals would make a good impression abroad, since they were able to visit foreign countries. This situation was regarded as temporary, corresponding to the definition of socialism where everybody gives according to his capacities and receives according to his *work*. Under communism each person would continue to give according to his capacities, but each would receive according to *need*. Due to this system of unequal supply and material privilege, the personalities honored by the Soviet regime, such as cosmonauts, presented no exception with regard to their interest in luxury. For example, the first female cosmonaut, Valentina Tereshkova, attended the presentation of the spring-summer collection in the Molyneux haute couture house in 1965 while paying an official visit to France.[53] Such examples might be seen as political gestures had they been covered by the Soviet mass media. Newspapers in the U.S.S.R. kept silent, however, on these more private aspects of the journeys. French TV broadcasts, meanwhile, discussed the subject openly.

Some actions of representatives of the U.S.S.R. Chamber of Commerce who organized foreign exhibitions and were thus familiar with luxury suggest they were seeking ways to satisfy the demand for French luxurious artifacts. In 1957 the president of the Chamber of Commerce, Nesterov, asked Robert Bordaz, economic adviser to the French embassy in Moscow, for his opinion concerning a project to sell dresses from Paris department stores at GUM (State Department Store). Nesterov also initiated the invitation of French haute couture houses to Moscow.[54]

The organization of retailing in Leningrad reveals the same phenomenon. In 1959 the local soviet and Party committee decided to open three shops by 1969 which would specialize in clothes of the best quality for men and women.[55] The Arcade (Passazh) department store in Leningrad was also oriented toward the sale of luxurious goods under Khrushchev.[56]

Thus the Thaw facilitated the establishment of Western luxurious clothing practices in the Soviet Union. The fact that only some restricted categories of the population could have access to the best-quality clothes produced in the West made the presence of social hierarchies in Soviet life visible. Soviet elites, being orientated toward French haute couture, tried to adopt a Western upper-class lifestyle. According to classic sociological explanations for the spread of fashion, developed by Herbert Spencer, Georg

Simmel, and other thinkers, ordinary people tend to imitate the fashion preferences of the elites. Is this theory applicable to the Soviet case?

The Aspiration to Luxury in Soviet Clothing Consumption

Interviews with ordinary Soviet consumers whose youth coincided with the 1950s and 1960s suggest an idea of a vertical dissemination of fashion in Soviet society. The Soviet elites' devotion to luxury shows that they were eager to distinguish themselves from the "masses." But ordinary people imitated their clothing practices, and this contributed to the wide adoption, in Soviet society, of tendencies borrowed from French haute couture. As in the West in the same period, Soviet actresses were fashion idols:

> We copied the fashion silhouettes of actresses . . . When Peletskaia appeared in the film *Different Fates* wearing a luxurious dress with a bow on one side, everybody began to do the same. Soviet actresses or the wives of actors (Cherkasov's wife, for instance) loved French fashion. We ordinary people did not know what one wore in Paris. We imitated our actresses.[57]

The real success of the Dior "new look" style is due to Riazanov's film *Carnival Night*. Soviet women tried to reproduce Liudmila Gurchenko's stage dresses using all possible means: making them at home, or ordering such models from private dressmakers or from state workshops.

Thus Soviet society is no exception as regards the mechanisms of social distinction and the spread of fashion. The possession of symbolically charged artifacts had a function in social positioning. But because these mechanisms operated in a society of shortage, they had even more significance. That people resorted to various techniques, including illegal ones, in order to provide themselves with "prestigious" artifacts, emphasized the symbolic significance of such goods.

This was the case with furs, for instance (which are discussed in more detail in Anna Tikhomirova's chapter in this book). Furs were traditionally considered luxurious attire and for this reason played a role as social markers. The lack of furs in the state shops in the second half of the 1950s resulted in a huge rise in their prices on the black market. Black market retailers increased official prices threefold (even for pieces of furs, as well as complete garments). For example, some Leningrad consumers could buy an otter's hide for 1,200 rubles while its state price was 412.5 rubles, and three marten's hides for 2,250 rubles while their state price was 558 rubles.[58] Taking into consideration the average income mentioned earlier, it is clear that the acquisition of a fur coat for 3,000 rubles from black market resellers who bought it for 2,230 rubles in 1960 was only possible for well-off consumers.[59] Despite the obvious official efforts to make luxurious artifacts accessible to the masses, in reality their consumption was reserved for a very small category of people.

The state shop clerks themselves derived profit from shortages of furs when they sold them to either acquaintances or black market retailers for a higher price.[60] The high demand for furs contributed to the thriving of numerous underground undertakings composed of people connected with the fur industry. They stole fur garments or fur materials from the factories in order to produce clothes illegally (without the requisite license for handicraft activity) and then sold them on the market.[61] The case of a great fur robbery from the Second Moscow Fur Factory in 1956 exemplifies perfectly what kind of fur clothes Soviet consumers valued most. Fourteen criminals stole 80 "gorgets" in silver fox fur, 28 semi-pelerines of the same fur, 34 collars in astrakhan and silver fox fur, 9 fur coats, and other clothes for the sum of 362,000 rubles.[62] The denomination of most of these goods in French (the transcription of French words in Russian is the following: *gorzhety, polupeleriny, manto*) demonstrates the symbolic significance of these artifacts associated with luxurious clothing practices. The heist was organized by the vice director of the factory, who had a criminal past: as a workshop chief in another fur factory he had been prosecuted for plundering a fur workshop in 1951.[63] The "speculators," who were keen to off-load the stolen goods quickly, sold many at half price; a mink coat was on the market for 9,500 rubles instead of 19,000.[64] Sadly the identity and social profile of the customers buying the coats is not described in the sources.

Conclusion

The attitude toward luxury was not homogenous in Soviet fashion. It was complicated by the superimposition of various factors: the political context of the Cold War; the planned organization of the economy; the professional culture of Soviet clothing designers fascinated by Western haute couture; the partial opening up of Soviet society during the Thaw to external influence; and a growing tendency toward social distinction through the possession of luxurious artifacts.

The public repudiation of luxury in Soviet discourses could be construed as an attempt to maintain social consensus in a society where the material conditions of ordinary people were defined by shortage. The utopian promise of abundance in the communist future played a similar role by turning people's attention away from their real standards of living. Claiming that the Soviet economy would trump capitalism, this promise was central to the rehabilitation of socialism during the period of de-Stalinization. Soviet clothing designers contributed by producing designs which represented the material advantages of the socialist way of life. Transposing some elements of Western haute couture into Soviet fashion, they set out to educate the "good taste" of Soviet consumers, as well as to regulate clothing practices (by insisting on "compulsory" evening dresses, for instance). Yet at the same time, designers tried to escape from subjection to the demands of industry. Creating examples that could not be made by Soviet industry, their status as designers drew closer to that of Western haute couture designers. Their passion for luxurious clothes—common in all socialist countries—infected some of the more fortunate social groups. Soviet elites tried to provide themselves with prestigious French dresses or ordered clothes in high-class dressmaking workshops. Such consumer strategies marked the social stratification of Soviet society. "Ordinary" people followed fashion trends that trickled down from the top of the society, a popularization of luxury that offers parallels with Simmel's scheme. They also adopted various consumption strategies to draw closer to the upper classes. In a society of shortage, luxury obtained a highly charged symbolic significance.

Notes

1. L. Efremova, "Moda dvukh stolits," *Dekorativnoe iskusstvo SSSR*, no. 4 (1963): 34.

2. N. T. Savel'eva, *Moda i massovyi vkus* (Moscow: Legkaia industriia, 1966), 8.

3. RGAE (Russian State Archive of the Economy), f. 523, "U.S.S.R. House of Clothing Design," op. 1, d. 205 ("Report of a group of specialists about a trip to France with the aim of becoming acquainted with clothing design and production, creation of new patterns, and structures of fabrics for garment industry, 1965") l. 5, 7.

4. N. S. Khrushchev, "Iz doklada N. S. Khrushcheva na chetvertoi sessii Verkhovnogo Soveta SSSR 'O merakh po vypolneniu programmy KPSS v oblasti povysheniia blagosostoianiia naroda,'" *Dekorativnoe iskusstvo SSSR*, no. 9 (1964): 1.

5. P. S. Nazarov, V. M. Siniutin, and Iu. L. Shnirlin, *Potreblenie v SSSR i metodika ego ischisleniia* (Moscow: Gosudarstvennoe izdatel'stvo torgovoi literatury, 1959); I. Iu. Pisarev, ed., *Metodologicheskie voprosy izucheniia urovnia zhizni trudiashchikhsia* (Moscow: Izdatel'stvo sotsial'no-ekonomicheskoi literatury, 1959); V. V. Shvyrkov, *Pokazatel' elastichnosti potrebleniia i ego prakticheskoe znachenie pri izuchenii urovnia zhizni trudiashchikhsia* (Moscow, 1959); V. V. Shvyrkov, *Metodologicheskie voprosy izucheniia struktury potrebitel'skogo biudzheta* (Abstract of *Kandidat* dissertation, Moscow Institute of National Economy Moscow, 1959); V. V. Shvyrkov, *Zakonomernosti potrebleniia promyshlennykh i prodovol'stvennykh tovarov* (Moscow: Izdatel'stvo Ekonomika, 1965); V.V. Shvyrkov, *Voprosy modelirovaniia potrebitel'skogo sprosa*, part 1: *Metodika prognoza sprosa i planovogo rascheta roznichnogo tovarooborota* (Minsk: NII ekonomiki i ekonomiko-matematicheskikh metodov planirovaniia pri Gosplane BSSR, 1969); Iu. L. Shnirlin, *Nauchno obosnovannye normy potrebleniia* (Moscow: Gosudarstvennoe

izdatel'stvo "Vysshaia shkola," 1961); V. F. Medvedev, V. V. Shvyrkov, and L. P. Chernysh, *Modeli prognozirovaniia potrebitel'skogo sprosa dlia tselei planirovaniia* (Minsk: NII ekonomiki i ekonomiko-matematicheskikh metodov planirovaniia pri Gosplane BSSR, 1969); V. S. Tiukov, *Planirovanie roznichnogo tovarooborota: V pomoshch' ekonomistu i planoviku* (Moscow: Gosplanizdat, 1960); V. S. Tiukov and R. A. Lokshin, *Sovetskaia torgovlia v period perekhoda k kommunizmu* (Moscow: Ekonomika, 1964); A. Korneev, "K voprosu o proizvodstve i potreblenii tekstil'nykh izdelii v SSSR," *Voprosy ekonomiki,* no. 7 (1956): 43–58; N. Ia. Bromlei, "Uroven' zhizni v SSSR (1950–1965)," *Voprosy istorii,* no. 7 (1966): 3–17.

6. *Nekotorye voprosy razvitiia sovremennoi odezhdy* (Kiev: Obshchestvo "Znanie" Ukrainskoi SSR. Kievskii dom nauchno-tekhnicheskoi propagandy, 1964), 31–32.

7. Ibid., 32–33.

8. Thorstein Veblen, *Théorie de la classe de loisir* (1899; Paris: Gallimard, 1970).

9. Tatiana Strijeňova, *La mode en Union Soviétique, 1917–1945* (Paris: Flammarion, 1991), 38, 70, 74, 91, 93.

10. Larisa Kashuk, "Alternativnoe iskusstvo 60–kh godov," in *Net!—i konformisty: Obrazy sovetskogo iskusstva s 50–kh do 80–kh godov* (exhibition in the Xawery Dunikowski Museum, Warsaw, May 1994, and Russian Museum, Saint Petersburg, July–August 1994), 50–52.

11. V. A. Ivanova, "O napravlenii mody v odezhde na 1963–1964 gg.," in *Novaia tekhnika i tekhnologiia shveinogo proizvodstva,* 2nd ed. (Leningrad, 1963), 4.

12. L. M. Litvina, I. S. Leonidova, and L. F. Turchanovskaia, *Modelirovanie i khudozhestvennoe oformlenie zhenskoi i detskoi odezhdy* (Moscow: Izdatel'stvo "Legkaia industriia," 1964), 16.

13. L. M. Shipova, "Novoe v modelirovanii legkogo zhenskogo plat'ia," in *Mody i modelirovanie* (Moscow: Gosudarstvennoe izdatel'stvo torgovoi literatury, 1960), 3.

14. M. Il'in, "Iuvelirnye izdeliia i moda," *Dekorativnoe iskusstvo SSSR,* no. 5 (1959): 26.

15. RGANI (Russian State Archive of Contemporary History), f. 5 (Central Committee *apparat*), op. 43 (Department of Industrial Goods for Mass Consumption), d. 69, l. 83, 89.

16. RGAE, f. 9480 (State Committee for Science and Technology of the U.S.S.R. Council of Ministers), op. 3, d. 1417 (correspondence with ministries, departments, and other organizations on questions of missions in France), l. 81; RGANI, f. 5, op. 43 d. 77, l. 1; RGAE, f. 523, op. 1, d. 205. On Soviet designers' assignments to France, see Larissa Zakharova, "Kazhdoi sovetskoi zhenshchine plat'e ot Diora (frantsuzskoe vliianie v sovetskoi mode 1950–60–kh godov)," *Sotsial'naia istoriia: Ezhegodnik [Yearbook] 2004* (Moscow: Rosspen, 2005), 339–67; Larissa Zakharova, "La mode soviétique et ses sources d'inspiration occidentales dans les années 1950–60," *Matériaux pour l'histoire de notre temps* 76 (2004): 34–40.

17. V. Aralova, "Na vystavke v N'iu-Iorke," *Zhurnal mod,* no. 4 (1959): 36.

18. On the incompatibility of Soviet clothing designers' preoccupations with the planned economy, see Larissa Zakharova, "Fabriquer le bon goût: La maison des modèles de Leningrad à l'époque de Hruščev," in "Repenser le 'Dégel,' versions du socialisme, influences internationales et société soviétique," ed. Eleonory Gilburd and Larissa Zakharova, special issue of *Cahiers du Monde russe* 47, nos. 1–2 (2006): 195–225.

19. TsGA SPb (Central State Archive of Saint Petersburg), f. 9610 (Leningrad

House of Clothing Design), op. 3, d. 94 (plan of organizational and technical measures for 1961), l. 17; d. 112 (annual report on the main activity in 1960), l. 50.

20. See, for example, *Zhurnal mod* and *Modeli sezona* (both published by the Institute of the Culture of Clothes); *Odezhda i byt* (published by the Moscow combine of applied arts); *Mody* (published by GUM, the State Department Store).

21. Roland Barthes, *Système de la mode* (Paris: Éditions du Seuil, 1988).

22. Material concerning the organization of these congresses can be found in RGAE, f. 523 (U.S.S.R. House of Clothing Design), op. 1, d. 111, 112, 114, 125, 143, 159. See also Larissa Zakharova, "La mise en scène de la mode soviétique au cours des Congrès internationaux de la mode (années 1950–60)," *Le mouvement social* 221 (2007): 33–54.

23. RGAE, f. 523, op. 1, d. 159 (Material concerning the organization of the XI International Congress of Fashion in Prague), l. 102.

24. For example, E. Semenova, "Letniaia odezhda," *Rabotnitsa*, no. 6 (1959): 30.

25. Veblen, *Théorie de la classe de loisir*, 112.

26. Litvina, Leonidova, and Turchanovskaia, *Modelirovanie i khudozhestvennoe oformlenie zhenskoi i detskoi odezhdy*, 276–77.

27. *Mody odezhdy na 1962–1963 g.* (Moscow: Vsesoiuznyi zaochnyi institut tekstil'noi i legkoi promyshlennosti Ministerstva vysshego i srednego spetsial'nogo obrazovaniia RSFSR, 1963), 105.

28. Ibid., 106–11.

29. A. Blank, "Vashe novoe plat'e," *Rabotnitsa*, no. 5 (1957): 24.

30. *Novoe v konstruirovanii i modelirovanii odezhdy i napravlenie mody na 1963–1964 gg.* (Simferopol: Krymizdat, 1963), 11.

31. L. Kramarenko, "Ob iskusstve odezhdy: Zametki s Vsesoiuznogo soveshchaniia po modelirovaniiu odezhdy," *Dekorativnoe iskusstvo SSSR*, no. 5 (1964): 21.

32. Shipova, "Novoe v modelirovanii," 3–4.

33. RGAE, f. 523, op. 1, d. 125 (stenographic report of meeting of Soviet clothing designers devoted to results of the XIX International Congress of Fashion, July 28, 1958), l. 14–15.

34. TsGA SPb, f. 9610, op. 1, d. 176 (stenographic note of the public presentation of models, 1954–55 season), l. 20.

35. Ibid., l. 24.

36. Ibid.

37. RGAE, f. 1562 (Central Statistics Authority of the U.S.S.R.), op. 26 (Department of Budget Statistics), d. 473 (Materials [tables sent to U.S.S.R. Planning Committee, to the State Economic Commission, and other organizations]), l. 40.

38. TsGA SPb, f. 9610, op. 1., d. 188 (stenographic report of meeting of the garment industry workers), l. 7, 14, 17, 18.

39. TsGA SPb, f. 9610, op. 1, d. 204; d. 176 (stenographic note of public presentation of models, 1954–55 season), l. 26.

40. Ibid., d. 204 (meeting of the employees of the House of Clothing Design with functionaries of the municipal and regional committees' *apparat* of the Communist Party on the subject of trends in design, January 14, 1955), l. 5.

41. Ibid., l. 3, 4.

42. Ibid., l. 16.

43. RGAE, f. 635 (U.S.S.R. Chamber of Commerce), op. 1, d. 566, l. 40.

44. Ibid., d. 566a, l. 27.

45. Center of Diplomatic Archives in Nantes, collection: French embassy in Moscow, set B, box 272 (French exhibition, correspondence [November 1959–February 1962]); letter from M. Dejean to Couve de Murville on the lessons learned from the Japanese and Hungarian exhibitions in Moscow in mounting the French exhibition of 1961, August 31, 1960).

46. Ibid., box 271 (private commercial operations [U.S.S.R.-France], 1951–64; letter from the commercial attaché of the French embassy, Jean Bernard, to the secretary of state for economic affairs, on the presentation of Christian Dior fashions, June 25, 1969).

47. Interview with actress Nataliia Vlasova, September 18, 2004, Moscow.

48. TsGA SPb, f. 9798 (trust for individual sewing and repairing of clothes "Leningradodezhda"), op. 1, d. 59 (orders of the R.S.F.S.R. Ministry of Trade and of the direction of trade with industrial goods of Leningrad on improving the work of dressmaking establishments, 1955), l. 7.

49. GARF (State Archive of the Russian Federation), f. 9401 (special file of N. S. Khrushchev), op. 2, d. 478, l. 12, 20, 29, 170–72.

50. RGANI, f. 5 (*apparat* of the Central Committee), op. 14 (Commission for Foreign Travel), d. 19 (about serious shortcomings in the work of the Ministry of Culture in sending assignments of artistic personalities, January 9, 1960).

51. *Journal de nuit,* April 1, 1960, INA (National Institute of Audiovisual Documentation), BNF (French National Library).

52. Tamara Kondratieva argues that this way of "nourishing" the Party and state officials in order to get their loyalty derived from the practices of the old Russia's princes. Tamara Kondratieva, *Gouverner et nourrir: Du pouvoir en Russie (XVIe–XXe siècles)* (Paris: Les Belles Lettres, 2002).

53. C. Désiré et al., "La haute couture et ses problèmes," *Panorama,* July 16, 1965, INA, BNF.

54. Center of Diplomatic Archives in Nantes, collection: French embassy in Moscow, set B, box 270 (commercial relations between U.S.S.R. and France); letter from the reporter to the state council, economic and commercial attaché Robert Bordaz to the secretary of state for economic affairs, June 29, 1957; report of the negotiations between Hubert Cau and Nesterov, April 24, 1956; note of the French commercial attaché in Moscow Hubert Cau on the problems of commercial expension between the U.S.S.R. and France, September 16, 1955.

55. TsGA SPb, f. 9610, op. 3, d. 59 (resolution of the Executive Committee of the Leningrad Soviet on the attribution of pieces to the House of Clothing Design, April 2, 1959), l. 5.

56. Ibid., d. 152 (stenographic reports of the meetings of the Grand Artistic Council, 1962, volume 1), l. 85.

57. Interview with L.V.M. (born 1941), Saint Petersburg, August 26, 2004. Cinema stars were mentioned as sources of fashionable trends in the following interviews: T.V.O. (born 1944), Novgorod, August 14, 2004; Z. P. Shch. (born 1932), Saint Petersburg, August 28, 2004; N.A.G. (born 1921), Kronstadt, September 2, 2004; G.G.S. (born 1924), Moscow, October 19, 2004.

58. LOGAV (State Archive of the Leningrad Region in Vyborg), f. 4380 (prosecuting magistracy of Leningrad), op. 3, d. 411 (supervision on the affair of accusation of Gurevich, Abel Genrikhovich, Rivlin Abram Natanovich, and Radushkevich Lev

Izrailevich according to articles no. 107 and 99 of the Criminal Code, 7.3.–13.5.57), l. 21.

59. Ibid., op. 3, d. 973 (supervision on the affair of Saleev A. Kh., Sadiykin Sh. P., Tuishev A. M., accused in the crimes according to article no. 107 of the Criminal Code of the R.S.F.S.R., 10.10–14.10.60).

60. Ibid., op. 4, d. 227 (information on the results of the analysis of speculation affairs during 1962), l. 8; op. 3, d. 540 (supervision on the affair of Nol'ken Aleksandr Abramovich, Malysheva Elena Alekseevna, Shchepaniuk Nikolai Parfirevich, and Dolbilov Petr Aleksandrovich. Articles 107, 109, and 2 of the Ukase of 4.6.47 [theft of state property] 1.7.58–9.11.58).

61. See, for example, LOGAV, f. 4380, op. 2, d. 1112 (supervision on the affair of Kulikov Konstantin Nikolaevich, articles 99 and 1 of the Ukase of 4.6.47, 30.4–30.6.53); op. 3, d. 411 (supervision on the affair of accusation of Gurevich Abel Genrikhovich, Rivlin Abram Natanovich, and Radushkevich Lev Izrailevich according to articles no. 107 and 99 of the Criminal Code, 7.3–13.5.57).

62. GARF, f. 8131 (prosecuting magistracy of the U.S.S.R.), op. 28, d. 3182 (supervision on the affair of the theft of fur goods from the Second Moscow Fur Factory, 23.3.56–28.11.57), l. 21.

63. Ibid., l. 21.

64. Ibid., l. 22.

МИНИСТЕРСТВО РЫБНОЙ ПРОМЫШЛЕННОСТИ СССР

ГЛАВРЫБСБЫТ

ИКРА

ЗЕРНИСТАЯ, ПАЮСНАЯ И ПАСТЕРИЗОВАННАЯ

Promotional poster and postcard for Soviet caviar designed by A. P. Andreadi, 1952

CHAPTER FOUR

Soviet Luxuries from Champagne to Private Cars

Jukka Gronow and Sergei Zhuravlev

We can find extensive references to luxury in official documents and the press in the Soviet Union in the 1930s. Luxuries could be invoked to indict excessive and politically harmful fascination with the material world of commodities which the authorities thought plagued some Soviet citizens. At the same time, they were presented as worthy aspirations that every Soviet man or woman would have a right to enjoy, at least in the near future, and, as such, things that the government and the Communist Party of the Soviet Union (CPSU) had an obligation to deliver. This aim mirrored Stalin's declaration in 1936 that Soviet society had reached the stage of overall abundance. Life had become more joyous.[1] The line between luxuries and necessities was not very clear in the minds of decision makers and economic planners. With increases in production, goods and services that had formerly been luxuries gradually became necessities; that is, not simply required for the satisfaction of basic human needs, but what were thought to be "normal" for the conduct of good and cultured living.

That Stalin's and his ministers' idea of mass-producing luxuries, like champagne and perfume, was in line with the promise of general well-being and abundance is well known.[2] After the war and the end of the Stalin era, the discourse on luxury—either as a negative or positive point of reference—was no longer as pronounced in Soviet (semi)public debates and official declarations.[3] The problems of definition, however, did not disappear, even though they were rarely discussed explicitly in terms of luxury and necessity. Throughout Soviet history, the state faced a problem legitimating the principles and standards by which scarce goods would be distributed. Somewhat to the surprise of the authorities, the scale of goods "in deficit" did not diminish with the rapid improvement in living standards in the 1960s and 1970s. On the contrary, the faster economic growth, the faster consumers' demands and expectations seemed to grow too.[4]

In this chapter we shall analyze the question of Soviet luxuries and the principles determining their distribution through three examples: champagne, the products of fashion ateliers, and private cars, each of which, we claim, is representative of three periods: the 1930s, the 1950s, and the 1970s, respectively. Their relative and changing status also reflects the development of Soviet consumption from conditions of considerable poverty to material well-being. A private car might only appear in the wildest fantasies of a Soviet consumer in the 1930s: in the 1970s they were acquired by Soviet citizens for the first time in relatively large numbers (though they remained in short supply). A mass-produced bottle of champagne—a luxury in the 1930s—became by the 1960s a rather common delight and an "essential" feature of many private and public celebrations in the lives of Soviet citizens. Fashionable clothing was a pressing problem for all Soviet citizens, and for women in particular, throughout the history of the Soviet Union, which the establishment of a comprehensive chain of fashion houses and ateliers after the Second World War was a serious attempt to resolve. Champagne, fashionable clothing, and private cars were by no means the only scarce or highly valued objects of desire by Soviet consumers. In fact, under the conditions of the planned and strictly centralized economy, the demand for most commodities was only rarely met and therefore there were, to various degrees and in different periods, serious shortages of the most ordinary consumer goods, food included. The particular Soviet luxury goods and services discussed in this essay, however, highlight specific and different aspects of the production, distribution, and consumption of goods under the premises of the planned economy. Each represented, in different ways, attempts to give some credence to the CPSU's promise of general abundance.

The early novelties among Soviet consumer goods from the 1930s were all cheap, mass-produced copies of "real" luxuries from the prerevolutionary period. They were, as we argue below, forms of Soviet kitsch. The new fashion houses and ateliers opened shortly before and after the Second World War, which openly copied the output of famous Parisian fashion houses, had, from the start, a twofold task of designing clothes both to individual order *and* for mass production in the clothes factories. The local fashion ateliers—or at least the "deluxe" ateliers—designed what might be described as Soviet "haute couture," while the large all-union or republican fashion houses produced designs for industrial production. Thus, Soviet fashion design stood with one leg firmly in the old world of luxury manufacturing, with famous Paris fashion houses as its ideal, and with the other in modern industrial production. Fashion designers and economic planners never really succeeded in bridging this gap.

When the production and selling of private cars started in earnest in the late 1960s, Soviet planners did not take their models from capitalist luxury markets as they had with the two earlier examples of Soviet luxuries.[5] They did not promise the Soviet worker a Mercedes Benz, a Rolls-Royce, or a Bentley but simply copied (this time quite legally) what they judged to be the most technically advanced European family car, the Italian Fiat. Paradoxically, this new Soviet "middle-class" car, the Lada, soon became a particularly Soviet kind of luxury and status symbol. Not only a real "deficit" in terms set by the command economy, it was also a drain on resources: many Soviet citizens queued on waiting lists for years or paid very high prices on the black market to acquire a new or secondhand one.

Our study is based mainly on historical archival sources and other written reports from journals and newspapers. It makes use of several recent, new studies of the history of Soviet and Russian consumption and consumer goods industries, the authors' own included. In addition, we use oral history to illustrate and enliven the story with memories of the lived past.

Scarce Goods, Rationed and Commercial

After the announcement of the First Five-Year Plan in 1928, two kinds of consumer goods became available in the Soviet Union: those sold in commercial shops open to all; and centrally rationed goods, distributed through "closed" outlets serving a restricted clientele. When strict rationing of basic foodstuffs and other consumer goods (first introduced during the years of the collectivization of agriculture) ended in the 1930s, it was thought that the newly opened commercial shops would only sell goods that were not in short supply (*defitsitnye*).[6] Gradually, with the increasing general abundance promised by Stalin, such "deficits" would, it was believed, disappear and all goods would become available in amounts that could fully satisfy demand. Soviet champagne was a typical early example of one of these commercial, high-quality goods.

These goods were, in principle, on open sale in shops, available to anyone who had money to buy them. The retail cost of these goods was not set by the market but was a "state price" centrally determined by calculating production costs and adding or subtracting an agreed margin. Some goods and services—including housing, gas and electricity, local transport, and basic foodstuffs like bread, as well as champagne and caviar—were

A boy modeling clothes designed by
the House of Clothing Design,
Kuznetskii Most, 1970s

available at low prices, heavily subsidized by the state. (Children's clothes and shoes were also subsidized, which, as a rule, made them even more scarce, since even small adults could wear them.) Others goods—including cars and furniture—were sold at high prices which far exceeded actual production costs.

Centrally rationed goods were distributed through other channels, mostly workplace organizations and trade unions in "closed" canteens and shops open only to a restricted clientele. Products and services could be given as gifts or as rewards for exceptional achievement, but they, as a rule, also had a price. Price, however, was not the main factor in their consumption: the privilege of access was decisive. One could not buy such goods without being entitled, for one reason or another, to them. These were, in other words, status entitlements, attached to one's position, ideally determined by one's performance or importance in the hierarchical order of work. Unlike market economies where consumer goods can be free-floating symbols because they can be bought by anyone with sufficient funds at their disposal, the socialist system in this respect was paradoxically reminiscent of systems of closed estates with strictly regulated status privileges (such as the sumptuary laws which operated in early modern Europe). Since such official hierarchies of value could never be drawn with crystal clear borders and since many rare goods and services could be acquired through informal and even illegal channels, as symbols, they could acquire independent "meanings" from those imposed by the Soviet authorities.

The apparently clear-cut division of goods and services into two separate classes was further complicated by the fact that the commercial goods were, as often as not, in "deficit" too: demand could exceed their supply by many times. Consequently, centrally rationed goods were often traded on the black market and on the official secondhand market for higher sums than their official price, as we shall see in the case of private cars. The same product could circulate in both distribution systems, free of charge (or at a very cheap price) in one and at a much higher price in the other. A peculiarity of the official retailing system was that the price mechanism could not correct the imbalances of the market. Prices were centrally fixed and could not be adjusted according to fluctuations in demand and supply.

Sales—in the sense of cutting prices to stimulate trade—were unknown in the U.S.S.R.[7] But comprehensive price cuts of basic consumer goods and food items were an important political and propaganda measure. For instance, between 1947 and 1950 Stalin lowered the prices of basic items for mass consumption on five occasions. Another peculiarity of the Soviet system was that in some cases consumers could only buy the consumer goods that they desired if they had other products to offer in exchange. Kolkhoz

Table 4.1. The production of consumer durables and sale of
private cars in the U.S.S.R. in 1955–65 (in thousands)[8]

	1955	1956	1965
Private cars (sold to private citizens)	64	62	64
TVs	495	1,726	3,655
Refrigerators (for domestic use)	151	529	1,675
Irons	87	895	3,430

workers could occasionally buy new clothes in their rural cooperatives only
if they offered meat, wool, or vegetables, raised and grown in their own
gardens, in exchange.

In general, "deficit" described those things and services in the U.S.S.R.
for which demand outstripped supply. In some cases—most notably in the
case of basic foodstuffs—shortages were caused or sustained by very low,
highly subsidized prices. In others, shortages arose and waiting lists formed
even when the price of the goods was very high in relation to average income. The prices of private cars, private garages, cooperative apartments,
TV sets, and other items of domestic technology in the 1960s might, for
instance, equal a worker's total earnings over several years.[9] In some product
categories like TVs and refrigerators, saturation was achieved (only in the
limited and technical sense that a great majority possessed them): in others,
like private cars and apartments, this never occurred. (In the production
of many consumer durables, a great leap forward took place in 1956; see
table 4.1.) At the same time, influential and well-funded state organizations
could take good care of their own workers. This meant, in many cases, a new
and better apartment rather than higher wages.

The Common Luxury of the 1930s

After the First Five-Year Plan and the forced collectivization of agriculture,
Soviet industry and trade aimed in the mid-1930s to offer their customers
much that was not self-evidently necessary for the satisfaction of basic human needs.[10] Why should the Soviet economy produce, for instance, millions of bottles of champagne (a decision made in the summer of 1936) or
promote the production of vintage wines or cognac (as decided in 1938)
instead of greater quantities of plain vodka and beer?[11] The former were

luxuries, but they were also goods that the Soviet authorities and directors of industry and trade now felt were almost desperately "needed" by common people. At a meeting of the directors of the newly established state department stores, the participants complained that supplies of many basic household utensils—bowls, brushes, scissors, shoelaces, and wooden hangers—were unavailable and could not be stocked. Many of these things were not produced at all in the Soviet Union. Consequently they had "the character of luxury."[12] The term "luxury" could, it seems, refer to very dissimilar things: those items which carried the aura of real or imagined luxurious lifestyles from the past; and others which, though "ordinary," were in fact very scarce or even unavailable.

Many of the self-proclaimed Soviet luxury consumer goods of the 1930s, like champagne, caviar, chocolate, and perfumes, were cheap mass-produced copies of the goods that were thought to have carried the "aura" of high social status under the old regime. For this reason, they can be called Soviet kitsch. Furthermore, they could at least in principle, it was thought, be produced in great quantities in the near future at a relatively low cost and thus be made available to almost every Soviet citizen.

Fashionable Designs and Mass-Produced Clothes

The case of fashionable clothes, discussed in more detail in Larissa Zakharova's contribution to this volume, was more complicated than many other *defitsit* products or services, i.e., those in short supply. The authorities were aware—at least to some extent—that they faced two principal problems. First, they had to work out the correct relationship of the design of individual garments (Soviet "haute couture") to industrial mass production. It was clearly not possible to imagine that "luxury" fashion ateliers could ever really satisfy mass demand. Working to individual orders, they produced custom-made dresses and tailored suits as well as custom-made hats, shoes, and other accessories in relatively small quantities. After the Second World War, the network of fashion ateliers spread to the major cities and capitals of the Soviet republics. Despite their rapid growth, Soviet planners did not imagine that hand-production could meet the sartorial needs of the great consuming masses. Nor was it possible to establish a fashion atelier within the reach of every factory or kolkhoz. In 1955 the Fashion Atelier at GUM, the State Department Store in Moscow, for instance, proudly reported that it had turned out over 5,000 coats, over 5,000 women's dresses, and 17,000 women's hats. With production totaling over 38,000 items per year, it was the biggest organization of its kind in the Soviet Union.[13] Even though this

Model wearing clothes made by the House of Clothing
Design standing in Red Square, Moscow, next to a
Volga GAZ-21 car, mid-1960s

fashion atelier was not the only one in Moscow, its output measured in tens
of thousands of garments could never fully satisfy total demand in a city of
two million inhabitants (a figure extended by millions of visitors and guests
from the provinces too).

The Soviet authorities gradually became aware of a second problem,
that of the rapidly changing nature of fashion (though they remained essentially suspicious of the phenomenon's disregard for utility). Fashion—by
definition—renders otherwise functional garments prematurely obsolete.
The "need" for novelty can never be fully satisfied: the very moment the
appetite for a new fashionable style is satisfied and the market saturated, a
new fashion arises. What makes fashion desirable is its very novelty.[14]

The first Soviet state fashion ateliers were established—at the same
time as the other major institutions of luxury production—in the mid-
1930s. They were, as a rule, attached to department stores in large cities. In

early 1944, while the Second World War was still being fought on all fronts, the Soviet government and the CPSU decided to open a big fashion house in Moscow. Soon after the war ended, several similar fashion houses were established by the Ministry of Light Industry—Minlegprom, responsible for mass production of clothes in the capitals of the Soviet republics and other major cities. By the end of the 1960s, their number had reached almost twenty. After four years, the Moscow fashion house was redesignated as the All-Union House of Fashion, becoming the leading fashion house in the country. It "supervised" the republican and regional fashion houses in setting general fashion trends. Although numerous, these fashion houses were by no means the only organizations active in fashion design in the Soviet Union. As a rule, all big department stores had their own fashion garment-producing workshops to which design units of various sizes were attached. The flagship of the Soviet department stores, GUM, opposite the Kremlin on Red Square, had, for instance, a huge department of fashion design founded in 1953. It was so large that it competed with the All-Union House of Fashion in size and importance.[15]

These two chains—the fashion houses and the fashion ateliers in department stores—were not the only influences on Soviet fashion. In addition, hundreds of local fashion ateliers belonged to the system of *indposhiva* (individual sewing) workshops, each with their own fashion designers and professional pattern makers who mainly modified existing designs to make them more practical and easier to make. They sometimes created new designs too. In the 1960s and 1970s large Houses of Everyday Life providing domestic services were established in urban and regional centers throughout the Soviet Union. Combining a hairdressing salon, a laundry, and a beauty parlor, they generally included a workshop in which local citizens could order custom-made clothing. They were classified by the quality and cost of the service they offered, with "de luxe" ateliers as the highest class. As if this range of fashion workshops and retailers was not enough, at the end of the 1960s the Ministry of Light Industry opened a central, experimental fashion institute, the VIALEGPROM (All-Union Institute for the Assortment of Products of Light Industry and Culture of Clothing) in a Moscow high-rise building with hundreds of employees.[16] Its main tasks were the future planning of Soviet fashion (i.e., "trendsetting") and the coordination of all branches of Soviet light industry in the fields of textiles, furniture, and, of course, fashion design.

In practice, from the 1960s on, three huge parallel fashion design organizations existed in the Soviet Union. They belonged to different administrative systems and worked under different ministries: the fashion houses were under the Ministry of Light Industry; the fashion ateliers and their design units were under the Ministry of Trade; and, finally, the ateliers of *indposhiva* operating within the Houses of Everyday Life were organized by the Ministry of Home Services. Separate fashion houses existed for the design of shoes, sportswear, work clothes, and so on. VIALEGPROM, the crown on the head of Soviet fashion, belonged to the Ministry of Light Industry—its tasks and functions overlapped to a great extent with those of the All-Union House of Fashion in Moscow.

In principle, if not in practice, a rather strict division of responsibilities distinguished these organizations. For instance, the fashion houses were charged with designing clothes for mass production in bigger clothes factories, while the ateliers in department stores and the *indposhiva* workshops were to produce one-off garments. But this division of responsibilities did not quite hold. In addition to designing clothes for industrial production, each engaged in two main tasks, albeit to varying degrees. Each took an interest in the design of clothes for production in "experimental" series, either made in their own workshops or in cooperation with local industry. Invariably made in small runs, such series usually consisted of a few hundred items. They were often sold in local clothes outlets, often connected to the factory or workshop. The second important task was the propagation of fashion, combined with education about good taste and etiquette in dressing. Making more fashionable and beautiful clothes available to the public at large was viewed as the most effective way of promoting "civilized" codes of dress. In addition to issuing numerous publications, fashion journals, and albums, these institutes regularly organized fashion shows and exhibitions, sometimes on their own premises and sometimes by touring towns, factories, or kolkhozes further afield. These publications and fashion shows not only entertained their audiences, they served a practical function by providing examples for Soviet women to order from local ateliers or to make at home. For those who lacked the skills with a needle and thread, talented neighbors, colleagues, or friends could be commissioned to make new fashionable clothing.

Although the importance of the task of introducing new designs to industry was recognized, the fashion houses and institutes faced major economic and technical challenges. The major factories were not very eager to adopt new and often technically more complicated designs offered to them by fashion designers. Since the fashion houses worked according to a centrally approved plan, they had to produce a preordained amount of garments in particular categories every year. Factory directors often preferred to fulfill their quotas by producing well-established, standardized goods rather than experimenting with new, often more expensive ones.

Soviet fashion institutes found it particularly difficult to respond to rapid changes in demand. According to historians of the Soviet Union, the centralized nature of Soviet planning was the main hindrance in this regard.[17] The Soviet fashion houses and ateliers faced, however, an even more fundamental challenge: How should they engage with the dynamics of change which define fashion? How did fashion fit into the Soviet system of a planned economy which explicitly aimed at the satisfaction of the needs of the population? Fashion is, by definition, neither functional nor strictly useful. As the Soviet specialists knew, in capitalism the rapid turns of fashion served the interests of profit by artificially "aging" otherwise useful products. As such, it was alien to socialism. They also had to admit that fashion was difficult, if not totally impossible, to predict. Nevertheless, economic experts and planners thought that fashion had somehow a rightful place even in socialist consumption. The solution generally proposed by those involved was to distinguish between extravagant fashion designs, characteristic of capitalist clothing culture, and those designs which were demonstrably functional or served the purposes of "real" beauty.[18] In this way, fashion could be presented as improvements in much the same way as technical inventions evidently were. Thus fashions could be welcomed and even praised as signs of social, cultural, and economic progress. The chief benefit of fashion understood in these terms was understood as higher aesthetic values. As one of the leaders of the Moscow House of Fashion stressed, it was important to "decide where the functionally beautiful form ends."[19] The question of where to draw the line was, however, impossible to answer in any general terms.

It was characteristic that when the All-Union House of Fashion in Moscow wanted to send a delegation to visit the Paris fashion houses at the end of the 1950s—an event discussed by Larissa Zakharova in this book— and asked the Central Committee of the Communist Party for permission, the answer was blunt: since the delegation had already visited Paris the year before, there was no need to go again. They had absorbed all that could be learned about fashion design.[20] Obviously, it never occurred to the members of the Central Committee that Paris was worth another visit to learn what the latest fashions looked like.

Soviet fashion professionals were obviously eager to develop a system of fashion closely resembling their Western counterparts in Paris. Soviet fashion houses and institutions illustrate a general pattern that Christoph Neidhart has observed of Soviet society.[21] The Soviet Union established and developed many of the main social institutions found in Western societies such as parliamentary elections, trade unions, academic institutions, and department stores. They were claimed to be even better than their Western counterparts: Soviet elections were more democratic, trade unions really represented workers' interests, and universities had higher academic standards. But they were never really like their Western counterparts. An essential aspect—like free elections, the right to strike, or freedom of academic thinking—was always missing. The same pattern was true of fashion houses. They were just like their Western namesakes, with one important exception: they did not really know how to cope with fashion. In effect, by maintaining numerous local fashion ateliers the Soviet Union preserved and encouraged forms of handicraft production and manufacturing which were already becoming a rare luxury in capitalism. At the same time, by establishing and encouraging a full-fledged fashion system with seasonal innovations, Soviet policy opened up the door to the perpetual production of new luxuries.

A Short History of Soviet Private Cars

While our two historical examples of Soviet luxuries, champagne and the products of fashion houses, fit well into Werner Sombart's classical definition of luxuries as finer versions of more ordinary goods (as refinement or *Verfeinerung*), Soviet passenger cars were different in this respect.[22] They were ordinary cars, and did not pretend to be copies of anything finer than they really were. Nevertheless, they were guaranteed the "aura" of luxury by being hard to get and expensive to buy. As such, they were objects of desire for the great majority of Soviet people.

Construction of the first two Soviet car factories began in Moscow in 1931 and in Gorky (Nizhnii Novgorod) in 1932. Until the early 1970s the majority of automobiles produced in the Soviet Union were trucks (see table 4.2). As early as 1936 the U.S.S.R. attained second place (after the United States) in truck production in the world.[23]

In the 1930s when the production of passenger cars first started in the U.S.S.R., they were only very exceptionally sold to ordinary citizens.[24] Cars were dedicated to "official use" only. In the rare cases where a private person owned a car, it was usually as a special reward from the government or, in rare cases, had been bought with "hard" foreign currency.[25] High-ranking

Table 4.2. The production of trucks and cars in the U.S.S.R., 1932–74 (in thousands)[26]

	1932	1935	1939	1945	1950	1955	1960	1965	1970	1974
Trucks	23.7	76.9	178.8	68.6	294.4	328.1	362	279.6	524.5	666
Cars	0.03	19	19.6	5	64.6	107.8	138.8	201.2	344.2	1,119

members of the *nomenklatura* (the Party and administrative elite) did not own their cars but were driven by a chauffeur in a vehicle that came with public office. Ordinary citizens could only dream of owning an automobile by buying a ticket in a state lottery which had a car as the first prize. For them, ownership of a vehicle might only extend as far as a bicycle or, in rare cases, a motorcycle.

The Second World War gave a strong stimulus to the production of Soviet cars. About 50,000 (Willis and Ford) cars were leased from the United States for military purposes, thus allowing many Soviet soldiers to become car drivers or, at least, to make their first personal acquaintance with a passenger car.[27] Hundreds of thousands of Soviet soldiers also came into contact with private cars in the countries they occupied and liberated. After demobilization, many tried to take a car that they had requisitioned home and then become its legal owner. The authorities, however, prohibited such efforts at privatization.

After the war, the Soviet leaders decided to increase the number of Soviet car models and started producing new cars at Gorky (the GAZ-20 or Pobeda "Victory") and at Moscow (the Moskvich). According to the central plan, the Moscow factory (MZMA) should have produced three hundred cars as early as 1946, but the first model was not to leave the factory gates until January 1947. At first, Moskvich cars were sold only to citizens who had earned the right to purchase them because of their status or work achievements, but later they were, at least in principle, allowed to go on open sale.[28]

In 1956 a new model was put into production in Gorky, the GAZ-21 (generally known as the Volga), a car that was to become quite prestigious in the U.S.S.R. As a rule, state and Party officials, officers of the KGB, and other important people were driven by chauffeurs in black Volgas. The highest ranks of the leadership, however, traveled in a Chaika, a black limousine with seven passenger seats, which was produced in relatively small numbers at the Gorky car factory after 1958. While Chaikas were exclusively for the use of high-ranking public officials, Volgas could be bought by ordinary citizens, although only in relatively small numbers. To drive one's own Volga was probably the highest dream of many Soviet citizens. (The Russian leader Vladimir Putin only realized this dream a few years ago when he bought a white Volga. Russian television showed a happy Putin driving his "new" car on holiday.)[29]

The Zaporozhets, the smallest Soviet car, went into production in the early 1960s. It was designed in MZMA by the constructors of the Moskvich. The Zaporozhets was smaller, cheaper, and had a two-stroke engine. It was more popular among collective farm workers than among city dwellers, partly because of its relatively cheap price. With the Zaporo-zhets, the number of car models available to private drivers in the U.S.S.R. reached three. But the levels of production remained quite modest in the 1960s when measured in terms of the numbers that were actually sold to Soviet citizens. A relatively large proportion was exported, used as taxis, as official vehicles, as police cars, or as army vehicles. It was a sign of the times that the production of buses and other forms of public transport increased at a faster rate than the production of cars.

Until the mid-1960s, official Soviet policy did not encourage the sale of cars to private citizens. Between 1955 and 1964, an average of 61,000 cars per year were sold to individuals, that is, 45 percent of all the cars produced in the country.[30] The CPSU program of 1961 included a chapter on "The Tasks of the CPSU in Increasing the Material Well-Being of the Popula-tion" which caused lively debates. The general secretary of the CPSU, Ni-kita Khrushchev, argued that—in the fight against individualism—it was more rational to promote public forms of transport, including state-owned taxis, than privately owned vehicles. These taxis should be cheap to hire and widely available to the population. Since professional drivers would be behind the wheel, it was claimed that one of its social benefits would be a reduction in the number of road accidents. In addition, ordinary citizens would not have to worry about parking or servicing their cars and could, therefore, spend their leisure time in more productive or cultural activities. Once this system was extended, Soviet citizens would, it was claimed, come to prefer taxis to the private ownership of cars. Khrushchev expressed his strong opinions on the question in a speech to the workers of the city of Vladivostok on October 6, 1959:

> The Americans often boast that they, by the way, have more private cars than we in the Soviet Union. But we do not set it as our goal to compete with the Americans in producing more private cars. We in-crease and shall increase the production of cars but not like the Ameri-cans ... We want to establish another system of car use than in the capitalist countries, where they reason in the following way: it is a wreck, but it is my property. Cars will be utilized more rationally in our country than in America; we shall develop more taxi companies, from which people can hire a car for their necessary journey. Why should a person have to worry where to leave his car, why all the fuss? Such a system will better satisfy people's demands and it will be more in line with the interests of the society as a whole, as well as of those of each and every citizen.[31]

Cars for the People

When, in 1964, Party Secretary Leonid Brezhnev and Prime Minister Aleksey Kosygin (a figure with a background in "light" industry) came to power, the Party changed its policy toward private car ownership.[32] At this time the old MZMA factory in Moscow which had produced Moskvich cars was rapidly becoming obsolete, and the authorities took the view that it was not possible to expand production to the levels required there. A decision was made to build a new plant nearby instead. In the spring of 1968, the construction of a major industrial zone started in the Moscow region Tekstil'shchiky. In 1971 the Moscow factory changed its name to the Lenin Komsomol Car Factory (AZLK). It was organized—together with the new VAZ factory at Togliatti discussed below—to manufacture family cars for the "middle" strata of Soviet society.[33] The first VAZ-2101 (Lada-Zhiguli) rolled off the factory line at Togliatti at the end of 1971; the first Moskvich-412 was manufactured at the new Moscow factory in September in the same year. While both factories competed fiercely with each other for export opportunities, they did not have to compete at home, where the demand for private cars always far exceeded the supply.

The new VAZ car factory at Togliatti which opened in 1970 was the result of close and, in Soviet terms, unique technical and economic cooperation with Fiat in Turin, Italy. For the first time, ordinary Soviet citizens enjoyed the real possibility of being able to buy a private family car, a Lada (or Zhiguli, as it was also called). As an illustration of how very exceptional this was, it is worth noting that most of the newly appointed directors of VAZ could not drive. (With official cars and chauffeurs, they had little need to learn.) As if to signal the revolutionary change in the Soviet automobile industry, the general director of VAZ, V. N. Poliakov, ordered that all members of the factory leadership should attend an obligatory three-month driving course to acquire driving licenses.[34]

Despite the impressive production figures of the new factory (it had been set a production target of seven hundred thousand cars per year),[35] which far exceeded the total capacity of all the previously existing passenger car factories in the U.S.S.R., the "automobilization" of the country was very slow and took place much later than in Western Europe and some Eastern European "satellite states." In 1975 the ratio of people to cars in the U.S.S.R. was 54:1 compared to 2:1 in the United States, 4:1 in the United Kingdom, and 7:2 in West Germany.[36] In 1970, 2 percent of Soviet households owned a car: ten years later this had increased to 10 percent (and in 1985 to 15 percent).[37] Compared to the rather rapid spread of electronics in Soviet homes, car ownership lagged far behind.[38] Nevertheless, a "great leap" undoubtedly took place in the U.S.S.R. in the 1970s, when the average number of private cars increased from six to thirty for every thousand people in a single decade.

It is interesting that no overall target for the planned level of the auto-mobilization of the country was ever declared publicly. It is, however, obvious that the original targets were rather modest compared to the international standards then prevailing.[39] Soviet planners and economists obviously never envisioned that almost every Soviet family would own a car in the future. Various modes of public transport were available at relatively cheap prices and were the main ways in which Soviet citizens traveled.

One might also seriously wonder whether the Soviet authorities and planning officials ever really understood the full economic and social consequences of their decision to make private cars available.[40] Obviously, it was not enough simply to build and operate car factories. Increasing numbers of cars needed more and better roads, service and repair stations, spare parts, oil and gasoline supplies, and so on. In 1971 there were only 447 service stations and 3,320 car mechanic workshops in the sprawling territories of the Soviet Union. The Togliatti factory (VAZ) was particularly eager, following the lead of its Italian partner, Fiat, to create a network of service stations of its own. These stations had a right to sell cars too. It is interesting that the Lada service network was the first of its kind in the whole country in any field of technical consumer durables. However, during the first five years of operation, Lada only opened 30 car centers, as well as 130 fixed garages and 100 mobile repair units. These were expected to service all the 2.2 million Ladas produced in this period. The resources invested by the state in maintaining private cars on the road were totally inadequate. The situation was much the same in the production of spare parts. They were never produced in numbers which equaled the increasing amount of private cars, a state of affairs that was well known to the planners and decision makers. This, of course, accentuated the value of spares on the black market.

This state of affairs could not but influence the psychological attitudes of Soviet drivers toward their cars. An owner would wash and wax his car regularly, check its shock absorbers and springs, and cover it carefully with a tarpaulin to protect it both from the sun and the snow. Before embarking on longer trips, the driver would entreat his car not to let him down. Like a horse, a car became used to its master's habits, and so only one driver could take the reins in his hands. If someone dared to ask to borrow a car, its owner would probably react with surprise and decline the request. According to a common saying, there were only two things that a man should never lend: his wife and his car.

Who Was Entitled to Own a Car?

In the last decades of the Soviet Union, a private car was unmistakably a luxury item in the sense that it was both expensive to purchase and difficult to obtain.[41] In the early 1970s when the first Ladas were sold, it took four to five average annual salaries to buy one. Compared to the price of a relatively spacious family apartment in a cooperative building in Moscow, a private car was not only as expensive but was, in fact, more desired. Since all prices were determined by the state, this differential was not an accident but a policy. In the mid-1970s, for instance, a new, prestigious, three-room apartment in Moscow was worth about 10,000 rubles. Although many people had difficulty saving the down payment of 3,000–4,000 rubles, the remainder could be repaid over ten years at rates which an ordinary family with an average annual income could afford. At the same time, the price of a new Volga was 16,000 rubles; different models of Lada-Zhigulis ranged from 6,000 to 8,000 rubles, and a new Moskvich-412 was priced at 6,000 rubles. Even though the evidence is, according to Lewis Siegelbaum, mostly anecdotal, the relative worth and status of these different cars in the minds of Soviet car enthusiasts as well as the population at large matched their differences in price rather closely.[42] Chaikas and ZILs were totally out of the reach of ordinary citizens. Even the cheapest cars were almost as expensive as a relatively luxurious new family apartment. But cars, unlike apartments, could not be bought on credit. However difficult it was to buy a car, many preferred to save their money for a vehicle rather than a home. A family of two working adults could, perhaps, buy a new car by saving the earnings of one wage earner over four or five years, but usually they had to be prepared to wait even longer (on average eight years). Secondhand cars were also expensive. As one interviewee told us, in 1974 he bought an old Moskvich which was badly in need of repair for just over 2,000 rubles. Another person bought a ten-year-old Moskvich in 1978 for 3,500 rubles.[43]

The black market prices of cars could be higher than the official prices. Many people saved money and queued on a waiting list for the best part of their lives in order to buy one. A car preserved its value well too. After six or seven years a car owner could still sell his vehicle for the same price— or even higher—than he had originally paid for it. Therefore, it is understandable that a car was expected to serve its owner for a very long time. Citizen Klimenko from Moscow, a satisfied car owner, wrote in 2005 that "my 'Kopeika' [the pet name for the Lada-2101, the first model produced by VAZ] from 1970 became like a family member long ago. Over thirty years it has outlived my mother, my husband, and my sister-in-law. Now my 21-year-old grandson helps me take care of it. Therefore it is no wonder that the car has a feeling of responsibility to its masters."[44]

The car economy changed little during the last years of the U.S.S.R. Demand always far exceeded supply. New and more expensive models of the Lada with minor improvements were introduced, but essentially the Togliatti factory produced three basic models of car: the VAZ-2101 with some modifications (2102–07); the city jeep NIVA; and two variations of the Lada-Samara (VAZ-2108 and 2109)—a front-wheel-drive vehicle which was introduced in the 1980s. The VAZ-2101 (the "Kopeika") based on the old "standard" (Fiat) model remained the market leader in the U.S.S.R.

For most aspiring car owners the main objective was simply to buy a car; the model or even price were of secondary importance.[45] Since the official price was always fixed by the authorities, the problem of shortage could not be solved by raising prices, nor was it possible to increase production and thereby satisfy demand by further investment, as might have been the case in a market economy. Increased investment and production figures were possible only if approved by the Party and the government and adopted into the official Five-Year Plans. In 1980 an academic economist, Gavriil Popov, suggested a radical solution to the problem of the shortage of passenger cars in the Party newspaper *Pravda*. He argued that a new car plant should be constructed, financed with funds collected from people on the waiting list for cars who would—once the plant went into production—receive its products first. Popov's unheeded proposal pointed to a kind of people's capitalism.[46]

To cope with the huge discrepancy between supply and demand, a special system of distribution was created. The total annual production of cars was allocated by the planning offices to all the different economic and social organizations—largely employers and trade unions—which were then required to distribute them to their members.[47] These institutions took over the process of managing the waiting lists for cars and, using more or less explicit criteria, decided who among their employees and members had the strongest right to buy one.

When the first Ladas went on sale and huge queues formed, the Soviet motor journal *Driving (Za rulem)* asked its readers to send proposals for how best to organize the sale of private cars. It received thousands of letters. Some suggested formal criteria like the possession of a valid driving license and the place of residence. Previous car ownership, for some, should be a negative criterion. The most egalitarian correspondents proposed an open lottery.[48] The suggestion with the most support from its readers was to assess the social and professional "worth" of potential buyers. Here is evidence that a moral principle of distribution, according to which the relative social merits of the individual (measured in terms of his or her contribution to the common good) should be taken into account when deciding entitlements, really enjoyed strong popular support among the Soviet people. People and state concurred that such "status symbols"—or rather "status entitlements"—should be awarded to those who had earned them by dint of their achievements. The practical application of this principle was not without its problems, as is shown, for instance, by the fact that the authorities tried other methods of distribution too. In Moscow, in 1974–75, the local traffic police were given the right to keep lists of the potential car buyers.

When the news spread, at the end of the 1960s, that the huge new car factory at Togliatti was commencing production, many people who wished to buy a car started to organize waiting lists (in a tried and tested manner). The list of potential car buyers in Moscow soon included hundreds of thousand of names, even before the first car had left the factory.[49] Similar, though much shorter, waiting lists were reported as early as 1954: 20,000 people were then queuing in Moscow for the Pobeda cars. Only 6,300 Pobedas were sold to private persons annually. The self-nominated organizers of the list, headed by three major generals in the Soviet army, decided who was entitled to buy a car next. As the director of the Moscow official trade organization declared, he had nothing to do with this system. Reportedly each person in the list had to pay one ruble to cover the costs of maintaining the list.[50] As the head of the Moscow Police car inspection (the Moscow Regional Office of State Automobile Inspection) reported, it was obvious that the system was corrupt since five persons—three chauffeurs, a professor, and a popular performer—had managed to buy and sell as many as three or four Pobedas each between 1949 and 1953. In order to prevent such abuses of the system, the police inspector suggested that a new rule should be introduced: an owner of a car which was three years old or less should not be allowed to buy a new one. In addition, half the price should be paid in cash when placing the order.[51] It is interesting that the very same practical measures were suggested and adopted again when sales of the Lada started in 1971.

However well reasoned in abstract moral terms, there were two major problems built into the distribution system of the passenger cars and other scarce objects of consumption in the Soviet Union. Obviously, the system could be and was misused. Corruption, stimulated by seductive and simply scarce commodities, was the main enemy. The system also presumed that the hierarchy of merit on which it was built was generally accepted by the great majority of the society. Judging from various sources, the idea of rewarding extraordinary or outstanding work or achievement *was* widely accepted as the basic moral principle of socialism ("to each according to his labor"). But the lurking possibility of administrative arbitrariness could easily cial change. In socialism, social status was—at least ideally—not ascribed but achieved, and the hierarchical order was open to social mobility. The ideological basis of social status could not be disputed or challenged. To lose one's office or job meant that one also automatically lost the privileges that came with the position. The state and the CPSU, just like the earlier autocratic states, were the guarantors and guardians of this social order and the general well-being of citizens. Therefore, like in early modern Europe, the problems of luxury presented themselves as a natural moral discourse on economy. Early modern European concerns with luxury were usually focused on what was perceived to be the threat of corruption of the social order presented by the prospect of social imitation.[56] Social mobility and prosperity threatened to put luxuries into the "wrong" hands. In the Soviet Union luxuries awaited all hardworking citizens in the future, but they were entitled to them only in a strictly regulated manner.

In the Soviet case, novelties and luxuries, in the sense of scarce or exceptional things and experiences, were, in principle, reserved for those who had earned them by their skills and performance at work and, for those reasons, officially "deserved" them. These people had a higher official social status in Soviet society. The main difference between early modern Europe and the U.S.S.R. was, however, that it was possible to move through the hierarchies of status. In principle, anyone could reach the highest positions by his or her own efforts (with the important reservation that the CPSU was the final gatekeeper of social ascent). And what is even more important, the hierarchy itself was only needed for the time being.[57] As soon as the rest of the society became as equally dedicated to socially useful tasks and performed them with as much vigor as the vanguard, they too would automatically be entitled to new and higher cultural standards and material well-being. Thus, at least in ideal terms, increased production of consumer goods, the product of improved work performance, would go hand in hand with growing and socially legitimate demands.[58] The economic moral was simple and followed Saint-Simon's maxim, which Karl Marx had adopted, according to which the remuneration of work should follow the principle of socialist distribution: "to each according to his work." If people worked harder and better, they would produce more of the things that they needed and would also be entitled to receive their share of the increased fruits of their collective labor. Increasing demand thus went closely hand in hand with increasing supply, and vice versa.[59] There is good reason to believe that the majority of the Soviet population accepted and adopted this socialist work ethic. Somewhat to the surprise of the authorities, though, scarcity did not disappear with economic growth but reappeared in new forms and changing shapes. The socialist consumers blamed the government and the CPSU for not satisfy-

ing their legitimate demands.[60] At the same time, the system was open both
to corruption as well as to the emergence of pervasive and corrosive doubts
about existing entitlements and privileges. What if, the Soviet citizen might
wonder, these were not measures of real social and moral worth on the part
of those who enjoyed them, but signs of corruption?

Notes

1. For a more detailed analysis, see J. Gronow, *Caviar with Champagne: Common
Luxury and the Ideals of the Good Life in Stalin's Russia* (Oxford and New York: Berg,
2003).

2. See N. S. Timasheff, *The Great Retreat: The Growth and Decline of Communism
in Russia* (New York: E. P. Dutton, 1946); S. Fitzpatrick, *Everyday Stalinism: Ordinary
Life in Extraordinary Times. Soviet Russia in the 1930s* (New York and Oxford: Oxford
University Press, 1999); R. Stites, *Popular Culture: Entertainment and Society Since
1900* (Cambridge, Eng.: Cambridge University Press, 1992).

3. For the use of luxury in the discourse on consumption in the German Democratic Republic in the 1950s and 1960s, see M. Landsman, *Dictatorship and Demand:
The Politics of Consumerism in East Germany* (Cambridge, Mass., and London: Harvard University Press, 2005), 78.

4. See P. Hanson, *The Rise and Fall of the Soviet Economy* (London: Longman,
2003), 118.

5. Two comprehensive histories of Soviet car production and distribution have
been published recently, marking a new interest in Soviet material culture among
historians. Lewis H. Siegelbaum, in his pathbreaking study *Cars for Comrades: The
Life of the Soviet Automobile* (Ithaca, N.Y.: Cornell University Press, 2008), paints
an overall picture of the history of Soviet car production and the place of the car in
Soviet society. S. V. Zhuravlev et al., *AvtoVAZ mezhdu proshlym i budushchim: Istoriia
volzhskogo avtozavoda, 1966–2005 (AvtoVAZ Between the Past and the Future: The
History of the Volzhskii Car-Building Factory, 1966–2005)* (Moscow: RAGS, 2006), is
the first comprehensive history of AvtoVAZ, the largest car producer in the U.S.S.R.
(and still operating today), which produced Ladas.

6. See Gronow, *Caviar with Champagne*, 88. Rationing of basic consumer goods
and food was once again adopted in the U.S.S.R., like in many other European countries, at the outbreak of the Second World War. The rationing of food ended first in
December 1947. The Soviet government had, however, to ration food at later times:
as late as 1982, for instance, food rationing was introduced in a number of provincial
towns of the U.S.S.R. (see Hanson, *Rise and Fall*, 135).

7. Hanson, *Rise and Fall*, 89. Sales were not entirely unknown in the U.S.S.R., even
though they were not advertised and promoted as such. Shoes and clothes for which
there was inadequate demand could, at times, be sold at lower prices. To draw a contrast with capitalist marketing and sales, this was explained as the government's wish
to make these consumer goods available for the people as cheaply as possible.

8. Compiled by V. M. Iamashev from various editions of *Narodnoe khoziaistvo
SSSR*. See V. M. Iamashev, "Volzhkii avtozavod: Prervannyi ryvok za mirovoi mod-
ernizatsiei," in *Istoriia OAO AvtoVAZ: Uroki, problemy, sovremennost'. Sbornik trudov*

I-i Vserossiiskoi nauchnoi konferentsii po istorii OAO AvtoVAZ (Tol'iatti: AvtoVAZ, 2003), 234.

9. A plan for a promotional movie about GUM in the mid-1950s illustrates the picture the authorities wanted to present about increasing demand for more valuable and modern consumer goods due to higher general standards of culture and living. One scene was to present a picture of a long queue in the store's home electronics department of people eagerly wanting to buy new TV sets at the huge price of two thousand rubles each, a sum that was the equivalent of one and a half year's wages for an average worker. TV sets were in the 1950s a luxury item, but a luxury which everyone "needed" and to which everyone would, sooner or later, be entitled. (See RGAE [Russian State Archive of the Economy], f. 7971, op. 1, d. 2384, l. 231.)

10. Timasheff, *Great Retreat;* and A. K. Sokolov, ed., *Obshchestvo i vlast': 1930-e gody: Povestvovaniie v dokumentakh* (Moscow: Rosspen, 1998), 162–229.

11. Gronow, *Caviar with Champagne,* 17–28.

12. Ibid., 68–69. Chewing gum was a later example of such "small things" which had the character of luxuries because they were not produced and sold in the U.S.S.R. until the 1980s. East Germans in the 1950s spoke of the "thousand small things," meaning all the small household utensils and other ordinary consumer goods whose availability was taken for granted in the West but which were rare and difficult to find at home. See Ina Merkel and Felix Mühlberg, *Wunderwirtschaft: DDR-Konsumkultur in den 60er Jahren,* ed. Neue Gesellschaft für Bildende Kunst (Cologne: Böhlau, 1996), 12–15.

13. A. Kozlova, "Atel'e individual'nogo poshiva," *Sovetskaia torgovlia* 1 (1956): 20.

14. See G. Simmel, "Fashion," in *Perspectives on Fashion,* ed. G. B. Sproles (Minneapolis, Minn.: Burgess, 1981) (English original in *International Quarterly,* no. 10 [1904]: 130–55); and J. Gronow, *The Sociology of Taste* (London and New York: Routledge, 1997), chap. 4.

15. For the early history of Soviet fashion design and its institutions, see S. V. Zhuravlev and J. Gronow, "Vlast' mody i Sovetskaya vlast': Istoriia protivostoianiia," *Istorik i khudozhnik* 7 (2006), 9 (2006), and 1 (2007); and S. V. Zhuravlev and J. Gronow, "Krasota pod kontrolem gosudarstva: Osobennosti i etapy stanovleniia sovetskoi mody," *Soviet and Post-Soviet Reviews* 1 (2005): 1–92.

16. VIALEGPROM was established in 1958 but was given broader tasks and a new building in the center of Moscow in the 1960s.

17. See J. Gronow, "Oliko sosialismissa muotia? Neuvostokulutuksen historiaa," in *Arjen talous: Talous, tunteet ja yhteiskunta,* ed. P. Jokivuori and P. Ruuskanen (Jyväskylä: SoPhi, 2004), 185–207.

18. L. Zakharova, "Kazhdoi sovetskoi zhenshchine—plat'e ot Diora! Frantsuzskoie vliianie v sovetskoi mode 1950–1960–kh gg," in *Sotsial'naia istoriia: Ezhegodnik 2004* (Moscow: Rosspen, 2005), 339–67.

19. Ie. Semenov, "Bol'she krasivoi i udobnoi odezhdy," *Sovetskaia torgovlia* 4 (1954): 16.

20. Zakharova, "Kazhdoi sovetskoi zhenshchine," 351.

21. C. Neidhart, *Russia's Carnival: The Smells, Sights and Sounds of Transition* (Lanham, Md.: Rowman and Littlefield, 2003).

22. W. Sombart, *Liebe, Luxus und Kapitalismus: Über die Entstehung der modernen Welt aus dem Geist der Verschwendung* (Berlin: Wagenbach, 1983).

23. L. M. Shugurov, *Razvitie avtomobilestroeniia SSSR v period pervykh piatiletok (1930–1941 gg.)* (Moscow: NIIN Avtoprom, 1969), 36–37.

24. In the 1930s private consumption was limited to about 1 percent of the passenger cars distributed in the U.S.S.R. See V. Lazarev and P. R. Gregory, "The Wheels of a Command Economy: Allocating Soviet Vehicles," *Economic History Review* 2 (2002): 330.

25. Ibid., 342–43.

26. Ie. A. Riadchenko, "Avtomobil'naia promyshlennost': Etapy stanovleniia, zadachi i perspektivy," in *Istoriia OAO AvtoVAZ: Uroki, problemy, sovremennost'* (2003), 126–28. See also A. D. Abramovich, *Kratkii ocherk razvitiia avtomobil'noi promyshlennosti i avtomobil'nogo transporta v SSSR* (Moscow: Znanie, 1958); and V. Ia. Selifonov, *Avtomobil'naia promyshlennost' SSSR v 1959–1965 gg* (Moscow: Znanie, 1959).

27. The U.S.S.R. received 477,485 trucks and cars from the Allies on lease (350,000 from the United States). In addition, it produced 240,000 trucks and cars of its own. See L. B. Kashcheev and V. A. Reminskii, *Avtomobili lend-liza* (Kharkov: ATF, 1998); B. V. Sokolov, "Rol' lend-liza v sovetskikh voennykh usloviiakh, 1940–45," *Journal of Slavic Military Studies* 4 (1994), http://militera.lib.ru/sokolov1/04.html; and A. Vislykh, "Spasitel'nyi lend-liz," *Nezavisimoe voennoe obozrenie,* October 12, 2001, http://nvo.ng.ru/history/2001–10–12.

28. K. Averyanov, S. Zhuravlev, et al., *Istoriia Iugo-vostoka Moskvy* (Moscow: Mosgorarkhiv, 2000), 280.

29. In 2009 Putin announced on TV that he had purchased another popular Russian car, a new 4x4 "Niva" (which had been produced from the 1980s by AvtoVAZ).

30. L. Siegelbaum, "Cars, Cars, and More Cars," in *Istoriia OAO AvtoVAZ: Uroki, problemy, sovremennost'* (2003), 245–47. See also L. Siegelbaum, "Cars, Cars, and More Cars: The Faustian Bargain of the Brezhnev Era," in *Borders of Socialism: Private Spheres of Soviet Russia,* ed. L. Siegelbaum (London: Palgrave, 2006), 83–103.

31. N. S. Khrushchev, *Mir bez oruzhiia—Mir bez voin,* vol. 2 (Moscow: Gospolitizdat, 1960), 327–28.

32. In many respects the new policy, however, was reminiscent of Khrushchev's first years in power in the mid-1950s. (See, for instance, Yu. E. Emel'ianov, *Khrushchev: Smutian v Kremle* [Moscow: Veche, 2005], 105–60.)

33. The town Togliatti or Togliattigrad was named after the famous Italian communist leader Palmiro Togliatti. It is written in the form Tol'yatti or Tol'iatti when transliterated from Russian.

34. E. D. Starenko, "Vsegda na linii ognia," in *VAZ: Stranitsy istorii: Vospominaniia i fakty,* vol. 5 (Tol'iatti: AvtoVAZ, 2005), 52.

35. M. R. Zezina, "Avtomobil 'Zhiguli' na sovetskom potrebitel'skom rynke," in *Istoriia OAO AvtoVAZ: Uroki, problemy, sovremennost'. Sbornik trudov II-i Vserossiiskoi nauchnoi konferentsii po istorii OAO AvtoVAZ* (Tol'iatti: AvtoVAZ, 2005), 67; see also A. K. Sokolov, "Rozhdenie volzhskogo avtogiganta v kontekste vnutrennego i vneshnego polozheniya SSSR," in *Istoriia OAO AvtoVAZ: Uroki, problemy, sovremennost',* 48.

36. V. T. Efimov, "Avtomobilizatsiia: Tendentsii i protivorechiia," *Sotsiologicheskie issledovaniia* 4 (1981): 171; see also Hanson, *Rise and Fall,* 117.

37. TsSU SSSR (Central Statistical Administration of the USSR), *Narodnoe khozaistvo SSSR v 1985* (Moscow: Finansy i statistika, 1986), 446.

38. The proportion of households owning a television and refrigerator rose from

24 and 11 percent, respectively in 1965 and to 92 and 89 percent in 1982. D. Lane, *Soviet Economy and Society* (Oxford: Blackwell, 1985), 58.

39. Siegelbaum, *Cars for the Comrades*, 239, refers to an official Gosplan (State Planning Office) target for the year 1985 of 93 cars per 1,000 people.

40. Siegelbaum, "Cars, Cars, and More Cars," 245–48.

41. For a detailed study of the system of car distribution in the 1930s, see Lazarev and Gregory, "Wheels of a Command Economy," 324–47.

42. Siegelbaum, *Cars for Comrades*, 241.

43. Interviews with S.A. and A.P., 2005. In selling an old car, one usually followed this procedure: the seller and the buyer agreed on the price of the car beforehand and then took it, following rules laid down in law, to the state secondhand shop (*komissionnyi magazin*). A representative there estimated the value of the car, taking into account its age and condition. The car was sold for this relatively low, official price and the necessary taxes were paid to the state. Then, after leaving the shop, the buyer paid to the seller the difference between the official price and the previously agreed real price.

44. *VAZ: Stranitsy istorii*, vol. 5, 186. It is no wonder that the inventory of cars in the U.S.S.R. consisted relatively of many old vehicles. When the AvtoVAZ celebrated its thirtieth anniversary in 2000 it was discovered that the factory museum did not have a singe example of its first model (VAZ-2101). Therefore, it announced in *Komsomol'skaia pravda* that the owner of the earliest and still running Zhiguli could exchange his car for a brand-new Lada. They received many calls and letters from the owners of thirty-year-old cars, all in very good condition. They even found the owner of the first car produced by the factory. This car stands in the factory museum now (Iu. K. Tselikov, "Vse chto udalos', vse s 'Kopeiki' nachalos'!" in *AvtoVAZ: Vospominaniia i fakty*, vol. 5. [Tol'iatti: AvtoVAZ, 2005], 109).

45. Unlike minor consumer luxuries like perfumes and chocolates, there was very little product differention in Soviet cars. See Gronow, *Caviar with Champagne*, 43–67. As late as 1970, Soviet consumer researchers recommended that the number of different perfume labels on sale should be reduced from 400 to the 20 or 30 whose sales constituted over half the total market (see I. Ostrovskii, O. Kostko, and I. Kochneva, "Shirokii assortiment i neudovletvorennyi spros," *Sovetskaia torgovlia* 1 [1970]: 28–29).

46. Hanson, *Rise and Fall*, 148. The idea was not new as such. For a short time in the beginning of the 1930s, individuals as well as various organizations could buy state auto-obligations which gave them a right to receive a car later, when produced. According to Lazarev and Gregory, in 1933 some 1,500 such obligations—one-third held by individuals and two-thirds by various organizations—represented claims to a new car (Lazarev and Gregory, "Wheels of a Command Economy," 343).

47. Unfortunately, there are no systematic studies available of these distribution practices after the 1930s. With the greatly increasing production figures and the increasing amount of recipients, it is likely that such schemes became more complex and less transparent. For an interesting study of the Hungarian car market in which the time spent waiting for the opportunity to purchases a new car in the 1960s and 1970s was usually just a year or two, see Z. Kapitány, J. Kornai, and J. Szabó, "Reproduction of Shortage on the Hungarian Car Market," *Soviet Studies* 2 (1984): 236–56.

48. Zezina, "Avtomobil 'Zhiguli,'" 70.

49. Ibid., 69.

50. RGAE, f. 7971, op. 1, d. 2384, l. 47, 61.

51. Ibid., 62–63.

52. Siegelbaum, *Cars for Comrades*, 236.

53. Zezina, "Avtomobil 'Zhiguli,'" 85. One could perhaps see here the birth of the modern consumer in the U.S.S.R., a consumer typical of modern capitalist societies who is, in principle, never satisfied. Her demands are always individual and rapidly changing. As Zygmunt Bauman has argued, unlike in capitalism, in socialism the consumer could always blame the state and the ruling party for her dissatisfaction. (See Z. Bauman, "Communism: A Post Mortem," *Praxis International* 3–4 [1990–91]: 185–92.)

54. S. Iu. Tselikov, "Avtomobil'nyi rynok Rossii: Istoriia formirovaniia i perspektivy razvitiia," in *Istoriia OAO AvtoVAZ: Uroki, problemy, sovremennost'* (2003), 263.

55. For post-Soviet developments in the Russian car industry, see S. V. Zhuravlev, "AvtoVAZ nachala 1990–kh godov: Istoriia privatizatsii," in *Sotsial'naia istoriia: Ezhegodnik* (Moscow: Rosspen, 2008), 103–49; S. V. Zhuravlev, "Vzaimootnosheniia gosudarstva i biznesa v usloviiakh perekhoda k rynochnoi ekonomike (na primere Volzhskogo avtozavoda)," in *Sud'ba Rossii: Vektor peremen*, ed. R. Pikhoia (Moscow: RAGS, 2007), 85–106; and S. V. Zhuravlev, "Rezhimnost' v epokhu smeny rezhimov (na primere OAO 'AvtoVAZ')," in *Rezhimnye liudi v SSSR*, ed. T. Kondratieva and A. Sokolov (Moscow: Rosspen, 2009), 184–214.

56. D. Roche, *A History of Everyday Things: The Birth of Consumption in France, 1600–1800* (Cambridge, Eng.: Cambridge University Press, 2000), 54–55.

57. In practice, this egalitarian ideology—in combination with increasing economic well-being—led to the growth of social differentiation which threatened to compromise the very same egalitarian principles of the politics of consumption. (For similar problems in the GDR, see I. Merkel, *Utopie und Bedürfnis: Die Geschichte der Konsumkultur in der DDR* [Cologne: Böhlau, 1999], 44–46.)

58. One should, however, keep in mind that throughout Soviet history the authorities systematically prioritized investments in heavy industry, metallurgy and machine building, and, above all, the military sector of economy. This meant that consumers were expected to be patient and wait in order to enjoy the fruits of their own labor.

59. As Elena Osokina has shown in her study *Za fasadom "stalinskogo izobiliia": Raspredeleniie i rynok v snabzhenii naseleniia v gody industrializatsii, 1927–1941* (Moscow: Rosspen, 1998), the Soviet government had followed similar principles when rationing basic foodstuffs during the First Five-Year Plan. Later, these principles were applied when distributing the often very modest—and relative—forms of abundance. All workplaces were ranked according to their national and economic importance, and then all work positions and jobs were ranked within an institution. The level of remuneration depended on the industry and factory or office in which one worked, as well as on one's position.

60. Z. Bauman, "Communism: A Post Mortem," 185–92.

worthy individuals who would serve as models for personal growth and civic
activism. In this way, Soviet enthusiasm for television imagined the medium
not primarily in terms of personal pleasure, but rather as collective progress:
TV was a revolutionary mechanism for building a new kind of Soviet community; TV viewing was productive leisure for a better, truer world.

Most Russian-language studies of Soviet television are written from the
perspective of its early enthusiasts; in fact, the most prominent scholars in
the field are all former professionals themselves.[4] Unsurprisingly, they tend
to take an uncritical view of TV's self-proclaimed humanism in the 1950s
and 1960s. The focus on "reality," "everyday life," and *lichnost'* is understood
to be an inherently progressive phenomenon with long-term positive effects. Like Thaw-era film and literature, television wins praise for having
nurtured respect for the individual and a hunger for greater openness in
political and social life. In the late 1960s, the story goes, conservative forces
in the Soviet regime moved to stifle the innovative, "liberal" spirit of TV,
ushering in a period of heavy-handed control and cultural stagnation. The
explosion of civic-oriented television in the Gorbachev era is then represented as a kind of resurrection: Soviet TV in the 1950s and 1960s as
glasnost smothered in the cradle.

In this chapter, I want to complicate this picture by exploring how key
enthusiast categories like *lichnost'* and "reality" functioned in practice and, in
particular, how they worked to structure the era's most famous program, the
game show known as *KVN*. Which individuals and whose reality belonged
on the home screen were far from neutral questions for TV's enthusiastic
pioneers, as the screen itself was far from a neutral space in their eyes. Early
Soviet TV professionals saw all culture as a mechanism for moral (usually
marked "spiritual") education as well as for political mobilization; in audiences, they saw needy patients rather than patrons. Overall, there was little
to distinguish this conception of culture from that of the Soviet political
authorities. (And indeed, the Soviet TV professional's sense of "public service" had a great deal in common with contemporary notions in Europe
and the United States as well.)[5] What marked the Soviet enthusiasts was
less their values per se than the way they saw themselves as a group and
the way they conceptualized television itself—two stances deeply rooted
in the tradition of the Soviet cinematic avant-garde and, more broadly, of
the Russian-Soviet intelligentsia.[6] TV enthusiasts believed it was *they* who
should decide which slice of reality was to be broadcast and who counted
as a *lichnost'* appropriate for the home screen, and they relished the role;
it was they, after all, who were inventing a new space in television for the
regeneration of Soviet individuals and community. For this reason, I argue,
the baseline conflict in television in the 1950s and 1960s was one mostly

obscured by enthusiast narratives of "liberal" experimentation versus regime control: the struggle for authority over Soviet audiences and, in no small way, for the pleasures of exercising that authority. As I hope to demonstrate with the story of the game show *KVN,* identifying winners and losers in Soviet TV culture is not as simple as it looks.

Television Art and the Enchantment of Live Broadcasting

The men and women who pioneered Soviet television programming called themselves "enthusiasts," but they also used terms like "dilettante" and even "loser."[7] Few people came to TV with a passion for the new medium, and none brought expertise; in fact, many had never seen a broadcast.[8] Rather, early TV workers were often people who had failed at or saw no future in the professions for which they had been trained. They were typically well educated—often in film, theater, or journalism—and overwhelmingly young. In the 1950s, it was possible for an educated young person literally to walk in off the street and land a job in TV. Leonid Dmitriev did just that in 1956: when he and a friend, fellow graduates from the prestigious Institute of International Relations, heard that the Moscow studio was looking for staff, they took a tram there and told the guard it was their dream to work in TV. (In fact, Dmitriev, at least, dreamed of a career in cinema, but had been rejected by the film institute, VGIK.) Ten minutes later, they met the director of the studio (known as Shabolovka), and in another ten minutes, they were employees of Soviet television.[9]

Dmitriev and his former colleagues are unanimous in describing the atmosphere of early TV as uniquely vibrant and egalitarian. L. Zolotareva recalled a workplace suffused with a "youthful, creative spirit" that "inspired hope." "You could sense a kind of freedom and a chance for creativity and self-expression," she commented in a recent interview.[10] A. Grigorian re-membered the 1950s as a time when "there were new faces in the hallway practically every day" and the use of *ty* (informal "you") predominated, even among people of different rank. "At that time, we were all equal before television's unexplored potential," he explained. "We were young, and that linked us [to television]. We happily hoisted a significant load of respon-sibility on our shoulders, and we carried it not because of fear, but because of conscience."[11]

The sense of freedom, hope, and community recalled by Soviet TV's first professionals was something many Soviet people experienced during the Thaw. Yet television was a special case all the same, thanks both to the newness of the medium and the composition of its staff. The remark-able fact is that well into the 1960s, faute de mieux, young, enthusiastic "dilettantes" did dominate Soviet studios, delivering programs that reached millions of TV sets all over the Soviet Union—nearly five million in 1960, around 16 million by 1965, and 44 million by the end of the decade.[12] The enthusiasts saw themselves as engaged in a process of pure invention. "No one knew what television was. No one had any idea how to make it," Dmitriev told an interviewer. "It was a time of constant discoveries."[13] And as enthusiasts like Dmitriev went about inventing TV, as they saw it, they were also inventing themselves as creative professionals in a new sphere. What Soviet TV's pioneers experienced was an unusually personal and intense identification with television—indeed, a happy confusion between self (or cohort) and the medium. The experience of working in early television was a dynamic process of self-discovery; successful TV broadcasting became for them a form of self-actualization.

As they tell it, many of TV's "dilettantes and losers" fast developed a messianic zeal about the medium, and rejected the very notion of TV as a mere medium, a purveyor of other cultural forms, as hopelessly backward. In the early years, when studios were the size of closets (and may well have been closets a month before), TV broadcasters had little choice but to rely on other cultural forms, particularly film and theater, to feed the hungry air.[14] But the enthusiasts' goal was not just to televise culture, but to "televisionize" it. If TV were to broadcast theater, for example, then it should be TV theater (*televizionnyi teatr*), designed for the specificities of the medium. The distinction between theater on TV and TV theater may appear insignificant at first glance, but it was crucial for the enthusiasts. "We thought of television as an art—as something which was not yet an art, but which was becoming one, and we were participating in that," recalled R. Kopylova in a recent interview.[15] Her contemporary, A. Iurovskii, was not so hesitant when he published his battle cry for TV in 1960—and in the leading Soviet film journal, to boot: "Television now is already a big and bright window on the world. Already now, today, television is a remarkable means of artistic expression, a new, attractive, and important art for the people."[16]

If TV was a new art, the task was to discover its distinctive aesthetic principles and modes of address, and so to unlock its true might. Among the enthusiasts, there was near unanimity that the key to the art was live broadcasting (*zhivoi* or *priamoi efir*). In the 1950s and for much of the 1960s—that is, before the spread of video technology—almost all original television programming was live by default, setting nerves on edge in studios across the globe.[17] The annals of TV history are filled with live gaffes, such as the story of the jittery American anchorman who, when required by contract to enjoy the sponsor's product on the air, lit cigarette after cigarette from the filter end.[18] But while the American anchor kept his job in this case, his Soviet counterpart would not have been so lucky. In one notorious case from the mid-1950s, an announcer was fired on the spot for accidentally replacing "a generation of Leninists" (*pokolenie lenintsev*) with "a generation of lazybones" (*pokolenie lenivtsev*).[19] Of course, any newspaper or radio show that fumbled in this way would not have gone unpunished. But newspaper articles were carefully edited before being typeset, and radio was typically taped and edited; live TV, by comparison, was a high-wire act without a net. As director Kseniia Marina recalled: "If a host blurted something out, we all had to pay for it. Our backs were wet [with perspiration] all of the time."[20] In the case of the "lazybones-Leninist" slip, not only was the hapless announcer barred from TV for life; the incident cost the head of the Moscow studio her job as well.[21]

TV personnel also paid the price if invited guests said something untoward in a live broadcast. It was standard practice for TV staff to meet with guests ahead of a program to go over what they would be saying.[22] This information was logged in a file (*mikrofonnaia papka*) that had to be approved and signed by the show's editor before anything was allowed on the air.[23] The level of preparation varied, but the general rule was: the more, and the more detailed, the better. In many cases, interviewees would memorize a script written by the show's staff ahead of time and rehearse their parts extensively. This was the most common scenario for live "man on the street"—or, more likely, "worker at the factory" or "engineer in the studio"—interviews. The arrangements with expert figures such as artists and intellectuals were often more open-ended and, for this reason, often more troublesome for TV staff.[24]

Given these difficulties, how can we explain the enthusiasts' enchantment with live broadcasting? Professional bravura? Certainly, the risky nature of live broadcasting added to the excitement and sense of camaraderie of early TV. Fear and enthusiasm, nerves and inspiration, were two sides of one coin. It is true that once videotape became more widely available, many people welcomed the technology as a professional step up. But the fact that many others did not indicates that there was far more to the romance with live TV in the early days than thrill-seeking or a dearth of options. For many of Soviet TV's early enthusiasts, live broadcasting was the essence of television and a powerful social and moral force.

The most compelling elaboration of this vision came not from a TV professional but rather from a theater critic, Vladimir Sappak, whose remarkable slender volume *Television and Us* (*Televidenie i my*) became the enthusiasts' bible.[25] Although Sappak was not among those ready to declare TV already an art, he did see art in the making, and one of the tasks of his book was to help define the medium's formal qualities and promote its development. The essence of TV, he maintained, was the *effekt prisutstviia* (the presence effect), or the ability of live broadcasting to transport viewers psychologically to the scene of the on-screen action. For Sappak, it was the ordinary made extraordinary—a magical effect.

> It is often difficult to tear ourselves away from that tiny little screen.[26] Why this is so, even we can't really explain. If I turn on the TV by chance and see that there's a movie or a theatrical performance on, I can turn it off right away with a fearless hand, as they say. But all it takes is for me to see those announcers we all know so well now reading the news, or a soccer field with bustling players, an English lesson, or kids in white shirts and pioneer scarves reciting poetry written for the occasion in their ringing voices, and my hand involuntarily hesitates on the off switch. Here [is a place] where you can look at any time and, without thoroughly investigating the heart of the matter, you can just observe the *movement of life* for a moment, and let the idler inside you wake up and gawk at how the birds are flying, how the grass is growing ... And your hand will not make a move to stop this living life on the screen, to turn it off, to cut it short.[27]

In Sappak's writing, the connection between television and the real world has a mystical power all its own: we sense that watching TV will—indeed must—change our relationship to lived experience, but in ways that we cannot anticipate. Sappak thought change inevitable because what live television offered the viewer was nothing less than "perfect pitch for truth"; with *podlinnost'* (authenticity) TV's very nature, any false note was immediately apparent on the screen.[28] Sappak gave multiple examples of this in *Television and Us*—not cases of gross deception, but of phoniness or, in his terms, the "little lie." A journalist has a traffic cop stop a driver "at random" for an interview, but it is clear from each person's delivery that the entire episode has been carefully rehearsed.[29] Two doctors discuss their experiences working in Iraq, but their stories are unconvincing and the program boring because the doctors, although identified as a married couple, never even look at each other.[30] In both cases, live television enabled viewers to see what would have been obvious had they been physically beside the camera, that is, the staged quality of the action or emotion; this was part of the magic of TV's *effekt prisutstviia*.

But Sappak took the point even further by arguing that the experience of watching live television actually improves our ability to see the world around us and improves us as people: television "sharpens our sense of truth," he thought, and opens our eyes to new vistas in everyday life, including the emotional and spiritual world of others.[31] Only television, Sappak argued, was up to the task of reporting on Iurii Gagarin's historic space flight because only television was able "to understand this person ... [and] break through to something internal, confidential, and intimate."[32] Sappak saw *intimnost'* (intimacy), like authenticity, as intrinsic to television, and *intimnost'* meant more than celebrity. Viewers needed to see and understand ordinary people and the everyday as much as they required knowledge of great figures and historic events; television, the "X-ray of character," would help them. In this sense, Sappak's vision of TV worked to resolve the paradox of the viewing experience—the private consumption of public culture—by socializing the medium. The intimacy engendered by the physical location of TV in the home was, for Sappak, a vital social link; thanks to the power of television broadcasting, solitary viewers gained new knowledge of one another and a new sense of community; viewership thus became participation, a civic act. The title of his book was not *Television and Me;* it was *Television and Us.*

It is difficult to overestimate the influence of Sappak on Soviet thinking about TV, and to this day it is rare to meet a former TV professional who fails to mention his genius.[33] Sappak was not, however, the only person then speaking in this idiom. The Soviet defense of television as art typically began with praise for live broadcasting as "realistic and convincing by its very nature" and evoked the hidden charms of ordinary life.[34] One pioneering TV documentarian (the father of the little atheist girl) spoke of "penetrating into the little secrets of the soul" in his films with titles such as *A Sakhalin Character (Sakhalinskii kharakter)* and *Journey into the Everyday (Puteshestvie v budni).*[35] And even the head of the radio and television administration sounded like Sappak when he complained to his staff about the forced, unnatural quality of Soviet TV in 1956. "If someone can't speak without a text, then sit him down at a table and let him use the text without hiding it from the viewer," he instructed. "People [on television] need to behave more simply and more freely."[36]

The enchantment with live broadcasting and putting "ordinary" people on-screen was an international phenomenon in television's early years, but in the Soviet context it had a distinctive resonance in both historical and contemporary terms. TV enthusiasm tapped into a powerful Soviet cultural tradition and, in particular, into the theoretical work of the filmmaker Dziga Vertov. In the 1920s Vertov famously anathematized fiction film as "mortally dangerous" and declared *"kinopravda"*—the filmed exploration of real life—to be the only true cinema of the revolutionary working class.[37] It was Vertov, too, who first hailed the camera or *"kinoglaz"* (film-eye) as superior to human sight, able to penetrate the essence of all phenomena, including the human character. And it was Vertov who first proclaimed that the consumption of "living reality" (or "life caught unawares") would improve viewers by perfecting their understanding of the world and each other; with *kinopravda*, one could "unite all workers scattered over the earth through a single consciousness, a single bond, a single collective will in the battle for communism."[38]

Although most enthusiasts did not cite Vertov directly (Sappak did), his vision—and, in a more general sense, the vision of the Soviet cinematic avant-garde—was latent in the enthusiasts' view of the medium and themselves. Embracing the ideal of "living reality" on-screen meant overcoming the Stalinist "varnishing of reality"; it meant returning Soviet culture to an earlier and, in their eyes, purer revolutionary era.[39] At a meeting of TV staff to discuss the recent Twentieth Party Congress in 1956, many people laid the blame for the poor quality of their broadcasts squarely at the feet of the "cult of personality." The culture of the cult—pompous, dogmatic, and artificial—had been a violation of television's nature. Now people would have to relearn how "to think and lay out their own thoughts" and how to listen to and trust one another.[40]

Television's enthusiasts could make common cause with many Thaw-era intellectuals in the project of overcoming the Stalinist legacy, but they also stood out in their belief that they alone had enlisted modernity, the incomparable *effekt prisutstviia* of live broadcasting, on their side. The TV camera was not only truthful for them, let us remember; it had "perfect pitch for truth," and the simple act of watching improved the viewer. Moreover, television for them had a populist sensibility (*demokratizm*, said Sappak) that no other medium or art form could match.[41] With its presumed natural connection to everyday life and ordinary people, television could not help but shift the focus of Soviet society from the leader to the community, from the cult of personality to the development and interaction of many personalities.

Yet this project, for all its language of *demokratizm*, assigned the pivotal role in this process to TV professionals and, here again, the tradition of the Soviet avant-garde was very important. While Vertov rhapsodized about the virtues of the camera as a "machine" with sensory powers superior to those of contemporary humans, he also stressed the role of the camera operator (or director) in what he called the "organization" or the "choice of facts" (to wit, the title of his most influential film: *Chelovek s kinoapparatom*, usually translated as *Man with a Movie Camera*). The "choice of facts" was critical, he argued, because "it will *suggest the necessary decision* to the worker or peasant."[42] In this scenario, viewers need the people behind the camera to apprehend *kinopravda* as much as the camera itself.

For TV enthusiasts, the promotion of "living reality" was a bridge over troubled Stalinist waters (a means to transport viewers in spirit to a purer revolutionary landscape), but it was also a connection to the "heroic" era of Soviet cinema in the 1920s, enabling TV enthusiasts to imagine their work as its modern-day counterpart. When Leonid Dmitriev and his colleagues spoke of early TV as terra incognita, they echoed Sergei Eisenstein, to choose one example, who once described Soviet cinema in the 1920s as having no antecedents whatsoever ("something not yet existent" was his phrase).[43] Although enthusiasts for television did not deny their creative debts in such a radical manner, they did position themselves in a similar fashion as pioneering Soviet artists. By making the bridge to the 1920s, the enthusiasts gained a vision of themselves as critical cultural authorities, a vision that stressed not only Soviet society's need for television's "truth" in the aftermath of Stalinism, but also Soviet viewers' need for TV professionals to organize and present it to them.

VVV and the Limits of Soviet "Reality TV"

Given the extremely modest resources of Soviet television in the mid-1950s (as of 1956, even Shabolovka, the best-funded studio in the Soviet Union, boasted only one mobile camera), there was little opportunity for enthusiasts to put their ideas into action. The first major break came in 1957 in conjunction with the International Festival of Youth and Students in Moscow.[44] As part of the run-up activities to the festival, a group of enthusiasts at Shabolovka designed a show they called *VVV*, for *Vecher veselykh voprosov* (*Evening of Merry Questions*).[45] In theory, the show was to be an engaging forum to educate young people about festival themes, and it took inspiration from two sources: the most popular program on Czechoslovak TV at the time, a quiz show called *GGG*, and the comedy-theater groups, or *kapustniki*, that had blossomed in student circles after Stalin's death.[46] Years later, people remembered *VVV* as a rallying cry for everyone who thought TV's festival programming should "proclaim the power and the capacity of television far and wide."[47]

How did this enthusiasm translate on the screen? *VVV* was live, interactive, person-centered TV and, unlike its distant American cousins, it was wide open; *VVV* did not preselect its contestants, but rather invited members of the studio audience to play at random—for example, by choosing seat numbers from a drum filled with ticket stubs. (Granted, the audience itself was not a truly random cross section of Soviet society, as the studio distributed many tickets through Komsomol and university channels.) One show invited newlywed couples onstage and quizzed them separately about their wedding day: "What was the weather like?" for instance. The winning couple was the one with the most matching answers. Another show asked contestants to specify how a cat climbs down from a tree: head first or tail first? *VVV* also included home viewers in the game, inviting them to the studio during the broadcast. On one show, the challenge was to bring a ficus plant, a samovar, and the third volume of Jack London's collected works to the studio; another called for babies with the initials V.V.V. who had been born on the day of the program's premiere.[48] Viewers who met the challenge were given a small prize (a frying pan, for instance) and interviewed right on the air.[49]

With its open-door policy and open-ended format, *VVV* was a radical departure from Soviet broadcast norms. But equally radical, perhaps, was its tone—its domesticity and sheer silliness. *VVV* did not just bring private people into public media space, it also invited them to share items from their personal lives—plants, books, memories. Although the show had a nominal connection to the Youth Festival, and it did incorporate some questions with a festival theme, there was no real reason for these competitions; *VVV* was indeed "an evening of merry questions." And from the perspective of its creators, it was also a demonstration of the power of television in its essential mode—a thrilling experiment in "living reality" on-screen.

Scandal came to *VVV* just a few short months after its debut. For its third broadcast in September 1957, the show's writers designed a contest around the Russian proverb "*Gotov sani letom, a telegu zimoi*" (lit: "Get your sled ready in the summer, and your cart ready in the winter"); the challenge was to show up during the broadcast wearing a sheepskin coat, felt boots, and a hat, and carrying a samovar. Earlier *VVV* competitions had attracted at most a few dozen contestants; this challenge brought in 600 to 700 people on a hot day—so many, in fact, that the main roads to the theater where they were broadcasting (on the grounds of Moscow University) were reportedly jammed with sweaty people, some on foot hauling samovars, others bundled up in their fur coats in buses and cars.[50] The head of Shabolovka described the crowd as "frightening." They were "drunk, wearing tattered, ripped sheepskin coats," he said, and "they forced their way through the gates of the university and broke down the door to the auditorium."[51] Someone brought a live chicken. With the cameras still rolling, the crowd rushed the stage, shouting and cursing, and the curtain was torn down.[52] The show's host, the popular composer Nikita Bogoslovskii, stood by in shock and was then toppled off the stage in the melee. (Ultimately, he would flee the scene altogether.)[53] The head of the university's Komsomol organization stood up from his seat, shouted "Komsomol members, gather around me!" and a group of students took control of the situation by form-

ing a human barrier to the stage. After some delay, *VVV*'s director decided
to cut the transmission, which left viewers at home with only a silent screen
announcing a station break "for technical reasons." Only later did the police
arrive, approximately forty-five minutes after they had been summoned by
Shabolovka's director.

The TV administration held a postmortem the very next morning,
soon to be followed by the Central Committee, and in short order the *VVV*
scandal had cost the head of the U.S.S.R.'s main TV studio and numerous lower-ranking personnel their jobs.[54] What emerged from the official
investigations was a series of mishaps and miscalculations. Apparently Bogoslovskii, the host, had failed to mention a key element in the contest that
would have made it far more difficult and presumably lowered the number
of would-be contestants.[55] No one had anticipated that large numbers of
workers from the nearby housing construction projects would stream in,
and that these people, living in dormitories, would have all of their winter gear at hand. Even once the crowd had grown, *VVV*'s director, Ksenia
Marinina, had hesitated to cut the transmission because she had nothing
on hand to replace it. While it was standard practice to have a feature film
available in case of technical problems, in this case, the reserve film was
locked in a safe, and the young man who held the keys had left work early
to go on a date.[56] Besides, as Marinina reported to the postmortem meeting,
the studio was getting phone calls from viewers pleading with them *not* to
cut the transmission—itself an interesting comment on at least some viewers' taste.[57] And who could blame them? *VVV* under siege must have made
for a gripping spectacle, particularly in its context. Television broadcasting
itself was still an exotic and exciting phenomenon in these early years, and
what happened that September night was something more than just television; it was an eruption of everyday Moscow life and Muscovites, messy and
unpredictable, inside Soviet media space.

In the official discussions that followed, television and Party authorities
repeatedly returned to the question of who had been allowed into that space
and especially how they had looked. The head of the TV administration,
D. I. Chesnokov, exclaimed: "You let ragged and drunk people on television—it's a kind of sacrilege [*profanatsiia*]."[58] And: "Just the fact that the
program was cut off midway, even if it had been a good one in all respects,
is already a scandal. But it is not only that. Everything here has marks of a
political nature. We saw a crowd, dirty people, people dressed for the dirti-
est jobs. This borders on provocation."[59] The Central Committee went so
far as to suggest that people had been "clearly seeking to underscore their
poverty and slovenliness" on Soviet television.[60] But whatever the motives
of either TV professionals or would-be contestants, the end result, from the

perspective of the Soviet authorities, was the same: Soviet TV had broadcast "a large group of unorganized and random [*sluchainye*] television viewers who *cannot be shown on television.*"[61]

VVV was already challenging convention by inviting ordinary people to participate in the shows as themselves—not as scripted props or social categories brought to life (the "leading worker," the "prizewinning athlete," the "model plant manager," and so on) but as contestants, Muscovites, ordinary people. What the *VVV* scandal exposed was the uneasy status of the "real" and the "ordinary" inside Soviet media space. As the head of Soviet TV Chesnokov said, there were some people who simply *could not be shown.* Soviet television was no place for the workaday world with its dirt and disarray. No one denied this workaday world was real; the point was that Soviet media space was not that world.[62] For Chesnokov, who had joined the Party in 1939 and made a career in the Stalinist era, the image of the *VVV* crowd was nothing short of sacrilege; Soviet media space was sacred. But even outside the quasi-religious idiom of Stalinism, all Soviet media had an "otherworldly" quality because they were fundamentally aspirational and instructional. If drunken, dirty people were to appear in Soviet media, then they were to be clearly marked—as "hooligans," for example—and whether in a satiric or a serious context, they were there to make a point. But the people who erupted on-screen during *VVV* (and even the show's usual contestants) were "random" or undefined. They were parasites in Soviet media space; they had no *work* to do there. Worse still, their very presence ran the risk of degrading ideals altogether. While the discussion at the TV administration focused largely on the issues of control—how the contest had been approved, why staff did not respond sooner, and so on—officials at the Central Committee damned *VVV* altogether for its *poshlost'* (vulgarity) and lack of ideological principle. Citing the "which way does a cat climb" question and others, they concluded that the show's content was "calculated to make fools of and degrade the dignity of Soviet people." In the eyes of the Central Committee, the problem with *VVV* began long before the scandal; by design, the show was a "mockery" of the Soviet citizenry inspired by "the worst methods and morals of bourgeois television."[63]

In recent times, *VVV* has been presented as a symbol of the Thaw era and the dreams of the *shestidesiatniki* (people of the 1960s). A 1995 article (written, not coincidentally, by the wife of Sergei Muratov, one of the show's designers) set the stage for its account of the scandal by invoking the "sun of freedom" that rose over the country in 1956. "The youthful minds of the 'children of the Twentieth Party Congress' . . . were filled with joyful hopes, creative projects, and brilliant ideas," one of which, we are given to understand, was *VVV.*[64] A 1998 TV program from the series *The Way It Was*

(*Kak eto bylo*) struck a similar bittersweet tone, as Muratov, Bogoslovskii, Marinina, and other people involved in the show reminisced onstage, and the show's host played for laughs by reading from the Central Committee decree with mock gravitas. The most recent history of Soviet television presents the *VVV* scandal as one deliberately pursued by the Soviet authorities to put young TV workers "in their place," lest the success of their festival programming go to their heads and, in a broader sense, as part of Khrushchev's crackdown on the intelligentsia in the latter part of 1957.[65]

While the timing of the scandal places it in the midst of one of Khrushchev's periodic cultural campaigns, the fact is, the authorities were undoubtedly right, on their own terms, about the inappropriateness of a show like *VVV* for Soviet television. *VVV was* meaningless entertainment, in context, and this was a problem in itself. But even if *VVV* had been an evening of serious rather than merry questions, its wide-open format would still have made it incompatible with Soviet media practices. The brainchild of young TV workers experimenting with the medium, *VVV* shows many elements of TV enthusiasm I have described: the romance with live television and its ability to break the screen barrier between subject and viewer, the ideal of audience participation, the interest in ordinary people and everyday life, and the open, unpredictable quality implicit in the idea of "life caught unawares." By design, *VVV* extended an open-door invitation to anyone, and thus to anyone's problems (alcoholism, poverty), without providing a context for their incorporation into a broader ideological framework. What the *VVV* episode demonstrated, then, was not so much the impossibility of the real and the ordinary on Soviet television as the necessity for framing and packaging them; "life caught unawares" demanded an interpretation.

There would be no more live, open-access shows like *VVV* on Soviet TV until the days of perestroika, and in this sense, the events of September 1957 demonstrate the defeat of a certain idealized vision of television. Yet at the same time, the subsequent evolution of Soviet TV programming shows that the same enthusiasts who had devised *VVV* also supported and developed the idea of packaging the real and the ordinary for viewers. In this light, the *VVV* episode looks less like a defeat than a learning experience. TV enthusiasts stepped up to the plate to fulfill the interpretive demand on Soviet television—to replace the random with the marked, give purpose to the purposeless, and provide models for *lichnost'* and social activity.

KVN and the Model Individual

Soviet TV turned its back on the game show format for four long years after *VVV*. Around Shabolovka the show was a "symbol of calamity," remembered

Elena Gal'perina, who joined the staff after its demise. Although Gal'perina heard the warnings of her colleagues, she admired *VVV* as, she said, "the kind of real television for which so many of us—print journalists, theater critics, actors—had switched our vocations."[66] In 1961, as head of the youth *redaktsiia* (editorial group), Gal'perina enlisted *VVV* veterans and other enthusiasts to work on a new game show. The result was a live contest of wits they called *KVN,* for *Klub veselykh i nakhodchivykh* (*Club of the Merry and Quick-Witted*)—a clever name, not only because the concept of "clubs" as a way to organize youth recreation was then current, but because the initials K.V.N. were well known from the KVN-49, one of the first Soviet TV sets.[67] *KVN* went on to become one of the most popular Soviet television shows of all time and an important cultural phenomenon as well. In the 1960s and beyond, young people all over the Soviet Union competed in local *KVN* teams.[68] A number of contestants on the televised show went on to become well-known performing artists, and the show itself was resurrected in the glasnost era and still runs on Russian TV today.[69]

   KVN's origins in Soviet TV's flirtation with "merry questions" are not difficult to detect. Like *VVV, KVN* was broadcast live before a studio audience, and it was meant to be funny, zany, and somewhat irreverent. But *KVN* was also different in important and telling ways. First, *KVN* took care of the social category problem—the troublesome randomness of *VVV*—by limiting contestants to one group: students, overwhelmingly male, who competed in teams to defend the honor of their institutes. (This was the initial design; only under pressure did the show expand its base in later years to include teams from factories and, ultimately, cities and republics.) Moreover, *KVN* had none of the uncomfortable domesticity, no intrusion of personal objects and problems, that was evident in *VVV;* the contestants were on the air in a semiprofessional capacity as students (or later as workers, Kievans, etc.), and they had a job to do: to win for the honor of their group. Second, all of the young people who appeared on *KVN* were well screened and well scrubbed; they were models of youthful energy, camaraderie, and wit. And although the program was broadcast live, television workers did their best to rule out unpredictability by standardizing the competitions.[70] *KVN* teams were required to think on their feet—one contest presented them with a briefcase full of odd items and had them devise a story on the spot about its owner and how he had lost it—but they were also allowed to prepare some material (skits, songs, verse, etc.) ahead of time which was thoroughly vetted by the show's editors. For example, there was a standard contest called "BRIZ" for *Biuro po ratsionalizatsii i izobretatel'stvu* (Office for Rationalization and Inventiveness) that had competitors present their ideas for, say, a university on the moon.[71] Finally, *KVN,* unlike *VVV,* worked to censor shows in progress; in theory, as soon as contestants began to tell a joke that had not been cleared or was considered too controversial, the sound would be cut off and the camera would cut to a shot of one of the show's young assistants sitting in the audience.[72] As of 1968, the show was also videotaped and edited.

KVN earned a reputation for daring, and it is true that there were instances when contestants pushed their satire further than the authorities felt acceptable, with predictable consequences for the show's staff.[73] But *KVN*, unlike *VVV*, was controlled entertainment, and, perhaps more important, it could be said to have a clear purpose. It was, after all, not just a *vecher* (evening), a passing fancy, but a club, a collective and useful activity. And while the emphasis was always on wit and humor, with its contests on themes like improving the educational system and its satires on so-called shortcomings, *KVN* also had an obvious civic element that *VVV* had lacked. Even *KVN*'s studio audience was brought into the orbit of purposefulness by competing in a set "fan contest" (*konkurs bolel'shikov*) to win points for their teams. For viewers at home, *KVN* offered itself as one solution to the problem of youth recreation; in the words of its creators, the game was the answer to that "very topical question: 'what to do when there's nothing to do,'" and *KVN*, the TV program, encouraged thousands of local competitions as offshoots.[74] Muratov and his colleagues published how-to books for homegrown competitions complete with sample competitions and scripts for would-be hosts.[75]

KVN was also purposeful and meaningful in a way *VVV* was not because it was said to present positive role models for Soviet youth. Mikhail Kharlamov, head of the radio and TV administration, certainly thought so; he even objected to broadcasting a contestant who wore a beard to cover a facial defect because it projected the wrong image.[76] Soviet print media also discussed *KVN* in these terms. In the mid-1960s, a reviewer who had previously criticized the show for focusing on students and failing to relate to the "mass TV viewer" praised its presentation of "new heroes"—military academy students and workers in a watch factory. "Perhaps this contest did not shine with sharp wit, but it was merry and unconstrained, and young TV viewers could at least see the manners of a Soviet warrior, the masculine grace with which he offered his hand to a girl to help her . . . off the stage, how he escorted her back to her seat, and the maidenly modesty and dignity with which she thanked her opponents."[77] Another reviewer was impressed by a competition between students in physics and medicine in which the medical students produced two posters on the spot: "Hippocrates was a hundred times smarter than Archimedes!" (a clever rhyme in Russian) and "Physics is the medicine of the future!" Reflecting on the second poster, the reviewer decided it was more than "simply a gentleman's gesture toward his opponent" (although it did win an extra point from the jury for sportsmanship), but "far deeper in meaning" because it made people think about the "evolution of science ... and the atmosphere of science ... in which today's youth naturally lives." In their "sincerity and determination," he saw *KVN* contestants as "expressing their generation."[78]

The search for "young heroes" was a leitmotif of Soviet culture, and so the fact that reviewers looked to *KVN* contestants to fill these shoes is certainly no surprise. The important thing from the perspective of the evolution of Soviet TV programming, however, is that the people who worked on *KVN* also considered its contestants to be role models; the modeling idea was, in fact, central to the show's design. Muratov and his colleagues created *KVN* as a form of "intellectual soccer." Each team had a captain plus ten main contestants and two on reserve, and they had positions, in the sense that people tended to specialize in different sorts of tasks (musical, verbal, and so on).[79] Although the program did ultimately open its doors, the initial concept was entirely oriented toward students and was, in a broader sense, a celebration of the young, male intelligentsia. Founding editor Gal'perina emphasized this point at a 1964 meeting at the Filmmakers' Union. *KVN*, she told her audience, was not entertainment, as some people thought, but "100 percent propaganda." "What do we propagandize?" she asked rhetorically.

> We propagandize the intellect of student youth. We propagandize their positive frame of mind ... their optimism ... their sense of humor, [and] their ability to laugh at themselves. What difference does it make to the viewer if all of this improvisation is set up by the editors ahead of time? For the viewer, it's 100 percent improvisation. But the editors have tamed this improvisation and directed the discussion where it has to go.[80]

VVV and *KVN* clearly had a great deal in common, and their creators have always spoken of them as older and younger siblings. Like *VVV*, *KVN* was live and largely improvisational TV (at least in its initial design), and while the authorities repeatedly pressured staff to film the program, they resisted for years because, for them, live broadcasting remained "the ne plus ultra of television art."[81] *KVN* also put a premium on audience participation and made the creation of community—the community of teams and fans and also the wider community of *KVN* lovers united by television—a central feature of its design.[82] Finally, *KVN* was a show that put ordinary people at the center of viewers' attention and banked on the presumed intimacy of television as a medium. The show's contests were designed to "reveal the character" of its young contestants.[83] As Gal'perina detailed in a 1967 article, their tactic was "to find interesting people, create a natural and un-inhibited atmosphere and, finally, figure out a situation which like a magic 'Open, sesame!' exposes people in front of us." When the show succeeded in this, she thought, it was nothing less than television art.[84]

Like its commitment to live broadcasting, *KVN*'s drive to "expose" or "open up" the person on-screen is of a piece with the ideals of TV enthu-siasm. But it is worth lingering for a moment on Gal'perina's formula for success: the first requirement for TV art is finding not just any subject, but "interesting people." She went on to say that *KVN*'s staff had found many people unable to overcome their inhibitions in front of the camera and, more important, incapable of thinking on their feet. Students, they discov-ered, were their perfect subjects—less reserved, as young people generally were, but also more "interesting" and worthwhile subjects than the average person. Much the same might be said about the show's general attitude to female contestants, who were comparatively rare; the general assumption appears to have been that men made better players at "intellectual soccer" because they were naturally bolder and wittier.[85] This, then, was no *VVV*, with its wide-open doors, its sloppy populism, its lack of purpose. *KVN* delivered a neat and useful package by design: "the thinking person on the screen" (a male figure marked universal) as a model for Soviet viewers.[86]

In contrasting the two shows, it is possible to read *KVN* as a sort of middle ground between a more radical, open-ended vision of television rep-resented by *VVV* and its polar opposite: seamless, scripted, and, preferably, filmed and edited TV. It was, after all, toward the latter vision of broadcast-ing that Soviet TV was organizationally and ideologically inclined. Even as enthusiasts rallied for live, spontaneous TV, the organization of Soviet broadcasting, with its *mikrofonnaia papka* system and ex post facto punish-ments, was evidently pulling in the other direction. The year *VVV* went down taking leading figures in Soviet TV with it, 1957, was also the year when the regime began to train its eyes more sharply on television over-all, restructuring the administration for broadcasting entirely and creating the first targeted group for television within the Central Committee ap-paratus.[87] Perhaps *KVN*'s format in this context was a shrewd compromise brokered by idealists—the best that TV enthusiasts could do under the circumstances?

In their recollections of *KVN*, Gal'perina and her colleagues have often described the pressure they felt from political authorities, and the show has entered Soviet historical memory as one of the archetypal signs of youthful guts and verve in the 1960s.[88] *KVN*'s reputation for daring was formed at the time with its sometimes edgy satire, but it was sealed and delivered by its cancellation in 1972.[89] In the absence of any official explanation, many Soviet viewers concluded that the authorities had found the program too politically threatening; there were widespread rumors that the host was under arrest. In fact, spooked by the role of mass media in the Prague Spring, the regime did take serious measures to combat what it saw as dangerous permissiveness at home; many longtime employees in print and broadcast media lost their jobs in a late 1960s purge, and harsh new censorship regulations in 1969 ratcheted up the pressure on editors.[90] But arguably, when it came to TV, the most effective tool at the regime's disposal was not political, but technological: videotape entered widespread use in the late 1960s, replacing live broadcasts and giving TV staff unprecedented control in the form of editing. Since *KVN* made the switch from live to video as early as 1968, it seems unlikely that the decision to cancel four years later reflected fears of its uncontrollability.

If anything, *KVN* was moving in the direction of increased control of a different type altogether: professionalization. (And there were signs of this tendency even before the show shifted to videotape.) Over the years, the improvisational, amateur quality of *KVN* diminished and the number of prepared skits increased dramatically; some teams even hired theatrical coaches and writers to boost their competitive edge.[91] With *KVN* teams representing not just institutes but also cities and even republics, the stakes of the game ran higher in many eyes. Party and Komsomol organizations were likely to get involved now as sponsors and managers. One Baku newspaper reported that more than sixty people flew to Moscow weeks ahead of the all-union competition in 1968 to help the city's team get ready. Newspapers, magazines, and letters from Baku were also flown in on a daily basis to keep team members up-to-date for the competition, although one wonders when they had time to read: according to the paper, Baku's *KVN-shchiki* (*KVN* players) were in rehearsals eight to ten hours a day. On the eve of the contest, eighty fans, handpicked from more than a thousand applicants, were flown by the Baku Komsomol to take part in the show. And when Baku won, the victors were met at the airport by the head of the city and the republic's Komsomol organizations.[92]

KVN, in short, was looking less like amateur night and more like show business. The changes were criticized in the Soviet central press, and there were also more or less open allusions to the backstage element as a corrosive influence on the game.[93] One possible reason for the show's cancellation in 1972 is that TV's overseers in Moscow agreed, and saw a "professional" *KVN* as needlessly divisive and a waste of resources. It is also very likely, as many people around *KVN* have argued, that personal passions were instru-

mental. The new head of the radio and television administration as of 1970,
Sergei Lapin, reportedly despised the show, according to some, because it
had a large number of Jewish players.[94]

Yet while *KVN* ended its first phase on Soviet TV cloaked in controversy, this should not cloud our understanding of its origins. *KVN* was not
an oppositional program by design, nor did its design represent artistic compromise in the eyes of its creators. *KVN*, they thought, was a step ahead for
Soviet TV—a move toward packaging and promoting a particular image
of real life and individuals and a certain kind of community consciousness.
KVN was still person-centered, interactive TV, very much in the enthusiast
idiom of *VVV*. But *KVN* went further: it offered model people and model
forms of interaction, both of which were, in a large measure, reflections of
the show's creative milieu. All of the attributes of *KVN*—youth, intellect,
optimism, daring, team spirit, civic consciousness—were also the attributes
of Shabolovka, at least in the eyes of those who worked there. By design,
KVN was a projection of its creators' sense of self into Soviet media space,
an emanation of their cultural authority.

Cultural Authority and the Soviet Audience

For many former TV professionals, the early 1960s were Soviet TV's "golden
years," thanks to *KVN* and a series of other new shows that placed a premium on enthusiast values.[95] They were all live and conversational—they
broadcast people talking to one another rather than solely *at* viewers—and
they prided themselves on introducing viewers to interesting individuals in
an intimate setting, one-on-one; the new shows were conceived as televised
spaces for social interaction (*obshchenie*) on the screen as well as across the
screen barrier. And like *KVN*, all of these programs made choices about
their subjects that demonstrated a hierarchy in the idea of *lichnost'*. Where
KVN highlighted the young, usually male intelligentsia as a group, most of
the other programs from TV's "golden years" put an authoritative male host
(*vedushchii*) center stage.[96]

Television's enthusiasts were convinced that this kind of original programming performed a valuable public service. Sergei Muratov called thirty
minutes with (host) Sergei Smirnov "a civic event," and he emphasized that
it was time with a man like Smirnov that mattered for viewers: "social interaction with these people may be no less aesthetically valuable than the
subject of the conversation itself."[97] Yet while Smirnov's show and some of
the other new programs did draw substantial audiences, on the whole, viewers in the Soviet Union demonstrated a rather different set of priorities. In
letters to the press and TV stations alike, they consistently asked for one

thing above all: more movies. Researchers found that viewers tuned in for feature films more than any other kind of programming, often by wide margins. At the next level of popularity came *KVN*, the most popular original TV broadcast, and programs with performers (such as *Little Blue Flame*).[98] Viewers also reported regularly watching broadcasts from theaters, concert halls, and sports arenas. News and public affairs programming—indeed, almost all *original* television programming—ranked lowest of all.

"Living reality," it seems, was far less compelling a proposition to most viewers than to the enthusiasts who kept Sappak's bible on their nightstands. But while the renaissance in Soviet sociology of the 1960s meant that audience behavior became a topic of scientific study, audience taste never loomed large in the minds of TV professionals. It was, in effect, superfluous information for people who made Soviet television; as Gal'perina explained, what was important was that they know how to direct the discussion where it had to go. And in this conviction, this attitude to audiences, TV's enthusiasts and its political overseers were very much on the same page.

I would not wish to downplay the impact of political control and conflict on television's production process. As Soviet enthusiast-historians emphasize, the constant pressure to avoid slipups and to keep upwind of scandal discouraged risk-taking and helped produce a great deal of dull, scripted programming, even in TV's "golden years." This pressure increased throughout the 1960s, and when videotape technology became available, many TV workers embraced it not only because it offered greater technical precision, but also because they hoped it might help protect their jobs. Nonetheless, the clash between TV's overseers and creators was less fundamental than the trail of reprimands and firings would imply. TV enthusiasts saw television in an anti-Stalinist, yet Soviet framework. The journalist G. Kuznetsov, to wit, described the news program he worked on in the 1960s as "a little island of freethinking on the airwaves, but not in the sense that we cast the virtues of our native party and Soviet power into doubt. On the contrary, we tried to portray them in as human a manner as possible."[99] Kuznetsov went on to comment that their work "anticipated the notion of 'socialism with a human face' that appeared in Prague a year later."

For Soviet television, the critical question was whose face would represent socialism on the screen, and for Soviet TV workers and their overseers, who would be responsible for selecting and controlling that face. Enthusiasts sought to replace the Stalinist *kul't lichnosti* with *lichnosti*—a concept that, though pluralistic, did not include all comers. A *lichnost'* was someone worth emulating, a person with something to teach, a cultural authority. And given their educational and moral goals and their sense of superiority over their audiences, *lichnosti* were a natural choice for TV enthusiasts to foreground

in their programming; they were an extension of themselves, as they understood or wished themselves to be. Soviet television was a means for an entire
new group to write themselves into the ranks of the intelligentsia as the
people's conscience and teachers.[100] When conflicts with the regime arose,
they were sometimes ideological in an obvious way, as in questions about
whether a particular person—the poet Evgenii Evtushenko, for example—
was an appropriate *lichnost'* for Soviet TV. But the more basic problem was
one of authority: who would determine the appropriateness of any *lichnost'*?
What was not in question at any time was the position of Soviet viewers,
who were seen by all parties, enthusiasts and their political overseers, as
needing an authority to direct their desires. Television, the new medium
in the 1950s and 1960s, did not present a new model for Soviet culture.

Still, television as a cultural institution and television watching as an
experience were not, of course, the same thing. Even as enthusiasts struggled—with technological constraints, with the political authorities—to
realize their ideals in broadcasting, Soviet viewers continued to show a
marked preference for filmed fiction. From the perspective of the enthusiasts, Soviet TV was worse off in many respects in the 1970s and 1980s than
in its early years. Technologically, of course, broadcasting grew far more
advanced. Made-for-TV movies came into their own, and sports and news
programming were far more sophisticated. With video came an end to most
of the glitches that had plagued early broadcasts, as well as an increased
capacity for surveillance and control; there were far fewer scandals in the
1970s and 1980s than in TV's early years. But for enthusiasts who believed
that the essence of television was live broadcasting and the special relationship between viewers and model individuals, these technical advances only
worked to make broadcasting more artificial and superficial and—paradoxically, considering that audiences were now far larger—less valuable.[101] *This*
Soviet television was not the new art form of their youthful dreams. Soviet
audiences watched anyway. Indeed, they watched even more, and not, to the
enthusiast eye, as active, civic-minded individuals, but rather as a mass of
media consumers. In living rooms across the Soviet Union, it was the pleasures of spectatorship and stasis—an unproductive leisure, they said—that
had won the day. The success of Soviet television broadcasting, it seemed,
had undone the best intentions of its enthusiastic postwar pioneers.

Notes

I would like to extend my heartfelt thanks to the staff at Gosteleradiofond in Moscow
for their assistance in the research for this project. I am grateful to the participants
of the Russian History Workshop at Columbia University for their comments on an
earlier version of this essay. Some of the material presented here is also to be found in

my forthcoming book, *Soviet Culture in the Media Age*. My thanks to Cornell University Press for allowing its inclusion in this volume.

1. *Goluboi ogonek (Little Blue Flame)*, 1967 (Gosteleradiofond). The story has an apocryphal whiff, but it does also appear in a book about television's young enthusiasts written by a friend of the girl's father. G. Fere, *Tovarishch TV* (Moscow: Molodiia Gvardiia, 1974), 29.

2. According to the principal history of the Soviet era, the number of people employed by Soviet television rose from 402 in 1955 to 17,813 in 1965. A. Ia. Iurovskii, *Televidenie: Poiski i resheniia* (Moscow: Iskusstvo, 1983), 108. "Soviet television" for the purposes of this chapter refers primarily to the work of Central TV in Moscow, which not only employed the majority of TV workers but also set the standard for studios throughout the U.S.S.R. While some regional studios did generate innovative programming, the vector of influence generally ran from Moscow outward; regional studios tended to copy Moscow's formats and methods. Moreover, there is little to suggest that the staff of regional studios differed significantly in social background from their Muscovite counterparts or developed an understanding of the medium inconsistent with theirs.

3. "Enthusiast" is a word Soviet television workers often used to describe themselves. Boris Firsov drew a distinction between the "enthusiasts" of the Thaw and the people who came to work in TV in the 1970s and 1980s, whom he has characterized as careerists. Boris Firsov, "Televidenie i my: K istorii nashikh otnoshenii," in *Televidenie: Vchera, segodnia, zavtra*, no. 9 (1989), 8–22.

4. S. A. Muratov, A. Ia. Iurovskii, V. V. Egorov, and R. A. Boretskii are perhaps the most prominent of the scholars of Soviet television who worked in the Central Studio (Shabolovka) in the 1950s and 1960s. The first and, to date, only comprehensive post-Soviet history, *Ocherki po istorii rossiiskogo televideniia* (Moscow: Voskresen'e, 1999), is a collective effort, drawing upon the work of all of the important Soviet-era scholars of TV. In English, the political scientist Ellen Mickiewicz is the only scholar to have written extensively on Soviet TV. See her *Media and the Russian Public* (New York: Praeger, 1981) and *Split Signals: Television and Politics in Soviet Society* (New York: Oxford University Press, 1988). See also Mark Koenig's unpublished dissertation, which follows the interpretation of the Soviet enthusiasts very closely: "Media and Reform: The Case of Youth Programming on Soviet Television (1955–1990)" (Ph.D. diss., Columbia University, 1995); and Kendall Bailes, *Soviet Television Comes of Age: A Review of Its Accomplishments and a Discussion of the Tasks Facing It* (New York: Radio Liberty Research Paper, 1968).

5. For an overview, see Anthony Smith, "Television as a Public Service Medium," in *Television: An International History*, ed. A. Smith (Oxford: Oxford University Press, 1998), 38–54.

6. On *lichnost'* in Russian cultural history, see Catriona Kelly and David Shepherd, eds., *Constructing Russian Culture in the Age of Revolution, 1881–1940* (New York: Oxford University Press, 1998), 13–26.

7. R. Boretskii, "Otkroveniia dilettantov," in *Shabolovka, 53: Stranitsy istorii televideniia*, ed. A. Iu. Rozov (Moscow: Iskusstvo, 1988), 148–58. Boretskii also quoted his colleague, Igor Beliaev, on this point: "Losers [*neudachniki*] landed on Shabolovka's shores" (148).

8. Television was not altogether new to the postwar Soviet Union, which had seen experimental broadcasts as early as the 1920s and the advent of regular broadcasts

from Moscow and Leningrad in 1939. World War II interrupted Soviet TV development, and it was not reinvigorated until the 1950s: dozens of cities across the U.S.S.R. built new TV centers in the early and mid-1950s. On the pre–World War II period, see Iurovskii, *Televidenie*, 29–39; and A. Iurovskii, "Pervye shagi," in *Problemy televideniia i radio* (Moscow: Iskusstvo, 1971), 95–108. On the 1950s, see Kristin Roth-Ey, "Finding a Home for Television in the USSR, 1950–1970," *Slavic Review* 66, no. 2 (Summer 2007): 278–306.

9. Rozov, *Shabolovka*, 96–97; L. Dmitriev, Gosteleradiofond Oral History Project interview, 2002.

10. L. S. Zolotareva, Gosteleradiofond Oral History Project interview, 2002.

11. Rozov, *Shabolovka*, 125.

12. Iurovskii, *Televidenie*, 43. Figures on the growth of television vary significantly in the Soviet sources.

13. Dmitriev, Gosteleradiofond interview.

14. The studio at Shabolovka, the largest and best equipped in the U.S.S.R., measured only three hundred square meters. Shabolovka had neither facilities for developing film, nor a costume and prop department, nor even rehearsal space at this time. Many other studios were the pet projects of technological enthusiasts (typically connected to radio clubs) who had enlisted the support of a local factory, and they made do with a room there for broadcasting. Given the low quality of Soviet equipment, every studio was forced to flood its sound stage with several times more lighting than typically used in foreign TV production, raising temperatures to forty degrees Celsius and higher.

15. Interview with R. D. Kopylova, St. Petersburg, June 2002.

16. A. Iurovskii, "Pogliadim na ekran," *Iskusstvo kino*, no. 4 (1960): 125. Iurovskii was responding to an earlier article by the film director M. Romm, "Pogliadim na dorogu," *Iskusstvo kino*, no. 11 (1959). When Dmitriev, Boretskii, and Grigorian presented their own battle cry, "Televidenie—Eto iskusstvo," to *Sovetskaia kul'tura* in 1957, they fought against the newspaper inserting a question mark at the end. Dmitriev recalled long debates on TV art at the House of Journalists attended by Vladimir Sappak, among others. Rozov, *Shabolovka*, 100–101.

17. The United States was exceptional in this respect, because of both its heavy use of other technologies (film, kinescope) early on and its rapid adoption of video. While approximately 80 percent of programming on American TV was live in 1952, by 1961 that figure had dropped to 27 percent. Jeff Kisseloff, *The Box: An Oral History of Television, 1929–1961* (New York: Viking, 1995), 272.

18. For this and other amusing tales of live TV in the United States, see Kisseloff, *The Box.*

19. *My nachinaem KVN* (Moscow: Izdatel'skii dom "Vostok," 1996), 7.

20. Ibid.

21. Dmitriev reports that the Moscow studio head lost her job over this affair and names the announcer as Andrei Khlebnikov. Dmitriev, Gosteleradiofond interview.

22. For a cinematic representation of these practices, see the film *Moskva slezam ne verit'* (*Moscow Does Not Believe in Tears*), Mosfil'm, 1979.

23. Editors (*redaktory*) thus stood on the front lines of Soviet TV production. Censors from the main censorship organ, Glavlit, did work in TV, as they did in all publishing houses and newspapers, and technically, a program needed a Glavlit "visa" to go forward as well as editorial approval. But as of 1960, according to one

Glavlit worker appealing for better cooperation from TV staff at a Party cell meeting, there were only *four* censors on-site for all of radio and television. Clearly, this level of staffing was inadequate to the task of censorship, and the onus fell largely on TV workers themselves. TsAOPIM (Central Archive of Social Movements of Moscow), f. 2930, op. 1, d. 16, l. 7–10. A 1958 reorganization of Glavlit emphasized the "personal, party-professional responsibility" of the *redaktor*, and this responsibility was again ratcheted up significantly with a 1969 Central Committee decree. See T. Goriaeva and Z. K. Vodopianova, *Istoriia sovetskoi politicheskoi tsenzury: Dokumenty i kommentarii* (Moscow: Rosspen 1997). See also T. Goriaeva, "Glavlit i literatura v period 'literaturno-politicheskogo brozheniia v Sovetskom Soiuze,'" *Voprosy literatury*, no. 5 (1998). Self-censorship was also an extremely important—indeed, according to émigré media professionals interviewed in the 1970s, the most important—factor in production. See Lilita Dzirkals, Thane Gustafson, and A. Ross Johnson, *The Media and Intra-Elite Communication in the USSR* (Santa Monica: Rand Corporation, 1982), 37–61.

24. For examples of scandals from this period involving writers whose statements on live television veered into controversial territory, see Kristin Roth-Ey, "Mass Media and the Remaking of Soviet Culture, 1950s–1960s" (Ph.D. diss., Princeton University, 2003), chap. 5.

25. Sappak's thinking on television also had a broader resonance thanks to the publication of portions of *Televidenie i my* in the thick journal *Novyi mir* in 1960.

26. The first TV sets were truly tiny. The screen for one of the first sets in mass circulation, the KVN-49, was a mere 18 centimeters (measured diagonally). Popular sets like the Rekord and Start had 35-centimeter screens. *Ocherki po istorii*, 68–69. People attached magnifying lenses for this purpose.

27. V. Sappak, *Televidenie i my* (Moscow: Iskusstvo, 1962), 42 (italics mine).

28. Ibid., 98.

29. Ibid., 58.

30. Ibid., 117–22.

31. Ibid., 61.

32. Ibid., 45.

33. Sappak's writing about the transformative power of watching the everyday world from one's home takes on added poignancy in light of his personal situation. Chronically ill since childhood, Sappak was forced to spend much of his short life indoors. *Televidenie i my* was his first and last book. He did not live to see its publication.

34. Iurovskii, "Pogliadim na ekran," 126. More than forty years later, Iurovskii still averred that "live shows are what television was invented for." A. Iurovskii, Gostelradiofond Oral History Project interview, December 2001.

35. Fere, *Tovarishch TV*, 23.

36. GARF (Main Archive of the Russian Federation), f. 6903, op. 1, d. 500, l. 9. Here Puzin sounds remarkably like Sappak. "There is nothing more awful in television than carefully rehearsed improvisation . . . You can speak without notes (if you know how). You can read from a text openly laid out in front of you. But you must not sneak 'hidden' peeks at crib notes or play act an obviously written, obviously edited dialogue with a free-and-easy tone."

37. Annette Michelson, ed., *Kino-Eye: The Writings of Dziga Vertov* (Berkeley: University of California Press, 1984), 5–9.

38. In the 1950s and 1960s, the Vertovian phrase "living reality" (*zhivaia realnost'*) was more common than "life caught unawares" (*zhizn' v rasplokh*), although both were in use. Vertov also saluted Soviet experiments with television, which he called "radio-cinema." Michelson, *Kino-Eye*, 49, 56.

39. This leapfrog maneuver (jumping over Stalinist formulations and into the arms of something defined as Leninist) was a key mechanism of Thaw culture. See Katerina Clark, "Changing Historical Paradigms in Soviet Culture," in *Late Soviet Culture: From Perestroika to Novostroika*, ed. Thomas Lahusen and Gene Kuperman (Durham, N.C.: Duke University Press, 1993), 298; Stephen V. Bittner, *The Many Lives of Khrushchev's Thaw: Experience and Memory in Moscow's Arbat* (Ithaca, N.Y.: Cornell University Press, 2008).

40. GARF, f. 6903, op. 1, d. 502, l. 1–26.

41. Sappak, *Televidenie*, 112.

42. Michelson, *Kino-Eye*, 49 (italics mine). Consider, too, the imagery of the film itself: the legs of the man with the movie camera are gigantic and striding; he dwarfs the city and ordinary folk.

43. See Ian Christie, "Canons and Careers: The Director in Soviet Cinema," in *Stalinism and Soviet Cinema*, ed. Richard Taylor and D. W. Spring (London: Routledge, 1993), 146. Christie has argued that the negation of Russia's rich, prerevolutionary cinematic heritage was the keystone of a "creation myth" for Soviet cinema, establishing it as a "quintessentially 'Soviet'" art form founded by Eisenstein and four other pioneers (the "Five").

44. The festival was a turning point for Soviet TV. Shabolovka's enthusiasts successfully lobbied for better equipment and facilities and were able to provide nearly dawn-to-dusk coverage: 221.5 hours over a period of roughly two weeks. Soviet reporters used new mobile cameras to put literally thousands of ordinary people on the air, Soviet and foreign, individually and in mass groups. There were also dozens of interviews with delegates and live performances from the studio. Filmed copies were flown to Leningrad, Kiev, and several other cities for broadcast during the festival as well. For the lobbying (which involved a letter delivered directly to Khrushchev), see R. Boretskii, Gosteleradiofond Oral History Project interview, 2002. For Central TV's activity during the festival, see RGASPI-m (Russian State Archive of Socio-Political History-Komsomol), f. 4, op. 104, d. 30, l. 169–83; A. Iurovskii, *Televizion-naia zhurnalistika* (Moscow: Nanka, 1998), 65.

45. The initial idea for *VVV* is credited to Sergei Muratov, who worked in Shabolovka's "Festival'naia" *redaktsiia* and had met the director of the Czech show, Stanislav Strnad, in Moscow. (*GGG*, or *Gadai, gadai, gadal'shchik—Guess, Guess, You Guessers—* is the Russian translation of the show's name.) Muratov wrote a first draft of a script for *VVV* with Andrei Donatov and Mikhail Iakovlev; Al'bert Aksel'rod and Mark Rozovskii, two well-known *kapustnik* performers (see note 46), were soon brought on to the project. Interview with Sergei Muratov, Moscow, June 2002; "KVN: Vzgliad cherez chetvert'veka," *Televidenie: Vchera, sevognia, zavtra*, no. 7 (1987): 84–85; Masha Topaz, "VVV, ili bochka s porokhom," *Sem' dnei*, no. 29 (1995).

46. The term *kapustniki* generally refers to improvisational comedic (often satiric) performances. Historically, *kapustniki* were associated with turn-of-the-century Russian actors who, it is said, performed for each other after hours and, too poor to buy meat, shared cabbage *pirozhki*. (Hence, the name *kapustnik*, from the word for "cabbage.") *Kapustniki* were also associated with prerevolutionary university culture,

and many Thaw-era student groups saw themselves in the *kapustnik* tradition. Although the *kapustniki* sometimes skirted the edge of political propriety, they were also encouraged by the Soviet regime, along with other forms of amateur performance (*samodeiatel'nost'*), as one solution to the youth recreation problem. Their success at the 1957 Youth Festival boosted their popularity even further. See L. P. Solntseva and M. V. Iunisov, eds., *Samodeiatel'noe khudozhestvennoe tvorchestvo v SSSR: Ocherki istorii* (St. Petersburg: Izd. Dmitrii Bulanin, 1999), especially M. V. Iunisov, "Studencheskii teatr estradnykh miniatur," 281–306. See also Iunisov's interesting monograph that attempts to locate *KVN* within a rich tradition of student subculture, *Mifopoetika studencheskogo smekha* (*STEM i KVN*) (Moscow: Gos. institut iskusstvoznaniia, 1999).

47. E. V. Gal'perina et al., eds., *KVN? KVN . . . KVN!* (Moscow: Komitetpo radioveshchaniiu i televideniiu, 1966), 9.

48. Each of the people involved in these programs remembers the details a bit differently. (One says it was the seventh volume of Jack London, another, the third; someone recalls a primus stove instead of a samovar, and so on.) But there is general agreement on the main features of the program's format.

49. *VVV*'s creators flirted with the idea of offering more substantial prizes, but decided this would run counter to the spirit of the show and settled on funny, token ones. Contemporary Radio Moscow did offer prizes (including some expensive ones, such as cameras and watches) to international listeners to write-in quizzes, usually about Soviet history. U.S. State Department report, "The Soviet Bloc Exchanges in 1957" (January 1958), 12.

50. According to one of the ushers at the theater, the would-be contestants who came to the studio that evening were agitated because the prize was a comparatively luxurious one: a new bicycle. *Kak eto bylo* (*The Way It Was*) (ORT, 1998).

51. GARF, f. 6903, op. 1, d. 532, l. 5. Boretskii, who was in the fourth row of the audience, recalled a "huge crowd" of "construction workers . . . some sort of *zeks* (ex-cons) who, since it was a Saturday, were three sheets to the wind." Boretskii, Gosteleradiofond interview.

52. Topaz, "VVV, ili bochka s porokhom."

53. There are varying accounts of what happened to Bogoslovskii. One report has it that he hid in a wardrobe. *My nachinaem KVN*, 9. He remembers fleeing in a car with his cohost. N. Bogoslovskii, *Chto bylo i chego ne bylo i koe-chto eshche* (Moscow: Olma Press, 1999), 277.

54. The *redaktsiia* in charge of festival programming (and by extension, youth programming, as there was no youth-specific group then) was liquidated entirely. Sergei Muratov was not officially fired for the incident, but when asked for his resignation, he complied.

55. The missing element was a copy of a newspaper from December 31, 1956. Muratov was out of town at the time, but he recalls rejecting the idea for this contest because he knew it would be too simple, and also that the director of the Czech *GGG* had warned him about crowd-control problems with easy contests. Aksel'rod and Iakovlev approved the *gotov sani letom* idea at the last minute and only after another contest had fallen through, but they added the newspaper element to make it more difficult. Bogoslovskii forgot this element. Interview with Muratov; "KVN: Vzgliad cherez chetvert' veka," 86.

56. *My nachinaem KVN*, 9.

57. GARF, f. 6903, op. 1, d. 532, l. 15. The indispensable Sappak was watching, and he was among those who found the spectacle rather exciting. In *Televidenie i my*, he joked that those responsible should have been rewarded rather than punished. Sappak, *Televidenie*, 64.

58. GARF, f. 6903, op. 1, d. 532, l. 8.

59. Ibid., l. 26.

60. "'Veselye voprosy's pechal'nym otvetom," published in *Sem' dnei* in 1995. From the personal archive of Sergei Muratov.

61. GARF, f. 6903, op. 1, d. 532, l. 2 (italics mine).

62. According to contemporary codes of conduct, wearing work clothes anywhere outside of work was *nekul'turno* (uncultured). See Olga Vainshtein, "Female Fashion, Soviet Style: Bodies of Ideology," in *Russia—Women—Culture*, ed. H. Goscilo and B. Holmgren (Bloomington: Indiana University Press, 1996), 66–67. I am arguing that the nature of Soviet media culture made broadcasting the violation of this work/ nonwork boundary even more transgressive.

63. "'Veselye voprosy's pechal'nym otvetom." The Central Committee's comments may have been motivated in part by the presence of foreign correspondents in the audience. Muratov and his colleagues are convinced to this day that the *VVV* scandal was reported widely in American media outlets. One of the show's staff, Iurii Zerchaninov, recalls seeing an American journalist shooting film of the event, which he later heard from Shabolovka director Os'minin was made into a sensationalist documentary about the desperation of Soviet consumers entitled *Ubiistvo za skovorodku* (*Murder for a Frying Pan*). *Kak eto bylo*. R. Boretskii also reports seeing foreign correspondents. I have found one report in a Washington, D.C., newspaper: B. J. Cutler, "Soviet Giveaway Show Takes Station Off Air," *Washington Post and Times Herald*, October 1, 1957. Cutler reported that "a flood of booted and fur-hatted comrades . . . clumped around the stage waving to friends still at television sets at home and demanded their prizes" while the announcer was nowhere to be seen "but could be heard shouting gamely from the background." He attributed the chaos to the lure of free prizes, as did NBC's Moscow correspondent, who later wrote about the show as well. Irving R. Levine, *Main Street, USSR: Selections from the Original Edition* (New York: Signet Books, 1960), 68. It is unclear whether either man was in attendance.

64. Topaz, "VVV, ili bochka s porokhom."

65. According to this account—again, not coincidentally, penned by former enthusiasts—the *VVV* scandal "came in handy" in the "large-scale 'working over' of insufficiently principled creative types" that followed the publication of Khrushchev's main policy paper on the arts, *Za tesnuiu sviaz' literatury i iskusstva s zhizn'iu narod* (*For a Close Tie Between Literature and Art with the Life of the People*), in August 1957. *Ocherki po istorii*, 78–80. Regional branches of the creative unions all over the U.S.S.R. met to discuss the policy paper that fall, with widespread publicity in the central press. State Department intelligence report, "The Soviet Union in 1957: A Review of Internal Developments" (February 1958), 14.

66. Rozov, *Shabolovka*, 206.

67. The KVN-49 set was named for its three designers (V. K. Kenigson, N. M. Varshavskii, I. A. Nikolaevskii) and the year it went on the market. For the history of TV technology in the U.S.S.R., see V. A. Urvalov, *Ocherki istorii televideniia* (Moscow: Nanka, 1990). *KVN* debuted in November 1961 and was broadcast monthly (and sometimes less often), typically on Sunday evenings.

68. *KVN* competitions also appeared on regional TV, and there were local *KVN* teams in schools and factories, on kolkhozy and in the armed forces, among taxi drivers and shop clerks. *KVN-shchiki* today claim that the popularity of the game was so great that even Soviet prisoners set up teams. *KVN,* they say, was and remains a "way of life." Although the importance of the game in Thaw-era culture has now taken on mythic proportions, it is clear that the *KVN* idea did have an extraordinary social resonance. *My nachinaem KVN,* 15. Its popularity was not always welcomed. Some clubs were accused of giving civic and educational themes short shrift: a Komsomol review team was disturbed to find "passionate arguments about the question: 'How fast does a hippopotamus run, and does it run at all?'" and jokes about hemorrhoids at a 1963 *KVN* in Latvia. RGASPI-m, f. 1, op. 32, d. 1106, l. 132.

69. Among the most famous *KVN-shchiki* who went on to careers on the stage were Gennadyi Khazanov, Leonid Iakubovich, and Mikhail Zhvanetskii. On the work of Khazanov and Zhvanetskii, see Richard Stites, *Russian Popular Culture* (New York: Cambridge University Press, 1992), 184, 167–68. Many *KVN* team members, especially captains, were as popular as film stars. See Petr Vail' and Aleksandr Genis, *60–e: Mir sovetskogo cheloveka* (Moscow: "Novoe literaturnoe obozrenie," 1996), 151; interview with Iurii Makarov (former captain of the Odessa team), New York, May 2002. In recent years, *KVN* has become a truly global phenomenon, with organized clubs and competitions in many former Soviet republics as well as the United States, Israel, Germany, and other countries. For more information on today's "International Union of KVN," see the official site at http://www.amik.ru.

70. Interview with M. E. Krasn'ianskaia (former *KVN redaktor*), Moscow, July 2002.

71. For descriptions of contests, see V. Grigor'ev, "Televizionnaia mechtaniia," *Teatr,* no. 5 (1963): 121–28; "KVN: Vkhod tol'ko telezriteliam," *Sovetskoe radio i televidenie,* no. 2 (1968): 15–17; "KVN: Vozvrasheniia k skazke," in *TV-publitsist: Sbornik tsenariev,* ed. E. V. Gal'perina (Moscow: Iskusstvo, 1971), 110–63; "*KVN:* Vzgliad cherez chetvert' veka," *Ocherki po istorii,* 106–9.

72. Soviet television's technical capacity to perform this function consistently is doubtful at best. See "Igroki-starozhily ne liubiat segodniashnii *KVN*," *Komsomol'skaia pravda,* October 11, 1999.

73. Interview with Krasn'ianskaia. *KVN* spent its first year on Central TV's Second Program (which reached far fewer homes than the First), according to TV workers, because it was perceived by the central authorities as too risky.

74. A. Aksel'rod, S. Muratov, and M. Iakovlev, *Klub veselykh i nakhodchivykh* (Moscow, 1965), 3.

75. Ibid. See also E. V. Gal'perina and B. I. Sergeeva, eds., *KVN otvechaet na pis'ma* (Moscow: Iskusstvo, 1967). *KVN* games could have broad applications. The organizers of a Latvian "Contest of Atheists" in 1965 told Komsomol authorities they had found a *KVN* how-to book very helpful. RGASPI-m, f. 1, op. 32, d. 1198, l. 88–155.

76. Kharlamov stuck to his guns when told about the defect. "They're also abstractionists [a reference to Western artists], they need to be removed from society. Long-hairs, bearded ones, and so on. These are all phenomena of the same type. Peter shaved off beards forcibly, and we have to do the same." GARF, f. 6903, op. 1, d. 777, l. 56–57. The image of the hosts was as important as that of the contestants. *KVN* was ordered to drop its first female host, actress Natalia Zashchipina, after she took the role of a prostitute in a play. *My nachinaem KVN,* 15.

77. V. Nemtsov, "Neskol'ko vecherov u televizora," *Sovetskaia kul'tura,* August 18, 1965, 2.

78. Grigor'ev, "Televizionnaia mechtaniia," 123.

79. In the days when the contests were still largely improvisational, the show's staff might tell teams ahead of time how many "artists" or "musicians" they would need to have ready. *My nachinaem KVN,* 12–13.

80. RGALI, f. 2936, op. 3, d. 106, l. 7.

81. Rozov, *Shabolovka,* 218.

82. Teams who showed extraordinary "civic wit" (*grazhdanskaia ostrota*), demonstrating that they saw *KVN* "not only as a game, but also as a means of struggle," could win extra points from the jury. "*KVN:* Vzgliad cherez chetvert' veka," 90.

83. Rozov, *Shabolovka,* 218.

84. E. V. Gal'perina, "V gramm dobycha, v god trudy," in *Iskusstvo golubogo ekrana,* ed. G. Mikhailova (Moscow: Iskusstvo, 1968), 109.

85. M. E. Krasn'ianskaia made precisely this point in my interview with her in July 2002.

86. "*KVN:* Vzgliad cherez chetvert' veka," 89.

87. The restructuring led to the formation of the State Committee for Radio and Television under the auspices of the U.S.S.R. Council of Ministers (soon followed by analogous committees at the republic level). The working group for TV (*sektor televideniia*) was within the Central Committee's Department of Propaganda and Agitation. See Roth-Ey, "Finding a Home for Television."

88. This has been a leitmotif for the various *KVN* anniversary shows broadcast on post-Soviet Russian TV. In print, see, for example, Iunisov, *Mifopoetika;* L. Brusilov'skaia, *Kul'tura povsednevnosti v epokhu "ottepeli": Metamorfozy stiliia* (Moscow: Universitet Rossiiskoi akademii obrazoraniia, 2001), 141–46; Vail' and Genis, *60–e,* 151. This reputation has been beatified in a way by the fact that, as Muratov and others often mention, Vladimir Vysotskii was present when they were hashing out the initial design for *KVN.* (He was a neighbor in Iakovlev's *kommunalka* and liked to listen in.) Although Vysotskii is more of a 1970s than a Thaw-era figure, and he was not a dissident, he is associated with many of the Thaw tropes—truth-telling, authenticity, youthful daring, and so on.

89. According to the researcher Bella Ostromoukhova, who has interviewed several former *KVN* players, the main thrust of the program shifted from wit to politically charged satire around the mid-1960s. Ostromoukhova argues that players picked up on this desire of a certain segment of the audience to see criticism of the regime and ran with it; "humor on 'dangerous' themes even became fashionable" among participants. Bella Ostromoukhova, "KVN-'molodezhnaia kul'tura shestidesiatykh?'" *Neprikosknovennyi zapas,* no. 36 (2004).

90. See Kristin Roth-Ey, *Soviet Culture in the Media Age* (Ithaca, N.Y.: Cornell University Press, forthcoming), chap. 5.

91. "*KVN:* Vzgliad cherez chetvert' veka," 90–97; *My nachinaem KVN,* 15–20; interview with Makarov. Makarov reported that he and fellow members of the Odessa team coached teams from Riga, Minsk, and Baku in the late 1960s. Although they were paid, he said, their motivation was not financial: they wanted to help provincial teams win in the face of what they saw as the jury's pro-Moscow bias.

92. F. Kasilov, "KVN: Sem' funtov pod kilem," *Molodezh' Azerbaidzhana,* June 18, 1968.

93. See, for example, G. Kuznetsov, "Kogda otgremeli batalii," *Sovetskaia kul'tura,* July 9, 1966, 3; A. Aksel'rod, "Klub? Veselykh? Nakhodchivykh?" *Literaturnaia gazeta,* February 25, 1970. The *New York Times* reported on viewer disappointment with the first program in the 1970–71 season: "'Quick-Witted' Variety Show Returns to Soviet TV," *New York Times,* October 29, 1970.

94. Interview with Makarov; *My nachinaem KVN;* "*KVN:* Vzgliad cherez chetvert' veka." Former host Svetlana Zhil'tsova said the formal reason for the cancellation was the Odessa team's defiance of a ban on long hair and beards, while the real reason was that the show was "too controversial and too free." Aleksandr Mel'man, "Geroi vcherashnikh dnei. Svetlana Zhilt'sova: Ia ne o chem ne zhaleiu," *Moskovskii komsomolets,* September 13, 1999.

95. "Golden years" is the term used in *Ocherki po istorii rossiskogo televideniia* (see note 4) for the period from 1957 to 1970. Also included in the pantheon are the "TV-café" *Goluboi ogonek, Kinopanorama* (on cinema), *Klub kinoputeshestvii* (on geography and travel), *Muzykal'nyi kiosk* (on classical music), *Estafeta novostei* (a weekly news magazine), and *Rasskazy o geroizme* (a program about and for World War II veterans). For more on these shows, see Roth-Ey, *Soviet Culture,* chap. 5.

96. *Estafeta novostei, Kinopanorama, Rasskazy o geroizme,* and *Klub kinoputeshestvii* all had male hosts. *Goluboi ogonek* was an exception in that it typically used TV announcers (*diktory*) or invited actors to act as hosts. *Muzykal'nyi kiosk* was hosted by a woman.

97. Sergei Muratov, "Kofe i liudi," *Sovetskaia kul'tura,* January 21, 1965, reprinted in his *Televidenie v poiskakh televideniia* (Moscow: Izd. Moskovskogo universiteta, 2001), 43–46. Not everyone agreed that TV hosts were skilled in the art of *obshchenie.* For a blistering critique of *Estafeta novostei's* host, Iurii Fokin, see M. Mikriukov, "Razmyshleniia u pogasshego ekrana," *Teatr,* no. 1 (1967): 65–76.

98. The best overall source on viewer taste is B. M. Firsov, *Televidenie glazami sotsiologa* (Moscow: Iskusstvo, 1971), 126–30. One 1966 study from cities across the U.S.S.R. found that 74 percent of viewers aged 14–30 reported "always" tuning in for *KVN;* for the 14–18 age group, the number approached 90 percent. *KVN* was also popular with older viewers, and second in overall popularity only to feature films. GARF, f. 6903, op. 3, d. 329, l. 11–13.

99. G. V. Kuznetsov, "Zapiski lishnego cheloveka," in *Televizionnaia mozaika,* ed. Ia. N. Zasurskii (Moscow, 1997), 38.

100. In this sense, the story of the professionalization of TV production follows a similar pattern to that identified by Sheila Fitzpatrick for intelligentsia-regime relations in the 1930s. See Sheila Fitzpatrick, *The Cultural Front: Power and Authority in Revolutionary Russia* (Ithaca, N.Y.: Cornell University Press, 1992), 1–15.

101. *Ocherki po istorii,* 154–70; Sergei Muratov, "The Structure of Broadcasting Authority," *Journal of Communication* 41, no. 2 (Spring 1991): 172–84; Firsov, "Televidenie i my."

Chapter Six

Women on the Verge of Desire: Women, Work, and Consumption in Socialist Czechoslovakia

Paulina Bren

The American journalist Tad Szulc described Czechoslovakia's cultural atmosphere during the 1960s as synonymous with "jazz and the big-beat sound" and with "blue jeans and beards," "as if in retaliation against years of Stalinist monotony and boredom."[1] Not only the politics but the very appearance of socialist Czechoslovakia changed rapidly during this time, connecting directly and indirectly with similar movements flowering on the other side of the Iron Curtain.[2] The initial debate about the injustices of Stalinism further expanded into probing critiques of the present-day socialist experience, in particular the glaring discrepancies between the promises of the communist state and the realities of socialist life. Among this laundry list of exploding complaints was the lot of women under communism.

This is not to say that feminism found a permanent foothold in the Prague Spring, but critiques of gender roles and expectations did find their way into the popular culture of the 1960s, if not its legislation. Mindful of the relationship between politics and popular culture in the Eastern Bloc from the 1960s onward, in this chapter I trace the various adventures, and their purpose, of two iconic female characters in popular culture: Marie, the 1960s tram driver, who looks to the promises of the coming Prague Spring; and Anna, the 1970s supermarket counter girl, who, in the aftermath of the Warsaw Pact invasion, brings those same promises to heel.

Marie, the Tram Driver

The 1960s debates about the postwar communist project collided with the
theme of women's liberation in the deliciously amusing 1966 film musical
A Lady on the Rails (*Dáma na kolejích*).[3] The title role of tram driver Marie
Kučerová was played by one of Czechoslovakia's most popular actresses, the
petite and feisty Jiřina Bohdalová, who danced and sang her way through a
finger-snapping score that incorporated jazz, big beat, and modern opera,
while also featuring the latest hip 1960s fashions. *A Lady on the Rails's* starting point is Marie's discovery of her husband's adultery. Early one morning,
as fog hangs over the streets of Prague, Marie the tram driver is stuck at the
intersection in Malá Strana Square (Little Quarter). While she waits in the
driver's seat of her Number 12 tram, she glances around the street and spies
her husband, Václav, kissing a young and very fashionable blonde woman
(or, as Marie will later remark, "She's no Lollobrigida but she knows how
to put herself together").

This shocking discovery comes after a morning during which Marie
has been fuming over her workload at home—an unending list of domestic
tasks that seem to go unappreciated and certainly unaided. Her anger over
her double burden had been temporarily allayed when a chorus of well-
heeled young women entered the tram singing the musical's opening number, which proclaims that the work of mother and housewife is worth it
"as long as you know he loves you." Now, having caught him in the act of
adultery, Marie is no longer sure that he does love her, and her grievances
over the home drudgery take over, as suggested by the song she belts out
next as she marches angrily through the streets of Prague, staring at the film
camera head-on: "For you I slogged like this . . . To you I gave what I had . . .
my innocence, my youth."

During this sighting of her husband's adultery, which sets off the film's
events, Marie is wearing her tram driver's uniform. It is a curious mix between what looks like a flight attendant's outfit (a winged insignia is attached to the front peak of her pillbox hat) and a Russian commissar's
hand-me-down coat (made of a thick, scratchy gray wool, with sleeves
at least two inches too long for her). Marie's sexual desirability has vanished, the costume seems to say, lost in the enormity of her unfashionable
coat. Along with Marie's sexual allure so too goes the 1950s communist
ideal of womanhood. It was a beauty shaped, as the Czech literary historian Vladimír Macura noted, by "the fact that she abandons her home and
takes up work in the public domain."[4] While Marie has not abandoned her
home, she most certainly has taken up work in the most public of domains;
but this decision has seemingly backfired. Judging by Marie's husband's

choice of mistress, the bourgeois beauty is back. Socialist men (or at least her man) are blind to the kind of beauty shaped by taking on masculine professions and garb, which by their very definition leave no time for a woman's "self-maintenance."

In *A Lady on the Rails*, Marie's frustrations with her role as a run-down mother of two small children, pursuing a full-time job outside of the home along with full-time work at home, were expressed in a way that was both amusing and recognizable. Two years later, once the Prague Spring was in full swing, the Czechoslovak Association of Women (Československý svaz žen) would echo Marie's specific complaints when it stated in an open letter that "at many levels, women are forced to pay dearly for motherhood, because the weight of responsibility and accountability in bringing up the young generation seems to rest largely upon them."[5] In other words, women were doing all the work of childcare and home maintenance, in addition to their jobs outside of the home.[6] But it was not until 1968, when the corridors of the Czechoslovak Association of Women were finally aired and its Stalinist-era director replaced with a pro-reform communist, that the association could speak for Czechoslovak women rather than for the interests of the Communist Party. In 1966, it was left to Marie to voice women's real concerns.

Driving Off Course

Marie plays out one of the most extreme fantasies of women living with the double burden: she responds to her husband's betrayal (a betrayal that is as much about the difference between her thick gray coat and his mistress's fashionable outfit as it is about her husband's sexual promiscuity) by emptying their joint bank accounts. She then spends the money on a shopping spree followed by a visit to a day spa. Her adventure does not begin in a state-run department store with empty shelves but in a modern couturier's showroom where immaculately dressed, bourgeois-looking women of all ages sit commenting on the live models that parade among them showing off the latest designer fashions. When the show finishes, girlishly delighted by what she has seen, Marie stands up on her chair, slaps her banknotes against her palm, and shouts in glee: "I'm taking it all!" She replaces her tram driver uniform with another uniform entirely: a red shift dress and a leopard print three-quarter-sleeved coat and matching hat. With her heart set on an entire makeover, Marie's next stop is the spa where fellow pampered clients on massage tables join her in singing the Latin conjugation of the word "woman."

In the meantime, her husband, Václav, is at home getting sloshed after

learning that Marie knows about his affair. Even so, he excuses his philan-
dering, grumbling that "when a woman stops paying attention to herself,
she shouldn't be surprised." When Marie arrives home, changing out of her
red dress and leopard coat into a Marie Antoinette–style lounging robe, she
fully concurs with Václav: his adultery is her fault, she admits, it is the result
of her not having taken proper care of herself as a woman. But she is going
to do so now and she is going to pay for it from their bank accounts. Her
husband objects that she already gets paid: Marie responds, "Oh, I don't
mean that little salary I get from the state! I'm talking about the salary from
my other job, my second shift—which is much harder." Even though the
going rate for housework, she says, is seven crowns an hour, she has generously calculated at merely four crowns an hour and thrown in "moments of
love" for free. After having added up the cost of five years of cleaning, cooking, laundry, and childcare, she has paid herself accordingly. Václav objects:
"Well, then any woman could claim that." Marie replies defiantly: "Well,
she should!"

But Marie is not as happy-go-lucky as she appears. The internal conflict
she feels between taking a firm stand against her double burden and being
a loyal and submissive wife and mother is played out through two of the
film's songs. The first song becomes a refrain throughout the film, sung in
whispers at different moments by a chorus of women who live in the same
building as Marie and her husband, and who stand clustered in the building's stairwell dressed in floral housecoats. Together they sing quietly and
persuasively: "Be reasonable, Mrs. Kučerová . . . Forgive him, Mrs. Kučerová,
whatever it was . . . You have children. A woman must think of the children.
Forgive him, and start over again . . . A woman must know how to suffer."
The second song that speaks to Marie's conflict is sung by Marie herself at
her company dance that same evening after her whirlwind shopping spree.
Dressed in a white evening gown that is the envy of every woman there,
Marie leads the other wives at the dance into a frenzied protest song titled
"Pluck Up Your Courage, Women!" ("Zmužte se ženy!"). It is a war cry with
a mixed message, for the word for "courage" in Czech—*zmužit se*—literally
means "to become a man/to make oneself a man."

At the end of the evening, after depositing her drunken husband at
his mistress's apartment with instructions on how he likes his breakfast
made and his shirts washed, Marie heads off to one of the new jazz clubs
now thriving in Prague in the 1960s. At the club, however, she is promptly
picked up for prostitution by a plainclothes policeman: he suspects her because of her expensive clothing and her single status. When Marie dic-
tates her statement at the police station, she turns it into an impassioned
speech, which begins: "I, the detained, throw myself upon the mercy of the

Czechoslovak Socialist Republic that guarantees women equal rights ..."
But the dream of equality is just that. As the film comes to an end, there is
an abrupt shift back to reality. It turns out that none of what we have seen
in fact happened: Marie did not go on the warpath. All that remains real is
Marie's husband's infidelity. We see Marie again as in the opening scene: in
her coarse wool coat standing at the intersection observing her husband kiss
the blonde. But instead of abandoning her tram at the intersection and taking action, as she did at the start of the film, she now merely stares miserably
down at her coat, and returns slowly to her tram, defeated.

Marie is a "lady on the rails" in both a real and metaphorical sense. She
drives the Number 12 tram on its prescribed route on its fixed tracks, day
in and day out. Cloaked in her unattractive wool coat, sexual desirability
evades her. When her consumerist desires are satiated, it reveals itself to
have been a dream. But the desire that is most censured is her longing to
escape from the inevitable predictability of her route, to deviate from her
role as self-sacrificing wife, mother, and socialist worker. Even when she is
momentarily "derailed" by the sight of her husband's betrayal, she fails to
grasp the moment and succumbs to the siren song of her equally frustrated
female neighbors who sing: "Be reasonable, Mrs. Kučerová ... A woman
must know how to suffer." In a general sense, the film's message could (and
most probably still can) speak to women on both sides of what was called
the Iron Curtain. It is the story of many a woman's overburdened life, and
the ease with which her sacrifices are taken for granted.

But what makes *A Lady on the Rails* unique is its willingness to spot-
light women's double burdens under socialism and, more interestingly still,
to offer up a decidedly non-socialist lifestyle and consumption as a potential means to liberation. Admittedly, Marie's consumerism turns out to
have been mere fantasy, but this plot twist does not undermine consumerism as such; instead, it underscores the difficulty encountered by Marie in
becoming a serious consumer, presumably not only because she lacks the
courage to do so but also because she lacks the means as a citizen of a socialist country.

A Woman's Work Is Never Done

The Prague Spring, it should be remembered, was not so much a revolution
as an unleashing of a multitude of desires, both serious and playful. These
included a desire for the end of censorship, free elections, a multiparty system, rock and roll, American films, Parisian clothes, and travel to the capitalist West. In this sense, *A Lady on the Rails* fit well with the atmosphere of
reformist Czechoslovakia during the 1960s.

The August 1968 Soviet-led Warsaw Pact invasion put an end to these desires. What followed for the next twenty years was a Communist Party–led program of "normalization." Gustáv Husák, Czechoslovak general secretary from 1969 to 1987, would later explain: "The concept of normalization was not my invention. We all voted for it as the only possible outcome. If some country experiences an earthquake—what then? It tries to normalize life. And what can it do when a 100,000-plus-strong army descends upon it?"[7] But after the army of 100,000 had left, leaving behind a small core that now represented the permanent Soviet occupation of Czechoslovakia, "normalization" came to mean the active rebuttal of ideas, questions, and, indeed, desires introduced during the Prague Spring.

Among the ideas to be eschewed was the 1960s critique of women's double burden. In a 1974 radio program for women, the Prague Spring government was now accused of promulgating "bizarre theories of market socialism" that had envisioned "the return of women into the home, to the stove and the spatula." The radio commentator added that during the 1960s "questions began to be bandied about as to whether the employment of women is even necessary or justified. If perhaps women's access to employment does not harm women, families, and society as a whole . . . The bourgeois model of woman was brought back into circulation, in which she should return to her rightful calling in the home."[8] While conceding that in "real and existing socialism," gender relations were still developing and, much like the economy, had not yet been perfected, the post-1968 leadership also insisted that the Prague Spring reformers had exploited "these shortcomings in a struggle against the employment of women."[9] In contrast, *they* were committed to supporting women working. Normalization's leadership was not exactly a pantheon of forward-thinking, feminist-friendly men, however.[10] What they really meant was *not* that they were committed to supporting working women but that working women would be central to socialist society after 1968.

Television Redefined

As much as tram driver Marie Kučerová was an iconic female of 1960s Czechoslovak popular culture and reform socialism, so delicatessen counter girl Anna Holubová would define normalization. Whereas Marie appeared on film, Anna appeared on the television screen. That Anna was a television rather than a film character was appropriate: the post-1968 Party leadership went to great lengths to create a dialogue with its citizens through the television screen. In particular, soap opera–like serials became instrumental in this dialogue, and constituted a key feature of late communist political culture in Czechoslovakia.[11]

By the 1970s the Czechs and Slovaks were enamored of the television serial. First introduced on the television screen in the early 1950s, the genre's popularity had much to do with Jaroslav Dietl, Czechoslovakia's most successful and popular television writer. It was Dietl who created Anna Holubová, one of normalization's best-known working women, in the 1977 serial *The Woman Behind the Counter*.[12] Each of the twelve episodes represented a month in the year following Anna's divorce after she leaves her high-status job as a supermarket manager at one end of Prague to move with her two children to the other side of the city, where she takes on the less prestigious job of supermarket delicatessen counter girl. This twelve-episode serial was watched by over 80 percent of Czechoslovak citizens who owned a television set.[13] This was no small number. Czechoslovak state television first broadcast in 1953, and by 1972, 80 percent of Czechoslovak families owned a television set.[14] By the mid-1970s, when *The Woman Behind the Counter* was on the air, nine out of ten families owned a television set.[15]

The history of post-1968 Czechoslovakia is almost always narrated as a political struggle waged against the regime by dissidents; both the casual and serious student of postwar Eastern Europe will most likely think first of the playwright Václav Havel, the underground rock band Plastic People of the Universe, and the dissident group Charter 77, when asked to conjure up an image of late socialism in Czechoslovakia. But there is a competing history, one much more likely to be recalled by the ordinary citizen who lived through late socialism and had little or no knowledge of political dissent and certainly no direct contact with it: the familiar names and images in this other history interconnect with the lead characters of Jaroslav Dietl's popular television serials. As one commentator remarked, "Normalization and its 'mass culture' are significantly different from one another," but Jaroslav Dietl's television serials were unique in that they brought the two worlds together: "Just like the television heroes in these serials, most citizens of this state were not badly off. Similarly, most of the nation also lived with the absurd worries of those times, fulfilled the Five-Year Plan, went to the May Day parades, and voted for members of the National Front."[16] Another article noted that "viewers immersed themselves in the pseudo-world of these television serials, which carried idealized touchstones of their everyday lives."[17]

Anna, the Supermarket Counter Girl

In *The Woman Behind the Counter*, the lead role of Anna Holubová was played by Jiřina Švorcová. She was not Jaroslav Dietl's first choice, and when he was instructed to cast her, his frustration not only centered on Švorcová's notorious political profile (she had welcomed the 1968 Soviet invasion) but also her appearance and age—she was ten years older than Dietl's thirty-nine-year-old fictional creation.[18] On the television screen, Švorcová's Anna Holubová is indeed no great beauty. She is somewhat overweight, with the overdyed raven-black hair then thought to add youth to age, and a faint moustache. But it is these "flaws" that on television transform her into "every woman." What further identifies her as such is her familiar double burden. But unlike Marie the tram driver of the 1960s, who felt impossibly stretched by her multitude of tasks, Anna Holubová, 1970s counter girl extraordinaire, is able to fit more hours and minutes into the day than seems humanly possible. She is a single mother of a needy seven-year-old son and a difficult seventeen-year-old daughter; she begins her job at 5:30 a.m. in order to be ready for 6:00 a.m. opening hours; and, most significantly, she is a "mother" to the entire staff at the supermarket, determined to solve problems where need be, to help out when necessary, and to create order and calm where originally there was none.

On her very first day on the job, when lesser mortals would simply be orienting themselves, Anna is a catalyst for change. The deputy manager's wife rules the store like a queen bee although she is not even an employee there; it is Anna who tells her what's what and makes it possible for the affable head manager to send her on her way. In the second episode, Anna tries to help the stuttering Jiřina by taking her to a speech specialist. When he explains there is nothing he can do, Anna does not give up but convinces the supermarket manager to put Jiřina in charge of the vegetable department, which in turn so elevates her self-confidence that a new beauty shines through, despite her speech impediment. In episode 4, when the salesgirl from the meat department is found by her mother in the cellar with the stock boy, it is Anna who tries to help negotiate between them. This heroic tempo seldom slows throughout the twelve episodes of the serial.

Significantly, Anna's wounds from her failed marriage begin to heal because of the part she plays in the "supermarket collective" as a curative symbol and a soothing maternal figure. Her colleagues, the recipients of her untiring help, refer to her affectionately by her diminutives of "Andulka" and "Anička." Anna is tireless despite the burden of her own private problems: by being so, she is truly the ideal socialist heroine. Because of the need for the double burden—on the one hand, the state would face a major labor shortage without it; on the other hand, few households could get by with just one income—being tired and overworked became valorized by the state. The result was that the official media frequently helped to connect women's fatigue with virtuousness. For example, a 1982 women's radio program interviewed a woman named Dana, a thirty-two-year-old mother of two small children, with the apparent purpose of getting its women listeners to think about their own "time management" issues:

> Interviewer: Most of the time in this context [of family and work ob-
> ligations], when someone is complaining, when she says that she just
> won't manage something in time, or doesn't have time for something,
> in fact she's really just making excuses and blaming her lack of time.
> Do you think this is really just a question of time?
>
> Dana: Well, on the one hand it could be a question of time. But time,
> there are 24 hours in the day, time can be used better. You can't blame
> everything on time. In my opinion at least ... Maybe it would help to
> be more organized, more persevering, not to be a lazy person.[19]

The expectation that women should work themselves to the bone—and that this best defined them as women—was reflected not just within the official culture at large but similarly in the unofficial world of dissent, which for the most part was an exclusively male club. For example, in a 1983 debate carried out on the pages of a respected Czech samizdat journal, *Obsah* (Contents), the dissident and literary critic Jan Trefulka argued (seriously it seems) that women's very industriousness barred them from the pantheon of great writers:

> Of course I don't really think that women's and men's intelligence and
> creativity, psychology and abilities differ much at all. But the truth
> is also that women are differently directed in life, they always have
> more to do, and so they develop certain characteristics—for instance,
> industriousness, diligence, endurance, the ability to withstand some
> sort of mechanical work—which are for them indispensable in ev-
> eryday life, but I would say quite disadvantageous when it comes to
> literary work.

Being forced by society to be industrious, Trefulka speculated, once a woman does have time later in life, "the pen appears in her hand as the knitting needle once appeared in her grandmother's hand." And so she writes and writes, "but about things she doesn't really know anything about, for which she doesn't have the ability, she writes without really having to think about it or feel it, basically only so she can amuse herself, chat, lecture someone or pass on some juicy gossip." Men are better creators, Trefulka concludes, because "laziness is the best safeguard against bad literature— and blessed laziness unfortunately is missing even from most of the smart and otherwise good female authors."[20] When it came to this issue, at least, the world according to the political dissidents did not differ so much from the world according to the Communist Party: a woman was defined—for better or worse, seriously or not—by her willingness (or unwillingness) to work tirelessly.

Normalization's Desires

The drudgery of this double burden, as Marie the tram driver demonstrated so eloquently, left little room for desire. And yet *The Woman Behind the Counter* was filled with things to desire. The setting of the television serial was an ultramodern supermarket in which everything one lusted for in socialist Czechoslovakia existed and was forever available. Food was not only desirable in late socialism but was also a political commodity: bananas were as scarce as political idealism, and a good reason (probably the only good reason) to attend the yearly May Day parade and its mass proclamations of socialist brotherhood was that one might actually find oranges and other sought-after goods on sale there that day. Even the Czechoslovak secretary of ideology, Vasil Bil'ak, among the most orthodox of the normalizers and characteristically uninterested in the superfluous whims of ordinary citizens, understood this. In 1971, soon after the invasion and just prior to the Fourteenth Party Congress that was to define normalization, he stated:

> [In 1948] we had posters in the shop windows about how socialism is going to look, and people were receptive to it. That was a different kind of excitement and a different historical time, and today we can't put up posters about how socialism is going to look, but today shop windows have to be full of goods so that we can document that we are moving toward socialism [*sic!* communism] and that we have socialism here.[21]

Even as early as December 1969 the normalization regime had boastfully announced a price freeze on all basic foods as a way to curry favor with the disgruntled population. The price freeze was subsidized by loans from the Soviets intended for modernizing antiquated industries in Czechoslovakia.[22]

Not only was it not incidental, then, that *The Woman Behind the Counter* was set in a *super*modern, *super*clean, *super*stocked *super*market, but that Anna chooses to position herself behind the delicatessen counter (*lahůdky*) is also relevant. It is a glass-fronted counter filled with sausages, cheeses, and the typical Czech party favorite, *chlebíčky* (small circles of white bread aesthetically crowded with Soviet Bloc delicacies such as salami, ham, mayonnaise-based salads, and hard-boiled eggs), each open-faced sandwich sporting its own special name. In this way, *The Woman Behind the Counter* showcased a smorgasbord of plenty. The food, as much a lead character as the human personae, is fussed over, fiddled with, touched, stacked, caressed, clucked over, and commented on by the women who staff the store. (The manager and deputy manager as well as the two stock boys are male; those who serve its customers are all women.)

The very seductiveness of what is on offer behind these polished glass panels and on the well-dusted shelves is suggested by Dietl's opening lines written out at the beginning of each episode's script:

> Have you ever seen a supermarket empty of people, a quietly resting supermarket? Five abandoned cash registers like gates into a forbidden paradise guard the entrance. (Music full of suspense begins here.) Shelves with canned goods and syrups, shelves lined with packets of sugar and salt, shelves with refined flour, with unrefined, whole wheat, extra quality, farmer's and even soy, shelves with Prague bread, Šumava bread, with rye and small graham loaves, shelves with baked goods of all kinds—all the shelves filled to maximum height, shelves with bottles of wine and liquors, their labels shining, one outdoing the other, while wire baskets filled with milk bottles create a jagged pyramid, beer is stacked all the way up to the ceiling in metal crates, lemonades and sodas, freezer shelves protect chickens, ducks, Hungarian geese, and turkeys. Other freezer shelves are full of boxes of peas, spinach, carrots, and tomatoes, others have fish ... and the bloody flanks of beef, ten types of salami ... pork knees are pale and powerless ... While one glass partition over, piled high, are lemons, oranges, and bananas that announce their *joie de vivre*.[23]

While in the script Dietl called for a voice-over that would not only utter these seductive lines but refer to the sum total as a "paradise," the director instead let the images speak for themselves. In the opening shots for each episode of *The Woman Behind the Counter*, there is no voice-over but instead the gentle strains of orchestral music as the camera, like a greedy viewer's eye, sweeps across store shelves and greengrocers' crates, lingering enticingly here and there, loitering among the plethora of fruits, vegetables, cognacs, and bloodred flanks of meat.[24] Staff and customers nibble and taste; viewers salivate.

Consumerist desire exists and, most important, is satiated in Anna's Prague supermarket. Here, unlike in *A Lady on the Rails*, the setting is not a dream sequence, but is "real"—in the sense that the viewer is to believe it is real, real food in a real supermarket, not a mirage that will disappear as did Marie the tram driver's fantasy of consumerism. This sense of the real permeates despite the fact that, as someone working on the set later recalled, "every morning they delivered deli foods and no one was allowed to touch anything unless it was written into the script. Cheeses, *chlebíčky*, salamis— the only people to carry those out wrapped up in paper were the [episode's] 'customers.'"[25] So while some such items had not been available in stores all day or else had sold out by the afternoon, Anna's supermarket remained fully stocked.[26] But audiences did not seem to be bothered too greatly by this discrepancy: on the one hand, they were used to state media dishing up the hoped-for future of socialism in lieu of the present-day reality and, on the other hand, as was recently pointed out, Czechoslovakia was not Romania, after all, and many goods rare in other Soviet Bloc countries at this time were frequently available in Czechoslovakia.[27] Moreover, the audience must have also gained some pleasure—visual at least—in viewing the ripe produce, the juicy meats, the imported bottles of liquor.

Notably, in this showcase of consumer plenty, women rule over the gastronomical pleasures. But what is key is that they do not fall victim to its excesses (as does Marie in *A Lady on the Rails*); rather, they are there to control and regulate consumption. Consumerism during normalization was intended to be a marker of the dynamic times, as the very existence of such a splendid supermarket suggests. At the same time, the Husák-led government was perpetually faced with its self-made conundrum: having put consumerism and consumption at the heart of its attempts to secure support for normalization after 1968, it could not sustain the tempo of consumerist desire, a quandary which Katherine Verdery suggests determined the ultimate downfall of Eastern Bloc socialism.[28]

Normalization's Triple Burden

Despite the decision to incorporate a modern-day consumerism into the program of late socialism, Czechoslovakia's normalization government still went to great lengths to insist on a distinction—however artificial or fragile—between a "socialist way of life" and a "capitalist way of life." Both included consumerism, they argued, but those who practiced a capitalist way of life allowed themselves to be defined by consumption, whereas those who experienced a socialist way of life did not. As an article in the Czech communist daily *Red Right* (*Rudé právo*) entitled "To Be Does Not Only Mean to Have" explained: in socialist society material objects were intended as a means for one's "self-actualization," and not as an end unto themselves.[29] "Self-actualization" and "self-realization" became official catchwords during normalization, intended to hint at the nonconsumerist but nevertheless fulfilling possibilities of life under socialism.[30]

Women like Anna fit into this model of a socialist way of life (a term that was frequently employed in the media) because as caretakers of both their families and the larger family of socialist society, they were to be at the forefront of moderating consumerist desire and, therefore, of building and supporting socialism. In a sense, this was to be their third burden: they were to rationalize consumption so that it did not overextend into capitalist-like consumerism. This third burden was a sign of women's traditional powerlessness but also of their new powerfulness during late socialism. As Susan Reid has written with reference to Khrushchevist discourses and policies in the Soviet Union, "while attributing to women an ideologically inferior role, [they] simultaneously ascribed to them, in their capacity as consumers and retailers, a particular kind of power and expertise as the state's agents in reforming the material culture of everyday life."[31] More specifically still, she writes, "shop assistants were to be not merely purveyors of material goods but of communist values and behavioral norms, whereby the corrupting potential of consumption might be mitigated."[32] The shop assistant was, in this sense, to be the vanguard of socialism.

Anna Holubová, as mother, divorcée, and counter girl, was the model of moderation and was applauded for being so. In contrast, Marie in *A Lady on the Rails* was a whirlwind of excess: emptying bank accounts, tossing money to the wind, buying more clothes than she could possibly wear, visiting jazz clubs alone. She was a woman filled with consumerist and sexual desires. Anna, on the other hand, is able to manage what is on offer in late socialism. She is able to temper her own desires, despite some significant hand-wringing on her part (which merely humanizes her). The reward for her steadfastness, her untiring nurture of family at home and at work, and her determination to live a socialist way of life are ever present in the polished chrome and glass delicatessen counter, the marble tiled floor beneath her feet, and the freshly cleaned tongs ready to scoop up the *chlebíčky* dripping with salami, eggs, and *Český camembert*.

Unchecked Desire

In *The Woman Behind the Counter*, women not only work hard to regulate the intake of food but also of sex, albeit less successfully. In this regard, the overindulgence in food and sex are analogous. And once again, it is women who must hold the men in check for they are too weak to do so themselves; they are apt to give in to their desires.[33] Certainly the men that surround the women in the supermarket seem unable to control their lust and their hands. Anna has left her husband because of his young girlfriend, and when he finally weasels his way back into her life, with the help of her unsuspecting but self-centered children who remain devoted to their father, he yet again embarks on an extramarital affair. Another character, still madly in love with her husband after many years of marriage, discovers that he is having an affair with a shop assistant in a textile store, and she forcibly brings him back into the home by sending their children after him to shame him publicly for his misdeeds. The deputy manager of the store, whom Anna dislikes, becomes so smitten with our heroine that he tells her he has left his wife and attempts to lure her into his arms; to put a damper on his absurd claims of love, she finally locks him into the walk-in refrigerator.

But poor Anna, so busy putting the brakes on others, finds it hard to take her foot off the brake in her own love life. Anna's love interest is Karel, customer and ideal socialist man; a successful engineer with graying hair, he is also a gentle, soft-spoken man deeply attached to his mother, with whom he still lives. But despite his stellar qualities, Anna at first finds it hard to take the first step, even though she is angry at herself for failing to show her interest in Karel. She is often frustrated by this, particularly when she foolishly lets her ex-husband back into her life and, despite wanting to be with Karel, cannot seem to kick the husband out. When she does finally bed Karel, it is an uncomfortable scene, partially because of the stamp of communist-era prudishness, and partly because of the character of Anna herself: she and Karel sit awkwardly side by side in the small, narrow bed in which Karel sleeps at his mother's, dressed in almost identical men's pajamas—carefully done up to the last button and rumple-free.

But there is another young woman in the television serial who does not abide by these rules, who does not take seriously her woman's third burden of controlling desire. Her name is Olinka and she too works at the delicatessen counter, and is in fact Anna's affable sidekick. Fun-loving Olinka has failed to rein in her desires, both consumerist and sexual. Although Dietl's original script suggested a buxom, vampish blonde, Olinka on the screen is a toned-down version—slim, with black, shoulder-length hair, pretty but not extravagant. Nevertheless, her "role" on the page and on the television screen remains similar. Olinka cannot possibly bring moderation to socialist society, for she knows nothing of moderating her own pleasures. An only child of wealthy parents (she is automatically read as "wealthy" because her father is a taxi driver and her mother is the head of a building enterprise; both were lucrative jobs under socialism because of the unofficial "skimming benefits" they offered), she lives in a villa, and does not take her job at the supermarket seriously because she fully expects to quit it as soon as she finds her man, who will perpetuate her extravagant lifestyle and consumerist value system. She is an appealing character, however, adored by her fellow staff; she is the "happy hooker" that everyone loves to love.

Much to her colleagues' surprise, Olinka finally finds her man—also a much-prized engineer, but significantly older than she, and decidedly unattractive. In fact, he looks as if he had just stepped out of a Central Committee meeting. Wedding plans proceed, but Olinka continues dating her biker boyfriend, Fany. Olinka has her last date with him a few days before the wedding day. Feeling rejected, Fany follows her wedding convoy back to her parent's villa, barges in, and makes a scene during the wedding lunch. Olinka's mother shouts at him to behave himself and lists the purchase price of the objects that he is in danger of knocking over any minute with his drunken antics. Fany indicates to her that he could not care less. Finally, he charges up to Olinka and plants on her a passionate kiss, which she returns. To appease her new husband, Olinka then offers him her chaste cheek to be kissed.

But despite this ambiguous start, postmarriage Olinka is a changed woman, a socialist Stepford wife. She has thrown her lot in with the balding communist man and not with the aged biker in his Bambi-brown leather jacket who stormed into her villa. Olinka now wants to attend courses to increase her qualifications, has every intention of keeping her job, and makes frequent jabs at her money-grabbing side of the family. She has rejected their consumerist values in favor of wholesome socialist ideals (represented by her new husband) rather than rebel-like, negative attitudes (represented by Fany, and disdained by the state as much if not more than mad consumerism).

Anna Holubová/Jiřina Švorcová

In 1977 Anna Holubová, delicatessen counter girl, was normalization's heroine. But earlier that very same year Jiřina Švorcová, the actress who played Anna, had been normalization's heroine in a yet more official sense. In January 1977 the normalization leadership first received word that Václav Havel, along with some other fellow political dissidents, was organizing an oppositional group called Charter 77. Upon learning of this, Secretary of Ideology Vasil Bil'ak informed his fellow Politburo members that most likely tens of thousands of Czechoslovak citizens, perhaps even hundreds of thousands, would sign their names to the Charter.[34] No such thing happened. But in anticipation, the regime organized its own official protest, the so-called Anti-Charter rally (Anti-Charta), and Jiřina Švorcová (soon to be "Anna"), as head of the Artists' Union, was called on to lead it.

The Anti-Charter was the largest and most formative of public political spectacles to take place in the period between the 1968 invasion and the 1989 "Velvet Revolution." In a move that was unusually shrewd, the regime trotted out the nation's film, theater, and television entertainers and publicly called upon them to condemn the dissidents. This enormous gathering of the nation's celebrities and popular culture icons in Prague's gilded National Theater was televised live. As participants entered the theater, television cameras swept across the arena, cataloging attendees, neatly linking them to normalization in the most public manner. Some of those sitting in the National Theater saw their participation as yet another meaningless gesture of loyalty toward a regime that fiercely demanded it; others sat sheepishly in their seats, ashamed and embarrassed; and a few genuinely believed in the rally and its message.

Actress Jiřina Švorcová, as head of the Czech Theater Artists' Union but also as an ideological "true believer," stood at the podium and read out loud in her well-trained voice the gathering's declaration of censure against the Charter 77 signatories: "Thus we will hold in contempt those who irresponsibly write high-handed conceits out of self-interest, or who for lowly financial gain ... choose to extricate themselves and isolate themselves from their own people—and even among us here such a group of opportunists and traitors has been found."[35] When Švorcová was finished, the participants lined up to sign a document laid out on the table ("their Charter") that promised, according to its title, "New Creative Works in the Name of Socialism and Peace." Apart from the role of Anna that would come later that year, this was Švorcová's greatest and, for better or worse, most memorable role.[36] She stood before her fellow actors as well as her fellow citizens to curb the most censured of desires—political desire.

Conclusion

Jiřina Švorcová took center stage in 1977 before being quietly moved to the sidelines. But ordinary women continued to exercise a unique centrality in normalization's script. Petra Hanáková points out that while women were exhausted and stressed, their increased workload also "created a sense of omnipotence."[37] Jacqui True argues that although the original promise had been for emancipation via collective labor, now the regime "increased the prestige of private consumerism and [thereby] the power of women within the family-household given its association with consumption and personal happiness."[38] Václav Havel, as spokesman for Charter 77, and Jiřina Švorcová, as spokeswoman for the Anti-Charter, represented a rarefied world in which politics were still black and white, us versus them. More identifiable for the majority of citizens was someone like the delicatessen counter girl, Anna, because her private and public lives and goals were intertwined. Anna never speaks of the Communist Party, of her obligations to build socialism. Instead, it is her double burden of work and family, as well as her third burden of consuming in moderation and keeping others' unbridled consumption under control, that makes her a loyal member of the larger socialist family, of which she is its ultimate caretaker.

Notes

1. Tad Szulc, *Czechoslovakia Since World War II* (New York: Viking, 1971), 194.

2. The goals of student protest movements, East and West, were not as similar as frequently presumed. For more on the difficulties that Czech students encountered in talking to their peers across the Iron Curtain, see Paulina Bren, "1968 East and West: Visions of Political Change and Student Protest," in *Transnational Moments of Change in Postwar Europe: Europe 1945, 1968, 1989,* ed. Padraic Kenney and Gerhard-Rainer Horn (New York: Rowman and Littlefield, 2004).

3. *Dáma na kolejích,* dir. Ladislav Rychman (Prague: Barrandov Film Studios, 1966).

4. Vladimír Macura, "Domov," in *Šťastný věk: Symboly, emblémy a mýty* (Prague: Pražská Imaginace, 1992), 37–38.

5. "ÚV Československého svazu žen všem československých ženám. Otevřený dopis vyzývající k účasti na demokratizaci politického života a k přípravě Akčního programu ČSSR," April 1968, Prague: document reprinted in *Občanská Společnost (1967–1970): Emancipační hnutí uvnitř Národní fronty 1967–1970,* ed. Jindřich Pecka, Josef Belda, and Jiří Hoppe (Prague: ÚSD, 1995), 258.

6. In 1968, already 46.1 percent of the workplace was occupied by women, and by 1989 that number was up to 48.4 percent. At that time 94 percent of women of working age in Czechoslovakia had some form of employment outside the home. (Jiřina Šiklová, "Are Women in Central and Eastern Europe Conservative?" in *Gender Politics and Post-Communism: Reflections from Eastern Europe and the Former Soviet Union,* ed. Nanette Funk and Magda Mueller [New York: Routledge, 1993], 75).

7. As quoted in Jiří Pernes, *Takoví nám vládli: Komunističtí prezidenti Československa a doba, v níž žili* (Prague: Nakladatelství Brána, 2003), 285.

8. Open Society Archives, Budapest: Rádio Praha, "Vysílání pro ženy" ("Broadcasting for Women"); author of the piece, Marie Houšková; February 28, 1974: 1100 hrs.

9. Open Society Archives, Rádio Praha, "Vysílání pro ženy"; author of the piece, Jaroslava Bauerová; November 13, 1973: 1100 hrs.

10. As concerns the normalization leaders and their attitudes to women, it is probably fair to say that these men were openly sexist and felt little need to abide by any ideological notions of equality between the sexes. According to a recent account of normalization's general secretary, Gustáv Husák, at evening get-togethers at his home, and later at the Prague castle, once dinner was over, and as the men readied themselves to relax, light their cigarettes, and pour their wine, Husák would shout out to his partner and any other women present, "And *baby* out!" And "that was that" (see Pernes, *Takoví nám vládli,* 303).

11. For more on this, see Paulina Bren, *The Greengrocer and His TV: The Culture*

of Communism After the 1968 Prague Spring (Ithaca, N.Y.: Cornell University Press, 2010). The Czech scholars now working on communist-era media include Irena Reifová from Charles University's Department of Sociology (see, for example, her "Kryty moci a úkryty před mocí," in *Konsolidace vládnutí a podníkání v České republice a v Evropské unii II* [Prague: Matfyzpress, 2002]); Petr Bednařík, also from the Department of Sociology as well as the Institute of Contemporary History (see "Dějiny televizního vysílání v datech," in *Dějiny českých médií v datech—Rozhlas, televize, mediální právo* [Prague: UK, 2003]); and Šimon Dominik (see "The Narrative Structures in Jaroslav Dietl's Serials," M.A. thesis, Department of Sociology, Charles University, Prague, 2006).

12. *Žena za pultem;* produced in 1976, broadcast in 1977; 12 episodes; written by Jaroslav Dietl and directed by Jaroslav Dudek.

13. ČT APF (Czech Television's Written Materials Archive), Prague: Fond Inf., k. 66, ev.j. 377: "Rozbor dopisového ohlasu za prosinec 1977."

14. *Radio Free Europe Czechoslovak Situation Report/10,* March 14, 1973 (based on an article in *Tribuna,* January 17, 1973). This number is calculated according to the number of television licenses purchased in the country.

15. In 1980, Czechoslovak Television's first channel could be seen in 94.9 percent of the country, and the second channel in 73.5 percent. Jarmila Cysařová, *Československá televize 1985–1990* (Prague: ÚSD, 1999), 20.

16. Zbyněk Petráček, "Jen houšt' a větší kapky," *Respekt* 14 (April 4, 1994): 3.

17. Jiří Peňás, "Pod kuratelou seriálu," *Respekt* 10 (March 4, 1996): 18.

18. According to Dominik, Czechoslovak Television at first refused to spend the money to produce *The Woman Behind the Counter* since they did not think it was sufficiently political to warrant their financing it. The go-ahead came when someone decided the serial would provide a good opportunity to cast Jiřina Švorcová, who "deserved it" for her loyalty to the Communist Party (Dominik, "Narrative Structures in Jaroslav Dietl's Serials," 72).

19. Open Society Archives, Rádio Praha, "Vysíláni pro ženy," February 26, 1982: 11:05 hrs.

20. Libri Prohibiti Archive, Prague: Jan Trefulka, "Odpověd popuzené čtenářce," in *Obsah,* no. 6 (1983): 2.

21. NAČR (National Archive of the Czech Republic), Central Committee of the Czechoslovak Communist Party [ÚV KSČ]: Fond 10/10, sv. 1, a.j. 3, bod 0: "Záznam: Pro 3. schůzi ideologické komise ÚV KSČ" (October 19, 1970) (Bil'ak).

22. Pernes, *Takoví nám vládli,* 293.

23. This description continues at some length in the script. ČT APF, Prague: script for *Žena za pultem,* Czechoslovak Television (1977), dir. Jaroslav Dudek, written by Jaroslav Dietl; Episode no. 1.

24. A premiere of selected episodes of the television series was organized for the Party elite at the Blaník cinema in Prague, with Secretary of Ideology Vasil Bil'ak and normalization's cultural spokesman Secretary Jan Fojtík on the guest list. The November 1977 premiere, as the invitation stated, was being co-organized with the general directorship of the country's supermarket chain, Podník Potravin (Groceries Enterprise). ČT APF, Ve-2 Fond, k. 117, ev.j. 794: letter from the Central Director of Czechoslovak television to Josef Kempný, member of the Presidium and Secretary of the Communist Party Central Committee, October 31, 1977.

25. Televize.cz, http://www.televize.cz/scripts/detail.php?id=22828 (accessed June 27, 2006).

26. Moreover, what was on open display "behind the counter" on *The Woman Behind the Counter* was more typically "under the counter" during normalization—the phrase used to describe the better or scarcer goods reserved for family, friends, and special customers under the counter where ordinary shoppers could not have access to them.

27. Zdeněk Fekar, "Propagandistka za pultem? Hloupost!" in *Tramvaj Načerno*, http://www.tramvaj.cz/021004_M.htm (accessed May 3, 2007).

28. Katherine Verdery, *What Was Socialism, and What Comes Next?* (Princeton, N.J.: Princeton University Press, 1996), 28.

29. See, for example, Miloslav Chlupáč, "Být neznamená jen mít," *Rudé právo*, April 21, 1978, 4–5.

30. For more on "self-realization," see Paulina Bren, "Mirror, Mirror, on the Wall . . . Is the West the Fairest of Them All?" *Kritika: Explorations in Russian and Eurasian History* 9, no. 4 (Fall 2008): 831–54.

31. Susan E. Reid, "Cold War in the Kitchen," *Slavic Review* 61, no. 2 (Summer 2002): 220–21.

32. Ibid., 233.

33. Indeed, just as one could make an argument that Anna's healing process following her divorce hinted at Czechoslovakia's healing process following the Prague Spring, one might also draw parallels between men giving in to their sexual desires and giving in to the persuasive charms of the Prague Spring. The year 1968 was officially re-remembered by the normalization regime as a feminine hysteria that lured the weak.

34. Jiří Peňás, "Držet lyru a krok," *Respekt* 7 (February 10, 1997).

35. As quoted ibid.

36. It needs to be said that unlike most normalization-loyal Communist Party members, Švorcová did not change her political allegiances after 1989, never renounced her earlier ideological stance, and in 1996 ran (and lost) on the Communist Party ticket in the Czech elections.

37. Petra Hanáková, "The Viscitudes [*sic!*] of Czech Feminism" (1998), http://www.cddc.vt.edu/feminism/cz.html: 5 (accessed April 10, 2006).

38. Jacqui True, *Gender, Globalization, and Postsocialism: The Czech Republic After Communism* (New York: Cambridge University Press, 2003), 35.

Chapter Seven

Camping in East Germany:

Making "Rough" Nature More Comfortable

Scott Moranda

In the summers of the 1970s, East Germans celebrated sunny weekends by eagerly flocking to popular campgrounds in the countryside. The flourishing of outdoor leisure, however, comes as somewhat of a surprise; after all, the regime conducted a merciless assault on nature and proudly promoted the collectivization of farms, strip mining, and the clear-cutting of forests. Despite the destruction of numerous rural landscapes, the enjoyment of the outdoors nonetheless became an important part of everyday life—enjoyed by both successful SED (Sozialistische Einheitspartei Deutschlands; Socialist Unity Party) members and grumbling outsiders. Even with the ideological emphasis on urban landscapes and heavy industry under Marxism-Leninism, more recognition must be given to the continued importance of nature enthusiasm within Soviet-dominated Eastern Europe. Dissident environmentalists in the 1980s demanded the dissolution of the East German state, but they were not alone in their concern for green spaces. Rural landscapes remained central to attempts to imagine and perfect East German society even as regime leaders praised the triumph of technology over nature. The manner in which citizens of a socialist state should interact with the natural world, though, remained a matter of some dispute. What role would luxury and comfort play?

One model for proper vacationing was found in Soviet efforts in the 1920s to fashion a "proletarian tourism" that gave purpose to leisure time.

A proletarian tourist did not relax or escape into "pure" nature, but joined official organizations to engage in physically vigorous activities free of consumer excesses.[1] The East German regime, in this tradition, promoted the virtues of struggle and austerity in official free-time activities. Sports and education planners offered sports enthusiasts and youth groups political pageantry, military marches, war games, and athletic competition in the countryside—all to help transform suspect Germans into model socialist personalities. Romantic nature enthusiasm was suspect and bourgeois; nature, here, served as an empty stage for rituals of rejuvenation at a safe distance from the threatening Westernized pleasures of the urban landscape. As the sociologist Hasso Spode has written, the Socialist Unity Party had an ambivalent, but sometimes openly hostile, opinion about camping, which it understood as a "petty bourgeois" and "capitalist" phenomenon.[2] In large part, it was the camping enthusiast's embrace of consumer goods to create an individualistic travel experience that posed such a threat to the regime.

National Socialism had offered its own model for tourism and nature enjoyment that was both similar and different to Soviet "proletarian tourism." Nazism, on the one hand, was more comfortable with individual family vacations; the Autobahn and the Volkswagen, after all, were supposed to provide the "little man" with new travel and consumer opportunities once limited to the wealthy. The Strength Through Joy travel programs (beach resorts, cruise vacations, and day hikes) strove to overcome class divisions and create a unified national community. In an example of "socialism of the deed," Strength Through Joy offered vacation opportunities that had previously been out of reach to workers. On the other hand, Nazism imagined travel not as a fundamental right of all citizens but rather as a reward for racial purity and political mobilization. Outdoor recreation would improve the health of the race and prepare citizens for struggle against racial enemies. First and foremost, leisure would discipline and steel citizenry on vacations that were structured to be free of selfish and "degenerate" commercialism.[3]

In post-1945 Eastern Europe, though, more individualistic vacation practices actually began to flourish. The East German regime thus lauded "proletarian tourism" even as conditions changed on the ground. In postwar Germany, weary survivors rejected mass politics and its demands for sacrifice and mobilization.[4] Even in the Soviet Union, promises of more vacation opportunities suggested to citizens that they would now be able to live the good life after years of suffering and violence.[5] "Wild tourists" began to strike out on their own to enjoy rest and relaxation at undesignated campsites, and they found their excursions more satisfactory than those spent at state-sponsored resorts.[6] Camping vacations were, in fact, part of a Pan-European, postwar leisure boom fueled by increasing automobile ownership.

Given the regime's ill-timed attempts to politicize leisure, the increasing number of community gardens and campgrounds in the 1960s have often been identified by scholars as places where an old-fashioned, even "petty bourgeois" culture survived as a refuge from "Real Existing Socialism."[7] Some scholars, in addition, suggest that the enjoyment of "niche society" hinted at a specifically political, anti-regime agenda. Camping enthusiasts hoped to escape the "coercion of the collective" and carve out independent political space for at least one or two weeks every year.[8] Similar conclusions are reached by Stephen Lovell in his investigation of the relationship between the Soviet state and dacha owners. According to Lovell, the state's vision of a uniform, collective countryside encountered challenges—sometimes even political ones—in the form of dacha communities.[9] Other historians stress the distinctively innocuous qualities of Eastern European vacationing cultures. Paulina Bren argues that Czech authorities cherished dacha life as a distraction from political activism; by permitting private worlds to flourish at dacha colonies, the regime seemingly made good on its promise of economic rewards under socialism.[10] As Hasso Spode suggests, regime leaders in East Germany also recognized that camping served a ventilating function and ensured silence instead of open criticism.[11] If citizens retreated to the countryside to escape political realities, the state welcomed it.

While some campers openly rejected the regime and the SED may have recognized that leisure distracted citizens from their powerlessness, analyzing popular camping culture as a "world apart" from the normal functioning of dictatorship has its limitations. In particular, it erroneously suggests that leisure only mattered when attached to overt political activism, even as it assumes that consumerism was a mindless distraction from "what really matters." Recent scholarship on consumerism in Europe, however, has emphasized consumer practices as part of the history of everyday life and essential to the creation of collective identities and the negotiation of power.[12] Camping did not just serve a "ventilating function"; rather, camping enthusiasts daily engaged in local politics. They criticized authorities, pushed for better management of landscapes, and engaged in letter-writing campaigns to improve amenities at campgrounds. Campers, it must also be stressed, were often career-oriented citizens—not merely outsiders clinging to bourgeois culture or dissenters opposed to socialism. They often insisted on greater (not less) state intervention to ensure social equality and better living standards.

Recreation landscapes (campgrounds, landscape preserves, and bungalow colonies) were thus a product of daily politics and the confrontation between popular expectations, utopian visions, and communal identities (local, regional, and national).[13] The pertinent question here is this: did the camping landscape created by vacationers offer a nostalgic alternative to socialist modernism, or did the built environment of campgrounds primarily reflect the regime's ideological objectives? In answer to this question, I suggest that rather than spaces of oppression, refuge, or dissent, East German campgrounds should instead be reconsidered as unstable and hybrid spaces—both divorced from and intimate with larger social and political transformations. Rather than a distraction from politics, the outfitting of a campground was a way to imagine and even recast an East German collective identity.

Initially, sports and tourism planners promoted "proletarian tourism," even as they clung to older German notions of health associated with social hygiene and eugenics. The countryside served as a realm apart from urban commercialism and a setting for political indoctrination free from dangerous influences. Would East Germany be a community of austerity, citizen obligations, and heroic struggle untainted by frivolous consumerism? As I argue below, however, recreation spaces in the rural countryside largely became cluttered domiciles with many of the comforts and amenities of an urban apartment. Was this transformation a rejection of state ideology? Not necessarily. Even if state-endorsed Marxism did not appeal to many citizens, the welfare dictatorship's promises of equality and better living standards resonated widely. Instead of rebellion or a political obligation, recreation was now a right owed to citizens in a socialist welfare state. What was most remarkable about camping in East Germany, therefore, was not dissident politics or meek escapism. More remarkable was the common assumption (by vacationers, tourism planners, economists) that the state must intervene to protect citizen rights promised by socialist modernism—which included the enjoyment of nature.

As recreation evolved from a communal obligation into an individual right, common assumptions about nature and luxury also changed. East Germany's vacationers ultimately reimagined the German countryside as a comfortable domicile or cozy backyard. In doing so, East German vacationers both built upon and moved beyond previous visions of nature in Central Europe—as a romantic or masculine escape from artificial and effeminate civilization into a more primitive (but nobler) past of medieval and agricultural landscapes, as an incubator of racially pure Aryans, as a stage for political indoctrination, or as sacred nature unsullied by commerce. With constant reminders of West German wealth from relatives and on television, camping enthusiasts chafed at the primitivism and austerity celebrated by nature conservationists, ideologues, eugenicists, and medical experts of various political inclinations. Vacationers agreed with many sport and tourism experts that uncluttered green spaces with fresh air, strong sunlight, and inspiring vistas were essential to a healthy lifestyle. As technological changes (increasing automobility, for example) and geopolitical realities (limited foreign travel opportunities) contributed to an overcrowded countryside, campers bickered among themselves about how to combine comfort and luxury with healthy nature experiences. Some requested greater protections of landscape preserves from all development, but planners and consumers of camping vacations generally demanded that the desires for consumer pleasures be addressed. Nature was by the 1970s less a primitive space apart and more just another everyday space (home, factory, neighborhood, countryside) that should be managed by a welfare state so that citizen rights and living standards were protected and improved.

Roughing It

Early East German sports authorities concluded that hiking and mountaineering promoted a flight from modern economic reality. Yet outdoor leisure nonetheless persisted in the German Democratic Republic. Educators, for instance, tirelessly shaped outdoor leisure programs that downplayed escapism and prepared youth and workers for the great struggle against capitalism. Here Soviet "proletarian tourism," as described earlier, provided a key model.[14]

Another group from the 1950s—landscape architects, health officials, and bureaucrats responsible for planning tourist activities—encouraged the public to enjoy undeveloped natural spaces for the sake of their physical and psychological health. For these technocrats, the SED had failed to adequately improve public health and organize leisure opportunities, and their concerns for social hygiene (the maintenance of public health and well-being) conditioned their imagining of outdoor activities. A therapeutic state, they believed, would create a utopian future through science and social reform. Architects and doctors, in fact, held opinions informed by the pre-1945 eugenics movement—with its stress on improving the health of a nation or race.[15]

Among regime elites, therefore, political hard-liners and social hygienists understood progress in different terms, yet they shared a belief in an interventionist, centralized state dictating popular behavior and managing leisure practices. For the modern, bureaucratic state, consumerism and commercial comforts threatened the ability of experts to control and educate—instead allowing for individual freedom and possibly counterproductive leisure activities. For social hygienists, commercial culture degraded the natural landscapes that offered mental and physical rejuvenation. Both groups, therefore, envisioned enlightenment through roughing it in untainted rural spaces—nature parks, landscape preserves, athletic festivals, or summer camps secluded from urban commercial culture.

The attempt to privilege rough outdoor experiences forced planners to confront the legacy of German nationalism and racism that identified the natural world as a source of distinctly German values. Hiking, after all, had traditionally been associated with the "back to nature" movement of the late nineteenth and early twentieth centuries. In the late nineteenth century, middle-class reformers touted the curative effects of nature outings (especially the powers of strong sunshine and fresh air to eradicate moral degeneracy) to address crises in urban health and social disorder.[16] *Heimat* (homeland) preservation groups imagined preindustrial landscapes as sources of regional and national identity and celebrated a vision of harmonious nature that held the promise of unifying a nation fractured by class and political conflict.[17] *Wandervögel* youth hiking clubs at the turn of the twentieth century encouraged youth to escape the stuffy confines of the classroom for hikes in the countryside and to rebel against the "iron cage" of middle-class morality and careerism.[18] Later, Nazi ideologues and landscape architects insisted that Germany's racial health depended on the planning of pure Aryan landscapes unharmed by Slavs and Jews, the latter becoming key symbols of undisciplined consumerism in German culture.[19]

The growing popularity of camping in the 1950s and 1960s only made the coordination of cultural and athletic programs more important.[20] According to authorities responsible for planning sport and leisure, the increasing number of campers should not just drink, tan, and grill, but be trained in more enlightened and progressive leisure activities.[21] The Ministry of the Interior developed an Ordinance for the Establishment and Administration of Camping Grounds in May 1957 to regulate camping fees and reservations and to establish "rules of behavior" similar to those in youth hostels.[22] In a magazine published by the state's youth organization, editors encouraged experienced campers to form a council at every campsite in order to educate the inexperienced and ensure courtesy toward neighbors.[23] Camping grounds, they believed, could even provide theaters, cinemas, museums, and libraries to properly channel vacationers toward cultural education.[24]

In particular, many experts involved in regulating camping enthusiasm hoped to ensure that campers actually interacted with nature and "roughed it" during their vacations—that is, they left behind urban consumer society. In guidelines for the planning and construction of campgrounds, landscape architects in Dresden planning offices asserted that "decisions about the technical accoutrement of a campground" should preserve the nature experience and encourage athletics.[25] Unregulated camping, they feared, created dens of urban squalor in previously undeveloped natural landscapes—physically harming the environment, breeding unsupervised behavior, and disturbing local residents. By roughing it in unspoiled spaces, they assumed, vacationers abandoned the softness and weakness supposedly characteristic of modern man. A sympathetic social hygienist, for instance, wrote in a tourist magazine, "Civilization, as beneficial as it is, has distanced us from nature to a great degree." "We are hindered," he added, "by our civilized comforts that offer us the greatest degree of convenience."[26] Urban residents, he noted, no longer had any vitality or energy.

Proponents of "roughing it" made a particular point of distinguishing between *Zelten* (traditional German, meaning "to camp") and *Camping* (an English word introduced to German in the mid-twentieth century in reference to auto camping). The critiques of *Camping* fit well into the SED's disdain for consumerism as the satisfaction of false desires nurtured by exploitive capitalist advertisers.[27] At the same time, the focus on roughing it by tent also reflected a belief in state guidance and simplification desired by any modern state hoping to control popular behavior.[28] Architects condemned *Camping* for being too dependent on expensive consumer goods and encouraging "passive" amusements rather than active exercise. Campers, so they believed, did not learn more about the countryside or improve themselves while *Camping;* instead, they "took it easy" and took pleasure in lazy afternoons. Landscape architects in Dresden, for instance, defined *Camping* as *Zelten* with comfort and associated it with bourgeois weekend cottages.[29] The preferred "tent life" encouraged vacationers "to voluntarily reduce their life needs to the basic physical needs"; as a result, "the relationship between the physical and psychic energy would be effectively influenced and a biological restitution would be the immediate consequence."[30] After visiting a Leipzig trade exhibit in 1962, a representative from Dresden's planning offices complained that "the tent, previously shelter for a night, became here a living room; living in nature became life 'near nature.'"[31] With camping trailers, "the home furnishings of urban life could be brought along" and the tent "became a living space [*Lebensraum*], with physical activity limited to the campground and its immediate vicinity."[32] The Dresden architect hoped to return campgrounds to their true purposes—providing a space for vacationers to live "in nature," not "near nature."[33]

Wrapped in Marxist rhetoric, these comments resembled to a remarkable degree the concerns of National Socialists about "feminized" Western civilization and its threat to true German culture. To counteract the comfort of modern life, vacationers needed to exert themselves and shed their consumer goods. One doctor echoed a traditional "back to nature" philosophy of pre-1945 German hiking organizations and suggested, "We must escape

from stimulus satiation, from monotony and convenience. We must redis-
cover our biological rhythm; must unwind and be able to evolve. In short,
we must be active and pursue recreation daily." This doctor argued, "We
only need to compare factory noises, telephone rings, and the clatter of a
typewriter with the sounds of the forests . . . Through the experience of the
calm and the discovery of silence, through the opportunity to get to know
nature better and to become part of the Whole and to feel a part of a community, hiking also forms the personality of young folks."[34] Unfortunately,
leisure planners believed, campers escaped to the countryside for pure
"amusement"—in other words, for the satisfaction of every base desire.[35]
Campgrounds, one doctor insisted, had to be kept primitive; they needed
to remain "sites of relaxation and silence," free of distracting noises—especially music from portable radios.[36] While seemingly "antimodern," such
sentiments could be translated relatively easily into the anticapitalist vitriol
of socialist modernism. Campers needed to learn to live simply or to "rough
it"—to distance themselves from the luxuries and corruption of capitalist
culture. In this way, leisure planners almost certainly influenced by non-
socialist traditions found a home for themselves within a regime that feared
consumerism and attacked capitalist culture.

Making Rough Nature More Comfortable

The regime also realized that it had to build popular legitimacy by creating
more leisure opportunities for workers. By the mid-1960s, the state had
introduced the five-day workweek and paid vacations for many of East Germany's seventeen million citizens, and in 1967 over a million vacationers
registered at public camping sites, with daily campground capacity officially
approaching a quarter of a million.[37] Leisure organizations—from the Culture League to Free German Trade Union League's Travel Service—busied
themselves with better accommodating the millions of new vacationers.
In just one administrative district (Rostock) on the Baltic, the number of
campsites had increased from 15,000 in 1957 to 71,050 in 1964.[38] These
numbers only told part of the story, however; many vacationers camped at
"wild" campsites unregistered with authorities, and a significant number of
business firms and government institutions owned or leased campgrounds
to make available to their employees. Reflecting the popularity of camping, a series of attractive photographic postcards from the 1970s featured
many scenes from bungalow colonies, children's summer camps, and campgrounds. Images of lakeshores and rolling hill country featured Trabants
(East Germany's diminutive "people's car"), motorcycles, and mobile homes
parked right in the middle of a meadow or in a small grove of trees.[39] Such

scenes became quite common; according to market researchers, almost half of all households owned some camping equipment by 1976.[40]

While social hygienists and ideologues imagined nature as a realm of less commercialized and nobler lifestyles, German camping enthusiasts reimagined the natural world as a type of outdoor parlor or living room—complete with modern amenities and small luxuries. Vacationers saw consumer purchases as means for better enjoying green spaces—not for ignoring them. The new material culture of camping owed a debt to new directions in East German economic planning. In the 1960s Walter Ulbricht's New Economic System celebrated plastics, the chemical industry, and cybernetics as the key to creating a socialist modernity that would provide high living standards and outperform inefficient capitalist economies. Scientific planners, at the same time, were given some latitude to put economic considerations and popular desires ahead of political indoctrination to guide social programs. In the late 1960s and early 1970s, Erich Honecker reacted harshly to the proliferation of new programs proposed by technocrats and sought to reassert central control by the Politburo. Yet Honecker also paid greater attention to putting consumer goods on the shelves. In particular, he promised more tourist opportunities for citizens. While Ulbricht's reforms had encouraged creative thinking in how to reform the economy and political system to promote creativity, Honecker now demanded political conformity and ensured consumer goods by taking on debt instead of embracing economic reform. One institution reflecting this new consumer socialism was the Institute for Market Research, which closely tracked consumer desires in East Germany.[41]

Citizens desiring comfort found support among some representatives of the regime as early as the 1950s. The proponents of the modern, futuristic campsite could be found especially among the designers of plastic consumer goods and in offices coordinating the advertising and production of "socialist modernism." For them, social improvement came through science and technology, rather than roughing it. The *Wochenpost* (*Weekly Post*), a popular weekly newspaper, published one such defense of consumer goods in a 1956 promotion. According to the author, "hiking and camping are not always only affairs for the young or the childless. Decades ago the equipment became modern ... Today, family excursions by tent, boat, or bicycle—in short, camping—have become very fashionable."[42] Camping was no longer solely the domain of Spartan purists who carried camouflage tents on their backs like soldiers. In fact, "1956 sees the overshadowing of monotone greens or green-browns by brilliant red, yellow, or blue colors."[43] Modern innovation, the article suggested, led to greater consumer satisfaction and better leisure experiences:

Lady Nylon also goes on hiking excursions in 1956. One can doze
away the next vacation day soft and warm in a sleeping bag with a
nylon lining . . . The outer layer is made out of colorful and inventively
patterned cotton and spun rayon; a rust-free zipper keeps occupants
"fastened tight." These nylon sleeping bags are largely less expensive
than those filled with down.[44]

Developments in the East German plastics industry made it easier and
less expensive to enjoy a vacation; consumers could choose from a variety of plastic equipment for their camping tour. Advising vacationers to
treat nature with care, the newspaper recommended that families regard
the campground as a domestic space—something virtually unthinkable to
many nature enthusiasts, landscape architects, or social hygienists. Mother
Nature would always welcome you, the newspaper suggested, if "you keep
your campsite as in order as many women keep their own household."[45]

The promotions of consumer pleasures such as those published by
Wochenpost became most common in the 1960s. In the 1950s the SED had
tooled the East German economy to produce heavy machinery and focus on
iron and steel—virtually ignoring luxury goods. After Party leader Walter
Ulbricht introduced the New Economic System in 1963, however, it became
official state policy to invest in technological innovation and to direct the
economy toward the production of consumer goods. A belief in "roughing
it" now clashed with the regime's pronounced desire to build a modern, innovative society enriched by its technological progress.[46] Reflecting the shift
in attitudes, the producers of consumer goods notified the SED's sports
authorities of a 1967 exhibition of products that would improve life for East
German citizens.[47] Featured items at the exhibition included fashionable
holiday outfits made from synthetic materials created by the chemical industry.[48] In Dresden at a 1968 meeting of the district parliament, delegates
enjoyed a "Camping Show" that included a fashion show. Organizers displayed a diverse array of consumer goods, including ten different styles of
tents, as well as boats, camping equipment, and beach gear.[49]

When Erich Honecker came to power in 1971, he ushered in an era
of consumer socialism to appease a population increasingly envious of
Western consumer wealth.[50] In the 1970s an Institute for Market Research
thus began to pay close attention to consumer demand for camping equipment. This institute did not always approve of the emerging social divisions
among vacationers (including the predominance of white-collar workers
among camping enthusiasts), but it accepted the growing accumulation
of expensive camping equipment among vacationers with relatively little
criticism. In its internal reports, the institute even suggested that the state

needed to invest in more consumer production to respond to demand. For instance, researchers analyzed spending patterns and noted that most vacationers hoped to one day own their own camping equipment.[51] In 1971 they reported that even though production of camping goods had tripled, consumer demand had not been satiated.[52] Market researchers, designers of camping equipment, and admirers of "socialist modernity" thus modified the vision of an interventionist state; citizens would be educated and reformed not just through austere physical activity that celebrated the antifascist struggle, but also by constructing material worlds that encouraged the adoration of the state that provided such colorful dream worlds.

Enjoying nature comfortably depended, in particular, on automobile ownership. The car had already become popular as a machine for enjoying nature in the United States as early as the 1920s.[53] In Weimar and Nazi Germany, however, a relatively smaller section of the population enjoyed the comforts of automobility. The Nazi autobahns, for instance, were hardly used. Ironically, a culture of motorized tourism did finally develop in the German Democratic Republic, where there were severe shortages of Trabants and other cars. Although the East lagged behind its neighbors in the West, a car-based tourist culture did exist. Parking lots, for instance, often reached capacity early during a holiday weekend since the regime failed to expand campgrounds to respond to growing demand. While many East Germans did not own a car, most camping enthusiasts did.[54] Moreover, the Trabant's poor construction only encouraged more local travel by making long journeys abroad with unreliable vehicles less appealing. In addition, a remarkably large number of East Germans owned motorcycles since they were unable to procure a Trabant, and the cycles were better suited for short jaunts in the immediate countryside.[55] Unable to travel freely to the West, East Germans also could only travel within socialist states. Some tourists visited Czechoslovakia and Hungary, but usually East Germans traveled domestically—crowding themselves into a few popular destinations. More vacationers than ever before in the history of Germany traveled within a small area bounded by the Baltic in the north, Czechoslovakia in the south, the Elbe River to the west, and the Oder River to the east. Natural landscapes within the republic's borders became very familiar to East Germans; the countryside became less a realm of rural values and rugged treks and more a space of short weekend jaunts in regional recreation centers nestled in between a handful of urban "islands."

Some motorists wanted to "get away from it all" and sought out the "primitive" and "rough," but historically a strong counter-discourse among motorists celebrated material comfort, the "freedom" of mobility, and the ease made possible by their machines.[56] Camping enthusiasts redefined

East German nature as a domesticated space, in part, because the car itself had already facilitated "a domestic mode of dwelling"—"a home away from home moving flexibly and riskily through strange environments."[57] With campers trailing behind them or camping equipment stored in the rear of the automobile, the car became even more of a "home away from home." Now cooking gear, beds, and even mobile "homes" could ensure a comfortable domesticity even when far from the city. In East Germany, in fact, families with automobiles began to spend a great deal of money on camping equipment to domesticate their campsites.[58] In the 1970s camping families tended to double the worth of their camping gear.[59] The car ultimately was a machine useful for getting closer to nature without sacrificing comfort.[60]

The automobile also offered freedom from "one size fits all" tourism planning. In particular, camping provided a contrasting experience to vacations at vacation lodgings provided by the Free German Trade Union's (FDGB) Travel Services. At campgrounds, vacationers did not depend on cafeterias with their limited hours, and a family had more flexibility to choose the length and time of their vacation without having to conform to itineraries set by an unseen FDGB bureaucrat.[61] One vacationer, for instance, reported that "the accommodations [at an FDGB guesthouse in the Ore Mountains] in most cases do not correspond with expectations." "Proportionate to the current building structure," he complained, "the rooms are too small, sleazy, and, in sanitary systems, too primitive."[62] A member of the Culture League similarly criticized the vacation lodgings provided to its members. On vacation, he expected "comfort [that], to a certain extent, correspond[ed] to the price."[63] Healthy, enjoyable camping vacations meant, above all, choice, rest, and comfort—all of which could be, in their opinion, better secured through self-reliance. Roughing it, as an escape from civilization, had often been associated with self-reliance, but now self-reliance became linked to greater comfort and pleasure. Primitivism would not lead to a more natural experience; instead, comfort—in making the outdoors more enjoyable—would.

The automobile even transformed the significance of certain consumer goods. A tent, for instance, came to have a different meaning in the GDR than it had in Nazi Germany. Tents at the beginning of the Nazi period suggested warfare, but they also served as ascetic shelters appropriate for rugged recreation in nature. Camping handbooks offered sketches of tent cities to guide organizations in the proper design of a "tenting community" that would effectively instruct young participants in the value of hard work while uniting social classes into one racial community that grew "organically" out of the landscape of *Heimat* and German forests.[64] By the end of World War II, tents and barracks would come to have very different meanings associated with ethnic violence, the horrors of war, and the forceful evacuation of refugees of all nationalities. Under the East Germany of the New Economic System, however, the tent would evolve into a mobile "living room" and even a semipermanent leisure dwelling adorned with consumer goods designed to make the outdoor experience more comfortable and relaxing.[65]

In East Germany, for instance, designers offered increasingly elaborate tents to consumers. While this trend was by no means unique to the German Democratic Republic, East German critics of *Camping* took special note of this evolution of the tent. One architect described new camping trailers as objects "more akin to weekend homes or bungalows. They are only different in the material composition."[66] Designers, for example, had named one structure the "Transportable Weekend Home," and it weighed 3,800 kilograms. Of course, most East Germans could not afford such trailers or even find them for purchase, but even simple tents were becoming more elaborate, according to critics. As the Dresden architects reported, it took much longer to set up these more complicated tents, and as the size of camping equipment increased, the space needed by each vacationer increased (thus reducing the amount of green space surrounding the campground). One architect despairingly added, "A campground outfitted with [small] two- or three-man tents had seven times the capacity as one outfitted with [these] new tents." New designs—with names such as "Dreamland" and "Vacation Bliss"—had multiple "rooms" and overhanging roofs to create a porchlike space for dinners and card playing. The Vacation Bliss tent even advertised itself as a permanent tent that could be set up for extended periods of time.[67]

Many of the material goods carried by vacationers also required more wiring and plumbing than previously "primitive" campgrounds. In response to consumer demand, market researchers now proposed better designs for resorts and camping grounds so that "their furnishing corresponds to the familiar standard of domestic surroundings." Vacationers, in their opinion, deserved access to "heated, running water, as well as separate restrooms." Campgrounds would need to become more than just "tent hotels," they argued.[68] One authority at the Institute for Market Research acknowledged in 1978 that some vacationers desired an old-fashioned camping experience "close to nature," but she clearly considered these vacationers as an afterthought to her concerns about tourists who desired "comfortable auto camping grounds."[69] She wrote, "The majority of camping grounds should be outfitted with modern sanitary facilities and utilities. For a growing number of recreational vehicles, camping sites with electrical connections should be provided."[70]

Reflecting the domestication of nature, camping aficionados made arrangements with local officials to obtain a long-term camping site that they could improve over time and return to year after year. Campers did not explore unknown landscapes, but returned to familiar, cozy environments. When one camping enthusiast discovered that community officials in Zschopau (in the Ore Mountains on the GDR's southern edge) canceled his permit for a long-term campsite, he made a plea to authorities in part by calling attention to the time and money he had invested in his campsite. He had purchased a high-quality tent from a neighbor for two thousand marks. This tent was particularly sturdy and served as a makeshift bungalow, for it could be left at the campsite for the entire warm season and had enough space to make long-term stays comfortable. Subsequently, he gained permission from campground administrators to construct a platform for the tent and even purchased a new paddleboat the previous summer.[71] For many similar campers, camping was thus more than a vacation—it was a passion associated not just with a nature experience, but also with the construction of a second home away from home. A good tent in the GDR cost more than a month's income, and air mattresses or sleeping bags could also break the budget; most campers were willing to spend this money, however, in order to better outfit their vacation experience. Savings, they also concluded, would appear as they used this equipment year after year.

Images of campsites on postcards and in advertising further revealed how material goods redefined natural landscapes as places of comfort and domesticity. In these scenes, lawn furniture was abundant, and families sat around the "dinner table" reading the newspaper while children played with their toys nearby. Tents even appeared to have curtains across windows, and camping families had plastic tea sets for afternoon gatherings.[72] Clearly, not all East Germans had equal access to this wide array of consumer goods. On the one hand, some camping enthusiasts had to piece together their campsites in an ad hoc fashion. Crates, for instance, made good picnic chairs. Better-connected citizens, on the other hand, had bungalows, or dachas, in or around campgrounds; local government officials tried to ban these private dwellings, but at any one campground, numerous buildings appeared practically overnight. Officials could do little to stop this and merely fined bungalow owners instead of tearing the structures down; essentially, the individuals or organization in possession of the home purchased the right to a plot of land with the payment of this fine. Nature enthusiasts, nonetheless, came from all social and political backgrounds, and for almost all of them, an intimate relationship with nature required an intense attachment to certain consumer goods that could provide both luxury and simplicity. Without the option of fairly cheap flights to Mediterranean islands or journeys to the

American West available to West Germans, the East German countryside became a well-used and somewhat cramped backyard "of the people."

Conclusion

While youth leaders, landscape architects, and social hygienists hoped that *Erholung* (recreation or recuperation) returned citizens to physical and mental purity by divorcing them from the comforts of consumer society, camping enthusiasts imagined *Erholung* as a combination of consumer pleasures, healthy fresh air, strong sunshine, and calming vistas. These different attitudes toward the nature experience, however, did not necessarily correspond with political sympathies. The most avid advocates of "roughing it" had their grievances with the SED, but many other camping enthusiasts enjoyed stable careers within the Party. Technology introduced greater mobility into East German life, made new social groupings possible, and threatened state-led attempts to create a new socialist society. Communal identities no longer (if they ever did) emerged only at the factory or in the neighborhood, but also at vacation resorts and among enthusiasts of certain vacation pleasures.[73] In new social spaces, individuals could begin anew and ignore the state and its promises. Campers, however, redefined nature not as an antiauthoritarian space but as a realm for enjoying the good life and modern amenities promised by the regime. Tourism planners and product designers in the 1960s simultaneously worked to improve camping equipment with modern plastics and synthetic fibers as a way of creating a new and better world. The dominant tension between camping enthusiasts and the regime did not evolve from differing opinions on political domination and resistance, but rather from an unresolved debate within mainstream GDR culture. Would the workers' and peasants' society be one of austerity and struggle or of pleasure without remorse?[74]

Nor could one claim that campgrounds only allowed the state to "bribe" citizens with pleasures that distracted them from political grievances. Vacationers often wrote letters to local officials and actively pestered the state; after an unexpected eviction from one campground, one vacationer wrote officials and demanded greater state attention to planning leisure spaces.[75] Vacationers thus engaged in everyday politics at the communal level in order to secure protection for campgrounds and bungalows, and they often vocally pushed the social welfare state to live up to its promises of a comfortable and modern quality of life. In fact, camping and politics often intertwined, but not because camping enthusiasts, as some historians have suggested, were prone to join antiauthoritarian political movements or sacrificed their political interests for luxuries. If gardeners and vacationers have been labeled as "niche dwellers" by historians, it is in part because scholars have failed to recognize that nature was not just a victim of Stalinist economic policy or a refuge from hard-liners; it was also central to how socialist citizens and planners imagined new social and political identities. For vacationers and their allies, a socialist political community was not made of brawny, austere, antifascist heroes but of enlightened citizens who enjoyed nature and the simple luxuries found at their homes away from home.

Notes

1. See Anne E. Gorsuch and Diane P. Koenker, eds., *Turizm: The Russian and East European Tourist Under Capitalism and Socialism* (Ithaca, N.Y.: Cornell University Press, 2006).

2. Hasso Spode, "Tourismus in der Gesellschaft der DDR: Eine vergleichende Einführung," in *Goldstrand und Teutonengrill: Kultur- und Sozialgeschichte des Tourismus in Deutschland 1945 bis 1989*, Berichte und Materialien no. 15, Institut für Tourismus—FU Berlin (Berlin: Moser Verlag, 1996), 19.

3. On National Socialist tourism, see Shelley Baranowski, *Strength Through Joy: Consumerism and Mass Tourism in the Third Reich* (Cambridge: Cambridge University Press, 2004); Rudy Koshar, *German Travel Cultures* (Oxford: Berg, 2000); and Kristin Semmens, *Seeing Hitler's Germany: Tourism in the Third Reich* (Basingstoke: Palgrave, 2005).

4. For more on Germany's particular debates about consumerism, see Michael Geyer, "Germany, or the Twentieth Century as History," *South Atlantic Quarterly* 96, no. 4 (1997): 663–702; Alon Confino and Rudy Koshar, "Regimes of Consumer Culture: New Narratives in Twentieth-Century German History," *German History* 19, no. 2 (2001): 135–61; and Michael Geyer and Konrad Jarausch, *Shattered Past: Reconstructing German Histories* (Princeton, N.J.: Princeton University Press, 2003).

5. Anne E. Gorsuch, "'There's No Place Like Home': Soviet Tourism in Late Stalinism," *Slavic Review* 62, no. 4 (Winter 2003): 760–85.

6. See Christian Noak, "Coping with the Tourist: Planned and 'Wild' Tourism on the Soviet Black Sea Coast," in Gorsuch and Koenker, *Turizm*, 281–304.

7. Günter Gaus, *Wo Deutschland liegt: Eine Ortsbestimmung* (Hamburg: Hoffmann und Campe, 1983).

8. Judith Kruse, "Nische im Sozialismus," in *Endlich Urlaub! Die Deutschen reisen* (Bonn: Haus der Geschichte, 1996), 106–7.

9. Stephen Lovell, "Soviet Exurbia: Dachas in Postwar Russia," in *Socialist Spaces: Sites of Everyday Life in the Eastern Bloc*, ed. David Crowley and Susan E. Reid (Oxford and New York: Berg, 2002), 105–22.

10. Paulina Bren, "Weekend Getaways: The *Chata*, the Tramp and the Politics of Private Life in Post-1968 Czechoslovakia," in Reid and Crowley, *Socialist Spaces*, 127.

11. Spode, "Tourismus in der Gesellschaft der DDR," 19.

12. Katherine Pence and Paul Betts, eds., *Socialist Modern: East German Everyday Culture and Politics* (Ann Arbor: University of Michigan Press, 2008); David F. Crew, "Consuming Germany in the Cold War: Consumption and National Identity in East and West Germany, 1949–1989: An Introduction," in *Consuming Germany in the Cold*

War, ed. David Crew (Oxford: Berg, 2003), 1–19. Recent literature on consumption in the German Democratic Republic is rich, and Crew's bibliography cites many of these texts.

13. Barbara Bender, "Introduction: Landscape—Meaning and Action," in *Landscape: Politics and Perspectives,* ed. Barbara Bender (Oxford and New York: Berg, 1995), 3.

14. Scott Moranda, "East German Nature Tourism, 1945–1961: In Search of a Common Destination," in Gorsuch and Koenker, *Turizm;* Ulrich Mählert, *Blaue Hemden, Rote Fahnen: Die Geschichte der Freien Deutschen Jugend* (Opladen: Leske + Budrich, 1996); Helga Gotschlich, ed., *"Links und links und Schritt gehalten . . ." Die FDJ: Konzepte-Ablaeufe-Grenzen* (Berlin: Metropol, 1994); Mark Fenemore, "The Limits of Repression and Reform: Youth Policy in the Early 1960s," in *The Workers' and Peasants' State: Communism and Society in East Germany Under Ulbricht 1945–1971,* ed. Patrick Major and Jonathan Osmond (Manchester: Manchester University Press, 2002), 171–89; and Leonore Ansorg, *Kinder im Klassenkampf: Die Geschichte der Pionierorganisation von 1948 bis Ende der fünfziger Jahre* (Berlin: Akademie Verlag, 1997).

15. See Young-sun Hong, "Cigarette Butts and the Building of Socialism in East Germany," *Central European History* 35, no. 3 (2002): 327–44; Donna Harsch, "Society, the State and Abortion in East Germany, 1950–1972," *American Historical Review* 102, no. 1 (1997): 53–84; Annette Timm, "The Legacy of *Bevölkerungspolitik:* Venereal Disease Control and Marriage Counseling in Post–World War II Berlin," *Canadian Journal of History* 33, no. 2 (1998): 173–214.

16. See, for instance, Brian Ladd, *Urban Planning and Civic Order in Germany, 1860–1914* (Cambridge, Mass.: Harvard University Press, 1990), 46; Richard Evans, *Death in Hamburg: Society and Politics in the Cholera Years, 1830–1910* (Oxford: Oxford University Press, 1987), 512; Thilo Rauch, *Die Ferienkoloniebewegung: Zur Geschichte der privaten Fürsorge im Kaiserreich* (Wiesbaden: Deutscher Universitäts Verlag, 1992), 58, 189.

17. *Heimat* translates directly as "homeland," but it evokes much more, often referring to a place where one feels at home. In Germany, the nation was often imagined as a collection of local *Heimats.* See, among others, Celia Applegate, *Nation of Provincials: The German Idea of Heimat* (Berkeley: University of California Press, 1990); Alon Confino, *The Nation as a Local Metaphor: Württemberg, Imperial Germany, and National Memory, 1871–1918* (Chapel Hill: University of North Carolina Press, 1997); and Thomas Lekan, *Imagining the Nation in Nature: Landscape Preservation and German Identity, 1885–1945* (Cambridge, Mass.: Harvard University Press, 2003).

18. See Manfred Kappeler, "Jugendverbände in Deutschland: Zwischen Selbstbestimmungswünschen von Jugendlichen und Funktionalisierungsabsichten von Erwachsenen," in *Aber nicht im Gleichschritt: Zur Entstehung der FDJ,* ed. Helga Gotschlich et al. (Berlin: Metropol, 1997). For further reading on youth movements, see John Alexander Williams, *Steeling the Young Body: Official Attempts to Control Youth Hiking in Germany, 1913–1938,* Occasional Papers in German Studies 12 (Edmonton: University of Alberta Press, 1997); Walter Laqueur, *Young Germany: A History of the German Youth Movement* (New Brunswick: Transaction Books, 1984); and Peter Stachura, *German Youth Movement, 1900–1945: An Interpretative and Documentary History* (New York: St. Martin's, 1981).

19. See Lekan, *Imagining the Nation in Nature,* as well as Thomas Zeller, *Strasse,*

Bahn, Panorama: Verkehrswege und Landschaftsveränderung in Deutschland von 1930 bis 1990 (Frankfurt: Campus, 2000); Joachim Wolschke-Bulmahn and Gert Gröning, *Liebe zur Landschaft: Drang nach Osten* (Munich: Minerva, 1986); Gert Gröning, ed., *Planung in Polen im Nationalsozialismus* (Berlin: Hochschule der Künste, 1996).

20. FDGB Bundesvorstand, "Vorschlag zur Verbesserung der politisch-kulturellen und der sportlichen Erziehungsarbeit auf den Zeltplätzen an der Ostseeküste," April 29, 1960, pp. 1–2, Stiftung Archiv der Parteien und Massenorganisationen der DDR im Bundesarchiv (hereafter SAPMO-Barch): DY34 1/293/084.

21. Ibid.

22. Ibid.

23. "Zelten—aber wie?" *Unterwegs*, no. 4 (1958): 1–2.

24. KTW (Committee for Tourism and Hiking), "Konzeption für die Beratung mit zentralen Dienststellen, welche mittel- oder unmittelbar das politisch-kulturelle und sportliche Leben auf den öffentlichen Zeltplaetzen unserer Republik beeinflussen können," 1965, pp. 2–3, SAPMO-Barch: DY34 5968. The KTW noted, "Political, cultural, and athletic life at public camping grounds had evolved very poorly in the last few years." See also Gerhard Wenzel, "Das entscheidende Jahr," *Unterwegs*, no. 1 (1961): 1.

25. Fritz Menz, Deutsche Bauakademie, "Öffentliche Zeltplätze: Anlage und Ausstattung," February 1, 1958, Sächsisches Hauptstaatsarchiv—Dresden (hereafter SäStArchD): Büro für Territorialplanung (hereafter BfT) 52.

26. H. Köntopp, "Wandern und Gesundheit," *Unterwegs*, no. 12 (1958): 14–16.

27. Jonathan R. Zatlin, "The Vehicle of Desire: The Trabant, the Wartburg, and the End of the GDR," *German History* 15, no. 3 (1997): 363–65.

28. James C. Scott, *Seeing like a State: How Certain Schemes to Improve the Human Condition Have Failed* (New Haven, Conn.: Yale University Press, 1998).

29. L. Geyer, Entwürfsbüro für Gebiets-, Stadt- und Dorfplanung des Rat des Bezirkes Dresden, "Berichte und Auswertungen zur Zeltplatzordnung im Bezirk Dresden," December 1961, p. 2, SäStArchD: BfT 50.

30. Ibid., 4.

31. L. Geyer, Entwürfsbüro für Gebiets-, Stadt- und Dorfplanung des Rat des Bezirkes Dresden, "Besichtigung der Camping-Artikel auf der Leipziger Herbstmesse 1962," September 22, 1962, p. 1, SäStArchD: BfT 52.

32. Ibid., 4.

33. Ibid., 8.

34. Ibid., 16.

35. "Diskussionsbeitrag Abgabe Dr. Boye, 5 Tagung des Bezirkstages Dresden," April 29, 1968, p. 2, SäStArchD: Bezirkstag/Rat des Bezirkes, 25664/1.

36. Ibid., 2–4.

37. KTW, Information über einige Fakten der Entwicklung der Touristik im Jahre 1967 in Auswertung der Jahresberichte der BKTW, March 18, 1968, SAPMO-Barch: DY34 5961.

38. KTW, "Tatsachen und Zahlen über die Entwicklung der Touristik und des Wanderns in der DDR," October 22, 1958, p. 2, SAPMO-Barch: DY34 1/293/5084; KTW, Bericht über die Zeltsaison 1965—Rostock, p. 1, SAPMO-Barch: DY34 5967.

39. Erasmus Schröter, ed., *Bild der Heimat: Die Echt-Foto-Postkarten aus der DDR* (Berlin: Schwarzkopf und Schwarzkopf, 2002).

40. Hans Dietrich, "Zu Problemen der Gestaltnng der Freizeit und des Verbrauchs von Freizeitkonsumgütern, 1979, p. 20, Bundesarchiv (hereafter Barch): DL102 1266.

41. Renate Graefe and Annelies Albrecht, "Ergebnisse einer Befragung auf Campingplätzen, Tabelle 9," in "Analyse des Personenkreises der Camper und Meinungen zum Versorgungsniveau auf Campingplätzen 1978," Barch: DL102 1253. Recent literature on consumption in the German Democratic Republic includes literature cited in note 12, but also Mark Landsman, *Dictatorship and Demand: The Politics of Consumerism in East Germany* (Cambridge, Mass.: Harvard University Press, 2005); Eli Rubin, *Synthetic Socialism: Plastics and Dictatorship in the German Democratic Republic* (Chapel Hill: University of North Carolina Press, 2009); Katherine Pence, "'You as a Woman Will Understand': Consumption, Gender and the Relationship Between State and Citizenry in the GDR's Crisis of 17 June 1953," *German History* 19, no. 2 (2001): 218–52; Ina Merkel, "Consumer Culture in the GDR, or How the Struggle for Antimodernity Was Lost on the Battleground of Consumer Culture," in *Getting and Spending: European and American Consumer Societies in the Twentieth Century,* ed. Susan Strasser, Charles McGovern, and Matthias Judt (Cambridge, Eng.: Cambridge University Press, 1998); Ina Merkel, "Der aufhaltsame Aufbruch in die Konsumgesellschaft," in Ina Merkel and Felix Mühlberg, *Wunderwirtschaft: DDR-Konsumkultur in den 60er Jahren,* ed. Neue Gesellschaft für Bildende Kunst (Cologne: Böhlau, 1996); Ina Merkel, *Utopie und Bedürfnis: Die Geschichte der Konsumkultur in der DDR* (Cologne: Böhlau, 1999).

42. "Zelten und Wandern mit Kind und Kegel," *Wochenpost,* no. 29 (1956): 14.

43. Ibid.

44. Ibid.

45. Ibid.

46. For a discussion of plastics and technology in the GDR, see Rubin, *Synthetic Socialism,* as well as Raymond G. Stokes, "Plastics and the New Society: The German Democratic Republic in the 1950s and 1960s," in *Style and Socialism: Modernity and Material Culture in Post-War Eastern Europe,* ed. Susan E. Reid and David Crowley (Oxford and New York: Berg, 2000).

47. Memo from Abteilung Leicht, Lebensmittel und Bezirksgeleitete Industrie to Hellmann, Abteilung Sport, "Hinweise für die Ausstellung neu und weiterentwickelter Konsumgüter zum VII Parteitag der SED," 1967, p. 1, SAPMO-Barch: DY30 IV A 2/18/14.

48. Ibid., 3.

49. "Campingschau," 5 Tagung des Bezirkstages Dresden, April 29, 1968, SäStArchD: Bezirkstag/Rat des Bezirkes, 25664/1.

50. Zatlin, "Vehicle of Desire," 368.

51. Annelies Albrecht, "Zur Entwicklung des Campingwesens in der DDR" (Teilstudie 4: Prognose der Entwicklung des Bedarfs nach Sport und Campingartikeln), 1971, p. 5, Barch: DL102 629.

52. Ibid., 5.

53. See Warren James Belasco, *Americans on the Road: From Autocamp to Motel, 1910–1945* (Baltimore: Johns Hopkins University Press, 1997).

54. According to the Institute for Market Research, only 14 percent of households in 1970 owned a car, but nearly 65 percent of houscholds at campgrounds arrived by automobile. Albrecht, "Zur Entwicklung des Campingwesens."

55. On the shortages of automobiles, see Zatlin, "Vehicle of Desire."

56. Belasco, *Americans on the Road,* 82; Wolfgang Sachs, *For the Love of the Automobile* (Berkeley: University of California Press, 1992), 160.

57. John Urry, *Sociology Beyond Societies: Mobilities for the Twenty-first Century* (London: Routledge, 2000), 191.

58. Annelies Albrecht, "Ausstattung und Kaufabsichten der Camping Gemeinschaften bei Freizeitkonsumgütern—Ergebnisse einer Befragung auf Campingplätzen," 1978, Barch: DL102 1251.

59. Ibid., Tabelle 2.

60. Sachs, *For the Love of the Automobile,* 156.

61. Annelies Albrecht, "Zu Problemen der Entwicklung des Campingwesens in der DDR," 1970, p. 21, Barch: DL102 511.

62. Letter from H.F. to Abteilung Feriendienst, June 22, 1975, SAPMO-Barch: DY34 10614.

63. Letter from G.L. to the Kulturbund, July 26, 1961, SAPMO-Barch: DY27 3465.

64. Walter Riem, *Deutsches Lagerhandbuch: Gesamtband* (Potsdam: Der Weisse Ritter Verlag, 1926).

65. Such a biography of the tent reflects the approaches to material culture and consumer society advocated by Kopytoff in his call for a social biography of things that should lead historians to study the life of a consumer good from design to production and marketing to consumption and use. See Igor Kopytoff, "The Cultural Biography of Things: Commoditization as Process," in *The Social Life of Things: Commodities in Cultural Perspective,* ed. Arjun Appadurai (Cambridge, Eng.: Cambridge University Press, 1986).

66. L. Geyer, Entwürfsbüro für Gebiets-, Stadt- und Dorfplanung des Rat des Bezirkes Dresden, "Besichtigung der Camping-Artikel auf der Leipziger Herbstmesse 1962," September 22, 1962, p. 1, SäStArchD: BfT 52.

67. Ibid., 2–7.

68. Wolfgang Stompler, "Zur Bedarfsentwicklung im Freizeittourismus der DDR Bevölkerung bis zum Jahre 1990," 1976, p. 34, Barch: DL102 1069.

69. Graefe and Albrecht, "Ergebnisse einer Befragung auf Campingplätzen, Tabelle 9."

70. Peter Stöckmann and Annelies Albrecht, "Tendenzen der Entwicklung der Urlaubs und Reisetätigkeit und der damit verbundenen Geldausgaben der Bevölkerung für Waren und Leistungen," 1978, pp. 24 and 36, Barch: DL102 1252.

71. Letter of complaint from H.R., February 12, 1973, Kreisarchiv Marienberg-Zschopau (hereafter KarchMZ): 6117.

72. See Annette Kaminsky, *Kaufrausch: Die Geschichte der ostdeutschen Versandhäuser* (Berlin: Ch. Links, 1998); Annette Kaminsky, *Illustrierte Konsumgeschichte der DDR* (Erfurt: Landeszentrale für politische Bildung Thüringen, 1999); Erasmus Schröter, ed., *Bild der Heimat: Die Echt-Foto-Postkarten aus der DDR* (Berlin: Schwarzkopf und Schwarzkopf, 2002).

73. On new social identities based on leisure, see Urry, *Sociology Beyond Societies;* and Rudy Koshar, "Germans at the Wheel: Cars and Leisure Travel in Interwar Germany," in *Histories of Leisure,* ed. Rudy Koshar (Oxford and New York: Berg, 2002).

74. The slogan "pleasure without remorse" could be found in West German advertisements in the 1950s and summed up the attractions of West Germany both to its own citizens and to envious East Germans across the border.

75. Letter from M.T. to VEB Naherholung, February 18, 1973, KarchMZ: 6117.

Cover of *Das Magazin*, December 1973, with an illustration by Werner Klemke

The flip side of East German pricing policy was that such "luxuries" were sold for extremely high prices. In 1989 a color television cost 5,297 marks—six months' wages for the average worker.[6] Elevated prices offered a means of subsidizing the five-pfennig bread roll and other basic goods, as well as a way of gaining access to the millions of marks in savings squirreled away by the population; but they were also a reflection of the regime's priorities. In describing state socialist economies János Kornai has written: "The leaders of the economy believe they know what is really good for the consumers better than the consumers themselves; they are ready to defend them from their own faulty consumer decisions."[7] The goods that were cheap and plentiful were those that were considered necessary for work—a roof over one's head, bread, potatoes, margarine, cigarettes, a tram ticket. Certain other goods, such as books, newspapers, and theater tickets, were considered to be culturally or politically worthy of subsidy. But prices remained high for products which were not essential to a worker's existence—butter, coffee, and cars.

The paternalist efforts of the state to encourage consumers to buy useful and functional goods which would make them better workers and socialist citizens were not always appreciated. Long waits for cars, televisions, and telephones added insult to injury.[8] High prices, combined with scarcity, led to similarly high levels of frustration and grievance. Demands for luxury goods were not an issue with which the Party leadership had much patience. Schooled in the Stalinist ranks of the Weimar-era communist movement, and with the sacrifices of the Nazi period ever fresh in their minds, the old communists of the Politburo instinctively felt more at home with work and necessity than leisure and luxury. Nevertheless, the question of consumption was not one the regime was able to escape.[9] The worst crisis of communist rule, the workers' uprising of June 1953, was triggered by a simultaneous hike of work norms and prices, and brought the regime to the point of collapse. Eight years later, the Berlin Wall was built as a direct response to the migration of millions of workers to the higher wages and living standards of the West. Ignoring consumers' demands was simply not an option. Concerted efforts in the 1960s and 1970s to make life under communism more attractive included opening specialist shops which sold luxury goods, often imported from the West, at vastly inflated prices. Exquisit shops stocked fashionable clothes, and the Delikat chain specialized in luxury foods such as Western coffee and jam. Most contradictory of all were the Intershops, which only accepted Western currency. At first they were open solely to foreign visitors, but demands from the general public that they too be allowed to spend hard currency sent to them from the West led to the opening of the Intershops to all East Germans in the 1970s.[10] The hypocrisy of this was unmissable: the regime asked its loyal adherents to break off contact with relatives in the West, but rewarded those who did not with access to Nescafé and Nutella.

Like the hard currency gold mine of the Intershops, the production of erotic goods played a role in holding together the East German economy, and also provides a telling example of the confused nature of socialist policy toward consumption. Not only did erotica raise difficult questions about the influence of the West and equality of access to consumer goods, but it combined them with the equally knotty subject of sex. The production of socialist erotica demonstrates how far the regime was prepared to go to provide the population with the goods they desired.[11] While claiming that pornography was anathema to socialism, the authorities authorized the printing of nude photographs both for export and for the domestic market. As we shall see, this gulf between moral rhetoric and economic policy quickly became an open secret.

Following the repressive line taken by the Soviets since the 1930s, early East German policy toward sex and the body was deeply conservative.[12] Abortions were difficult to obtain legally, prostitution and adultery were frowned upon, the ban on homosexuality was zealously implemented, and attempts were made to ban nudism.[13] This brand of reproductive heterosexuality was handed down from the highest levels. Walter Ulbricht's Ten Commandments of Socialist Ethics and Morals in 1958 left little doubt as to how citizens should lead their lives. "You should live cleanly and decently and respect your family," thundered commandment number nine.[14] The regime condemned Western pornography and erotica as bourgeois, decadent, and reactionary. During the early Cold War, pinups, striptease, and prostitution were portrayed as typical of an Americanized, profit-oriented West German sexuality, which was contrasted with the healthy sexuality of the East, based around marriage and childbearing.[15]

The capitalist exploitation of vulnerable women fitted neatly into a Cold War narrative of capitalist brutality versus socialist humanity. An article published in 1952 claimed that nude photographs were used by American magazines to distract the population from the horrors of the war in Korea.[16] This was "the Strength Through Joy tradition in American portions," concluded the author, underlining not only East Germany's moral superiority to its Cold War rival, but its antifascist credentials too. The Western sexual revolution of the late 1960s and early 1970s—of which East Germans were kept well informed by the West German media—posed a new challenge to East German propagandists. Their solution was to describe developments in the West as a "sex-wave" (sometimes "sex-flood" or even "sex-hurricane") which commodified sex and nudity in order to sell magazines, newspapers, films, and books. "Flooded" with sexual stimuli, the capitalist consumer became a "slave to his urges." The results: "moral sellout, brutality, loss of control, and deformed emotions."[17] Such moral panic could be mobilized against dissenting voices within socialism too. At the infamous eleventh plenum of the Central Committee in 1965, delegates attacked novelists and filmmakers for their "sex propaganda," "disgusting bed scenes," and "pornography," as well as the influence of "American amorality and decadence."[18] As Erich Honecker famously proclaimed from the podium: "Our GDR is a clean state. Here there are immovable ethical and moral standards for decency and morality."[19]

For all its public moralizing, however, the regime consistently used publications with sexual content as part of its strategy to win popular acceptance. Despite their criticisms of West German and American sexualities, the East German authorities had long been aware of the seductive power of sex. Advertisements featuring semi-clad women appeared as early as 1952 and were to remain a constant feature of East German life.[20] But the first specifically erotic consumer good appeared on the market in the wake of the workers' uprising of June 1953. Incensed by a 10 percent rise in work norms, which combined with price increases amounted to a total wage cut of 33 percent, workers in Berlin took to the streets. The protests soon spread through most of the country, and by the afternoon of June 17, four hundred thousand people were involved.[21] The SED leadership was forced to go into hiding, and the uprising was put down only with the help of Soviet tanks. It was clear that a rapid improvement in living conditions was necessary if the population were to be won over.[22] Reminded that austerity and ideology alone were not enough, the Central Committee increased the money supply and authorized the production of more consumer goods, including a new entertainment monthly called, simply, *Das Magazin* (*The Magazine*).[23]

Das Magazin contained little overt news or politics: its specialties were erotic short stories, racy articles about marriage and infidelity, and irreverent opinion polls with titles like "When Is a Flirt More Than a Flirt?"[24] Most shockingly of all, its editors were authorized to publish a nude photograph in every issue—among the only such pictures available in the 1950s and 1960s.[25] But despite its unusual content, *Das Magazin* was far from peripheral or marginalized in the East German publishing landscape. Its initial print run of 150,000 copies was highly significant in the context of paper shortages. Nor were its staff in any sense persona non grata: Hilde Eisler, editor from 1956 to 1979, had been a major figure in communist émigré circles during the Nazi period, and was married to the head of East German radio.

Although it was cheap and mass-produced, *Das Magazin* quickly became a collector's item. In April 1954, just four months after its launch, its publisher wrote to the Ministry of Culture requesting that the circulation be doubled to 300,000 copies. The magazine had sold out in Berlin within 24 hours, and in the Zeiss works in Jena, a key center of socialist production, there were only 50 copies between 18,000 workers.[26] By painting a picture of disgruntled customers and dissatisfied workers, the publisher hoped to persuade the ministry's planners to release more paper—a scarce and jealously guarded commodity in the socialist state. There was, after all, little point in launching a popular magazine if difficulties getting hold of it were going to increase consumer frustration. Nevertheless, circulation was increased only grudgingly and incrementally. As early as 1956, the publisher reported that *Das Magazin* was available only "under the counter" in many places.[27] By 1965 circulation had reached 425,000, reaching its high point of 565,000 in 1981.[28]

What was so appealing about this publication, and how was it able to inspire a level of devotion in its readers that the editors of *New Germany*, the Party organ, must have envied? Despite its low cover price, there was something undeniably luxurious about *Das Magazin*. Few of its articles referred directly to the building of socialism, nor was it oppressively ideological. The monthly nude sent readers an erotic signal, suggesting that socialist bodies could be used for pleasure as well as work. At a time when the sinewy frame of activist Adolf Hennecke was nearly ubiquitous, softly rounded female curves basking in the warmth of the sun were sumptuous indeed.[29] For readers whose freedom of movement was profoundly limited, *Das Magazin*'s features on foreign travel and lifestyles were an exotic glimpse of the unattainable,[30] as one fan described it, "a glass of champagne at the end of a working week."[31]

Das Magazin's popularity can also be attributed to the fact that it reflected how the majority of people chose to spend their leisure time—not working extra shifts or attending Party meetings, but spending time with the family, reading, traveling, talking about relationships, and putting on their glad rags. Even its cookery column was called "Love, Fantasy and the Art of Cooking" and featured recipes for dishes as adventurous as "Lord Byron Rice" (key ingredients: rice, white wine, sugar, cream, and tinned pineapple). This mixture of the exotic, erotic, and the everyday was exemplified by the magazine's distinctive cover art. The prolific graphic artist Werner Klemke produced 423 cover illustrations for it between 1954 and 1991.[32] His trademarks were a black tomcat, which appeared on every cover, and an irreverent, mischievous attitude toward sex and relationships. As early as June 1960, the magazine's cover featured a pretty blonde witch flying through the night sky clad only in fishnet stockings and red high heels.[33] In March 1968, a male insomniac counted Rubensesque women instead of sheep.[34] Klemke's covers often featured blissful couples, whose happiness was clearly based on a strong physical bond.[35] He could be extraordinarily suggestive; the Christmas issue of 1973 featured a kissing couple, naked but for a gold star tied over the man's genitals and a mask tied over the woman's, giving the impression of an artificial penis and pubic hair.[36] Clearly pleased with this motif, Klemke followed it in February 1974 with a cover in which a man, confronted with a naked woman, appears to wear a large pink dildo on his nose.[37] Only Klemke's humor and charm saved such covers from overt smuttiness or official censure.

The openness and irreverence about relationships present on *Das Magazin*'s covers was in evidence in its features too. East German mating habits were put under the microscope in a 1959 survey on flirting and seduction techniques, with respondents recommending the tried-and-tested formula of wining, dining, and flattery.[38] One outraged reader objected to these rather unsubtle suggestions. "What were you thinking of when you devoted three and a half pages to the primitive, kitschy opinions of these self-satisfied amateur Casanovas?" he fumed.[39] Other readers leaped to the publication's defense: "Even under socialism, we don't want to do without love," insisted one man, a phrase that could have been coined to describe *Das Magazin*'s philosophy.[40]

The cultural authorities appear to have agreed. *Das Magazin,* along with most other East German magazines and newspapers, was not officially censored before publication. While all books were vetted by the Ministry of Culture before publication, magazines were submitted to the press department of the SED's Central Committee only after they were printed. If the department's officials were really displeased by what they read, they could recall and pulp the entire edition. This drastic measure was never taken in the case of *Das Magazin,* although the editor was called to the press department for a dressing-down on a number of occasions.[41] On the whole, though, *Das Magazin* was spared the difficulties faced by other publications, such as the satirical *Eulenspiegel.*[42] This, of course, did not mean that censorship did not take place.[43] Authors and editors had a strong sense of what could and could not be said in the socialist public sphere, and self-censored accordingly. If a contributor's "inner scissors" did not trim sufficiently, a more cautious member of the editorial staff was sure to step in. This "censorship without censors" was perhaps even more effective than direct Party censorship would have been.[44] The lack of a safety net before publication, and the dire consequences if a publication had to be pulped, meant that editors tended to err on the side of caution. *Das Magazin,* for example, did not engage with politics in anything but the most gentle manner. Its articles on sex and relationships were certainly risqué by East German standards, but they did almost nothing to challenge the state's emphasis on heterosexual monogamy. Articles that did mention adultery, or extramarital pregnancy, were usually morally disapproving, or emphasized the unhappy consequences of such actions. For all its irreverence, *Das Magazin* published little that contradicted Ulbricht's exhortation to live cleanly and decently.

The nude photographs also chimed surprisingly well with the regime's emphasis on "clean," reproductive, heterosexual sexuality.[45] The typical East German nude was female, young, slim, and physically unblemished, lightly tanned, wore little makeup or jewelry, and was photographed out of doors. In marked contrast to Western "pinups," body hair was not a taboo, with armpit and pubic hair often on display.[46] It was generally agreed that it was best to photograph these "natural" models outdoors, preferably "playing sports and happy games."[47] That way, there were plausible grounds for their nudity, and the viewer would admire the beauty of the human body rather than using the photographs for sexual stimulation. Contexts that might imply sexual activity—the bedroom, group nudes—were to be avoided at all costs.[48] The attempt to make the nude body stand for health and strength, rather than sexuality, had of course important precedents in Nazi art and photography. And there can be no doubt that the "naturalness" of East German nudes, particularly the visibility of body hair, owed something to the conventions of Weimar nude photography too.[49]

In any case, *Das Magazin's* monopoly on nude photographs did not last for long. By the mid-1960s such images began to appear in other mainstream publications, including photographic, health, trade union, and youth magazines. As they became more commonplace, nudes also became more overtly sexual. Whereas early nudes tended to be prized for their natural, outdoorsy qualities, those published in the 1970s and 1980s were posed in altogether more come-hither attitudes, looked directly into the camera lens, and wore heavier makeup.[50] These developments were closely linked to the evolution of Western nude photography. East German photographers, publishers, and consumers did not inhabit a closed visual world: after all, the regular publication of nudes had been a direct response to developments in the West. Before 1961, the open border allowed East Germans to sample the racier side of capitalism. And even after the Berlin Wall was built East Germans experienced West German erotic consumer culture via TV, radio, and smuggled books and magazines. For all their protestations about Western pornography, the East German media too looked over the border for inspiration. The editorial staff of *Das Magazin* had a subscription to *Playboy* so that they could keep up with Western trends.[51]

The "Westernization" of the nude was accompanied by a new openness about the commercial value of erotica. From the 1950s onward, state-owned publishing houses produced pinups and glossy books of nude photographs for the lucrative overseas market.[52] By 1980 this was enough of an open secret for Inge von Wangenheim to publish a novel about it. *The Derailment* takes as its starting point the moment when a train comes off the tracks in a small Thuringian village. Its cargo, books of erotic photographs, printed in the GDR but destined for the Swedish export market, quickly disappears—with hilarious results. Supposedly based on a real incident, the novel sent up the hypocrisy of the Party and the old-fashioned morality of country folk in equal measure, and was a huge success with East German readers.[53] Rather like Werner Klemke, Wangenheim's humor and lightness of touch allowed her to address a potentially delicate topic for a mass audience.

Perhaps one of the reasons the book was passed by the censors was that in reality, East Germans no longer had to wait for a train to go off the tracks—erotic consumer goods had begun to find their way onto the domestic market too. Books such as Klaus Fischer's *Nude Photography* offered lavishly produced glossy nude photographs under the guise of an advice manual for amateur photographers.[54] By 1989, 27 out of 237 photographic posters on sale were of nudes.[55] The East German film industry, better known in the West for its hard-hitting social criticism, had a lucrative sideline in erotic slides for the home entertainment market. East German television got in on the act too, with *Nighttime Erotica*, soft pornography for the late-night viewer.[56] Even striptease, until now emblematic of the exploitation and gender inequality of the West, began to become an acceptable form of entertainment at factory work outings in the mid-1980s.[57] Even the celebrations to mark the 750th anniversary of Berlin in 1987 were marked by the presence of topless "mermaids."[58]

The population was equally aware that erotica was a commodity. A lively unofficial trade in professional and amateur photos ran parallel to the regime's activities, with books changing hands for hugely inflated prices.[59] Amateur nude photography was encouraged by the regime as a legitimate socialist leisure activity, and the results ranged from snapshots from the nudist beach to sexually provocative poses clearly imitating Western pornography.[60] Despite the fact that it was forbidden to bring or send pornography into the country, East Germans and their West German relatives went to great lengths to smuggle *Playboy* and other erotic goods across the border.[61] By the time the Wall came down, 30 percent of the population ad-

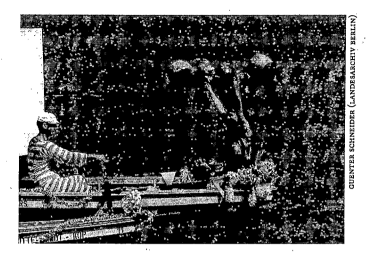

Participants in the parade of ships to celebrate the 750th anniversary
of the founding of Berlin, July 25, 1987

mitted to having been shown illegally smuggled West German pornography
at their place of work alone.[62] Erotica was not only a popular leisure activity but also a means of gaining access to scarce services such as car repair
and plumbing.[63]

As well as pacifying socialist consumers, erotica was also used to persuade them to part with their savings. In 1980 the Kiepenheuer publishing
house proposed the introduction of a new series, the Erotic Library. This
was part of a mini-boom in erotic publishing, centered around classics like
the *Kama Sutra* and Casanova's memoirs. Like the goods in the Exquisit
and Delikat shops, erotica was in such short supply that publishers could
set prices high and still expect an edition to sell out within weeks. The
Erotic Library took the concept of erotica as a luxury good to new extremes. Eighteenth- and nineteenth-century classics such as *The Adventures
of Fanny Hill* were to be published in tiny volumes, opulently bound, and
aimed at bibliophiles. The motivation for this was more economic than
cultural; in fact, the idea had come from the printing works rather than the
publisher's editorial staff.[64] The head of the publishing house also admitted
that the possibilities of the lucrative export market (and the resulting hard
currency) had proved decisive in the decision to produce the series.[65] Crucially, though, these publications would also be available to East German
consumers. The Ministry of Culture and the Central Committee quickly
acquiesced, and the series went into production.[66] Not only did the high

prices of these books (around ninety-five marks) promise a hefty profit for the publishing house, but they were also designed to keep their controversial content away from the general reader. Thus, it was possible to publish much more explicit material than in a mass-market paperback.

But despite the sound financial arguments for the series, the books still had to be justified on cultural terms, both to maintain Kiepenheuer's self-image as a serious literary publisher and to satisfy the demands of the East German censorship system. The publisher's usual tactic was to stress the manuscript's historical, literary, and cultural value and to refute any sugges-tion that the book might be published for its erotic content alone. Nerciat's *The Devil in the Flesh*, a romp through the bedchambers of the ancien ré-gime, was praised for its critique of prerevolutionary society. This book, the publisher was at pains to point out, "should not be seen as the facile sexual fantasies of an aging man" but rather as a valuable eyewitness account of life at the court of Louis XV.[67] Chorier's *The Dialogues of Aloisia Sigea*, a tale of sixteenth-century Italian courtesans, chastity belts, and male prostitutes, had no such political value. The reader's report admitted that it "verged on the pornographic" and that it would be disingenuous to attribute anticlerical intent to the sex scenes between priests and noble ladies. What did justify publication, however, was Chorier's rich and subtle use of language:[68]

But even the publisher itself was not always convinced by such justifica-tions. Roland Links, the head of Kiepenheuer, admitted in a letter to the Ministry of Culture in 1988 that members of his editorial staff had ex-pressed serious reservations about the series, doubts that he himself shared. He could not honestly say that any of the books in the series were "great literature," and he admitted that he had "not yet found an oracle that tells me exactly where the boundary between literature and pornography lies." Links balked at the suggestion that *Josefine Mutzenbacher*, the next book in the series, should be printed in an edition of 15,000 copies, and felt that it was unwise to include it in the Erotic Library at all.[69] Subtitled "The Life Story of a Vienna Whore," *Josefine Mutzenbacher* was unusually explicit. Its anonymous author, the publisher surmised, must have aimed to include every variant of sexual activity. However, they concluded queasily, even then "there is a limit to the number of human orifices, as well as the combina-tions of the sexes."[70] Links suggested a much smaller edition of 5,000, and a retail price of 160 marks, to restrict potential purchasers.[71] By the time the publisher officially sought permission to print, the price had been set at 200 marks, almost one-third of the average white-collar wage.[72]

Links's agonizing about *Josefine Mutzenbacher* neatly illustrates the eco-nomic pressures within the state socialist economy in the 1980s. It also demonstrates how keenly publishers like Links felt the gap between official rhetoric and economic necessity. However much they attempted to claim that they were producing a specifically socialist erotica—literary and aimed at the connoisseur—there was no getting around the fact that their motivation was primarily financial. Pricing potential purchasers out of the market was unusually elitist: East Germany prided itself on its reputation as a "land of reading" (*Leseland*), where literature was available to all. But even heavily subsidized publishing houses were expected to run one or two profitable sidelines. Links himself admitted that Kiepenheuer's erotic ventures had been "an excellent breadwinner."[73] Nevertheless, the profit motive would not have justified mass editions of pornography. State-owned enterprises were more dependent on the approval of their superior organizations—"the charity of the bureaucracy"—than on the market.[74] *Josefine Mutzenbacher*, as Links recognized, bordered on the unacceptably explicit. Packaging the work as a luxury good, stressing its literary credentials, and keeping circulation low was the only possible way to justify it. Setting the price high was supposed to limit its potential audience to bibliophiles and collectors. At the same time, the luxurious nature of the product, and the fact that such publications were in short supply, meant that a market was guaranteed, whatever the price. In fact, the extent to which such pricing policies put the Erotic Library out of the ordinary citizen's reach is questionable. Due to the lack of desirable consumer goods, and the low prices for everyday items, most East Germans saved considerable amounts of money. The small number published was likely to have proved a greater obstacle.

What, then, was luxurious about erotica? In economic terms, it was certainly expensive. In the case of the Erotic Library, the consumer bore the cost, but other products, notably *Das Magazin*, were heavily subsidized. Like all other newspapers and magazines, it was classified as a staple of socialist cultural production, which should be made available to the workers at an affordable price, and its cover price of one mark was never raised. This strategy proved counterproductive, however, as the fact that every extra copy cost the regime money made it difficult to justify further increases in circulation, with the result that consumer demand far outstripped supply. *Das Magazin* was continually oversubscribed, celebrating its twentieth anniversary in 1974 under the tongue-in-cheek motto: "In Short Supply for Twenty Years" ("Zwanzig Jahre Mangelware").[75] Readers complained that the only way to get a subscription was to inherit one—or marry a postal worker.[76]

Aesthetically, erotica had an air of luxury. Both *Das Magazin* and the Erotic Library enjoyed a distinctive and unusual look: *Das Magazin*'s colorful covers, dreamily photographed nudes, and "handwritten" headlines, and the Erotic Library's diminutive size, gilt embossed titles, and fancy endpapers. While the Erotic Library was deliberately targeted at bibliophiles, *Das Magazin* proved surprisingly collectible too. Treasured copies were passed from hand to hand, and eventually bound into volumes for future reference. Readers reported using the covers to wallpaper their homes,[77] and one man wrote, "I collect the nudes, my wife collects the recipes."[78] Both Klemke's *Magazin* cover art and the nude photographs were experienced by readers as a welcome relief from the dominant trends of socialist visual culture and the ever-present leitmotifs of school, factory, and collective farm.

Ideologically, erotica never really shook off its associations with the West, as *The Derailment* mischievously demonstrated. More than that, it made no reference to the worlds of work, politics, sport, or education. The lack of adornment, jewelry, or elaborate hairstyles (stressed by photographers and photographic manuals as crucial to the success of a nude photo) meant that nudes in *Das Magazin* appeared classless, a world away from the everyday politics of East German life. Most unusually for an East German cultural product, erotica did not make ideological demands on the reader or viewer, allowing him or her a rare opportunity to slip the political traces. This space for personal fantasy and escapism may have formed part of its appeal. Unlike the pinups in conventional men's magazines, the nudes in *Das Magazin* and elsewhere were aimed at a mixed mainstream audience, and there is evidence to suggest that readers of both sexes enjoyed looking at the monthly nude.[79] The outdoor setting created an implicit narrative based around good weather, leisure, and heterosexual sensuality. The idealized girl next door could act as an object of fantasy for both men and women. For the male viewer, the nude was a potential partner—young, and a little bashful. But for the female observer, there was also the possibility of seeing herself as the alluring object of desire.[80]

Sexually, erotica made the altogether luxurious assumption that the primary purpose of sex was pleasure, not reproduction. It is interesting that the predominant theme of East German erotica was of surrender, rather than domination. Even male sexual surrender was repeatedly thematized on the cover of *Das Magazin:* on the July 1972 issue, a tiny frogman sits in the palm of a monumental, topless blonde, imploring her to kiss him.[81] Later that year, a cover showed a man slumped in bed, clearly sexually spent, as his statuesque partner jubilantly claims victory.[82] However, although it was possible for Klemke to draw male sexual subordination, it was represented rarely if at all in photography. Male nudes were, to the intense frustration of *Das Magazin*'s female readership, in short supply. Hopes raised by the inclusion of a black male nude in the issue of June 1954 were to be disappointed. Despite dogged lobbying on the letters page, the next male nude did not appear until February 1975.[83] The reaction was delight mixed with disappointment, as the model's hand coyly concealed his groin. Seven readers spoke for many more when they versified on the letters page:

> Dear Magazin,
>
> Showing a man
>
> Without his full span
>
> Is really rather unfair
>
> If you expect the masses to stare,
>
> We seven Saxons hope and pray:
>
> Next time take the hand away![84]

But even such heartfelt appeals fell on deaf ears. The male nude remained a rarity, even as the female nude, propelled by the consumerism and increasing prosperity of the mid to late 1960s, spread beyond the niche of *Das Magazin* to other publications. Photographers and publishers clearly felt the male nude was inappropriate and unnecessary. The female subjects of nude photography were unmistakably passive objects of sexual fantasy. Male nudes rarely existed because they were difficult to fit into the photographic conventions of the nude: passive, sexualized, in thrall to the camera and the spectator. What was possible on Klemke's covers was not possible in the more literal world of the photograph.

For all the regime's rhetoric about gender equality, this world of leisure and pleasure, so self-evidently secondary to the realities of work and politics, was inhabited only by women. One only has to mentally substitute a male for a female model to realize how unthinkable it would have been to portray men in this context. Here the naked body was female, beautiful, heterosexual, and apparently apolitical. With their conservative gender politics, denial of class divisions, and unspoiled rural settings, mainstream nudes were curiously divorced from both the reality and the rhetoric of East German public life. So while these photographs may have been utopian, they were not progressive. It is difficult to agree with Dagmar Herzog that

> these photographs were remarkably tame compared with representations in the West and generally lacked the lascivious look and the non-average bombshell bodies so prevalent in western pornography. Meanwhile the heterosexual male anxieties that both funded and were fostered by the pornography typically available in the West were not provoked in the same way in the East.[85]

The presence of body hair and the natural settings should not lead one to assume that these were gender-neutral or positive images of women. If anything, East German erotica was fundamentally conservative, a reaction against a society where women made up an unprecedented percentage of the workforce, and had a high degree of economic freedom.

Ultimately, the place of luxury goods in a socialist society was ambiguous: were they a necessary evil to keep the population happy, a means of raising revenue, or could they contribute to the building of socialism? Thus, erotica fulfilled a number of often contradictory functions: as a crowd-pleasing strategy in heavily subsidized publications like *Das Magazin,* as a source of hard currency on the export market, as a profitable sideline for publishers, and as a means of projecting a pleasurable, even luxurious image of life under socialism. But as in other areas of consumption, it was unclear whether East German producers were supposed to emulate the West or to provide an alternative.

Thinking about sex was equally muddled. Attitudes toward sexuality became increasingly laissez-faire in the 1960s and 1970s.[86] In part this was an attempt to project an image of East Germany as a modern, progressive state, and to differentiate it positively from its more prosperous Western neighbor. But while openness about sexuality came to be seen as an integral part of a young, healthy socialist society, it was still overwhelmingly conceived of in terms of heterosexual reproduction. Sex manuals and sex surveys focused on penetrative sex within a monogamous relationship. Attitudes toward homosexuality ranged from grudging tolerance at best to Stasi surveillance at worst. But sex, despite its worthy associations with family, health, and happiness, also became increasingly commodified along Western lines, as the regime struggled to keep the population happy. The mixed messages about sex and gender inherent in East German erotica raised uncomfortable questions about the true values of socialist society. Publishers, photographers, and journalists clearly felt a need to compete with the West, but both economic limitations and ideological scruples meant that it was impossible to achieve either the production values or the variety of Western erotica and pornography.

Unsurprisingly, the books of the Erotic Library did little to shore up the ailing socialist economy or to assuage the grievances of the population. Following the collapse of communism, they are now only available through specialist dealers and Internet auctions, where they are sought for their rarity value rather than their erotic charge. *Das Magazin,* on the other hand, has been one of relatively few East German cultural products to survive the transition to capitalism. After German reunification, it experienced a short-lived and unhappy eroticization at the hands of a West German publishing house. Circulation plummeted, but a swift return to its tried-and-tested mixture of features, short stories, surveys, and the obligatory nude has resulted in a loyal, mostly Eastern, readership.[87]

Das Magazin showed that it was possible to promote the values of the regime and win a devoted readership. Luxury did not have to be expensive, and it did not have to imitate the West. In fact, *Das Magazin* was experienced as luxurious because it promoted the idea that socialist leisure time could be pleasurable and sensual too. The East German regime failed to fully grasp the implications of this, or the potential of a genuine alternative to the Western pattern of consumption. It was not the scarcity of material goods that sealed the fate of the East German regime, but its failure to provide a unique style of living.

Notes

My thanks to David Crowley and Susan Reid, and to the anonymous readers of Northwestern University Press for their comments on earlier drafts of this chapter. My research was generously funded by the Alexander von Humboldt Foundation, the British Academy Small Grants Fund, and the University of Bristol Research Fund.

1. Ina Merkel, *Utopie und Bedürfnis: Die Geschichte der Konsumkultur in der DDR* (Cologne: Böhlau, 1999); Ina Merkel, "Working People and Consumption Under Really-Existing Socialism: Perspectives from the German Democratic Republic," *International Labor and Working-Class History* 55 (1999): 92–111; Ina Merkel, "Consumer Culture in the GDR, or How the Struggle for Antimodernity Was Lost on the Battleground of Consumer Culture," and André Steiner, "Dissolution of the 'Dictatorship of Needs'? Consumer Behavior and Economic Reform in East Germany in the 1960s," both in *Getting and Spending: European and American Consumer Societies in the Twentieth Century*, ed. Susan Strasser, Charles McGovern, and Matthias Judt (Cambridge, Eng.: Cambridge University Press, 1998); Ina Merkel and Felix Mühlberg, *Wunderwirtschaft: DDR-Konsumkultur in den 60er Jahren*, ed. Neue Gesellschaft für Bildende Kunst (Cologne: Böhlau, 1996); Jeffrey Kopstein, *The Politics of Economic Decline in East Germany, 1945–1989* (Chapel Hill: University of North Carolina Press, 1997); Elizabeth A. Ten Dyke, "Tulips in December: Space, Time and Consumption Before and After the End of German Socialism," *German History* 19 (2001): 253–76; David Crew, ed., *Consuming Germany in the Cold War* (Oxford: Berg, 2003); Paul Betts, "The Twilight of the Idols: East German Memory and Material Culture," *Journal of Modern History* 72 (2000): 731–65.

2. Ina Merkel, "Luxus im Sozialismus: Eine widersinnige Fragestellung?" in *"Luxus und Konsum"—Eine historische Annäherung*, ed. Reinhold Reith and Torsten Meyer (Münster: Waxmann, 2003), 221–36.

3. See Kopstein, *Politics of Economic Decline*, 198.

4. See Felix Mühlberg, "Wenn die Faust auf den Tisch schlägt: Eingaben als Strategie zur Bewältigung der Alltag," in Merkel and Mühlberg, *Wunderwirtschaft*, 175–84. For a selection of petitions on the subject of material goods, see Ina Merkel,

ed., *"Wir sind doch nicht die Meckerecke der Nation!" Briefe an das Fernsehen der DDR*
(Berlin: Schwarzkopf und Schwarzkopf, 2000).

5. Merkel, "Luxus im Sozialismus," 231, 223.

6. Helmut Weiß, *Verbraucherpreise in der DDR: Wie stabil waren sie?* (Schkeuditz:
GNN Verlag, 1998); Kopstein, *Politics of Economic Decline,* 159.

7. János Kornai, *The Socialist System: The Political Economy of Communism* (Oxford:
Oxford University Press, 1992), 153.

8. Stefan Pahlke, "Warten auf ein Telefon, mit Permanenz und Penetranz," in
Merkel and Mühlberg, *Wunderwirtschaft,* 166.

9. On attempts to build prosperity in the 1950s, see Katherine Pence, "The Myth
of a Suspended Present: Prosperity's Painful Shadow in 1950s East Germany," in *Pain
and Prosperity: Reconsidering Twentieth-Century German History,* ed. Paul Betts and
Greg Eghigian (Stanford, Calif.: Stanford University Press, 2003), 135–59. On pressure from within the state bureaucracy to increase the supply of consumer goods, see
Mark Landsman, "The Consumer Supply Lobby—Did It Exist? State and Consumption in East Germany in the 1950s," *Central European History* 35 (2002): 477–512.

10. See Merkel, "Luxus im Sozialismus," 231–35; Merkel, *Utopie und Bedürfnis,*
243–77. On the Intershops, see Jonathan Zatlin, "Consuming Ideology: Socialist
Consumption and the Intershops, 1970–1989," in *Arbeiter in der SBZ-DDR,* ed. Peter Hübner and Klaus Tenfelde (Essen, 1999), 555–72; Katrin Böske, "Abwesend
anwesend: Eine kleine Geschichte des Intershops," in Merkel and Mühlberg, *Wunderwirtschaft,* 214–22.

11. I use the term "erotica" because it best encompasses the mixture of nude photographs and erotic literature discussed here. Much of this material, particularly the
photographs, could be classified as soft pornography.

12. On the repressive turn in Soviet sexual policy, see Daniel Healey, *Homosexual
Desire in Revolutionary Russia* (Chicago: University of Chicago Press, 2001); Janet
Evans, "The Communist Party of the Soviet Union and the Woman's Question: The
Case of the 1936 Decree 'In Defense of Mother and Child,'" *Journal of Contemporary
History* 16 (1981): 757–75.

13. Jennifer Evans, "Reconstruction Sites: Sexuality, Citizenship and the Limits
of National Belonging in Divided Berlin, 1944–1958" (Ph.D. diss., State University
of New York at Binghamton, 2001); Jennifer Evans, "The Moral State: Men, Mining
and Masculinity in the Early GDR," *German History* 23 (2005): 355–70; Uta Falck,
VEB Bordell: Geschichte der Prostitution in der DDR (Berlin: Ch. Links, 1998); Günter
Grau, "Return to the Past: The Policy of the SED and the Laws Against Homosexuality in Eastern Germany Between 1946 and 1968," *Journal of Homosexuality* 37
(1999): 1–21; Josie McLellan, "State Socialist Bodies: East German Nudism from
Ban to Boom," *Journal of Modern History* 79 (2007): 48–79.

14. *Protokoll der Verhandlungen des V. Parteitages der Sozialistischen Einheitspartei
Deutschlands: 10 bis 16. Juli 1958 in der Werner-Seelenbinder-Halle zu Berlin* (Berlin:
Dietz, 1959), 159. All translations from German are the author's own.

15. *Neue Berliner Illustrierte,* no. 13 (1952): 38.

16. *Neue Berliner Illustrierte,* no. 2 (1952): 7.

17. A. Jaritz, "Die 'Sex-Welle' oder Ausverkauf der Moral," *Humanitas* 19 (1970):
6. See also Walter Hollitscher, *Der überanstrengte Sexus: Die sogenannte sexuelle Eman-
zipation im heutigen Kapitalismus* (Berlin: Akademie Verlag, 1975), 16.

18. Günter Agde, ed., *Kahlschlag: Das 11. Plenum des ZK der SED 1965: Studien*

und Dokumente (Berlin: Aufbau, 2000), 241, 22, 245, 242. It should be noted that the filmmakers and writers who were the target of such virulent criticism were first and foremost political, not sexual, rebels. "Pornography" was a useful smear, but the eleventh plenum was directed primarily against political criticism and artistic autonomy. The SED's quarrel with the films banned at the plenum was not their occasional nude scenes—which were rarely sexual—but their unsparing view of life in East Germany.

19. Erich Honecker, "Bericht des Politbüros an die 11. Tagung des Zentralkomitees der SED, 15–18.12.1965" in Agde, *Kahlschlag,* 241.

20. See, for example, the advertisement for Mildana soap in *Neue Berliner Illustrierte,* no. 12 (1952): 6, in which the model's nipple is clearly visible. For a much later example, see *Das Magazin,* no. 11 (1975), inside back cover.

21. Gareth Pritchard, "Workers and the Socialist Unity Party of Germany in the Summer of 1953," in *The Workers' and Peasants' State: Communism and Society in East Germany Under Ulbricht 1945–71,* ed. Patrick Major and Jonathan Osmond (Manchester, Eng.: Manchester University Press, 2002), 112.

22. On 1953 as a turning point for East German consumer culture, see Katherine Pence, "'You as a Woman Will Understand': Consumption, Gender and the Relationship Between State and Citizenry in the GDR's Crisis of 17 June 1953," *German History* 19, no. 2 (2001): 218–52.

23. Stiftung Archiv der Parteien und Massenorganisationen der DDR im Bundesarchiv (henceforth SAPMO BArch), DY 30/J IV 2/3A /382.

24. *Das Magazin,* no. 2 (1961): 23.

25. There is not space here for a full account of *Das Magazin.* See the memoirs of its former editor, Manfred Gebhardt: *Die Nackte unterm Ladentisch: Das Magazin in der DDR* (Berlin: Nora, 2002); Evemarie Badstübner, "'Zeig, wie das Leben lacht und liebt . . .': Die Unterhaltungszeitschrift *Das Magazin* und ihre Leser zwischen 1954 und 1970," in *Befremdlich anders: Leben in der DDR,* ed. Evemarie Badstübner (Berlin: Dietz, 2000), 432–70; Evemarie Badstübner, "Auf 80 Seiten um die Welt. *Das Magazin* zwischen 1954 und 1970," in *Zwischen "Mosaik" und "Einheit": Zeitschriften in der DDR,* ed. Simone Barck, Martina Langermann, and Siegfried Lokatis (Berlin: Ch. Links, 1999), 189–201; Martina Freyer, 'The Indecent Legend of the Prudish East: *Das Magazin* as Source for Cultural and Historical Research" (M.A. thesis, Royal College of Art, 2002). My thanks to David Crowley for alerting me to the existence of this thesis and for kindly sending me a copy.

26. Bundesarchiv (henceforth BArch) DC9/9028, "Verlagsleitung (Letsch)," Verlag Das Neue Berlin, an Amt für Literatur und Verlagswesen, Abt. Planung und Plankontrolle, April 12, 1954.

27. BArch DC9/9028, "Verlagsleiter Das Neue Berlin (Müller) an Amt für Literatur und Verlagswesen," July 2, 1956.

28. BArch DC9/9028.

29. Hennecke was the figurehead of the East German Stakhanovite movement, who rose to fame by overfulfilling the norm by 387 percent.

30. See Badstübner, "Auf 80 Seiten um die Welt."

31. *Das Magazin,* no. 2 (1962): 3.

32. *Das Magazin,* no. 3 (2004): 85.

33. *Das Magazin,* no. 6 (1960).

34. *Das Magazin,* no. 3 (1968).

35. For example, *Das Magazin,* no. 11 (1975), which showed a newlywed couple

approach their wedding bed, on which the figure of a prone woman was outlined in flowers.

36. *Das Magazin,* no. 12 (1973).

37. *Das Magazin,* no. 2 (1974).

38. *Das Magazin,* no. 7 (1959): 28–30.

39. *Das Magazin,* no. 9 (1959): 3.

40. *Das Magazin,* no. 11 (1959): 4.

41. Gebhardt, *Die Nackte unterm Ladentisch,* 120–25.

42. Sylvia Klötzer, "Über den Umgang mit heißen Eisen: *Eulenspiegel* (eien)," in Barck, Langermann, and Lokatis, *Zwischen "Mosaik" und "Einheit,"* 105–15.

43. On censorship in East Germany, see especially Simone Barck, Martina Langermann, and Siegfried Lokatis, *"Jedes Buch ein Abenteuer": Zensur-System und literarische Öffentlichkeiten in der DDR* (Cologne: Böhlau, 1998).

44. Gunter Holzweissig, *Zensur ohne Zensor: Die SED-Informationsdiktatur* (Bonn: Bouvier, 1997).

45. Evans, "The Moral State."

46. American magazines such as *Playboy* and *Penthouse* only began to depict pubic hair in the early 1970s.

47. Gerhard Vetter, "Zum Thema Aktfotografie," *Fotografie,* no. 6 (1954): 165.

48. The idea that outdoor nudes were morally less worrying was nothing new. As Alison Smith shows in her work on the Victorian nude, pastoral settings were often a way of disassociating nudity from the questionable activities of the "demimonde" and transcending the "urban sexualised body." Alison Smith, "The Nude in Nineteenth-Century Britain: 'The English Nude,'" in *Exposed: The Victorian Nude,* ed. Alison Smith (London: Watson Guptill, 2001), 14.

49. See, for example, Gerhard Riebicke, *Photographien* (Berlin: Galerie Bodo Niemann, 2000).

50. On the commercialization of nudes, see also Ina Merkel, "Die Nackten und die Roten: Zum Verhältnis von Nacktheit und Öffentlichkeit in der DDR," *Mitteilungen aus der kulturwissenschaftlichen Forschung* 18 (1995): 80–108.

51. Brigitte Sellin, the photo editor of *Das Magazin,* interviewed in Uta Kolano, *Nackter Osten* (Frankfurt an der Oder: Frankfurter Oder Editionen, 1995), 37.

52. On the production of pinups in the 1950s, see BArch DR 1/7794, "Jüttner an Volkskammer," March 21, 1958; BArch DR1/822, "Deutscher Buchexport an VVV Leipzig," April 13, 1955. For an early example of a book produced solely for export, see *Internationale Aktfotografie* (Leipzig: Fotokinoverlag, 1966).

53. Inge von Wangenheim, *Die Entgleisung* (Halle: Mitteldeutscher Verlag, 1980). My copy, published in 1985, is the seventh edition.

54. Klaus Fischer, *Aktfotografie* (Leipzig: Fotokinoverlag, 1987).

55. "Das Fotoposter im Programm des Staatlichen Kunsthandels," *Fotografie,* no. 6 (1989): 2.

56. Torsten Wahl, "Zärtliche Zofen," *Berliner Zeitung,* July 7, 2003, 16.

57. Guenter Roessler interviewed in Kolano, *Nackter Osten,* 57–58.

58. Bundesarchiv Bild 183–1987–0704–042; Landesbildstelle Berlin, 289455, 289463, C14373, 289480, 289437. For more on this, see my "State Socialist Bodies."

59. Ulrich Backmann, "Als die Bilderwelten zusammenstürzten," in *Die nackte Republik: Aktfotografien von Amateuren aus 40 Jahren Alltag im Osten* (Berlin: Das Magazin Verlagsgesellschaft, 1993), n.p.

60. See my article, "Visual Dangers and Delights: Nude Photography in East Germany," *Past and Present* 205, no. 1 (November 2009): 143–74. For a collection of amateur photographs, see *Die nackte Republik.*

61. See, for example, Christian Härtel and Petra Kabus, eds., *Das Westpaket: Geschenksendung, keine Handelsware* (Berlin: Ch. Links, 2000).

62. Werner Habermehl and Kurt Starke, *Sexualität in der DDR* (1990), n.p.

63. Günter Rössler interviewed in Kolano, *Nackter Osten,* 52; Backmann, "Als die Bilderwelten zusammenstürzten."

64. BArch DR1/3704a, 480.

65. BArch DR1/3884a, 457.

66. Ibid., 453–56.

67. BArch DR1/3885a, 460.

68. BArch DR1/3884a, 459, 460.

69. BArch DR1/3704a, 480–81.

70. Ibid., 475.

71. Ibid., 480–81.

72. Ibid., 374. In 1988 the average monthly net wage of a worker was 899 marks, and that of a white-collar worker without a degree was 688 marks. Kopstein, *Politics of Economic Decline,* 159.

73. BArch DR1/3704a, 480.

74. Kornai, *Socialist System,* 265.

75. *Das Magazin,* no. 1 (1974): 4.

76. Das Magazin, "Leserpost zum Jubiläum" (accessed March 2004), http://www.dasmagazin.de/content/forum/lesermeinungen.php.

77. *Das Magazin,* no. 7 (1962): 2.

78. *Das Magazin,* no. 5 (1961): 2.

79. See, for example, the letter from an "avid reader" from Berlin complaining that the nude photograph in the previous issue did not show enough of the model's figure. *Das Magazin,* no. 11 (1968): 3.

80. On female identification with nude photographs, see Annette Kuhn, *The Power of the Image: Essays on Representation and Sexuality* (London: Routledge, 1985), 41.

81. *Das Magazin,* no. 6 (1972).

82. *Das Magazin,* no. 11 (1972).

83. *Das Magazin,* no. 2 (1975): 20.

84. *Das Magazin,* no. 4 (1975): 3. "Liebes Magazin, zeigst du den Mann / Nicht mit allem Drum und Dran, / kannst Du ihn auch weglassen, / so interessiert er nicht die Massen! / Wir sieben Sachen hoffen froh und munter: / Im nächsten Heft ist die Hand herunter!"

85. Dagmar Herzog, *Sex After Fascism: Memory and Morality in Twentieth-Century Germany* (Princeton, N.J.: Princeton University Press, 2005), 205.

86. Ibid., chap. 5.

87. A partial explanation for *Das Magazin*'s continued popularity is nostalgia for the vanished sexual culture of East Germany, particularly its ease with nudity. See ibid., 216–19, and my "State Socialist Bodies."

ROPOTAMO, THE SECOND BLEND
VARIETY WHICH FULLY SATISFIES
SMOKERS USED TO THIS TYPE OF
CIGARETTES.

Bulgartabak advertisement for a new "Bulgarian blend" of tobacco in publicity for an
international tobacco symposium organized in Plovdiv, 1965

CHAPTER NINE

Inhaling Luxury: Smoking and Anti-Smoking in Socialist Bulgaria 1947–1989

Mary Neuburger

At a meeting of the communist youth group "Septembrists" in 1947 Georgi Dimitrov, Bulgaria's first socialist leader, gave the following fatherly advice:

> Do not get carried away by superficial, temporary, and often harmful pleasures! I am a smoker and a passionate one. This happened in the last few years. But until 1927 I did not smoke. Septembrists should not smoke! For them there should be a law against it! In everything else, imitate me, but not in smoking—No! ... You should choose healthy pleasures, which increase your physical and moral strength, and not those which harm your health and break your will.[1]

Dimitrov's own "passion" as a smoker was in direct contradiction to his demand for "healthy pleasures" among the communist youth. The new regime's ideal of clean living was in part implemented by closing a large number of bars and other establishments that were known sites of public drinking and smoking.[2] But although the regime in theory "connected the struggle with Monarcho-Fascism with the struggle for abstinence," there were no laws to limit or prohibit smoking—even among youth—in the early years of state socialism.[3] In fact, there was a pervasive ethos of smoking among workers, partisans, soldiers, and the emancipated women that the regime actively courted. Though smoking was and continued to be connected with bourgeois excess, it was also part and parcel of working-class culture, masculinity, and socialist modernity. Far from nipping the admittedly "harmful" smoking habit in the bud, the new regime accelerated tobacco production, as it did other areas of agriculture and industry, and provided cheap tobacco products to the population at large. Tobacco was ultimately embraced as an integral part of the Bulgarian economy and socialist consumer culture.

The production of tobacco was firmly embedded in Bulgarian culture and the local economy by this period, with important repercussions for consumption. From the days of providing the coffeehouses of Ottoman cities to the penetration of Western European interests and technologies, tobacco was not only a local phenomenon but was also emblematic of Bulgaria's connection with the world. In communist formulations, however, its commodification was illustrative of "foreign" and Bulgarian bourgeois exploitation of the nation's precious national resources, namely its tobacco and its tobacco workers.[4] By 1947 the tobacco industry had been nationalized by the communist regime in the name of the Bulgarian *narod* (people or nation). Under state control, the state monopoly, now called Bulgartabak, was extremely successful, and by 1966 Bulgaria was the world's largest exporter of cigarettes, exporting 26.1 billion cigarettes in that year, surpassing even the United States.[5] Significantly, tobacco-processing workers were the largest contingent of Bulgaria's tiny prewar working class and were rapidly on the rise in the postwar period, playing a critical role in the success of the industry.[6] They were among the expanding pool of workers and professionals—a preponderance of them women—who also constituted a growing market for tobacco and other luxury goods within Bulgaria. The tobacco workers, with their much-celebrated history of strikes and participation in the socalled socialist revolution of 1944, were incessantly praised and wooed by the new regime as they had been by the prewar Communist Party. In large part, they were the workers on whose behalf the regime claimed to rule. And did they not deserve to reap the fruits of their own labor? At the same time, under a system that promised egalitarianism and the reclaiming of national wealth, shouldn't all Bulgarians be privy to this national treasure?

Tobacco and smoking in postwar Bulgaria exemplify the complexities of the shifting and necessarily contentious approaches toward luxury and consumption that proliferated under socialism.[7] For the Bulgarian apostles of Marx and Lenin, their vision of a workers' utopia included the promise of streets paved with gold. And indeed "Bulgarian gold"—as tobacco was frequently called—was central to the socialist pledge and possibility of material well-being and even *luxury* for the working class and the nation.[8] Few would imagine that Bulgarian communists would employ narratives of luxury or "pleasures" beyond a critique of "Western" or "bourgeois" practices. Luxury, after all, appears in stark contrast to the values and ideals of communism. It describes not only the "totally unnecessary" but also the lavish, the premium, and even a pleasure-seeking decadence.[9] How could luxury meld with a system that had theoretically annihilated the vilified bourgeois class in favor of an idealistic and ascetic working class? But in spite of seeming contradictions, a positive notion of deserved luxury was alive and well under socialism. And not just in the villas of state leaders and their Party coterie. In theory and in practice, luxury was promised and offered to the working class and socialist society more broadly. Increasingly, the ethos of consumer sacrifice for a socialist future was replaced by the idea of the "good life" here and now.[10] Luxury was part and parcel of the presumption of socialist success and, eventually, the promise of the imminent approach of communist utopia and the socialist society that preceded it. With consumption as one of the most critical battlegrounds of the Cold War, luxury became a crucial part of the socialist arsenal, a growing necessity to bolster state legitimacy and credibility.

By the 1960s the very legitimacy of socialism was riding on its ability to provide luxury, however begrudgingly this might have happened. In light of dramatic social changes as well as growing (although limited) knowledge of the Western "consumer paradise," luxury became necessity in the global competition between political systems. But this shift was not merely in response to changes or perceptions of the West, but rather because of a growing market at home of educated, urban consumers with new modes of leisure and taste, to which the regime felt compelled to respond. Indeed, in Bulgaria as elsewhere in the Eastern Bloc, there was a marked shift toward approval and provision of consumer goods and even "luxury" goods in the 1960s and early 1970s. Cigarettes, in their luxurious packaging and flavor variety, were among such goods, though tobacco sales also provided the revenue for the state to purchase and provide other kinds of consumer goods from abroad. These were the "golden years" for consumerism in Bulgaria (as elsewhere in the Bloc) and these conditions raised expectations for the future, perhaps even more than the socialist promise that "ripe communism" was just around the corner.

But by the mid-1970s and certainly the 1980s, shifts in the global economy required increasing consumer austerity in Bulgaria and in other parts of Eastern Europe under communist rule. Not surprisingly, as luxuries became harder to provide, they also came under increasing ideological scrutiny. In Bulgaria various socialist elites began vehemently to attack "prestige consumption" and "irrational consumption," and smoking was generally offered as a prime example of both. In addition to scarcity, socialist concerns about "irrational consumption" were also provoked by the rising number of smokers among women and youth. While both provided the needed labor to harvest and manufacture tobacco, their consumption of tobacco was seen as morally and ideologically unsound by Bulgarian communists as elsewhere in the Bloc.[11] By the mid-1970s vigorous anti-smoking campaigns were launched in Bulgaria and across the Bloc, with women and youth as prime targets. But such campaigns were in seeming contradiction to the ever-expanding production and supply of affordable cigarettes to Bulgaria and the Bloc. Such tensions were indicative of the conflicted nature of authority under state socialism. Indeed, the debates over smoking under Bulgarian socialism reveal the inherent tensions and paradoxes of socialist rule, namely the frequent clashes between ideology and economic and social realities.

Tobacco After Capitalism

In the immediate postwar years, the focus of the Bulgarian Communist Party was on the rapid expansion of tobacco production. In spite of Dimitrov's above-mentioned appraisal of smoking, he himself was often photographed with a pipe in his mouth and never hid from the Bulgarian public the fact that he was a "passionate" smoker. In addition, a large faction of the Bulgarian Communist Party also smoked and either did not view smoking as a widespread social problem or felt it needed to subordinate this issue to more pressing problems, such as the consolidation of power.[12] Indeed, the state's primary concern with tobacco in this period was to wrest it from the hands of the "fascist" Bulgarian bourgeoisie who had pillaged Bulgarian tobacco during the late interwar period and during the war years in the service of Nazi Germany. By 1947 tobacco processing and cigarette production had been consolidated under the umbrella of the state-run monopoly Bulgartabak. With the aid of Soviet credits that facilitated increased investment and mechanization, production of tobacco steadily increased throughout the socialist period, until by 1966 Bulgaria was first in the world both in terms of tobacco production per capita and of absolute volume of cigarettes exported.[13] By the same year, approximately one million Bulgarians were involved in the production of tobacco, or one-seventh of the total population. In Bulgaria tobacco was king, and some 90 percent of all tobacco was exported, mostly but not exclusively to Eastern Bloc countries. Tobacco export provided the continued resources that drove Bulgarian industrialization, bringing in the needed *valuta* (convertible or "hard" currency) to purchase tractors and machinery and to build infrastructure. From the beginning of the period, to a large degree "Bulgarian gold" was footing the bill for the building of socialism.

In the post-Stalinist era in Bulgaria, there was a major shift in government efforts toward fulfilling consumer demand. In the post-Stalin era this same *valuta* was increasingly used to import consumer goods such as cars, TVs, and washing machines, mostly from within the Bloc, to satisfy the newly urbanized population. In spite of its ultimate "failure" as an economic system—a statement that is certainly debatable—socialism also brought social mobility and spending power to large segments of the Bulgarian population. These changes, in essence, created a "market" for cigarettes and other luxury goods. It was a market that the regime had created, and one to which it was compelled to respond. To a certain extent, as Katherine Verdery and Jukka Gronow argue, the regimes behind the Iron Curtain "dictated" taste to such markets through decisions on exactly what and how much to produce.[14] In part, socialist state objectives to create the socialist man and eradicate backwardness were expressed through the engineering of a modern consumer.[15] But as Sheila Fitzpatrick also argues, since the mid-1930s the Soviet state had promised luxury goods, such as champagne, caviar, ice cream, and frankfurters, to fulfill "the rising demands" of Soviet toilers.[16] In the case of Bulgartabak, the enterprise quite clearly mapped and responded—as opposed to dictating—to the needs and desires of the population, including its desire for luxury goods.

By the 1960s Bulgarian economic specialists began to look for "scientific ways"—including Western economic theories like coefficients of elasticity—to predict and fulfill the consumer needs of the population. All such writings began with a variation of the following presumption: "With the victory of the socialist revolution in the country we were presented with the objective task of the uninterrupted improvement of the material and cultural well-being of the whole nation."[17] Tobacco was prominently featured in a significant number of these works as one of the top categories of consumption in the Bulgarian household budget. According to one study, by 1960 alcohol and tobacco together accounted for 11.1 percent of the average Bulgarian household budget, while by 1970 this figure had inched up to 12.1 percent.[18] In addition, tobacco, unlike alcohol, was reported to have one of the lowest measures of "elasticity of demand."[19] In other words, no matter how high the price of cigarettes was raised, the demand remained constant or actually increased. As one article in the trade journal *Bulgarian Tobacco* (*Bŭlgarski Tiutiun*) asserted:

> Tobacco products satisfy specific needs of smokers. Because of the constancy of demand, tobacco can be compared to consumption of products of the highest necessity. Generally, the volume of daily consumption is about 20 cigarettes. In the consumption of cigarettes there

is no seasonality as with many other products ... They are consumed
daily, even hourly.[20]

With this in mind tobacco consumption was mapped, predicted, and enabled to the extent possible, along with other consumer products. Indeed, in
many ways tobacco consumption was treated as a "necessity" for the modern
socialist worker.

But Bulgarian state goals clearly stretched beyond meeting the basic
needs of the population, for the regime recognized that a "new *modern* type
of consumption" had emerged, with the growing demand for quality non-
food items.[21] With this in mind, beginning in the 1960s the tobacco industry's intent to provide a premium product—an object of luxury and desire—
was openly elaborated. The Bulgarian state-sponsored tobacco trade journal
Bulgarian Tobacco provides the clearest articulation of such a shift. Already
in the early 1960s *Bulgarian Tobacco* discussed in lavish terms the specific
smoking attributes of Bulgarian Oriental tobaccos, which are characterized
by "flavor, exquisite aroma, and good burning properties," providing a "complete taste sensation and satisfaction when smoked."[22] *Bulgarian Tobacco*
also began to boast about the increased use of "luxurious packaging materials" such as metallic cartons, cellophane, and zip-fasteners, which "gave the
smoker comfort and aesthetic pleasure" and "associated the cigarettes with
their renowned luxury."[23] One brand of cigarettes exported to the U.S.S.R.,
which incidentally imported about 90 percent of Bulgaria's total tobacco
export, was actually called "Luks" (Luxe), though Bulgartabak's Shipka and
Stewardess were the most popular brands in the U.S.S.R.[24] The use of English words like "Stewardess" or "Sevens" in branding to imply luxury could
not have been accidental. On its export packs, Bulgartabak often had label-
ing information in French and German, even when the cigarettes were to
be sold in Czechoslovakia or Poland—the primary importers of Bulgarian
cigarettes, along with the GDR and the U.S.S.R.[25] The decoration of packages with Western words and languages would have heightened the association of Bulgarian cigarettes with the West and hence with a premium
product. But such associations were only meant to enhance the perception
of quality of a truly luxury product that Bulgartabak was producing and offering to ready consumers both at home and throughout the Bloc.

As the pages of *Bulgarian Tobacco* claimed, the industry was not creating but responding to customers who were increasingly demanding luxury
consumables. The articles of the journal incessantly referred to the changing tastes of buyers, which they connected directly with socialist progress
and achievement. As the material conditions and buying power of workers across the Bloc had risen, one article posited, "the taste and aesthetic

demands of consumers have risen to a new level, and from there demands
for quality of product and a greater assortment." Note that workers here
have become *consumers* who drive Bulgartabak to stabilize quality, improve
packaging, increase the volume of filtered cigarettes, and introduce different
aromatized tobaccos and tobacco blends.[26] Along with enumerating high
production numbers, the pages of *Bulgarian Tobacco* expressed pride in the
ability of their "highest-quality products with luxurious modern packaging"
to "satisfy even the most capricious smoker."[27] Providing satisfaction and
pleasure—especially olfactory pleasure—were pervasive goals of Bulgartabak, with the aroma of tobacco playing a primary role. Special labs apparently spent decades applying many of the principles of perfuming to ensure
that tobacco would have a pleasurable and consistent aroma and a taste that
would be palpable from the moment the package was opened until the last
drag on the cigarette. Throughout the 1970s and 1980s articles on aroma
and aromatization with synthetic and natural essences—such as vanilla,
cocoa, plum, and fig—were common. As one article ruminates:

> The aroma should harmonize with the taste of the tobacco and bal-
> ance it, so that neither the natural smell of the tobacco, nor its syn-
> thetic aromatic notes, dominate, that is, to achieve a complete fusion
> of olfactory sensations into one delightful perception, more specifically
> in tobacco terminology the "bouquet"... A harmonious expression of
> bouquet is the inherent mark of quality cigarettes and is manifest from
> the first until the last inhale with the same intensity and tone.[28]

In spite of the surprisingly indulgent forays into micro-details of pleasure
and sensation, the industry and the regime that controlled it never lost sight
of the justification and the audience for all of this luxury.

The achievements of the esteemed tobacco workers were the continu-
ous subject of both academic writings and popular culture in this period.
The historical plight of the tobacco workers, for example, was a central
theme in Dimitŭr Dimov's 1951 novel *Tobacco* (*Tiutiun*), the most widely
read and acclaimed—but also controversial—novel of the socialist period.
The novel depicts the evils of the Bulgarian tobacco oligarchy in the interwar and World War II periods against a background of workers' strikes,
with a denouement in the communist victory of 1944. Although workers,
who also participate in partisan resistance, are the real heroes in the novel,
the focus is on the trials and tribulations of the bourgeois characters—
however flawed they might be. Dimov's book was clearly not a work of
socialist realism, but it was published initially in 1951, however briefly, because of its recognized literary merits (in short supply in Bulgaria in 1951).

But the political controversy it sparked, the "Tobacco Affair," was enough to have the novel pulled from the shelves soon after publication, only to be released again after some revision in 1956 and made into a popular, award-winning motion picture in 1961. In the post-Stalinist period, many of the contradictions that were inherent in the message of the novel and the film were clearly in line with the regime's own duplicitous approach to tobacco.

For in the *Tobacco* novel and the film all of Dimov's characters smoke in socially circumscribed ways, with important and ambiguous implications. For the bourgeois characters, smoking generally signifies decadence and decay, a hastening of their death as a class. The main characters, Boris and Irina, are lower-class characters who sell their souls to the devil, in a sense, and become party to the profits and evils of the tobacco industry. They also partake of the excesses of the bourgeoisie, which in the World War II period take the form of opulent parties where they smoke, drink, and dance with German Nazis while locals beg on the streets for bread. For Irina, smoking is indicative of her emancipation, but also of her sexual promiscuity and lost morality; she is eventually married to Boris, but also has an open affair with one of their Nazi acquaintances. But in spite of such clear censure toward bourgeois smoking, the working-class characters in the novel and film also smoke. Their smoking, though, takes on a somewhat different character. It is permissible, part of their social solidarity and ethos of partisanship and masculinity (or, for women, positive emancipation). Partisans smoke, for example, as they perch in a mountain pass waiting to attack approaching Nazi vehicles. Smoking, then, is deemed socially acceptable as long as it is done in the context of productive or politically suitable pursuits. But while the dichotomy between the decadent and the productive smoker seems simple enough for viewers to digest, it is complicated by the particulars of such images. In scenes when Irina and Boris smoke, it is with all the glamour and flourish of Hollywood stars. Though they are fallen characters that the audience is supposed to hate, pity, and revile, they are also attractive, even sexy, and their enticing drags on cigars and cigarettes drawn from elegant silver cases only enhance this image. In contrast, the workers and partisans who smoke are rather rough and even ugly in appearance. When working-class characters smoke, including one female worker named Barbara, it is not with an air of luxury but rather in an atmosphere of utility and deprivation. And although the main bourgeois characters are indeed troubled and meet tragic and untimely deaths, their clothes, cars, apartments, and graceful inhaling of cigarettes is undeniably attractive to the average viewer. Significantly, of all these trappings of luxury, tobacco was specifically linked to the working-class struggle and, in part, was precisely what they were struggling for. The climax of the film and novel, after all, is the socialist revolution of 1944, which set the stage for the nationalization of the tobacco industry. This was now *their* tobacco. In theory, their alienation from the means of production would finally cease with the nationalization of tobacco interests.

As mentioned before, it was the growing needs—or the luxury become necessity—of the worker that remain at center stage of socialist writings, from tobacco industry trade writings to the works of economists. It was in the name of the working class that the socialists ruled, that they advanced the improvement of material conditions, and that luxury was justified. In *Bulgarian Tobacco*, for example, every issue was a veritable orgy of praise for the workers with their "golden hands" fulfilling and overfulfilling production quotas for tobacco. In a column called the "golden page," in-depth biographies and profiles extolled workers from various regions who played a part in the growing or processing of tobacco. In many such stories, workers who had been involved in the industry both before and after the transition to socialism presented comparisons of the miserable days before and the glorious days after 1944. Numerous articles asserted that the conditions of workers had vastly improved, as had their purchasing power, providing pictures of new apartment buildings and kindergartens that were provided for tobacco workers and their families. But such provisions went beyond these bare necessities. In numerous articles there were photographs and detailed descriptions of *pochivni stantsi* (rest stations—or resorts) that were built solely for the tobacco workers, some at the most desirable Black Sea locations. One 1963 article in *Bulgarian Tobacco* guided the reader through the rooms of the recently built "Palace Among the Dunes" at Sunny Beach with its twenty-three rooms and seventy beds:

> Of course on every table you will see various things according to the tastes of those staying in the room—books, fishing gear, needlework, cigarettes, toys, radios, letters, etc. . . . Is this not your house, workers with the golden hands, through which passes the gold of our homeland—tobacco![29]

Because they had hands of gold that produced "Bulgarian gold," workers were naturally deserving of their time in the sun, lounging on the beach, fishing, "playing cards," and of course smoking. No longer exploited by the bourgeois and foreign oligarchies, tobacco, like other luxuries, was now willingly lavished upon one and all. Or was it?

Irrational Consumers

Already by the early 1970s there were some rumblings among Bulgarian
economists about the increased demand and consumption of certain "luxury
and fashionable goods," but now with a decidedly disparaging tone. Instead
of lauding such developments as fulfilling workers' needs, economic specialists merely conceded that the consumption of such goods was "unavoidable." At the same time, as one author explained, "no one can be against
the increased production of luxurious, fashionable, and expensive goods"
because Todor Zhivkov (the leader of Bulgaria since 1956) had himself
ordered their increased production at the 1972 December plenum of the
Bulgarian Communist Party. At the plenum, Zhivkov had reportedly argued that the "market needs to have such goods" and at reasonable prices or
smuggling and the black market would take over, robbing and demoralizing
the population.[30] But in many ways Zhivkov set the tone for the years that
followed when luxury items—including cigarettes—became seen as a necessary evil. As tobacco production and consumption continued to increase,
so too did Party criticism of the many consequences and implications of
tobacco consumption.

   A more decisive shift within official circles on the smoking issue was
clearly palpable by the mid-1970s. As codified in a 1976 decree on abstinence, the Party now slated smoking for critique and limitation. Not surprisingly, health issues were central to the growing anti-smoking literature,
but behavioral and moral questions were equally fundamental, and smoking
as a "fashionable" and "luxurious" pursuit now came under direct fire. In a
1976 publication entitled "Conversations About the Harmfulness of Smoking," for example, a discussant opined:

> Humanity will sooner or later evolve and realize the truth. It will
> gradually sober up in its relationship towards fashion and in its at-
> traction to cigarettes. But it is humiliating and shocking that some
> wait for the ebb and flow of fashion to determine their behavior. For
> everyone it is clearly very hard to reject a vice that one has taken on
> voluntarily, devotedly, and from a wrongly understood notion of mo-
> dernity and elegance.[31]

Suddenly, smoking—embedded in freshly critical attitudes toward fashion and luxury—became equated with a failure to evolve in a sound and
socialist manner. Tobacco consumption was viewed as a malignant though
"unavoidable social phenomenon" explained by urbanization, the "scientific

technological revolution" (on the Soviet model) and other postwar changes in the Bulgarian way of life.[32] In short, smoking was a result of moderniza-tion, but it was also indicative of misplaced understandings of modernity, specifically a modernity that was not on a sound socialist footing. As the aforementioned discussant continued:

> Over time we ourselves will laugh at the absurdity and senselessness of many of today's fashionable pursuits. We will laugh, that is, if we are able to save ourselves from these excesses which the West has brought us. Because there is imitation, which in its most harmful form can only make us ludicrous and ugly, but there is also imitation which can liquidate us as a people and we will be lost.[33]

Smoking then, it is argued, far from being a sound pursuit for socialist workers, is a "Western" practice, connected specifically to the "contradictions of capitalism." Even more damning, these contradictions threaten not just to derail socialist progress but to liquidate the distinctiveness of the Bulgar-ian nation itself.

More and more, both smoking and luxury become associated not with healthy and deserved workers' leisure but, rather, with weakness, conformity, and snobbery and, by extension, the evils of the West. Smokers were de-scribed as having fallen prey to the lures of compliance and pretentiousness as they flaunted their "luxurious imported cigarettes or packs of tobacco."[34] Notably, *imported* cigarettes are highlighted in this and other texts which deplored the lures of luxury and "prestige consumption":

> With the continuing increase in wages and expansion of the *nomen-klatura* there is an increased demand for jewelry, artwork, and goods which demonstrate a high standard of living and social prestige. These goods are connected with the snobbery of certain groups of society. In connection with that, it is interesting that there is a change in the consumption of alcoholic beverages and tobacco products. With a rise in income, certain groups of the population, especially from the intel-ligentsia, have an increased demand and consumption of concentrated alcoholic beverages and above all "imported" and "luxurious" alcoholic concentrates and cigarettes.[35]

The fact that "imported" and "luxurious" are in quotes is telling. Most of the "imported" cigarettes in the Eastern Bloc in this period were actually produced in local factories, but with American technology and labels as well

as markedly higher prices. Bulgaria signed licensing and trade agreements
with both R. J. Reynolds and Philip Morris in 1975, which allowed Bulgaria
locally to produce, package, and sell Winston (R. J. Reynolds) and Marlboro
(Philip Morris) cigarettes.[36] Both brands were offered to the public in 1976.
Ironically, in the same year the State Council of Bulgaria issued its anti-
smoking decree with the aim of "curbing and gradually doing away with
this Western imperialist evil."[37]

   Bulgarian cigarettes were presumably the lesser of evils. It was as if the
evils of smoking could be at least partially contained in foreign packages. It
was even argued at this time the "American-type" tobaccos were carcino-
genic, while Bulgarian tobaccos had enough anticarcinogens to counter any
possible cancer risk.[38] Still, socialist governments were apparently willing
to take advantage of the population's attraction to the assumed "luxury"
of Western goods and sell their own tobacco with Western labels, recipes,
and technologies. Economic analysts, though, were appalled that consumers
were willing to pay the higher prices for these and other "luxurious" goods.
People's *veshtomania* (thing-o-mania) was reportedly so rampant that people
would often "limit expenditures on food or the fulfillment of other more
appropriate necessities in order to buy luxurious and new models of clothes,
furniture, and luxurious, imported drinks and cigarettes."[39] "Smoking," as
another author argues, "is an unnatural necessity ... it is deemed more
important than food, shelter, etc."[40] As smoking as a "luxury" seemed to
eclipse necessity, socialist concerns were heightened. Moral concerns aside,
in economic parlance smoking (and especially "luxury" smoking) was the
epitome of "irrational consumption."[41] The increase in purchasing power
among workers, though indicative of socialist achievement, also provoked
concerns by the 1970s and 1980s as Bulgarians supposedly squandered their
salaries on luxury items in a pattern of "irrational consumption." This, economic specialists argued, was indicative of a segment of Bulgarian consumers "abandoning the goals of socialist society."[42]

   Socialist efforts against smoking were not limited, of course, to academic
dialogue and reproof. In the late 1970s and 1980s public anti-smoking campaigns, though somewhat limited, were launched. Lectures and articles in
popular magazines and newspapers attempted to bring the message of tobacco's doom to a wider audience. In 1979 and again in 1984 there were
price hikes on cigarettes, but to no avail. In many ways the regime was
fighting a losing battle. Smoking was by this time embedded in Bulgarian
urban culture. It was interwoven into work and leisure as no other activity.
By 1982 approximately 50 percent of Bulgarian men and women smoked, a
large percentage of them an average of twenty or more cigarettes a day, that
is, more than one a waking hour.[43] In a period of increasing deficits of bare

necessities like certain food items and toilet paper, the declining legitimacy of the socialist regime made any serious attempts to require the population to give up cigarettes simply unrealistic. The supposed increased spending power and thing-o-mania of academic criticism is hard to reconcile with the reality of Bulgaria's consumer despair of that period that is so well known. But while many goods were in short supply, the regime continued to supply cheap and even "luxurious" cigarettes to the Bulgarian population and the Bloc more generally. Its legitimacy, its very survival, depended on it. As the anti-smoking literature itself admits and laments, smoking and smokers remained prominent in TV programming, films, novels, poems, and plays in which more often than not "some hero solves difficult problems with a cigarette in his mouth." Leisure, luxury, glamour, and entertainment seemed impossible without smoking.[44] The number of smokers in Bulgaria—as elsewhere in the Bloc—skyrocketed. The more the regime railed against smoking, the more Bulgarians smoked, with ever higher percentages of their income devoted to the purchase of tobacco.[45]

And as smokers became an increasingly large percentage of the population, more and more women and young people were included in their ranks. The rising numbers of women smoking presented particular dilemmas for socialist theory and practice. Significantly, the overwhelming majority of tobacco producers—both in the field and factory—were women. At this time there is a veritable deluge of biographies, profiles, and articles in *Bulgarian Tobacco* on women growers, pickers, factory workers, and specialists. Women in the factory are called the *"maistorki na tsigari"* (masters of cigarettes) and women in the fields are its nurturers, "leaf by leaf the gentle hands of women sort it."[46] In one article entitled "These Golden Hands" the life and work of a woman named Velika is explored, beginning with an adoring description of her hands: "Look at them—nimble, roughened by labor—pure gold. They can tell you many things."[47] In fact, women's significance was so great that in one map of tobacco-growing regions in Bulgaria in *Bulgarian Tobacco*, each region was marked by a woman in traditional Bulgarian dress. This is somewhat ironic, considering that many of these areas were heavily populated by Muslims (Bulgarian or Turkish speaking) who did not identify culturally with Bulgarians, although Bulgarians too were present.[48] Women's participation in the tobacco industry made them an important, if not critical, cog in the wheel of the Bulgarian economy; but it also provided the material conditions for their emancipation, a stated ideal of the socialist state.

But an increasing awareness of the link between smoking and women's emancipation presented a theoretical dilemma for state officials by the late 1970s and 1980s, as the number of women smokers skyrocketed. On the one hand, citing the American suffragettes as an example, numerous sources admitted that smoking was historically linked to emancipation and "progressive change" for women.[49] On the other hand, however, health officials and economists alike from the Bulgarian socialist elite were concerned by the phenomenon that "equality with men drives women to smoke." Ironically, they extolled the virtues of the village tradition—otherwise maligned as backward—for providing a shelter from the evils of smoking for Bulgaria's rural women.[50] But while the Bulgarian socialists had always gone to great lengths to promote and cultivate the image and economic reality of the modern emancipated woman, they also began to disparage newly urbanized and emancipated women who smoked to "appear modern."[51] Never mind the fact that images of women smoking were prevalent in films, novels, and tobacco "advertisements" from the 1950s and 1960s. By the late socialist period, these luxury-seeking, smoking creatures of "ripe" socialism presented the regime with a critical challenge.

Indeed, the anti-smoking writings of the late 1970s and 1980s incessantly expressed alarm about the particular problem of women smokers. Although a smaller percentage of women than men actually smoked in this period, the number of women smokers rose at an alarmingly faster rate. In a period when Bulgarian birthrates were lower than ever, the connection between smoking and women's reproductive capacity—and by extension their femininity—was a particular concern from the very beginning of the anti-smoking campaigns. In the 1976 "Conversations," the connections between emancipation, smoking, reproduction, and femininity are explicit:

> The cigarette has become one of the required markers of the emancipation of women, of their independence. In essence this ill-conceived independence is costly in terms of the unshakable dependence of the woman-smoker on the cigarette, with severe consequences for her health. For women the poisonous tobacco substances have negative effects on their ovaries. Their activities are disturbed, and as a result the appearance of the woman is changed—she takes on a masculine appearance. The tender color of her face takes on an earthy hue, the woman either grows thinner or, exceptionally, fatter. The regularity of her menstrual cycle is disturbed. Her voice becomes hoarse and with a bass tone.[52]

The image of the smoking woman was unflattering, manly. Smoking, it was argued, was customarily "connected with the image of a man." And as one source openly complained, "cigarette smoke coming out of the lips or nose of a woman is something uncommon that appears to us as something vulgar and unnatural."[53] In the lexis of the anti-smoking literature, smoking obscured and sullied the very essence of woman. The smoking woman was not only a "manly" and "unnatural" sight, she was also perilously desexed.

In fact, in succumbing to the vice of tobacco, women allegedly endangered the reproductive health of the nation. Women smokers, it was claimed, had an erratic cycle, and the practice purportedly "negatively affect[ed] her sexual desire."[54] According to state statistics, women smokers had more planned and spontaneous abortions and, in the miraculous event that they conceived, their lactation was depressed and their milk was "lacking in vitamin C."[55] But perhaps most significantly, researchers also argued that women's smoking had a significant impact on women's and men's sexual function:

> It is proven that smoking negatively affects the sexual potency of men and sexual desire of women. Nicotine depresses sexual function. As a result there is a sexual weakness in men and sexual frigidity in women . . . The smell of smoke from the lips of women diminishes the attraction for men and acts as an inhibitor to the sexual act . . . Many men said that they reacted negatively even to the smell of smoke on the clothes of female smokers.[56]

Admittedly, smoking men's "sexual weakness" and elsewhere "abnormal sperm" were evidently part of the reproductive predicament. But significantly, the sight and smell of smoking women as a supposed sexual turnoff is also central to such discussions.[57] As another source argues, "Men in our surveys said that a smoking cigarette in a woman's mouth lessens or eliminates their sexual attraction. Even if we accept that tobacco has no ill effect on the female organism, then isn't this last fact enough of an argument against smoking among women?"[58] It is unclear here whether the primary concern is with reproduction and smoking's effects on the nation as a whole, or more narrowly with men's sex lives. What is clear is that while for men smoking is more a matter of personal choice, for women the presumed social costs are much higher. At least among these social commentators, women's smoking was threatening to men, to the system, and to the nation.

In contrast, the link between masculinity and smoking was an unshakable one. Men smoked to be men, and the anti-smoking campaigns made virtually no effort to try and address or overcome such cultural connections. In one such pathetic effort, it was recognized that men habitually accepted a cigarette when offered because it "sounds more masculine and mature." As an alternative, the author suggested that men shouldn't "worry about saying no" and should instead eat cake or bonbons: "Many great men preferred bonbons over cigarettes and were not ashamed to admit it. Let's enumerate them: Robespierre, Napoleon, Pasteur, Pavlov, Sverdlov, Dzerzhinsky, and many others."[59] Significantly, other items associated with luxury consumption and with pleasure were offered as an alternative. Although both luxury and smoking were theoretically censured after 1976, the regime was not impervious to the population's continued demand for sources of pleasure and continued to supply them.

In the case of youth, the dilemmas of this scenario were equally glaring. Youth, like women, had a special place in the anti-smoking campaigns. Like women, their efforts in tobacco production were recognized. "Voluntary" youth brigades provided large contingents of seasonal labor for tobacco cultivation. Young workers were praised for their "limitless love for the homeland" as they made personal sacrifices to help sort "not dried lifeless tobacco leaves, but golden *valuta*, [to buy] machines for our factories, tractors and combines for our native fields."[60] But like women, youth were not encouraged to consume the products of their labor. Instead, Bulgarian authorities were openly concerned that youth were among the fastest-growing smoking segments of the population.[61] With this in mind, antitobacco lecturers traveled around to schools leading discussions and delivering lectures on such topics as "Tobacco—The Enemy of the People."[62] Smoking among youth was critically evaluated and, as with adults, analysts emphasized the role of negative phenomena such as "conformism, showmanship, snobbery," and a "passion for fashion."[63] Other sources explored youth smoking as a result of the need for boys to be "masculine" and fulfill their "internal needs for pleasure."[64] Researchers were also concerned with the misplaced desire among youth who smoked to appear "modern." As one Bulgarian youth who was interviewed admitted, "I have observed that some of my friends, even though they don't smoke, will take cigarettes so they don't look silly or backward in the eyes of their group of friends."[65] For youth, as for adults, smoking was connected with "irrational consumption" and even more so with the "irrational use of free time," of which they unfortunately had a surplus. The "problem" of free time, as numerous authors asserted, was that youth and adults alike were unable to use it in a "productive" way.[66]

With this in mind, the Bulgarian state opened a spate of youth clubs, restaurants, and discotheques with the express idea of countering "irrational consumption" among youth as well as adults.[67] The intention was for such establishments to provide a place to "satisfy the growing demands of both youth and adults, to appease the need to express social prestige and at the same time exclude the use of alcohol and tobacco products." The regime clearly recognized the need to appease the population's longing for leisure consumption, and so wanted to play a role in engineering such pleasures.

As a result it built and maintained a variety of venues that it claimed would somehow be infused with "refined taste and high culture."[68] As it turned out, such "high culture" was eclipsed by a more vibrant proliferation of popular culture and sociability that was apparently impossible without tobacco and alcohol. As one source on the problems of youth described:

> They [discotheques] were created for the more effective use of free time for youth. But do they fulfill these functions? In my opinion, categorically "no." Especially where they are under the control of Balkantourist ... discotheques have turned into places where young people spend a lot of money and learn how to smoke and drink imported alcoholic drinks. And if there is something that they learned from the propaganda on sobriety [and anti-smoking], then it is lost and forgotten in the atmosphere of these luxurious, smoke-filled venues.[69]

That these establishments, whose express purpose was supposedly abstinence from tobacco and alcohol, were neither smoke- nor drink-free is telling. Indeed, this fact epitomizes one of the fundamental contradictions behind the luxury "problem" in socialist Bulgaria. The regime both promoted (especially in the 1960s) and berated luxury. It supplied the venues and products for luxury consumption of tobacco, alcohol, and other products and then berated the population for its excess. It felt the need to reward its workers with a higher standard of living and the fruits of its own labors, but also regulated this consumption when it became "irrational." The closer "mature communism" approached in theory, the more the government had to appease the population with the good life it had promised them, while simultaneously scrutinizing how that actual life was lived.

Conclusion

Bulgarian cigarettes were by all accounts the "engine" of the Bulgarian economy under socialism. Tobacco workers, and indeed all segments of the population, deserved their share of "Bulgarian gold." Fortunately, tobacco was a national resource that was easily distributed to the population, and could be repackaged in the post-Stalinist years as a product now associated with the provision of quality and luxury to the working class. Bulgartabak provided luxury cigarettes as a directed response to perceived changes in worker demand that echoed their rise in social station under socialism. But in spite of the seeming symbiosis of smoking and Bulgarian socialism, smoking as a practice came under fire by the late 1970s and 1980s. Critics pointed to smoking as detrimental to health and indicative of lapsed moral-

ity and "irrational" consumption. Anti-smoking (and anti-luxury) appeals
were also justified on theoretical grounds. In other words, smoking and
"luxury" came under fire because they had no place in the ostensibly approaching communist utopia. Women and youth in particular, the bearers
and representatives of the next generation, became objects of state concern as they smoked in ever-greater numbers. In the final analysis, though,
anti-smoking rhetoric and activities were exceedingly weak and ultimately
unsuccessful among all segments of the population. In spite of holding the
reins of a command economy structure, the Bulgarian regime never took
action to decrease or eliminate the supply of cigarettes. In a period when
the Bulgarian state was hard-pressed to keep the shelves full of food, let
alone refrigerators and VCRs, the curtailing of cigarette supplies was out
of the question. Cigarettes were one of the few luxury goods that the state
could provide on a regular basis, and their sales were critical to the faltering
socialist economy.[70] Smoking, it seems, was grudgingly tolerated and even
promoted in spite of its apparent social downside. For although smoking,
as many sources admitted, "reflected poorly on the building of advanced
socialism," it also illustrated the Bulgarian socialist achievement in terms of
production and the provision of the "modern" good life to the consuming
class that socialism had itself created.[71]

Notes

1. Paun Genov, *S Fakela na Trezvenostta: Momenti ot Borbata protiv Pianstvoto
i Tiutiunopusheneto pres 1300–Godishnata Istoriia na Bŭlgariia* (Sofia: Natsionalen
Komitet za Trezvenost, Meditsina i Fizkultura, 1980), 43.

2. Ibid., 28.

3. Veselina Vlakhova-Nikolova, *Problemi na Tiutiunopusheneto i Alkokholnata Upo-
treba Sred Mladezhta* (Plovdiv: Nauchnoizsledovatelska Laboratoriia za Mladezhdta,
1983), 8.

4. See, for example, Todor Velchov, "Iz Borbite na Tiutiunorabotnitsite v Grad
Plovdiv, 1891–1920," *Godishnik na Museite v Plovdivski Okrŭg* 2 (1956): 11–37; and
Georgi Vangelov, *Tiutiunopabotnitsi: Spomeni iz Borbite na Tiutiunopabotnitsite* (Sofia:
Profizdat, 1955).

5. *Tobacco Reporter,* March 1974, 17.

6. Stefan Abadzhiev, *Spomeni ot Izminatiia Pŭt* (Sofia: Profizdat, 1982), 9.

7. Whereas in the "West" the history of the concept is far more complete, in Eastern Europe its study remains marginalized. On the West, see, for example, Maxine
Berg and Helen Clifford, eds., *Consumers and Luxury: Consumer Culture in Europe
1650–1850* (Manchester: Manchester University Press, 1999). On consumption under socialism see, for example, Susan E. Reid and David Crowley, eds., *Style and Socialism: Modernity and Material Culture in Post-War Eastern Europe* (Oxford: Berg, 2000),
and David Crew, ed., *Consuming Germany in the Cold War* (Oxford: Berg, 2003).

8. For a discussion of luxury consumption in the Soviet context, see Sheila Fitz-

patrick, *Everyday Stalinism: Ordinary Life in Extraordinary Times. Soviet Russia in the 1930s* (New York: Oxford University Press, 1999). See also Jukka Gronow, *Caviar with Champagne: Common Luxury and the Ideals of the Good Life in Stalin's Russia* (Oxford: Berg, 2003).

9. James Twitchell, *Living It Up: Our Love Affair with Luxury* (New York: Columbia University Press, 2002), 1.

10. Fitzpatrick, *Everyday Stalinism*, 91.

11. In the West attitudes toward women smokers have changed radically over time. Segrave argues that women smokers were only fully "accepted" in American society in the 1950s. See Kerry Segrave, *Women and Smoking in America 1880–1950* (Jefferson, N.C.: McFarland, 2005). At the same time, as in Bulgaria, there were rising concerns about American women and youth smokers in the mid-1970s. See *Tobacco Journal International*, no. 4 (1975): 264.

12. Kristo Stoianov, *Dvizheniie za Trezvenost v Razgradski Okrŭg* (Razgrad: Okrŭzhen Komitet za Trezvenost, 1983), 56.

13. *Bŭlgarski Tiutiun*, no. 2 (1966): 1.

14. Gronow, *Caviar with Champagne*, 8; and Katherine Verdery, *What Was Socialism and What Comes Next?* (Princeton, N.J.: Princeton University Press, 1996), 28.

15. On attempts by the Bulgarian regime to "modernize" Muslim women through consumption, see Mary Neuburger, "Pants, Veils, and Matters of Dress: Unraveling the Fabric of Women's Lives in Communist Bulgaria," in Reid and Crowley, *Style and Socialism*, 169–87.

16. Fitzpatrick, *Everyday Stalinism*, 91.

17. Rositsa Gocheva, *Rasvitie na Materialnoto Blagosŭstoianie na Bŭlgarskiia Narod* (Izdatelstvo na Bŭlgarskata Komunistichecka Partiia, 1965), 2.

18. Todor Iordanov, *Materialnoto-Tekhnicheska Basa na Razvitoto Sotsialistichesko Obshtestvo* (Sofia: Partizdat, 1973), 7.

19. Khristo Vladov, *Analiz na Domakinskite Biudzheti s Ogled na Predvizhdaneto na Potrebitelskoto Tŭrsene* (Sofia: Izdatelstvo na Bŭlgarskata Akademiia na Naukite, 1966).

20. *Bŭlgarski Tiutiun*, no. 10 (1971): 45.

21. Iordanov, *Materialnoto-Tekhnicheska Basa*, 7.

22. *Bŭlgarski Tiutiun*, no. 1 (1961): 26; and *Bŭlgarski Tiutiun*, no. 9 (1962): 32.

23. *Bŭlgarski Tiutiun*, no. 1 (1961): 26.

24. Ruth Mandel, "Cigarettes in Soviet and Post-Soviet Central Asia," in *Smoke*, ed. S. Gilman and Z. Xun (London: Reaktion Books, 2004), 184.

25. *Bŭlgarski Tiutiun*, no. 1 (1961): 57.

26. *Bŭlgarski Tiutiun*, no. 2 (1966): 3; and *Bŭlgarski Tiutiun*, no. 12 (1967): 32.

27. *Bŭlgarski Tiutiun*, no. 9 (1971): 18.

28. *Bŭlgarski Tiutiun*, no. 9 (1984): 46.

29. *Bŭlgarski Tiutiun*, no. 9 (1963): 37.

30. Zlatko Zlatev, *Tŭrsene, Predlagane, Tseni* (Sofia: Partizdat: 1973), 172.

31. Natsionalen Komitet za Trezvenost, *Besedi za Vredata ot Tiutiunopusheneto* (Sofia: Institut za Zdravna Prosveta, 1976), 13.

32. Vlakhova-Nikolova, *Problemi na Tiutiunopusheneto*, 9.

33. Natsionalen Komitet za Trezvenost, *Besedi*, 13.

34. Vasil Tsonchev, ed., *Tiutiunopushene i Zdrave: Sbornik Tezisi za Lektsii* (Sofia: Ministerstvo na Narodnoto Zdrave, 1979), 47.

35. Atanas Liutov, Boris Atanasov, and Kapka Stoianova, *Razvitie na Narodnoto Potreblenie* (Sofia: Izdatelstvo na Bŭlgarskata Akademiia na Naukite, 1982), 110.

36. *Tobacco Reporter,* January 1976, 47. The timing of such agreements coincided with the United States granting Bulgaria most favored nation status in 1975.

37. *Tobacco Reporter,* April 1976, 80.

38. *Bŭlgarski Tiutiun,* no. 11 (1967): 31.

39. Liutov, Atanasov, and Stoianova, *Razvitie na Narodnoto Potreblenie,* 116.

40. Tsonchev, *Tiutiunopushene,* 46.

41. Atanas Liutov et al., *Upravlenie na Narodnoto Potreblenie* (Sofia: Izdatelstvo na Bŭlgarskata Akademiia na Naukite—Ikonomicheski Institut, 1984), 86.

42. Ibid., 116.

43. See Vlakhova-Nikolova, *Problemi na Tiutiunopusheneto,* 59, 83.

44. Natsionalen Komitet za Trezvenost, *Besedi,* 34.

45. Liutov et al., *Upravlenie,* 116.

46. *Bŭlgarski Tiutiun,* no. 5 (1972): 38; and *Bŭlgarski Tiutiun,* no. 3 (1971): 20.

47. *Bŭlgarski Tiutiun,* no. 12 (1972): 4.

48. Tobacco growing was concentrated in the Muslim-populated Rhodope and Rila mountains and, to a lesser extent, the Dobrudja. While Muslims are discussed in *Bŭlgarski Tiutiun* as tobacco growers and, to a lesser extent, workers, they are absent in discussions here or elsewhere on tobacco consumption.

49. *Bŭlgarski Tiutiun,* no. 7 (1980): 43.

50. Vlakhova-Nikolova, *Problemi na Tiutiunopusheneto,* 6.

51. Natsionalen Komitet za Trezvenost, *Besedi,* 29.

52. Ibid., 26.

53. Ibid., 28.

54. Tsonchev, *Tiutuinopushene,* 32; and Natsionalen Komitet za Trezvenost, *Besedi,* 26.

55. Tsonchev, *Tiutuinopushene,* 9, 40.

56. Ibid., 32.

57. Ibid., 40.

58. Natsionalen Komitet za Trezvenost, *Besedi,* 29.

59. Ibid., 44.

60. *Bŭlgarski Tiutiun,* no. 8 (1961): 40.

61. Ministerstvo na Zdravookhraneniia—NR Bŭlgariia, Institut Sanitarnovo Prosveshteniia, *Shestoi Simposium Institutov Sanitarnovo Prosveshteniia Sotsialisticheskikh Stran* (Sofia, 1982), 104.

62. Ibid., 102.

63. Ibid., 91.

64. Ibid., 76; Vlakhova-Nikolova, *Problemi na Tiutiunopusheneto,* 26.

65. Natsionalen Komitet za Trezvenost, *Besedi,* 11.

66. See, for example, Zakhari Staikov, *Biudzhet na Vremeto na Trudeshtite se v NRB* (Sofia: Dŭrzhavno Izdatelstvo "Nauka i Izkustvo," 1964), 55–105.

67. Vlakhova-Nikolova, *Problemi na Tiutiunopusheneto,* 26.

68. Liutov et al., *Upravlenie,* 117.

69. Vlakhova-Nikolova, *Problemi na Tiutiunopusheneto,* 154.

70. Liutov et al., *Upravlenie,* 90.

71. Vlakhova-Nikolova, *Problemi na Tiutiunopusheneto,* 10.

CHAPTER TEN

Drink, Leisure, and the

Second Economy in Socialist Romania

Narcis Tulbure

They drank because life was difficult,
and because society made them drink,
and it was harmony ...
—G.F.

Only people who were ill did not go to the tavern ...
—N.M.

Conversations about everyday life with people who lived during late socialism in southern Romania are, most of the time, about the role of material
things in circulation, of the movements and activities that structured daily
schedules, and of the various forms of collective consumption that produced
social relations.[1] Reflections such as appear in this chapter's epigraph constitute an emotional description of the omnipresence of drinking and the
role of alcohol in the production of sociality during the recent past.[2] As my
informants and friends always told me, going to the village tavern (*MAT*)
or to one of the taverns in the working neighborhoods of the nearby town
where many of the villagers commuted to work was a privileged pastime for
men.[3] Since the overwhelming majority of the workingmen attended drinking sessions, the tavern became one of the main arenas for the construction
of masculinity, the reaffirmation of group boundaries, and the display of
reciprocity during late socialism. While moderate drinking and self-control
are said to have been appreciated qualities, both people who could not hold
their drink and those who did not usually drink were marginalized and

regarded ironically for not being manly enough and for not knowing how to drink. Most of those I interviewed seemed to enjoy remembering and sharing tales about their past drinking practices, describing social drinking as one of the most widespread sources of pleasure and occasions for having a good time (*a se simţi bine*).

An ethnographic reconstitution of the social life of alcohol in socialist Romania can be used to suggest an alternative perspective on socialism and the processes that constituted it. More precisely, the "social biography" of alcohol can shed light on some of the practices and locales that played an essential role in the social organization of leisure and the second economy in the last decade of socialism in Romania.[4] Drinking in taverns and restaurants situated in villages and the working-class neighborhoods of towns, a widespread and affordable form of leisure, was constitutive of a sphere of material and symbolic exchange. Consumption of alcoholic beverages was associated with the exchange of goods and services that were "taken" or stolen from state enterprises and which circulated in the sphere of the second economy in what became a generous arena for the display of reciprocity and the construction of masculinity. This form of leisure was not only permitted but actually facilitated by the state, which held a quasi monopoly over the production and distribution of alcoholic beverages as well as over the legitimate public and semipublic spaces of consumption. Drinking became a widespread pastime in the rural areas of Romania under socialism, managing to coalesce into a form of second economy driven by consumption. This chapter will propose that leisure and the socially productive practices associated with it can afford insights into some of the fundamental social processes of the period, facilitating a better understanding of the experience of socialism.

The romanticized presentation of the past and the idealization of drinking practices during the 1980s (emphasizing "harmony," reciprocity, and wide participation) illustrate the limitations of attempts to reconstitute the recent past based on the present narratives of those who lived in the times described. Narratives about the past are not simply reproductions of past practices that one witnessed or in which one took part; they should themselves be regarded as practices that are mediated by a historically constituted set of dispositions that facilitate a particular orientation toward the future. Following Peter Fritzsche and Alon Confino, it is useful to go beyond the "exclusively representational approach" to memory and understand that it forms social relations, being "embedded in social networks and ... a commingling of immaterial and material interests and motivations."[5] Therefore, present narratives about the past should be taken as practices situated in

time, while the social historian should make sure that the present conditions
in which these narratives are produced are not ignored.

In spite of the limitations outlined above, and even if obscuring most of
the strategizing that goes into practice itself, present narratives about the
past are able to reproduce the coordinates of the "ritualized" practices of
consumption as well as the ethos manifest in everyday interactions. More
specifically, talk about how one used to drink or how one should drink,
when, where, or with whom one drank, how one produced and exchanged
things, how one showed his appreciation toward a fellow worker or recipro-
cated a service of a friend, represents a discourse about practice that conveys
at least a sense of the fundamental dimensions of everyday life during the
socialist period.[6]

The Constitution of Socialist Leisure

The word "leisure," always an elusive theoretical category, lacks a direct
equivalent in the Romanian language.[7] Therefore, its transfer and use for
analyzing social phenomena in socialist Romania is not without problems.
During the socialist period, various categories were employed by different
state agencies or at the level of popular culture to describe the experiences
and practices that are associated with leisure in capitalist societies: "free
time" (*timpul liber*), "recreation" (*recreație*), "distraction" (*distracție*), "amusement" (*amuzament*), or "pastime" (*activitate liberă*). Nonetheless, the gulf
separating Romanian and Western academic or popular vocabularies is not
unbridgeable. Developed initially for capitalist Western societies,[8] leisure as
a historical category has been broadened and its genealogy has been traced
back to the early modern period.[9] In the early literature on the topic, several
definitions of leisure were proposed by various authors.[10] More recent literature indicates alternative directions of research rather than a theoretical
systematization of leisure. Not only would it be hard to derive a comprehensive definition of this category from the existing literature, but it is now
considered a more intellectually rewarding enterprise to "decenter" leisure
studies by critically scrutinizing the role leisure has played in society since
the advent of capitalism and modernity and to situate leisure within diverse
other historical and political formations.[11] Arguing for a renewed focus on
leisure and its defining activities, various authors reject approaches that define it only as the more obscure counterpart of work. They also propose to
broaden the analysis of leisure in historical, political, and geographic terms
beyond contemporary capitalist societies, projecting the category back in
time and onto noncapitalist societies.[12] This broadening of perspective

can create the premises for a reevaluation of the theoretical foundations
of leisure studies.

A number of authors have explored the relations between leisure and
related categories such as commitment, obligation, motivation, spontaneity,
or pleasure. Although some argue that pleasure is not a requisite of leisure,
most of the authors reviewed by Boas Shamir associate the two categories.[13]
The relation between leisure and pleasure is particularly revealing for the
social processes analyzed in this chapter, processes in which social drinking
plays a constitutive role. In this regard, it is useful to adopt the approach
which Jamie Hysjulien, following Foucault, has called the "archaeology of
social forms," that is, to analyze pleasure in connection with power and to
situate it within a political economy of capitalism premised on the relations
between leisure, pleasure, and reification.[14]

The present contribution is an attempt to illuminate the social practices constitutive of a particular form of leisure in late socialist Romania.
Rather than developing a comprehensive definition of leisure in socialism
or even in rural Romania (where most of my research was centered), here I
offer an understanding of how the category was produced under socialism
by focusing on some of the practices, spaces, times, and (material) objects
that constituted it. As several other forms of leisure developed during the
socialist period—state-sponsored holidays in seaside or mountain resorts,
popular sports events, concerts or theatrical representations, and membership in sports teams or folkloric ensembles associated with one of the local
factories, for example—it is useful to identify the main traits of the particular category of leisure analyzed in this chapter and to differentiate it from
other varieties.

The sphere of leisure analyzed here developed in rural areas or working-
class neighborhoods of provincial towns during the last decades of the socialist period. It emerged in the interstitial spaces between work time and
family time, between the sphere of work and that of the household, although
it was never entirely autonomous from either of those realms in terms of
the resources on which it drew continuously and which provided the main
criteria of affiliation among its actors. It was centered on the practices of
social drinking by workers who commuted between villages and industrial
towns that had grown under socialism. This became one of the main arenas
for the construction of masculinity and the display of reciprocity at the
time. Leisure was productive of specific configurations of time and space,
which were the object of ideological intervention by the state, the locus
of negotiation between state and people for the meaning of social life, as
well as the basis of counter-hegemonic models of the person opposed to
the "communist new man" (*omul nou comunist*) promoted by the socialist

state.[15] Last but not least, leisure progressively became a milieu in which the second economy, driven by localized acts of consumption and exchange, flourished during the socialist period.

Treated in this way, leisure provides an excellent window into some of the fundamental processes that constituted socialism in Eastern Europe. Furthermore, by "decentering" and broadening its conceptual boundaries, the study of leisure becomes an arena where various regimes of everyday life emerging during socialist, capitalist, or precapitalist periods can be defined, compared, and contrasted.

Socialist Policies on Alcohol and Drinking

An arena of material and symbolic exchange, as well as a context for the fashioning of masculine identity, public and semipublic drinking sessions certainly predated the advent of socialism. Alcohol has been a constant object of legislation, policy, and regulation by the modern Romanian state since the second half of the nineteenth century. It was part of a series of discourses—economic, nationalist, moral, or medical—and at times it was associated with eugenic arguments and discourses. Before socialism, the Romanian state had been more concerned with large-scale production and distribution capacities, and less so with regulating the burgeoning alcohol economy in peripheral areas. The taverns in the villages and provincial market towns in pre-socialist Romania were vibrant locales where social relations were acted out and economic contracts—land selling, agricultural products, or merchant goods transactions—were enforced.[16]

The advent of socialism with its policies of collectivization, industrialization, and the increasing control of public space determined the adaptive modification of public drinking, as well as that of the regimes of material and symbolic exchange associated with it. Central to these modifications was not only the criminalization of activities previously outside state control but also the imposition of new time schedules and practices with regard to public drinking. As with many other spheres of social life during the socialist period, alcohol policies were subsumed under the state measures for the nationalization of the economy and the project of creating the "communist new man."

The regulation of drinking and consumption should not only be seen as an instrument of public policy for the socialist state; it was also used to justify other areas of state performance and activity. Drinking has been used in socialist Romania as an alibi justifying the country's poor economic performance and socioeconomic conditions, especially through press campaigns stigmatizing "heavy drinkers," "young hooligans," or "promiscuous young women."[17] Romanian communist leaders were never ready to acknowledge openly the real magnitude of alcoholism and its social effects. Although inscribed in the general trend of increased consumption of alcohol and rising rates of alcoholism that characterized all Eastern European countries with the advent of socialism and its model of modernization based on forced industrialization and urbanization, in Romania statistical data on alcohol consumption and alcoholism disappeared progressively after 1980.[18] As in almost all sectors of the economy and society, Romanian leaders hid the statistical data that would have revealed the actual situation of the country.[19] Similar to most of the negative phenomena at the time, "alcohol abuse" and its adverse effects were presented in official discourses and bulletins as a problem that could soon be resolved. Expressions such as "unfortunately, still persist . . ." (*din păcate, mai persistă . . .*) or "unfortunately, there are still individuals who . . ." (*mai există, din păcate, indivizi care . . .*) convey the image of deviant individuals who resist the logic of the ideal society crafted by the socialist state. Responsibility for the delays in the creation of a society without problems was ascribed to such individuals. This may be considered a discourse by which the socialist state legitimized its power through defining the "problems" (illegalities, crimes) outside of its sphere and practices, yet within reach of its prophylactic measures.

The large number of laws and decrees that regulated alcohol directly or in an incidental manner fit broadly within three categories: those consecrating state ownership of most of the facilities of alcohol production and distribution, those regulating conduct and alcohol consumption in public spaces, and those setting work safety norms and prohibiting the consumption of alcohol at work. In the first instance, the socialist regime imposed its monopoly over the sphere of alcohol production and distribution with the nationalization of industry and commerce in June 1948. The sole exception—one that created some of the few areas of legality for the second economy—was granted to individual owners of small-capacity stills for the distillation of brandy (*cazane*). They were allowed to produce and sell (only from home) fruit brandy, subject to local council approval and payment of taxes on alcohol sales.

More consequential than the monopolization of material production were the measures the Romanian socialist state took to monopolize the social production of time and space which deprived its subjects of ever more social and personal resources.[20] Its measures were aimed at a progressive control over public space and time through either the criminalization or the regularization of previously semi-regulated or unregulated behaviors. Not only did areas of social life that had hitherto belonged to the "public sphere" become subject to increasing state control, but numerous other more or less

ambiguous social milieus were redefined as public, and therefore subject
to state regulation. Decrees enforcing rules of public order and conduct
sanctioned and even punished clients who refused to leave restaurants when
in advanced states of inebriation, as well as the sale of alcoholic beverages
to minors or outside regular schedules. The Penal Code of 1968 required
people with chronic drinking problems to attend treatment clinics on a
regular basis and even provided for the compulsory internment of alcoholics who, in classic Soviet style, could be compelled to work as a disciplinary
measure (if under the age of sixty in the case of men and fifty-five in the
case of women).

Several other state regulations regarding alcohol were part of a wider set
of policies meant to increase work efficiency (as in the entire Soviet Bloc)
and to enforce work safety measures in heavy industry.[21] Among the most
important purviews were those forbidding the sale of alcoholic beverages
in the stores inside factories or in their proximity, the sale of alcohol before
10:00 a.m. or after 1:00 a.m., or to minors and inebriated persons, and the
use of advertisements to promote alcoholic beverages. Concerned with work
safety and work efficiency, this set of laws can be taken as attempts by the
state to separate work from leisure (spatially as well as temporally) as realms
dominated by different attitudes, practices, rhythms, or linguistic registers.
However, similar to the measures aimed at the monopolization of alcohol
production, state attempts to separate the two realms were at best a partial
success. The efforts of communist leaders to master the social life of alcohol
and its socially productive potential were hampered by the structure of socialist policies and were continuously challenged by the everyday practices
of the subjects of law or of those meant to enforce the law.

The state's indecisiveness can also be described in terms of the conflicting interest of various agencies within it. Like most of its Central and
East European neighbors, the Romanian state has historically depended
on the fiscal revenues generated by the alcohol trade. The economic plans
of beverage producers and of a series of retailers (taverns, restaurants, and
even cafeterias) could not be accomplished without the revenues generated
by the alcohol trade.[22] Furthermore, public discontent was on many occasions powerful enough to compel the authorities to abandon attempts to
close pubs and taverns and even to announce an increase in the production
of alcoholic beverages.[23] Public policies and efforts to fight the spread of
alcoholism in the countryside through the program of "health education"
(*educaţia sanitară*) were systematically undermined by the alcohol commer-
cials posted on the walls of taverns and by the reduction in alcohol taxes.[24]

State categories were continuously challenged, sometimes being altered
and sometimes completely dismantled. Nonetheless, even as popular prac-

tices continuously eluded state control, they could never become completely autonomous. Everyday tactics intended to elude the vigilance of state representatives and to force the limits of restrictive state regulations inculcated dispositions that produced practices, attitudes, forms of speech, and even body postures, all of which betrayed the internalization of the state presence in everyday life. Examples of such internalization included the almost instinctive fear of militiamen, the euphemistic talk among drinking companions in the tavern to delude informers, avoidance of crowded public roads to avoid checks, or bending one's body to hide a bottle of alcohol hidden under one's clothes when entering a factory. These are only a few of the numerous such practices, some of which can be witnessed even today. Furthermore, as Katherine Verdery argues, the second economy developing under socialism was always dependent on the state sector, its resources and its channels of distribution, having a more or less parasitic condition.[25] As the following section shows, the shifting of perspective toward social drinking during leisure time and the practices of the second economy make it easier to understand the creative potential of consumption, as well as the various ways in which semiautonomous arenas of sociality were articulated with the official sector.

Social Drinking, Leisure, and the Second Economy Under Socialism

A product and object of ritual consumption and celebration of local hierarchies before socialism and the collectivization of land, alcohol gradually became a commodity during the socialist period, with drinking offering a milieu for the (re)production of social relations.[26] The introduction of new time schedules related to work and new modes of spatial organization, alongside other state attempts to rapidly modernize Romania, all had important effects on drinking patterns. According to Sam Beck, the basic transformations in Eastern European societies after World War II—collectivization, industrialization, urbanization, and the subsequent individualization—transformed alcohol into a symbol of consumerism, often the object of conspicuous and even competitive consumption.[27] While Beck's teleological representation of socialist modernization risks oversimplifying a more complex set of processes, it nevertheless shows how new categories of individuals—collective farm workers, commuters to the factories of Caracal, a growing administrative and educational apparatus in the villages—had increasing access to cash resources. Their regular payment by the state or state-owned factories meant that a wider range of people had the possibility to drink on a more frequent basis.

    Among the new consumers of alcohol, the daily commuters from the

countryside to the factories in the nearby towns (such as Caracal) can be recognized as the group with the highest and most frequent consumption among
all other social groups. Working in industry provided them with greater cash
revenues than most other villagers, while living in the village meant that they
faced lower expenses than workers living in town. The possession of both
recognized technical abilities and access to a variety of material resources
that were scarce in both villages and in towns gave worker commuters increased monetary resources and transformed them into constitutive agents
of the growing second economy. Simultaneously, their fixed work schedules
and their daily commuting routine afforded them several hours of free time
a day. Created in between work time and the time allocated for family life
or for work on the personal plot of land, free time offered an arena for the
constitution of the category of leisure under socialism.[28]

The focus on the category of worker commuters, as key actors in all the
social domains treated in this chapter, allows us to illustrate the confluence
between consumption, leisure, and the second economy under socialism.
Local classifications describe commuters as a distinct social category, although with considerable internal diversity. What set them apart were not
only their daily practices but also the way they were able to articulate their
sense of collective identity in relation (and often in opposition) to social
groups with whom they interacted: people working in the village, at the
cooperative farms—sometimes called *țărani* (peasants)—and the workers
living in towns—usually called *orăşeni* (townsfolk).[29]

Before the collapse of socialism in 1989, workers commuted to the factories in Caracal either by train or in buses rented by each state enterprise,
which made regular trips to the neighboring villages. For some commuters,
drinking after work offered an excellent opportunity for socializing with
fellow workers. For others who depended on a means of transportation
that left on a fixed schedule, usually from outside the factory, one possibility was to drink on the bus or train. As one of them remembers, this was
a solution that kept them out of trouble and brought them home quickly:
"We stopped at Complex [one of the district food stores] and took one
bottle of wine or *țuică,* and we drank it on the bus, and we left home with
a clear conscience [*cu fruntea senină*] ... We said 'Have a good day!' and
left!"[30] Those who had more free time enjoyed going "two on one" in one
of the district taverns.[31] Generally small and dirty establishments, smelling
strongly of cheap alcohol and tobacco, such district taverns were known better by the nicknames workers gave them. The best known in Caracal were
"Time Tunnel" (Tunelul timpului), "Drunken Bitch" (La cățeaua leșinată),[32]
and "Miss the Bus" (Pierde cursa). Here cheap brands of brandy or vodka
could be bought at accessible prices: Verdele ("Peppermint," also called

"Adio, Mama!"), *Secărică*, nicknamed "I have already seen your grave" (*te-am zărit printre morminte*), and "blue eyes brandy" (*ţuica doi ochi albaştri*), so named for the two plums drawn on its tag, were the most common ones.

Other commuters would buy a bottle of brandy and drink it on a bench at the bus station. (Examples of people consuming alcohol in public spaces were numerous in spite of the strictness of the laws.) Drinking was constructive of social relations in the most basic sense and can be considered responsible for the failure of state policies to enforce "appropriate" conduct in public or a strict separation between public and private behaviors. The topics of conversation during such drinking sessions were mainly linked to commuters' work, sometimes to their homes and families. In spite of their informal aspect, such discussions followed tacit rules with regard to what were or were not appropriate subjects, and how these were talked about. For instance, discontent with their supervisors or unhappiness over the hardship of life in general was rarely expressed, as people knew that "even the tables have ears."[33] Informers for the militia or for the factory organization of the Communist Party might be among the drinkers. In spite of their generally circumspect talk, people used such opportunities to provide each other with useful information and solutions to difficult situations: to identify a useful contact for dealing with a shortage; to set up the details of a transaction over goods and services that were hard to procure from the state sector; and subsequently, to celebrate such informal (highly personalized) exchanges.

A better option for those commuting by bus was to drink at the village tavern (*MAT*) after returning from work. As the bus station was in the center of the village and the *MAT* and village store were located just across the street, those returning from work did not have far to go.[34] Even those who commuted by bicycle preferred to drink at the *MAT* because they felt "more comfortable at home" (in the village). Throughout the entire socialist period the *MAT,* as the only official drinking outlet in the village, was the meeting place for those either working in town, on the local collective farm, or as tractor drivers in one of the local technical units. It was particularly crowded on paydays, when "people could not find seats inside and were forced to take their bottle and drink outside, on the side of the road or in the courtyard of *MAT,*" as one villager remembers.[35] The topics of discussion here varied more than in town since the attending crowd was more diverse. Such topics might include details of small businesses and arrangements involving, in one way or another, resources and time stolen from state factories (a few liters of petrol or machine oil, a handle of an axe made at the furniture factory, the plowing of a small personal plot by a tractor driver). Here services among friends were paid for and bargains were made and "lubricated" (*cinstea*).[36]

Alcohol consumption was intimately related to money, the allocation of which raised numerous material and moral issues. In the villages around Caracal, it was usually women who managed the daily affairs and budget of the household. Surprising though it may seem, given the gender hierarchies favoring men at the time, it was women who kept most of the money earned by their husbands and allocated it for daily expenses. Under these circumstances, negotiating over the part of one's wage to be spent on drink involved a serious amount of strategizing by men and provoked bitter arguments between spouses. Men had to come up with other ways of financing their consumption because the money they could openly admit for drink was rarely sufficient. Some of them could drink on credit from the villagers distilling *ţuică* or from the village *MAT.* This was not always possible, however, because credit was only available to a few people during the socialist period—close acquaintances of the seller or tavern keeper and people known to have regular access to cash to pay it back. Furthermore, since the tavern keeper adulterated the drinks of inebriated men and often charged extra drinks at the time when the debt was repaid, this was not a preferred option.

According to female informants, men often "pocketed" (*şmangleau*) money from the monthly wage, that is, they appropriated for drinks more than would have been morally acceptable. Various reasons were invented for explaining a reduced pay packet at the end of the month: having to pay for some piece of equipment used at work, having been penalized for a number of different reasons (the motif of the "tough work supervisor" had wide currency at the time), having to contribute to a public fund instituted by state authorities, or having been paid less due to extra days off were among the most frequently used. Such a strategy had its own downsides: understandably, there were numerous cases of wives inquiring at work about their husband's wage.

Another more or less spontaneous strategy was to talk those who had just cashed their wages into treating their drinking buddies. Since most worker commuters or tractor drivers in the village were paid biweekly and drinking circles could be quite wide, there was on any day a group of people able to buy drinks for their mates. Such practices tended tacitly to exclude those who did not reciprocate, whether because of poverty, lack of cash, or simply stinginess.

Throughout the period, one of the main sources of money for drinks for the *MAT* clients were the small but usually frequent revenues generated by transactions associated with the second economy. Constant sources of cash for my main groups of informants included selling goods stolen from state factories (tools, clothes, food items, small quantities of animal fodder), goods produced incognito at state facilities (crafted tools, a better spare part or component for home equipment, a small piece of furniture or a whole set patiently dismantled over a long period of time, even plowing one's personal plot with the cooperative farm's tractor), or goods and services that skilled workers and craftsmen were able to carry out. As one of the women informants let me know, "no man ever complained about not having money for drink . . . they always managed to get it."[37] Although this might be because drinking was not a legitimate reason for complaint, one gets the sense that men always managed to find ways of getting around temporary or long-term money shortages. While the regular income morally belonged to the family and appropriating too much of it could have been considered "theft," income obtained from transactions associated with the informal sector was considered even by women as belonging to men and to be used for their daily consumption.

While money was an important ingredient of the second economy under socialism, even more important, some would argue, were the locales of consumption and exchange (such as the village *MAT* or the backyard of a fellow villager who distilled moonshine *ţuică*) or the material goods that formed the object of exchange. Particularly important were the various goods and alcoholic beverages that circulated intensively within the second economy and came to play the role of local money substitutes.

The category of the second (or informal) economy has been treated extensively in the literature on socialism and has received sophisticated analyses. Classic accounts situate the second economy ("the third sector") in the interstices of the socialist system,[38] emphasize the structural aspects of the economic system,[39] attempt to integrate it within the theoretical model of socialism as a system based on "bureaucratic allocation" and "rational redistribution" of resources,[40] or focus on the cultural underpinnings and the importance of social networks for its development.[41] Although illuminating, these approaches tend to reemphasize the production and distribution of goods and services in the overall economic system and portray the second economy as the functional complement of the official sector, compensating for the shortcomings of the economic system.

Drinking and leisure can provide new insights into the organization of the second economy. They can help us move beyond the functionalism of earlier theories. Consumption and exchange during social gatherings such as drinking sessions not only explain the demand for goods "taken" from state factories but were instrumental in shaping the practices of production of goods circulating in social networks.[42] They created varieties of small-scale production in state factories that were hidden from official control, as well as small-scale services or home-based production by skilled workers. Realized at work or at home, both of these types of production evaded state surveillance and taxation.

Only by focusing on practices of consumption and exchange in a localized system of social relations can one understand how an important part of the second economy was formed. Rather than regarding the relations of the second economy as simple projections of wider realities at the local level, we can do the reverse: we can explore the generation of practices in a localized setting in order to understand the way wider realities (such as the second economy) are constituted by and through the innumerable acts of everyday life, as well as the way different spheres of social life (such as work, leisure, and family life) are articulated into more encompassing processes defining the socialist regime. This particular form of leisure, centered on social drinking, brings to light the interstitial practices, spaces, and times where social relations were constructed, and thus provides a lens into the constitution of the second economy and the texture of socialist societies.[43]

Social drinking was also productive of temporalities and social spaces that did not always respond to the normativity imposed by the state and tended to follow locally validated models of relations between persons. In spite of their creative potential, such arenas of sociality could not entirely escape the discipline exercised by the state through the regulation of consumption time and space, the numerous controls of the militia or the Party apparatchiks, and the seasonal limitations in the offer of alcoholic beverages. Numerous tactics were thought up to escape state-imposed constraints on drinking: these included bribing one's boss to allow one to drink at work or to "take" some of the goods produced there; buying alcohol from grocery stores the evening before to avoid the legal limitations of the times when drink could be bought; distilling one's own alcohol; drinking in apparently neutral spaces; or making arrangements with the tavern keepers using "moral" arguments that seemed to be easily accepted. While these tactics worked in many situations, such strategies of evasion nevertheless created dispositions (fear of control, the constant avoidance of militiamen) and body postures (rapid vigilant movements of eyes and limbs, bending to hide a bottle of liquor or a stolen sweater underneath one's clothes). Thus the state's gaze had been internalized and was present, at a more discrete and maybe more efficient level, in every act of consumption.

The constructive dimensions of social drinking generated a variety of motives and models playing into the emergence of social hierarchies during the socialist period. In this sense, the development of the second economy around alcohol produced popular models of the person that can, retrospec-

tively, be considered as alternatives to the "communist new man" the socialist state was supposed to create. The association between heavy drinking
and skilled craftsmanship became common knowledge and was repeatedly
stressed by most of my interviewees in Caracal and the surrounding villages,
to the point that statements such as "every skilled craftsman is also a drunk-
ard" became axiomatic. One may detect here a sort of vicious circle in which
skilled workers' breach of the "rules" of appropriate behavior was tolerated to
the extent of becoming taken for granted and self-justifying.

Drink, Skill, and Pleasure

The association between appreciated craftsmanship and excessive drinking was made possible and fueled by the structural model of the socialist
second economy. At the time, most skilled craftsmen (such as plumbers or
smiths) did work for neighbors, relatives, or acquaintances in their private
time in exchange for other services or just as part of a generalized system of
reciprocity. On payment they were almost without exception treated with
alcohol. The more skilled one was, the more drinks one received as a sign of
appreciation. No wonder, then, that the association between skill and drink
became a popular cliché.

Talking at length about the past, people who lived through the late
socialist period describe with nostalgia the heavy drinker/skilled craftsman
as a popular model, an alternative kind of person imagined by popular discourses that could be opposed to the "communist new man," the type of
subject constructed through state laws and discourses. While a simplistic
representation of the relation between the state and its subjects in terms of
the power–resistance dichotomy should be avoided, one should nevertheless acknowledge the creativity of local actors, their ability to imagine different kinds of persons than those privileged by the state. Appreciating, ultimately, some of the same virtues as those intended to be cultivated through
state policies (skill, knowledge, or industriousness), popular models tended
to be more flexible and better adapted to the practicalities of working and
living under socialism.

The productive dimensions of consumption become visible in the
specific construction of gender through drinking patterns throughout
the period. Alcohol consumption in public was constitutive of a male
realm. Women were rarely present in drinking outlets, especially the
cheap taverns. They rarely drank in public if not accompanied by one
male member of their family, and inebriated women were strongly stigmatized.[44] At the same time, the skilled craftspeople whose drinking was
regarded with understanding and sympathy were rarely, if ever, women.

Although alcohol legislation was gender-neutral, popular expectations saw such rules and regulations as affecting men above all.

Like most of the taverns in the working-class districts of towns, the *MAT* was essentially a gender-segregated space, one of the privileged arenas of masculinity. Women and children seldom entered, and when they did, to buy a box of matches or lamp petrol, they usually left in a hurry. When asked to comment on this topic, local people are usually intrigued by the idea. "A woman go into the *MAT*? Or a kid? A kid younger than fifteen or sixteen years to enter the *MAT*? It would have been very shameful . . ." When asked how she would have been regarded if she entered a tavern, a woman respondent from Dobrosloveni answered promptly: "Very badly! Personally, I was ashamed to enter the *MAT.* I would look around, I would look both ways in order not to be noticed by anybody when I entered to buy something."[45]

In contrast to the uneasiness of women and children in relation to alcohol, the village tavern was a realm of pleasant experiences for most of the men. (Of course, restraint in showing pleasure in drinking practices expressed by women also contributes to the differentiation of gender categories.) Although it was often an occasion for interested transactions, drinking together was almost always associated with pleasure and having a good time. For most men in Oltenia, sharing a couple of drinks with friends after a hard workday was something relaxing, especially during the harvest season. Furthermore, drinking at home, alone, was "simply not good enough" (*acasă, de unul singur, nu merge băutura*). Drinking at the *MAT* was much more enjoyable because "someone would be telling a joke, somebody else would be telling an anecdote . . ." On the other hand, drinking at home, without the company of friends and drinking buddies, was not as good: "Who was to tell jokes at home, one's woman [*cine sa spuie bancuri acasă, muierea*]?"[46]

At the same time, particular circumstances could turn drinking into an unpleasant experience. Coming home late, inebriated, and with no money was a constant source of conjugal fights and repeated reproaches. Furthermore, speaking too freely after a few drinks or drinking at inappropriate hours (in the middle of the day) could get one into trouble with the militia. Even so, drinking together during the socialist period is remembered and described most of the time as a pleasurable experience.

While attending the village tavern was almost exclusively a male pastime, drinking together was not only a masculine practice. Women did consume alcohol during the socialist period, but they mostly preferred to drink homemade wine or *ţuică* distilled by themselves or by one of their fellow villagers—at home, away from the watchful eyes of their co-villagers. Women admit to having drunk mostly in small groups, while paying visits to each other to agree on the conditions of small-scale domestic exchanges or to arrange for mutual help. Equally uneasy about the association between women and alcohol, men describe pejoratively women's drinking habits during the socialist period or their turn to public drinking during post-socialist times. One of the villagers, even more condescendingly, remembers that "they [women] drank, damn them! Some of them even drank industrial alcohol filtered through loaves of bread. Some didn't even filter it because they didn't want to waste the bread."[47] The motif of physical degeneration, caused by the strong industrial alcohol, standing for the moral degeneration of women who drink can be easily recognized when we situate the narratives of people who lived under socialism within the universe of daily consumption and exchange outlined above.

Under socialism, in Oltenia, women had to disguise pleasure and show discretion with regard to pleasurable practices as a sign of modesty and morality. Furthermore, spaces and times of moral ambiguity were almost always avoided. Being seen in the wrong place at the wrong time (being in the tavern or wandering in the streets at night) could easily be associated with sexual promiscuity, and this stigma would be something very difficult to shake off. Women themselves seem to have internalized such moral stances. They describe the unpleasantness of entering the tavern: "I was only going to the *MAT* to buy cigarettes. But after going in there my clothes smelled bad for a week; they smelled of alcohol and tobacco. The result was something foul [*ceva foarte scârbos*] . . . a terrible smell."[48] Moral discomfort was embodied in the form of unpleasant physical sensations.

The sense of female modesty conveyed by their relationship with alcohol is also transparent in conversation about free time and leisure. Like several other women I interviewed, one of the most articulate provided the following answer to my questions about her free time: "From my point of view, I did not consider that I had free time. I did not have enough time . . . ever."[49] She elaborated further, stating that "if I have ever lacked anything it was time . . . I think only an unconscientious, lazy woman can say 'I have nothing to do!'" Although during our discussion we identified several periods of relative inactivity throughout her daily schedule, she continued to stress that "a woman always has something to do! A woman has all her time filled. Maybe those who are too lazy . . . usually women who drink . . . have free time." Furthermore, even when visiting each other to chat, help one's neighbor, or set up the details of exchanges, women were supposed to give the impression that they were on the run and that they always had something to do. This socially appropriate performance for women, permanently conveying a sense of rush as an epitome for industriousness and diligence, prevented them from engaging in the practices and behaviors constitutive of the sphere of leisure.

Conclusion

In Oltenia, under socialism, leisure was the privilege of men and was constituted as a sphere of relative autonomy both from the state and from the family. In spite of the attempts by the socialist state to channel and control the organization of leisure, for the men I interviewed the favorite pastime remained drinking with their fellow villagers or workers. It was subject to a special ethos, as one had to know *how, when, with whom,* and especially *for what* one was drinking. Moderate drinking was seen as "normal," the sign of a healthy man, as has been shown earlier, local narratives associating it always with hard work and respectability. As long as one worked, was able to take care of one's family, and did not make a fool of oneself, one was expected to drink as much as one could.

Starting out from a social biography of alcohol, I have attempted to broaden the concept of leisure by writing about a provincial, mostly rural region in a socialist society. Taking it as a burgeoning arena for sociality and economic exchange, I suggested that the category of leisure can be used as a window into some of the processes that structured social life during the socialist period. Furthermore, in understanding the relations of the second economy as more than projections of wider realities at the local level, I have argued for the analysis of practices generated in localized contexts as a way of illuminating the production of the most encompassing social categories in everyday action, as well as the articulation between different spheres of social life (work, leisure, and family life) at the most mundane level.

The analysis presented here offers a starting point for developing a political economy of pleasure under socialism.[50] Such an approach, attentive to the historical contingency of social forms, would be all the more revealing because various ideologies of communism promised the rational administration and the equitable distribution of pleasure through the use in common of the basic commodities of life.[51] Meanwhile, a more detailed study of pleasure under socialism, situated in regard to the categories employed in this chapter, would not only shed light on the various forms of resistance to state policies for the rationalization of consumption, but might also illuminate the conditions of possibility for processes of subjection and resistance. This could be done by treating pleasure not as something extrinsic to and repressed by power, but as something that is produced by power. To investigate this, a phenomenological approach, paying attention to the ways pleasure is experienced and narrated, should be pursued in connection to a historically informed political economy of pleasure under socialism.[52]

The study of socialist leisure is also relevant, furthermore, for postsocialist studies. To focus on the changing patterns of alcohol consumption in the present day, especially by former commuters between villages and towns, opens up the possibility to understand some of the most important social and economic changes that have taken place in post-socialist southern Romania. Consumption has been considered secondary and has been overshadowed by the importance given to production in many scholarly attempts to understand what socialism was. Yet according to Katherine Verdery, the highly politicized role of consumption makes it an important topic of research that can reveal much about "actually existing socialism."[53] The main aim of such an approach is to attain a better understanding of what socialism was through an analysis of the essential experiences that defined and constituted it, since they form the basis on which post-socialist transformation comes into being, or, differently put, "the way the past enters the present, not as legacy but as novel adaptation."[54]

Notes

1. This chapter relies on ethnographic data from a study of the organization of work and leisure in Oltenia Region (part of southern Romania) during the socialist and post-socialist eras. It focuses mainly on the late socialist period of the 1980s. The study draws on interviews, discussions, observation, and archival materials. Extensive interviews and discussions were held with former worker commuters to Caracal—a small provincial town in Oltenia (where socialist policies aimed at rapid urbanization and industrialization had been implemented since the 1950s)—from the neighboring villages, as well as with work supervisors and engineers in socialist factories, people who worked in villages, and the female relatives of those involved in commuting. Observation was conducted in Caracal and Dobrosloveni (a neighboring village) in the village tavern and the newly opened bars and small shops after the fall of socialism, as well as during public gatherings on festive occasions. Documents, research reports, and newspaper articles from the period were consulted in the collections of the Open Society Archives in Budapest and those of the Library of the Romanian Academy in Bucharest. The research project set out to reconstitute a social history of the period with the help of some methods and techniques adopted from cultural anthropology.

2. The first quotation comes from an interview I held in 2003 with G.F.—the former chief of personnel of the train cart factory in Caracal. Trained as an accountant in one of the professional schools created during the first years of the socialist period, G.F. was a native of the town, lived his entire life in one of its peripheral neighborhoods, and had extensive kin in the neighboring villages. G.F. had been an employee of the factory his entire life and was practically contemporaneous with the creation of the socialist labor force through politics of rural-to-urban migration, on-the-job training, and evening schools for workers. During socialism he was in charge of the enforcement of work safety regulations, which included the measures against drinking during work. He was on the verge of retirement at the time of the interview and was witnessing with sadness the dismantling of the former socialist factory as a consequence of structural adjustment programs overseen by the World Bank.

The second quotation, a phrase repeated several times during an interview with

N.M., an agricultural engineer in Dobrosloveni, is an important component of the representation of masculinity in the region as intimately connected to drinking.

3. The acronym MAT stands for Alcohol and Tobacco Monopoly (Monopolul alcoolului şi tutunului—MAT) instituted in 1932. In rural Romania, village taverns continued to be called *MAT* throughout the entire socialist period, even after other establishments (village bodegas and stores) were allowed to sell alcohol.

4. Arjun Appadurai, "Introduction: Commodities and the Politics of Value," in *The Social Life of Things: Commodities in Cultural Perspective,* ed. Arjun Appadurai (New York: Cambridge University Press, 1992), 3–63; Igor Kopytoff, "The Cultural Biography of Things: Commoditization as Process," in Appadurai, *Social Life of Things,* 64–91.

5. Alon Confino and Peter Fritzsche, "Introduction: Noises of the Past," in *The Work of Memory: New Directions in the Study of German Society and Culture,* ed. Alon Confino and Peter Fritzsche (Urbana and Chicago: University of Illinois Press, 2002), 5.

6. According to Pierre Bourdieu, discourse about practice, being both a product of the semi-theoretical disposition that the researcher induces in the interlocutor and a reflection of a set of dispositions historically inculcated in social agents, should not be confused with practice itself; differently put, the *opus operatum* should not be taken for the modus operandi. See Pierre Bourdieu, *Outline of a Theory of Practice* (Cambridge and New York: Cambridge University Press, 1977), 16–22.

7. This is explained, at least in part, by the fact that disciplines such as social history, sociocultural anthropology, and cultural studies were almost nonexistent in socialist Romania. While the efforts of those trying to (re)create these disciplines in Romania after 1989 and their attempts to become conversant with "Western" academia are worthy of appreciation, there are still areas of relative "silence" because Romanian academic discourses lack many of the categories that became commonsensical in the West. Leisure is one such concept that has not yet been transferred or adopted.

8. Thorstein Veblen, *The Theory of the Leisure Class: An Economic Study of Institutions* (London: Unwin, 1970); Chris Rojek, *Capitalism and Leisure Theory* (London and New York: Tavistock, 1985); Chris Rojek, "Introduction," in *Leisure for Leisure: Critical Essays,* ed. Chris Rojek (Houndmills and London: Macmillan, 1989), 1–14; Colin Campbell, "Conspicuous Confusion? A Critique of Veblen's Theory of Conspicuous Consumption," *Sociological Theory* 13, no. 1 (1995): 37–47; Hans Mommaas et al., eds., *Leisure Research in Europe: Methods and Traditions* (Wallingford: Cab International, 1996).

9. Peter Burke, "The Invention of Leisure in Early Modern Europe," *Past and Present* 146 (1995): 136–50; Peter Burke, "The Invention of Leisure in Early Modern Europe: Reply," *Past and Present* 156 (1997): 192–97; Joan-Lluis Marfany, "The Invention of Leisure in Early Modern Europe," *Past and Present* 156 (1997): 174–91; Rudy Koshar, "Seeing, Traveling, and Consuming: An Introduction," in *Histories of Leisure,* ed. Rudy Koshar (Oxford and New York: Berg, 2002), 1–26.

10. In his introduction to *Leisure for Leisure,* Chris Rojek starts with a definition of leisure given by Joffre Dumazedier in *Towards a Society of Leisure* (New York: Free Press, 1967), 16–17. In this, leisure is understood as "activity—apart from the obligations of work, family and society—to which the individual turns at will for relaxation, diversion or broadening his knowledge and his spontaneous social participation, the free exercise of his creative capacity."

11. Chris Rojek, *Decentring Leisure: Rethinking Leisure Theory* (London: Sage, 1995).

12. Hugh Cunningham, *Leisure in the Industrial Revolution, c. 1780–c. 1880* (London: Croom Helm, 1980); Rojek, *Capitalism and Leisure Theory;* Jeff Bishop and Paul Hoggett, "Leisure and the Informal Economy," in Rojek, *Leisure for Leisure,* 150–70; Burke, "Invention of Leisure in Early Modern Europe," 136–50; Koshar, "Seeing, Traveling, and Consuming," 1–26.

13. Boas Shamir, "Commitment and Leisure," *Sociological Perspectives* 31, no. 2 (1998): 238–58.

14. Jamie Hysjulien, "Pleasure and the Economy of the Subject," *Cultural Critique* 20 (1990–91): 189–206.

15. David Crowley and Susan Reid explore the constitution of various spaces under socialism as sites of everyday life and arenas of ideological contest in *Socialist Spaces: Sites of Everyday Life in the Eastern Bloc* (Oxford and New York: Berg, 2002), 1–22.

16. David A. Kideckel, "Drinking Up: Alcohol, Class and Social Change in Rural Romania," *East European Quarterly* 18, no. 4 (1985): 431–46.

17. Excellently illustrating the above points, writers such as Ion D. Sîrbu (1997) and Alexander Zinoviev (1990) showed that the problematization of widespread drunkenness and the measures toward "compulsory sobriety" promoted by the Soviet leaders, and somewhat less intensely by the Romanian communist leaders, proved efficient means for controlling their subjects. The masses of convicts prosecuted for alcohol-related crimes or contraventions were an inexpensive resource (unpaid labor force) in the political economy of the socialist state. See Ion D. Sîrbu, *Adio, Europa!* (Bucharest: Cartea Românească, 1997); and Alexander Zinoviev, "Reforms and the Policy of Reform," in *Katastroika: Legend and Reality of Gorbachevism* (London: Claridge, 1990), 27–35.

18. Thomas Ilves and Carmen Pompey, "Alcoholism in Eastern Europe," in *Radio Liberty Research,* RAD Background Report (Budapest: Open Society Archives, 1987); Paul Gafton, "Heavy Drinking and Alcoholism in Romania," in *Radio Liberty Research* (Budapest: Open Society Archives, 1984).

19. Physicians working in the "Gheorghe Marinescu" Hospital of Bucharest are nowadays able to tell how they were treating "nonexistent alcoholics" before 1989. In spite of the fact that they were receiving 10 to 15 intoxicated persons a shift, physicians were not allowed to report them as alcoholics in order not to worsen the statistics. For a detailed report on this practice, see Daniela Georgescu and Romeo Neacsu, "A New 'Bet' Won: Alcoholism," in *Tineretul liber* (Budapest: Open Society Archives, 1991).

20. Katherine Verdery, *What Was Socialism, and What Comes Next?* (Princeton, N.J.: Princeton University Press, 1996), 39–57.

21. Of the various decrees of the period, the widest impact was exercised by Decree no. 76 regarding some measures concerning the retail sale of alcoholic beverages in the units of socialist commerce; Official Bulletin of Romania no. 73 from July 15, 1975, or Law no. 5 for the increase of work productivity and the perfecting of organization and standardization of production and work; and Official Bulletin of Romania no. 71 from December 20, 1985.

22. As Ilves and Pompey show, one of the adverse effects of Gorbachev's anti-alcohol campaign was that of leaving a whole area of Soviet state enterprises (producers and retailers) without the means of accomplishing their plan. At the same time, in

Poland, the state distillery was the country's most profitable enterprise providing the state with an important share of its annual income. In these circumstances, the Polish state not only did not do enough to contain the spread of alcoholism but, driven also by political motives, took measures against an independent temperance movement in 1985. See Ilves and Pompey, "Alcoholism in Eastern Europe," 4. .

23. Gafton, "Heavy Drinking and Alcoholism in Romania," 10.

24. "Hygiene Instruction in the Rural Areas," *Radio Liberty Research*, Item no. 1871/1968, Health and Recreation: Health Insurance, RU, 300, Open Society Archives.

25. Verdery, *What Was Socialism?* 191.

26. Kideckel, "Drinking Up," 431–46.

27. Sam Beck, "Changing Styles of Drinking: Alcohol Use in the Balkans," *East European Quarterly* 18, no. 4 (1985): 395–413.

28. As many of those living under socialism informed me, most of the worker commuters used to help their wives or parents fulfill their daily work norm at the cooperative farms, especially during the summer. For those whose close relatives were working for the local cooperative farm, exceeding the daily work norm meant higher monthly payments, higher ratios of agricultural produce from the cooperative at the end of the year, and potentially higher retirement benefits in the future.

29. Fredrik Barth, "Introduction," in *Ethnic Groups and Boundaries: The Social Organization of Culture Difference*, ed. Fredrik Barth (Prospect Heights, Ill.: Waveland, 1969), 9–39.

30. S.T., the villager from Dobrosloveni who explained to me the moral, legal, and practical implications of drinking while commuting, was in his seventies at the time of the interview; he was no longer drinking because of a heart condition, but was still active and taking his cows to pasture every day. Coming from a poor family of villagers, he lacked education. Working initially for the cooperative farm in the village, in his thirties he was retrained as a lathe worker. He later worked for several of the factories built in Caracal during the 1960s and commuted home daily (where he lived with his extended family) until he retired during the early 1990s.

31. The Romanian expression *să mergem doi pe una* has a powerful sexual connotation. While, in the context, it referred to the practice of two fellows contributing to buy a bottle of brandy, it hinted powerfully at the sharing of the same woman by two men. It was part of the games of allocating gender and playing with gender borders and roles in a realm that belonged almost exclusively to men. It can also be read as part of the play with meanings linking alcohol consumption and sexual promiscuity. The practice of contributing to buy a bottle of spirits ("making up a threesome") is also described by Alexander Zinoviev, *Perestroika in Partygrad* (London: Peter Owen, 1992), 75.

32. Literally "Faint Bitch," the tavern nickname alludes to the state of inebriation and its associated physical weakness, as well as to the sexually promiscuous practices performed or talked about after drinking alcohol.

33. S.M., a welder for the state railway company all his working life, told me repeatedly about the control and restraint that had to be exercised while drinking together with colleagues. Social drinking involved a complex performance during which the pleasure of being together and of moderate inebriation was always balanced by the self-control that had to be exercised both for the preservation of reputation and out of fear of informants. S.M. was a heavy smoker, a passionate drinker of spirits, and a

spirited joke teller. He commuted between the village and the various places where the railway company was working on specific projects, often having to live in barracks or dormitories improvised in train carts for several days in a row. In this male realm his qualities and vices were key ingredients for the construction of sociality.

34. Such a layout was common not only in nearby Caracal but for most of the villages in southern Romania under socialism. As in most villages, the tavern, store, culture house, town hall, and school were situated in or near the center, and the main bus stop was located there as well.

35. The remark was made by V.N., a villager from Dobrosloveni and worker on the cooperative farm of the village. Retired at the time of the interview and working his small piece of land received with the privatization of land in 1991, V.N. was frustrated both by the lower status of villagers in comparison with commuters to the factories in Caracal and with the loss of status after 1989 when the newly opened bars were dominated by a younger generation of villagers.

36. Drinking together could be both a symbolic function of exchanges and a form of payment for transactions in which the use of money would signify self-interest, distance, and amorality. As such, it created room for play with meanings in a region where reciprocity was the idealized form of exchange. The semiotic ambivalence of drinking practices created the possibility to misrepresent interested transactions as acts of generosity and to create the grounds for future reciprocal exchanges.

37. The remark was by A.M., the wife of a tractor driver in Dobrosloveni. Having completed only primary education, A.M. had worked all her life for the cooperative farm in the village. She managed to supplement household revenues by intensively working her small plot of land (the produce of which she sold in the Caracal vegetable market) and by being a daily laborer in the agricultural state farm on the outskirts of the village. She had a hard time allocating the small family revenues for the education of their children (all having obtained high school degrees under socialism) and got into frequent arguments with her husband over the portion of his salary and unofficial revenues that he kept for drinking.

38. Alain Besançon, *Economia Unui Spectru: Economia Politica a Socialismului Real* (translation of *Anatomie d'un spectre: L'economie politique du socialisme reel*) (Bucharest: Humanitas, 1992).

39. Steven L. Sampson, "The Second Economy of the Soviet Union and Eastern Europe," *Annals of the American Academy of Political and Social Science* 493 (1987): 120–36.

40. Katherine Verdery, "Theorizing Socialism: A Prologue to the 'Transition,'" *American Ethnologist* 18, no. 3 (1991): 419–39.

41. Gerald Mars and Yochanan Altman, "The Cultural Bases of Soviet Georgia's Second Economy," *Soviet Studies* 35, no. 4 (1983): 546–60.

42. Stealing from state factories was euphemistically called "taking" in discussions among my informants as well as during the interviews I conducted for this research.

43. Mary Douglas, ed., *Constructive Drinking: Perspectives on Drink from Anthropology* (Cambridge and New York: Cambridge University Press, 1987); Dimitra Gefou-Madianou, "Introduction: Alcohol Commensality, Identity Transformations and Transcendence," in *Alcohol, Gender and Culture*, ed. Dimitra Gefou-Madianou (London and New York: Routledge, 1992), 1–34.

44. Caution is needed when generalizing from my ethnographic findings in Ol-

tenia. Gender patterns of alcohol consumption and attitudes to drinking might have been different in the large cities or in other parts of Romania (such as Transylvania).

45. The confession about the uneasy relation with drinking and with spaces for the public consumption of alcohol was made by C.N., a teacher from Dobrosloveni, retired at the time of the interview. Being educated in one of the large cities in Romania and used to the discourses and practices of emancipated women there (including public smoking and drinking), C.N. had to fit into the gendered patterns of consumption and local ideas of respectability once she returned to teach in her native village.

46. All the quotations above come from an interview with S.M. (the welder introduced earlier in the chapter) conducted in the summer of 2004.

47. The confession was made by S.T. (introduced earlier in the chapter) during one of our more informal discussions.

48. The words of C.N., the woman teacher from Dobrosloveni, illustrate perfectly the embodiment of moral sanctions associated with trespassing the borders of the gendered realms existing at the time.

49. The quotations from this paragraph reproduce the assertions of L.M., a housewife and part-time laborer on the agricultural state farm in Dobrosloveni. She was seen as an ascetic and industrious woman who took good care of her household and large family. These qualities were appreciated locally, especially as her husband (S.M., the welder introduced earlier in the chapter) was away from home for several days in a row.

50. Hysjulien, "Pleasure and the Economy of the Subject," 189–206.

51. Edward Surtz, "The Link Between Pleasure and Communism in Utopia," *Modern Language Notes* 70, no. 2 (1995): 90–93.

52. Susan Winnett, "Coming Unstrung: Women, Men, Narrative, and Principles of Pleasure," *PMLA* 105, no. 3 (1990): 505–18.

53. Verdery, *What Was Socialism?* 13.

54. Michael Burawoy and Katherine Verdery, "Introduction," in *Uncertain Transition: Ethnographies of Change in the Postsocialist World,* ed. Michael Burawoy and Katherine Verdery (Lanham, Md.: Rowman and Littlefield, 1999), 3.

CHAPTER ELEVEN

Soviet Women and Fur Consumption

in the Brezhnev Era

Anna Tikhomirova

The Brezhnev period in the Soviet Union was marked by double standards in official attitudes toward commodities. On one hand, official ideological discourse condemned the taste for luxury, celebrating the divestment of things (*razveshchestvlenie*) as an ideal. The Khrushchev-era campaign against Stalinist *meshchanstvo'* (philistinism), emblematized in the taste for small elephant statuettes, rugs decorated with swans, gabardine coats, and so on, continued into the mid-1970s in the form of a critique of excessive consumerism (*veshchizm*).[1] Yet at the same time, a characteristic feature of late Soviet society was the "little deal" between the state and the middle classes and the *nomenklatura*, that is, the class of state and party functionaries who formed part of the Soviet intelligentsia (along with scientists, engineers, cultural workers, educationalists, and public health workers). In effect, the *nomenklatura* was the ruling class elite of late Soviet society, enjoying not only political power but also many privileges. The "little deal" legitimized these privileges.[2] Fur coats, as objects of prestigious consumption, were a highly visible marker of the luxury-oriented lifestyle of this elite; they contributed to the symbolic ordering of late Soviet society in which the *nomenklatura* may be distinguished from "ordinary" women of the intelligentsia. In this essay, the term "ordinary" women of the intelligentsia refers to people with higher education. Although well educated, these women were nevertheless "ordinary" consumers. For unlike the *nomenklatura*, they did not enjoy privileged access to official systems of distribution. And, in contrast to subcultural or oppositional groups such as *stiliagi*, hedonistic young consumers of fashion and pop music, their lifestyles and everyday consumption practices can be characterized as attempts to find a golden mean between necessity and luxury, rather than as a form of rebellion. In this way, their attitudes and practices were in harmony with official political attitudes and policies.[3] Thus I do not explore here those aspects of consumption which contributed to the destruction of the Soviet system; rather, I examine the mechanisms of Soviet consumer culture that held the system together and allowed it to exist for as long as it did.[4]

This chapter challenges the often overstated and even clichéd opposition of *nomenklatura* and "ordinary" intelligentsia women by identifying subtle social and class distinctions within late Soviet society. It suggests that Pierre Bourdieu's concept of the distinction-producing functions of consumption in general, and fashion in particular, may be brought to bear on socialist societies, while acknowledging their considerable differences from capitalist societies.[5] This essay sets out to explore why such social and class distinctions emerged and how they functioned, and to analyze the symbolic meanings ascribed to furs and the everyday practices in which these items of clothing were given a central role. "Consumption" here refers not only to the economic and utilitarian aspects of use but also to the production of symbolic meanings in the sense proposed by Jean Baudrillard.[6] His arguments about the various realities of commodities (linguistic, technological, emotional, and everyday) can also be applied to late Soviet consumer culture, a world of shortages, despite the fact that they were first applied to a context of relative prosperity, Western consumer societies. Baudrillard's concept of consumption—in addition to the ideas of Bourdieu—provide heuristic inspiration if not a specific analytical model for this essay.

The arguments offered here are based on an investigation of late Soviet official discourses on furs, particularly those appearing on the pages of fashion and women magazines, including the East German fur industry journal *Brühl*. This was the only specialist publication of its kind that appeared within the Comecon (Council for Mutual Economic Assistance) area. Although expensive, it was on sale on Soviet newsstands and was read by Soviet professionals working in the fur industry. Other titles consulted include *Fashion Journal* (*Zhurnal mod;* the leading Soviet fashion journal) and the satirical journal *Krokodil*. Particular emphasis is also given to interviews with consumers, specifically twenty-four women born between 1923 and 1974 and living in Moscow, Novosibirsk, and Yaroslavl. In treating their memories as a primary source, I draw on anthropologist Clifford Geertz's ideas of "thick description" in an attempt to understand the living universe of ordinary women.[7] The interview technique was informed by methods of qualitative social research, specifically those developed by Gabriele Rosenthal, whose techniques of "narrative analysis" exploit narrative-generating "how" questions (rather than analytical "why" questions).[8] These methods allow the interviewer to extract remembrances which draw closer to an individual's experiences.

The collapse of the U.S.S.R. initiated not only a change of the political system but also a transformation in the prevailing modes of consumption. In the 1990s a specific late Soviet "consumer culture" was transformed, through a chaotic and unbalanced process, into a kind of "consumer society" based on Western models. One concomitant of this process was the suppression of any "Sovietness" in the collective memory. The early years of the new century marked the next stage of post-Soviet consumer culture, with Vladimir Putin's rise to power functioning as a kind of watershed. Unlike the Western-minded 1990s, the years since have been characterized by marked anti-Westernism in Russia and a discourse promoting a kind of "national *Sonderweg*" (special path). This national discourse roots itself in a pre-Soviet past, imagining the years before 1917 in terms of glory and heroism. Yet at the same time the Soviet past, condemned until recently, has in some aspects been restored in the collective memory. Here too, one can identify a nostalgic emphasis on glory and heroism.[9] The Soviet past has been subject to much *(n)ostalgia* and transformed into something like a fashionable brand.[10] Nevertheless, my interviews expose a layer of memory which is, I suggest, still relatively close to individual experiences of the Soviet past, not only thanks to the techniques developed by Rosenthal but also because I conducted my interviews between 2003 and 2005, when Soviet *(n)ostalgia* was still nascent. In fact, the language and everyday perceptions of my interviewees remain colored by the ideological discourses of the late Soviet period and, to a lesser degree, by the subsequent post-communist discourses.

All my interviewees share, as part of their collective identity, a sense of their own "normality." They stress their place among "ordinary Soviet people" ("we") in opposition to the "elites" ("they"). In using the term "elite" they invoke people in high professional or Party positions with privileged access to the systems of distribution (whether of economic or social capital); their wives; and Soviet "high society" ladies, bohemians, and those in high positions in the field of Soviet trade. More specifically, the interviewees also feel a strong sense of belonging to the technical or cultural intelligentsia. Regarding their economic status, a chemist from Yaroslavl born in 1953 expresses a not untypical view: "Our family wouldn't be considered rich, of course; but, on the other hand, we didn't live in misery." Most displayed a strong interest in material things and forms of prestigious consumption, which might be taken to be characteristic of the late Soviet period. Their awareness of fashion was shaped by magazines (such as *Fashion Journal* and, as some reported, also the West German *Burda Moden* and *Sibylle*, *Für Dich* or *PRAMO* from East Germany, as well as *Siluet* from the Baltic republics) as well as the style of the Soviet elites. As the same woman reflected:

> How did a typical *obkomovets* [a member of a regional committee of the Communist Party] look? Well, he didn't stand out much, but his clothes were always of the highest quality. And, in conversation, he was known to mention his trips either abroad, or to the health resorts where he had vacationed with celebrities.

At the same time my interviewees, when asked about the defining features of good taste, stressed the importance of "modesty," "rationality," and "functionality." One, an economist from Moscow born at the end of the Stalin years, made the social pressure toward conformity clear:

> To stand out from the masses—no, it wasn't accepted. If your clothes set you apart (meaning originality), you were reviled behind your back. If your clothes were expensive or prestigious, questions immediately arose—with what money? And where did you get it (and through what connections)? This was true, of course, only for ordinary people: the *nomenklatura* was never bothered by such questions.
>
> Style was not the goal in itself, and outfits [*shmotki*]—not the main thing in life . . . I never thought about clothes, or that I wanted to set myself apart through fashion: it just happened. (Interview with T.I., female, born 1946, interpreter, lived in Yaroslavl)

Even for those who represented themselves as being particularly fashion conscious, everyday life was structured by a strong interest in culture (such as visits to theaters or concerts); by work; and by social collective practices such as organized tourism, or demonstrations.

Furs from Tsarist Luxury to Socialist Fashion

Fur played an important economic role in Soviet export trade throughout the Stalin years, serving the demand for luxury abroad. It was only in the late 1950s, with the emergence of a Soviet version of mass consumer society and, as Larissa Zakharova shows in her chapter in this book, with a reconsideration of the role of fashion, that official attitudes changed. Fur's status as an export commodity was modified by a new rhetoric representing it as inexpensive clothing that could satisfy mass demand at home. As a writer in the East German magazine *Brühl* put it in 1962:

> The timeless fur, which was possible to wear for decades, and which was more a status symbol than a fashionable item of clothing, belongs to the past. To own a fur is no longer a privilege of the idle rich. The circle of those who wear a fur today is so large that it can now be considered an item of daily winter use.[11]

The democratization of fur would at first sight appear to hark back to older versions of luxury. The meaning of this material, however, had changed. Expensive or "tsarist" furs such as sable were repudiated while inexpensive furs including sheepskin and rabbit were "ennobled." This was, at least in part, to reduce production costs. From the late 1950s on, efforts were also made to manufacture and promote artificial furs. The first winter coat made from artificial karakul appeared on the cover of *Fashion Journal* in 1955.[12] It seemed at the time that artificial furs would soon become "favorite women's wear."[13] And from 1960 insulated linings made of artificial furs were promoted ("peerless for any kind of work or travel").[14] At the same time, there was a regrading of fur clothing. From the 1950s central planners identified fur collars and caps (but not fur coats) as legitimate needs and set production targets for the Soviet fur industry.[15] This was reinforced by articles in fashion journals, which promoted these fur-trimmed products and at the same time argued for moderation in fur consumption. Arguments against a complete fur coat varied from pragmatic ones (the inconvenience of wearing one while traveling) to an aesthetic logic (concern, for instance, that an abundance of fur-muffled people could "spoil" a winter landscape).[16]

Yet contradictions abounded in the official representation of fur. Despite such—admittedly rare—comments that sought to discipline fur consumption, this material was continually legitimated by images of modernized versions of Russian national costume which appeared in the press. The "Russianness" of furs was also stressed in fashion shows abroad at events organized to promote an image of high living standards in the Soviet Union. Of a Soviet exhibition in Brazil in 1966, one Russian journalist wrote:

> The models appeared on the catwalk dressed in jazzy, ornamental ski-suits topped with fur jackets or fur coats made of squirrel, deer, karakul, in colored kerchiefs and boots, in everyday and holiday winter

clothes ... Many models were dressed in traditional Russian national
costumes ... They don't wear furs in Brazil, but nevertheless all the
furs of our collection were greeted very enthusiastically.[17]

The manufacture of fur caps was industrialized before the Second
World War. In the second half of the 1950s assembly lines were organized
for the production of collars and fur coats.[18] Official rhetoric made much
of increased production, with the output of collars increasing almost four-
fold and of caps by almost five times between 1950 and 1972.[19] By the late
1960s and 1970s, the rhetoric of dizzying quantity was supplemented by
new claims about the quality and fashionability of fur clothing. Brezhnev
himself turned furrier at the 1972 October plenary session of the Communist Party Central Committee when he said: "By the term quality we refer
not only to the durability but also to the decorations, the cut, and the relation to the fashion world."[20] At this time attempts were made to accelerate
the introduction of new models into mass manufacture. By the end of the
1970s official rhetoric increasingly talked of "fashionable fur clothing accessible to everybody." But with the growing shortages in the Soviet economy
and an accompanying discourse of asceticism ("just a few things"), the relation between furs and fashion was also a problem. In this context, the role
of communal services such as specialist sewing ateliers where one could
update and thereby prolong the life of a fur became important. Would-be
fashionable consumers were asked, "Is a new fur coat really necessary, when
it is possible to update an old one?"

As this brief excursion into history shows, the meaning and economic
significance of fur clothing shifted considerably through the Soviet period.
A good deal of effort was put into legitimating what had once been decried
as a symbol of tsarist excess. The words "fur coat" (*shuba*), a term associated
with tsarist luxury, prestigious consumption, philistinism, and commodity
fetishism, disappeared from official texts and was replaced by more neutral definitions such as "furs," "fur clothing," and "coat made of fur." But
what meanings were ascribed to furs by Soviet women themselves? Was fur
clothing a "luxury" for them?

Furs in Everyday Life

Attitudes to fur clothing were far from uniform. One respondent, born
in 1949, recalled: "I never wanted to own a fur coat, I was always indifferent to furs ... In Soviet times I didn't dream about furs at all." She,
however, appears to have been exceptional. For the overwhelming majority
of women it would seem that fur clothing was vitally important. Another

interviewee of the same generation stated: "I think that to have a fur coat [*shuba*] is the greatest dream for women of any age." What prompted such an all-conquering desire to possess a fur coat? First, there appear to have been what we might call "technological" reasons (drawing an analogy with what Baudrillard calls the "technological reality" of commodities as material objects with styles, cuts, fabric, colors, etc.), when the desire to have a fur coat was expressed not in terms of luxury but as a necessity relating to the conditions of life (such as the harsh climate). Second, interviewees expressed "emotional" reasons (close to the "emotional reality" of commodities described by Baudrillard as a category of feelings experienced by their consumers), verbalizing the desire to have a fur coat in terms of sensual perception (to touch the fur coat, the feeling of being "dressed in a fur coat"). What is striking is that such perceptions varied from negative emotions such as complaints about the slight odor produced by a fur coat, to ecstatic ones, and even to recollections tinged with eroticism and sensual pleasure.[21] Fur coats were "loved," "adored" by their owners; they were "comfortable," "cozy," and "warm." Finally, the possession of a fur coat was, for ordinary intelligentsia women—particularly of the older generations—a sign of an upward mobility from the working or peasant class. It embodied the availability of cultural, social, and economic capital in Soviet life.

Despite the official rhetoric stressing the democratic and utilitarian qualities of fur clothing, these objects retained their prestige as luxury goods and status symbols in the lives of these Soviet women. Furs in general were described in interviews as a "luxury," though the women interviewed tended to avoid explicit use of the word *roskosh'*, preferring to substitute it with near-synonyms like "prestigious," "smart," "original," and "favorite" (*prestizhnyi, shikarnyi, original'nyi, liubimyi*). The official view and that of consumers were not always divergent: the association of furs with "Russianness" was a shared understanding. Here the relationship with other prestige goods is significant. Asked which commodities had symbolized the "good life" for Soviet women, the interviewees ranked significant commodities: the more geographically remote and inaccessible its origins, the more "prestigious" the object. A key marker for Soviet women consumers was imported commodities such as clothes, shoes, or perfume. In this, they distinguished "authentic" items (from the West) from those originating in Comecon countries, which were to some degree considered as "ersatz."[22] The boundary between "foreign" and "our" clothes was very significant for Soviet women. The former connoted not only economic capital but also privilege and cultural capital. One interviewee, an economist born before the Second World War who had lived in Novosibirsk, recalled: "Prestigious meant imported, without a doubt. Even if somebody had clothes that were not bad but of

Soviet manufacture, she would quickly say that they were made to a foreign design." In the context of the seemingly unconditional preference for imported clothes in the symbolic economy of everyday life, the "Russianness" of fur coats marks a kind of exception. According to the fashion historian Alexander Vasil'ev, there was no autonomous Soviet fashion.[23] The names of designers—with the exception of Viacheslav Zaitsev—were unknown to the general public, and there was a host of ideological restrictions placed on fashion. By contrast, fur clothing had a clear and distinct Russian identity, first in serving the aristocracy and later in the form of gifts to Soviet leaders. As one respondent stated: "Furs—that is frost, snow, village, Russia" (interview with E.E., female, born 1960, nurse, lived in Moscow).

Furs, Gender, and Generation: Individual Distinctions

Women consumers understood fur clothing in terms of subtle distinctions. Let's try to deconstruct the often contradictory impression made by the Soviet crowd in winter. One of the basic stratification categories was that of age. Generally, a distinction was drawn, both in official fashion discourse and by women consumers, between "young girls" and "women of a certain age." In the minds of the interviewees of all ages, a fur coat was usually associated with mature women, over forty years old. As one respondent recalled: "Once I was walking with my younger brother, a military cadet, and a shopgirl on the street said to me: 'Mamasha, won't you buy some apples for your son. Look at him, he is so pale, he needs vitamins.' I was very embarrassed by this because at the time I was only twenty-five years old. Only older women wore fur coats, and that's why she took me for one of them" (interview with S.B., female, born 1950, economist, lived in Moscow). While mature women wore "serious" and "elegant" furs such as mink, karakul, baby beaver lamb, and sheepskin collars and caps, young girls favored either "queen's mohair," long-haired fur, or "fluffy" fur collars, particularly polar fox. Ordinary women of the intelligentsia appear to have internalized the official fashion discourses about age. This distinction echoed one of the fundamental stratifications of Soviet fashion throughout the Brezhnev era: two basic fur fashion lines were represented in the journals, "sports" clothes for young girls and "elegant" ones for "older women." This was a distinction which corresponded to body types (slender and "plump").

Another significant category was that of gender, or, more precisely, the distinction between women and men. Respondents expressed stereotypes, such as "fashion is the affair of women" and specifically that fur coats are female clothing. Furs were also divided into feminine and masculine types: fox fur and other long-haired furs were connoted in everyday practices as being explicitly "feminine," while others like sheepskin coats were gender-neutral.[24] This, too, reinforced official rhetoric. Similar gender distinctions appeared on *Brühl*'s pages. Its articles and accompanying photographs reproduced a very expressive iconography of "fur in action." Women appeared as fur consumers in the setting of luxurious theaters, operas, or restaurants, while men appeared as fur buyers or fur givers (themselves dressed in classical suits, smoking feverishly and excitedly offering escalating sums of money for furs).[25] In this regard, men were themselves represented in terms of conspicuous fashionable behavior that followed from the exercise of free choice. In this, lines can be drawn to other consumer identities such as those attached to the *stiliagi* (a subcultural movement of young men in the postwar period, distinguished by their love of American rock and roll and extraordinary sartorial codes, such as very narrow trousers known as *dudochki*), to "speculators" (*fartsovshchiki*), or to "legitimate" status distinctions enjoyed by the *nomenklatura*.[26]

What social distinctions could be identified in the consumption of fur clothing? The most significant categories of social stratification employed by the interviewees were those which separated "elites" from "ordinary" people. In distinguishing groups in this way, a corresponding distinction was often drawn between a "natural fur coat" and a "winter coat with a fur collar." As one respondent recalled: "Furs were expensive. Mink, polar fox, sable were in demand and considered 'prestigious.' [Whereas] the majority of people wore winter coats with only a fur collar" (interview with O.B., female, born 1948, engineer, lived in Moscow). Particular importance was attributed to the size of a fur collar: the bigger the collar, the wealthier its wearer was assumed to be. However, even the biggest fur collar was relatively modest when compared to the full fur coats worn by the elite. Some ordinary women interviewees aspired to own such prestigious commodities. One recalled, "By the end of the 1980s I bought a brown fur coat made of an artificial fur. I didn't like it very much, it was heavy and uncomfortable. I did not wear it for long. I already had a winter coat, with a mink and polar fox collar. I wanted a fur coat just to complete the 'collection'" (interview with T.N., female, born 1951, chemist, lived in Moscow). In this instance, not only economic wealth but also cultural capital was invoked. The fur coats worn by the elite could be understood as a benchmark against which one's own taste and that of others could be judged.

Significant distinctions could also be drawn between natural and artificial furs: "People from the party *nomenklatura* wore natural furs from the distribution center [*spetsraspredelitel'*].[27] People of my status didn't have access to natural furs and had to limit themselves to artificial furs ... Moscow in those times was synthetic and 'sparks flew' in the metro before 'antistatic'

was discovered" (interview with K.V., female, born 1935, economist, lived
in Moscow). In the satirical journal *Krokodil* there was much discussion
from the late 1960s about the stifling effects of artificial fur coats (they
were hot and uncomfortable).[28] Such scornful attitudes to synthetics persisted despite propaganda actively promoting the technical achievements of
Soviet chemistry and the practical advantages of artificial furs. The benefits
claimed for artificial furs over natural furs included their availability at low
prices, greater durability, elegance, and the variety of styles in which they
could be made, and they were often promoted as ensembles combined with
suede and leather, as well as coats made of artificial sheepskin. A slogan that
appeared in Soviet fashion journals in the 1970s was "modern artificial furs
for our youth."[29] This rhetoric reached its apotheosis in the 1980s when
artificial fur no longer imitated natural furs, but appeared as "quite new sorts
of material [with which] to model any kind of apparel."[30] However fine an
artificial fur coat—even the most scarce French imitation leopard skin coat
of the 1970s—Soviet women consumers always preferred a natural one.
As for artificial fur coats, respondents indicated that imported ones were
preferred to those made in the Soviet Union because of their better quality
and the possibility of washing them at home without damage.[31] Thus, the
example of artificial furs clearly demonstrates the gap between everyday
practices and official discourses.

It is also necessary to note the difference between heavy and simply cut
fur coats, accessible to ordinary women, and those produced in small numbers in small specialist sewing ateliers and intended for export but often
consumed by the elites. Very visible examples of the latter were the blue
squirrel fur coats worn by Svetlana Allilueva (Stalin's daughter) and Galina
Brezhneva (Brezhnev's daughter). Which furs symbolized membership in
the elites and, conversely, the status of being an "ordinary woman"? The fur
with least prestige was rabbit, despite great efforts to promote its advantages. Much was made of the "discovery" of this material by Paris fashion
houses in 1965–66. Thus rabbit fur was "ennobled" from abroad.[32] Meanwhile, the *Great Soviet Encyclopedia* in 1974 promoted the practice of dyeing
rabbit fur to imitate sealskin, mink, or sable.[33] Yet these efforts had little
effect. In fact, sheepskin (specifically a type of sheepskin known as "mutton"
[*muton*]) had a better claim to the title of "people's fur." As one respondent
residing in Novosibirsk noted: "Every member of our family had a 'sheep's
wool' fur coat. Although heavy, they were very warm and durable."

Mink was a dream, the height of luxury for Soviet women. The most
significant Soviet fur, it was always an enigma, carrying the aura of the
unknown, of elitism, of inaccessibility. Above all, it implied powerful economic capital: "We didn't even hear about mink. Maybe prominent actors,

big-time bosses and so on wore those furs" (interview with S.B., female, born 1950, economist, lived in Moscow). And "mink coats were incredibly expensive. It's hard to say who bought them because these were people who belonged to another class. They had a lot of money and probably they were actors, scholars, and so on" (interview with M.P., female, born 1952, engineer, lived in Moscow). In official texts mink was primarily an export good and not a material for mass consumption.[34] It was nevertheless possible—at least in principle—for ordinary women to buy a mink fur coat if they had enough money. (They were on open sale in Moscow in a specialized shop named "Furs—Shoes" ["Mekha—Obuv'"].) As one interviewee remembered: "Mink coats were sold in the fur departments of large department stores. They cost about six or seven thousand rubles (the same as a car!) and they were very beautiful. We didn't buy them simply because of the price" (interview with M.P., female, born 1946, engineer, lived in Moscow). At the same time Soviet power elites (for instance, the secretaries of various committees of the Communist Party) had their own channels to high-quality furs, including leather coats with small fur collars available from the end of the 1970s, or karakul coats. The sheepskin coat (*dublenka*) belonged to this category of furs only available through the "channels of power."[35] This particular item has an interesting history in that initially it had served as working clothes for watchmen, but it came into fashion in the Soviet Union in the 1980s. As one respondent recalled: "Once, my husband and I went to celebrate the New Year with friends whose parents worked for the regional committee [of the Communist Party] and were, therefore, very high authorities. We walked into the foyer and were stupefied—there were nothing but sheepskin coats on the coat-rack! My husband at that time wore a coat of imitation suede. Of course we were rather poorly dressed when compared to the rest of the guests" (interview with E.N., female, born 1949, chemist, lived in Yaroslavl). It was far more unusual to encounter "luxurious" furs such as fox, sable, or silver fox in Soviet life: "A silver fox collar was considered very 'prestigious.' There were no coats made entirely of silver fox fur, or maybe there were, but extremely rare and too expensive" (interview with A.A., female, born 1945, university teacher of Russian language, had lived in various Russian provincial towns).

An important marker of social distinction in Soviet society was the possession of a fur cap. On the one hand, it signaled command of political capital (or power). As one respondent recalled: "Workers wore, for the most part, rabbit caps, but members of the regional or the town committee [of the Communist Party] wore beaver ones. Authorities of lesser status wore mink caps (for men) or deer calfskin [*pyzhik*] caps ... Therefore it was possible to guess where a person worked by his hat" (interview with E.N., female, born 1949, chemist, lived in Yaroslavl). Fur caps also signaled the command over cultural capital as well: "I always wanted a fur cap. In those days fur caps were worn by the intelligentsia like doctors, engineers, and teachers" (interview with M.G., female, born 1923, doctor, lived in Yaroslavl).

Another form of social stratification in the consumption of fur was spatial: distinctions were drawn between Moscow and the provinces, and between town and village. Fashions in the provinces lagged behind Moscow: "In 1970 I came to Moscow from my village dressed in a green scarf and a winter coat with a beaver lamb collar, bought specially for Moscow ... Of course I felt like a provincial girl. People there looked better off. As far as I remember, Muscovites wore winter coats with 'big' furs like polar fox, or a mink" (interview with T.N., female, born 1951, chemist, lived in Moscow).

Detailed, thick descriptions of furs in the Brezhnev years allow us to "see" the social topography of Soviet society. We turn now to the question of why such lines of distinction operated. How did my interviewees understand the logic of the world of fur consumption? Their perspectives emerge in their descriptions of what can be called the "cultural biographies" of fur commodities in the embryonic realm of Soviet fashion in the Brezhnev years.[36] Such biographies encompass, first, the ways in which furs were acquired (the "emergence" of a commodity); second, the practices of using furs in daily life (the "life" of a commodity); and third, the life span of furs (encompassing the "disappearance" of a commodity).

Ways of Getting Furs

Soviet women were confronted with a dilemma. Mink clothing—the object of their dreams—was freely on sale, but was terribly expensive. Conversely, a "mutton" coat was more affordable but in short supply.[37] The latter constituted, therefore, a specific kind of socialist luxury, a theme developed by Ina Merkel in her chapter in this volume. That Soviet citizens developed strategies for coping with shortage—including furs—went without saying, or rather was not explicitly explained in interviews. Nevertheless, respondents described the social dimensions of life in a world of shortages. They described a philosophy of self-reliance, emphasizing the importance of being patient or of "hunting": "we were always in search of commodities"; "sometimes something was thrown out [put on sale] in the shop while we were on the hunt for goods." At the same time, it was sometimes important to "count on others," stressing the importance of "acquaintances" and "connections," or *blat* (like *spetsraspredelitel'*, *blat* had its origins in the 1920s, but survived after the rationing system ended), as well as the privileges which accompanied one's position in the social hierarchy.[38] Furs—as a luxury—

were acquired for special occasions like graduation from college. Yet one also had to be ready to obtain them at any time; Soviet women had to accept that chance was an important aspect of their lives by developing a "just in case" mentality. It should be noted here that respondents structured the hierarchies of acquisition in terms of ease/difficulty rather than in terms of legitimacy/illegitimacy.

The question of where to obtain furs was also significant. The sites of acquisition can be classified. First, furs could be bought in shops. In provincial towns, according to recollections of life in Yaroslavl, natural fur coats were only on open sale during the Khrushchev period. They disappeared from the stores during the Brezhnev years and, consequently, other acquisition strategies became necessary. Some consumers had access to shops which served a defined and limited clientele such as Voentorg ("military trade" stores that supplied Soviet army officers and their family members), which was better supplied with consumer goods, or the "Salons for Newlyweds" found in big cities and also in most smaller ones. Others exploited "connections" with any workers in Soviet trade. By contrast, artificial fur coats continued to be available in Yaroslavl until the early 1980s.

In this context of growing shortages, the possibility of shopping in Moscow was particularly significant. It was possible for women living in Yaroslavl to travel to the capital and back in a day (four hours each way on an electric train).[39] As respondents indicate, not only were the "terribly expensive" mink coats on open sale in Moscow: less expensive rabbit, goat, sheepskin, beaver lamb, and "mutton" coats could also be purchased there. They were sold either in specialized fur shops or in the fur departments of large department stores (GUM and TsUM), or in less well-known places (for instance, an atelier at Kuznetskii Bridge):

> Just by sheer chance my mother and I got lucky on our next trip to Moscow. We were able to buy a real sealskin coat. It was very expensive at that time ... The coat cost double my monthly salary of sixty-five rubles ... Hours of standing in line at GUM or TsUM were no guarantee that you would get that fur or winter coat. The line was three floors long, beginning somewhere in the street. Of course, to stay in the queue for hours was rather tiresome, even for young people, but in those days it wasn't considered a "humiliation." We were just very eager to buy something unusual and to separate oneself from the gray crowd. (Interview with I.D., female, born 1949, secretary, lived in Yaroslavl)

It was also possible to buy "prestigious" artificial fur coats in Moscow such as a "French" coat in imitation leopard skin or an artificial fur coat imitat-

ing sheepskin or suede. If one had the necessary funds and was prepared to
queue, one could also buy the object of many young women's dreams in the
1970s, a polar fox collar. As one respondent recalled:

> In 1974 I first acquired a winter coat with a natural fur collar. It was
> made of polar fox. To buy it, I stood in a long queue in Moscow all
> day. It was on a special shopping tour to Moscow that my friend and
> I took. There were winter coats of various colors and cuts. People were
> constantly coming out of the shop with coats. They were buying them
> and nobody knew which coats in which colors were going to be carried
> out next . . . while the queue was moving, all the colors I liked sold out,
> and I was stuck with a violet coat. It cost 200 rubles, while my salary
> was then 80 rubles, so this was money that I had saved up. (Interview
> with I.B., female, born 1953, chemist scientist with doctor's degree,
> lived in Yaroslavl)

Moscow was not the only place where furs could be purchased. In
fact, women bought furs anywhere, often "by chance" (on business trips,
when visiting relatives, etc.). In this regard, the Baltic republics—the Soviet "abroad"—stood out. What was distinct and significant for ordinary
women of the intelligentsia was the practice of getting furs in Comecon
countries (a widespread practice among army officers' wives). Respondents
recalled excellent natural fur coats (sealskin or "mutton") bought in East
Germany, which stood out in the Soviet winter crowd.

The second context in which furs could be acquired can be described
as the second or gray economy (discussed by Larissa Zakharova in this
volume). Furs were available at street markets, although the quality of these
goods was uncertain: "It was possible to buy both fur coats and skins in
the market, but we were afraid of the quality, because badly dressed skins
could fall to pieces or be worm-infested" (interview with I.B., female, born
1953, chemist scientist with doctor's degree, lived in Yaroslavl). Another
commented: "One could only buy fur caps at the flea market [the so-called
barakholka] in those times. They were not mass-produced and were sold
by hunters, so these fur caps were handmade. Those who couldn't afford or
didn't consider fur a necessity wore knitted hats, which were also popular"
(interview with I.D., female, born 1949, secretary, lived in Yaroslavl). One
could also buy a natural fur coat privately through a "speculator." As one
respondent recalled: "At the end of the 1980s the possibility of buying a
fur coat for double the price, 'on the side' arose. For instance, 'sheepskin'
coats that were sewn in Kaunas, in Lithuania. We bought fur coats in the
homes of honest Lithuanians, for four hundred rubles, and it was a good

deal" (interview with A.V., female, born 1950, chemist with a Ph.D., lived in Yaroslavl). The 1980s were an age of "barter," a symptom of the break-down of the Soviet economy: "In the 1980s there were so-called 'sales' at factories: when shops came to the factory and brought consumer goods for workers of this concrete factory" (interview with L.I., female, born 1961, engineer, lived in Moscow). Or: "They were bartered at the oil refinery, but not everybody could buy those goods: only those who won when they drew lots" (interview with I.B., female, born 1953, chemist scientist with doctor's degree, lived in Yaroslavl).

Thirdly, the most widespread acquisition strategy, particularly for winter coats with fur collars, was the practice of obtaining the skin usually at a street market and then having a coat made to order by a tailor in a sewing shop called an "*atel'ė*" (a "legitimate" service). The process of obtaining skins could be extremely energy- and time-consuming. These skins were variously farmed fur, "from under the bed" (that is, old furs passed down through the family), or the fur of trapped animals (such as marmots). Expensive karakul or mink skins could be purchased in Moscow in the GUM and TsUM department stores or, more likely, at the general consumer goods fair in Sokol'niki. A practical alternative to a demanding search for furs at such retail outlets, and one described by a number of respondents, was to collect "fur coupons." One outlined the system:

> There were times in the 1970s when there was no gold or fur but it was prestigious to own them. Coupons to have fur coats and caps made to order were distributed through the local trade union and Party committees in the institution where you worked as rewards or as a bonus. For example, you could get one as a young specialist for succeeding in socialist competition. Each institution was given between three and ten fur coupons ... This fur coupon only guaranteed permission to have the coat sewn. You still had to pay money for the actual work. My salary was 115 rubles, and that fur coat cost 750 rubles ... The whole process from the distribution of the fur coupon to the sewing of the coat took about two weeks: the committee gathered together and decided who would get this fur coupon (either chiefs, activists, or by drawing lots). Then you went with this fur coupon (just a piece of paper with an address of a sewing atelier) to the establishment and you were offered several different kinds of fur, and in two weeks the fur coat was yours! (Interview with L.I., female, born 1961, engineer, lived in Moscow)

In the absence of such a fur coupon, to have a fur coat made to order in an atelier was a nerve-wracking and potentially disastrous experience. The quality of the work was often catastrophically bad and led to disputes between clients and the shop. The gap between the much-proclaimed "high attention to the provision of cultural and living facilities" that such services were supposed to provide and reality was vast. It was typical to wait two months for an order to be completed, the result being something quite different from that which had been ordered (often the wrong fur collar or even the production of an ordinary coat when one had requested fur): "The way they sewed was just dreadful. There were quite a lot of fur sewing-shops, but finding a good tailor was a problem. Once they cut out a rectangle instead of a trapezoid! A scandal ensued, then they altered it ... it was terrible!" (interview with E.E., female, born 1960, nurse, lived in Moscow).[40] Such sewing shops were a favorite target of *Krokodil* and other Soviet publications in the 1970s.[41]

Let us now consider the acquisition practices of the elites, as reflected in the recollections of ordinary women. It is important to note here that the elites were differentiated in a range of ways that might be placed on a spectrum. At one end, some sections of the elite were considered "ours but also other" (these people included workers in Soviet trade such as heads of departments and warehouses, as well as the wives of army officers and salesmen), whereas others were so distant that the interviewees could only guess the concrete privileges they enjoyed or report rumors that circulated about their secret world. These "others" were first, party *nomenklatura;* second, chiefs of institutions; and third, members of the artistic bohemia. The means by which the elite acquired fur clothing inverted the practices of ordinary women. "Legitimate distribution" sites took the form of special "distribution centers" (*spetsraspredelitel'*) and specialist sewing shops for fur clothes to which only the elites had access. These were the fashion spaces patronized by elites from the "biotope" of Soviet institutions (the hierarchical pyramid of power which had a Communist Party Central Committee secretary, a secretary of the local trade union committee, and a chief of the department at its apex, supported by a second, larger "tier" which included "Party organizer" [called *Partorg*], the chairman of the department committee, and so on).[42] In addition, elites had access to "Beriozka" (special shops where foreigners could buy things with foreign currency after showing their passport), a fashion space described as the "enclave of Soviet luxury."[43] This realm was rendered exclusive by the fact that most women lacked the necessary economic capital to shop there. In official discourse, such ways of procuring furs were unspoken.

By an irony of fate, the elite also shared the most widespread practice of ordinary women: obtaining skins and having a fur coat made to order.

In this regard, it is notable that no interviewee expressed any surprise that these practices of custom-making prevailed in a country which constantly represented itself as a developed industrial state. While ordinary women had to invent a variety of strategies to secure the resources necessary to have a coat made, the elites—able to exercise their considerable political capital—needed only one. Moreover the channels for the two groups were different. Different sewing shops served the two markets, selling their goods and services to the elites at much cheaper prices. The elites had not simply "connections" but legalized privileges that reflected legally fixed social distinctions in late Soviet society. In other words, while the practices of fur acquisition for ordinary women and for elites appeared quite similar in formal terms, in reality they existed in parallel worlds.

The mechanisms for the distribution of products were highly centralized and interconnected:

> Clothes and food were distributed by the district, town, and regional committees [of the Communist Party]. There was one regional committee for Yaroslavl region (plus the equally important first, second, and third secretaries of the town and regional committee of the Komsomol, heads of large-scale institutions of federal significance, and chairmen of the regional and town Soviets of People's Deputies). The towns and districts of Yaroslavl region were structured according to the same hierarchy. The way shortages were managed corresponded to this hierarchy. From a mink fur (for their wives) and reindeer fur (for themselves) to ordinary sheepskin coats. (Interview with A.V., female, born 1950, chemist with Ph.D., lived in Yaroslavl)

Despite the considerable benefits they enjoyed, the elites also engaged in the illegal abuse of the distribution system. In many ways these practices echoed those of ordinary women who engaged in the practice of *blat* to secure their luxuries. However, the scale of these abuses was not only much greater; sometimes they turned into explosive political scandals.[44] As one respondent recalled:

> There was one more scandal, connected with the KGB. A lot of karakul skins were brought in, one or two railway carriages worth (an enormous sum of money). All these skins were "written off." It was in 1972 or in 1974. All the heads dressed themselves in these furs, the director, the chief engineer, basically all the "upper echelon" of Karaganda [a city in Kazakhstan]. Well, and then heads "rolled": the KGB came into play and all the chiefs found themselves in prison ... There were

constantly scandals because of furs! (Interview with I.S., female, born 1953, lived in various provincial towns)

Disputes also arose from the unwelcome intersection of the fur worlds of the elites and ordinary women. One respondent commented: "One friend of mine, a bookkeeper at a factory, 'squeezed out' a fur coupon and had a karakul coat made to order. Well, then she was afraid to wear this coat" (interview with T.N., female, born 1951, chemist, lived in Moscow). Her anxiety testified to the operation of unspoken "sumptuary codes" in Soviet society, which ensured that luxury was not perceived as "accessible to every-body" but was attached to definite "estates." Such social pressures had their roots in what I have already characterized as double standards in official attitudes to commodities characteristic of the Brezhnev period (i.e., official condemnation of luxury while, at the same time, brokering the "little deal"). The punishment for infringement of these codes was articulated in differ-ent ways, beginning with moral condemnations (expressed as "taste" dispo-sitions like "modesty") and ending with concrete sanctions, even including dismissal from work, an event with dire social consequences.

The distance between the "fur universes" of ordinary women and of the elites was enormous, but how different were these worlds? The idea that needs could be planned—whether for the elites or for ordinary women—was utopian and, as such, disconnected from the reality of life for both groups. What was more important was not only the fact that a specifically Soviet "acquisitive" mentality—common to both groups—emerged, but that their universes converged more closely the more "illegitimate" their practices for acquiring fur clothing were. Above all, they shared an all-conquering desire to possess luxury, irrespective of the fact that they differed in their abilities to realize it. The very practices involved in the acquisi-tion of furs and the fact that the Soviet fur industry could not meet their desires—even for those fur commodities like caps and collars which were inscribed in the economic plan as mass consumer goods—shaped notions of their status as luxuries.

Using Furs in Everyday Life

Here was a Soviet paradox. With the great variety of furs in her mind and great knowledge about their qualities as well as the manufacture of "off the peg" fur coats, the Soviet consumer was an expert.[45] Yet, for the great major-ity, there was only one "accessible" kind, that is, a "mutton" sheepskin. There was rarely—if ever—a choice of fur coats hanging in their wardrobes. Coats were replaced when they were worn out, not when they fell out of fashion or became "psychologically obsolete," a theme to which I will return below. Such limits corresponded to the spirit of official discourses. Such views as "it is not necessary for many women to have more than two coats: a warm winter coat and a light multi-season coat" expressed in the *Fashion Journal* were, as noted, typical.[46] So how should women wear their single fur coat? In addition to the matters of gender and age discussed above, the key determinants were those of time and place. There was, for instance, a clear opposition between winter and autumn. "Autumn" required—in their minds—a "transitional coat" (without a fur collar). The appearance of a coat with a fur collar or even a fur coat symbolized the coming of winter. In terms of "place," the most significant distinction and a commonly shared disposition was that between "going-out clothes" and "everyday clothes." "Going-out" natural fur coats were determined by "emotional realities," that is, pleasures of "festivities" or the desire to take others by surprise by "showing oneself off." As one respondent noted, "I always wore my fur coat. Everybody paid me compliments. For me it was a period of high popularity among men and in general, among my colleagues ... Usually if I had fine clothes, I wore them everywhere and always. I've never economized on clothes, on the contrary, it was very pleasing to be beautiful" (interview with S.P., female, born 1950, librarian, lived in Yaroslavl). Conversely, "emotional reality" also determined where a natural fur coat could *not* be worn, for instance, to the workplace or supermarket (thereby avoiding envy or "unnecessary" questions, or because in the supermarket no one could "assess the fur coat at its true value"). Natural fur coats were not to be left in the cloakrooms of theaters; they were not worn while carrying out the rubbish, or while watching sports events (because sports stadiums were associated with damage or theft). Such everyday places and times were appropriate places, from their perspective, for winter coats with fur collars and inexpensive fur coats. In this regard, they paralleled the lines drawn in Soviet fashion journals. On their pages this opposition was structured in terms of "everyday" (mainly "sports" fashion lines) and "festive" clothes for special occasions (mainly "elegant" fashion lines). Like the respondents, these magazines tended to place coats made with natural fur in the latter category. This was clear in a 1967 report: "Without a doubt, fur coats are festive clothes. The natural beauty of the fur, its shine, softness, variety of colors, warmth, and light are always magnetic. Fur suits everybody. It improves the clothing of every person. But you should make the right choice. Elegance should always prevail over luxury, and beauty over price."[47] But, of course, it has to be stressed that the range of fur clothing in the fashion journals was much more diverse than that in Soviet life.

An important disposition that represented what might be called legitimate taste was the ideal of the "complete ensemble," a concept that first appeared in official fashion discourse in the early 1960s. One columnist criticized "women [who] pay no attention to colors and wear, for example, a red hat with a wine-colored coat" and issued a prohibition against wearing a combination of artificial and natural furs.[48] These views were still being published at the end of the Brezhnev era.[49] The idea of the complete ensemble was internalized by respondents without any apparent divergence from the position of the magazines: "Caps had to be made of fur. It was obligatory. We tried to match our furs. For example, if I had a polar fox coat, I looked also for a polar fox cap; if I had a mink collar, I wanted also a mink cap. It was not considered beautiful and was in bad taste to wear different furs together" (interview with A.A., female, born 1945, university teacher of Russian language, lived in various Russian provincial towns).

The Life Span of Furs

Fur clothing lasted at least five years and on average more than twenty years. And most of the women interviewed still carefully keep their fur coats today: "I wore my fur coat throughout my time at the institute, and then three years more, even after graduation. The coat is worn out, but it is still 'alive' and hanging in my wardrobe. It is nearly forty years old! . . . It hangs in the wardrobe and I don't have the heart to throw it out" (interview with E.N., female, born 1949, chemist, lived in Yaroslavl). The reasons why coats were worn for such a long time can be put down to the cost and difficulties of acquiring a new one, but other factors have also to be considered. Although it was recognized that fur coats could be fashionable, they were subject to slower processes of change than other clothes. Discussion in the fashion press stressed the modern (but not ultra-fashionable) winter coat or the merits of classical tailoring which produced a coat that could be worn "with pleasure" for several seasons. Furthermore, older coats tended to be made from better-quality fur and were given "second" lives by being repaired or restyled.

Women prolonged the lives of their fur coats in a variety of ways. They looked after them with great care, cleaning the coats at home. When dry cleaning services became available, their effectiveness was subject to public doubt.[50] Respondents confirmed the poor quality of such services: "Once I took my fur coat to the dry cleaners, and they cleaned it without spoiling it. This was quite an exception, because the majority suffered from coats that had been spoiled by dry cleaners. Disputes with dry cleaners were a constant theme in radio broadcasts and, later, telecasts. It was impossible to find any complaint books there [obligatory for all shops and services], because managers of the dry cleaners concealed them" (interview with M.G., female, born 1923, doctor, lived in Yaroslavl). Old coats were also restored, repaired, lengthened, and dyed. They were also completely altered into "new" clothes like waistcoats, caps, and fashionable half-length coats. In effect, Soviet commodities never disappeared. They were continually consumed until they were totally exhausted, overcome by wear and tear.[51] Even then they were retained by their owners, a reflex of a deeply ingrained salvage mentality. Soviet society was a "society of repair."[52] This was, however, by no means antagonistic to the official view: the importance of prolonging the life of fur coats was frequently emphasized in the fashion press from the early 1970s on.[53]

Remodeling was sometimes carried out at home by the owner herself and sometimes in sewing shops. Like the dry cleaners, the latter were associated with negative experiences. Although widely promoted as important services which would liberate free time for the working woman, such facilities had the effect of stealing time from ordinary women either because consumers were forced to make good the poor work of Soviet dry cleaners and tailors or because they avoided such services. Emotional investments were also at risk in such failings: Soviet women were reliant on unpredictable sewing shops and dry cleaners for the maintenance of objects which carried an extraordinary emotional charge. Tremendous difficulty and suffering, as well as a lack of independence, were folded into these luxuries.

Conclusion

The Brezhnev years marked a significant break in what might be called the cultural evolution of the Russian intelligentsia. Even before the revolution, the intelligentsia could be characterized by an ascetic attitude toward clothes and a scornful view of comfort in everyday life (*byt*). This stance was a way of opposing "philistine" and petit bourgeois values. Such attitudes were sustained as late as the 1960s, boosted by the romantic appeal of space exploration and a rediscovery of nature in camping trips with guitars. It was in the Brezhnev period that what might be described as philistine and petit bourgeois taste revived, with "prettiness" and "elegance" becoming key aesthetic categories in the articulation of "good taste." The fact that not only the elites but also ordinary intelligentsia women came to desire prestigious objects is telling. The spread of an appetite for luxury, as well as the establishment of mechanisms for the distribution of material privileges for the *nomenklatura*, allow us to define the Brezhnev period as the second stage in the legitimization of luxury in the Soviet Union. The first had been Stalin's project of "democratic luxury," as Jukka Gronow has demonstrated.[54] But in comparison with the Stalin years, the Brezhnev period was marked by the absence of terror as an instrument of power, and by the emergence of a mass consumer society, albeit one with a Soviet imprint. As this chapter demonstrates, many of the contradictions of the Soviet order came to a head in these years. These include the conflict between the much-promoted image of woman as a producer and the resurgence of traditional notions of woman as a housewife and consumer, and the appropriation of petit bourgeois values by the Soviet official fashion discourse and in everyday consumer practices. The world of socialist fashion became petit bourgeois in this period.[55] The self-representation strategies of ordinary Soviet women were in accord with the spirit and contradictions of the official Soviet fashion discourse. This is clear if we consider women's apparent disavowal of social distinction and the emphasis they placed on individuality. Their narratives stress the "singularity" and "uniqueness" of the commodity in order to counterbalance the associations of "luxury" with "philistinism." At the same time, there was what must be described as self-deception concerning their attitudes to social distinction in the Brezhnev era. Moreover, the double standards evident in late Soviet ideology "trickled down" into the "living universe" of ordinary women. The "connections" and *blat* practices of the elites were perceived as natural. It was clearly difficult to draw a line between legitimate and illegitimate ways of marking social distinctions through the consumption of clothes and between legitimate and illegitimate tastes for luxury.

Postscript—And Today?

Despite the dramatic change in modes of consumption which occurred in Russia after the collapse of the Soviet Union, the new consumer culture continues to be based on petit bourgeois dispositions of "good taste" which emerged in the late Soviet period.[56] There has not been the dramatic break or watershed that is so often claimed. Furs remain a luxury, organized along the same hierarchy of significance (as are imported clothes). But unlike the Soviet period, attempts to limit the taste for luxury—whether through distribution mechanisms or through discourse—have ended, or rather they have been replaced by their opposite, a cult of excessive luxury. (This is sometimes called "backlog demand," refering to pent-up consumer desires which women have sought to fulfill since the end of the Soviet Union.)[57] The gap between the object of dreams and the possibility of consuming it has been reduced. Social capital ("connections," *blat,* "access," "privileges") no longer plays a determining role. This has been given over to economic capital ("easy to buy," "save money"). Alongside the residual Soviet tactics ("altering," "making everything out of nothing"), new post-Soviet strategies have arisen. Today every provincial town is choked with natural fur coats on sale in all large public buildings. Soviet women have been rescued by the market. Shopping tours to Greece—where mink is inexpensive though not of high quality—have become normal. Mink has not lost its symbolic status. What is more, its association with the "mature woman" has been erased, with both women and young girls dreaming of possessing a mink fur coat and abandoning their former favorite, the polar fox. The mink fur coat is still a symbol of membership of the elites, though now not symbolizing power but money. Sheepskin coats have become a democratic alternative to the fur coat and, because of their sporting and universal character, have many devotees. But other symbols of the Soviet "fur garment universe"— such as the inexpensive rabbit fur, the "mutton" sheepskin coat—no longer have symbolic value. Moreover, the once stable distinction between "going-out clothes" and "everyday clothes" has collapsed; the sight of young women dressed in a floor-length mink fur coat on the metro has became an everyday phenomenon. What has also changed is the number of natural fur coats in a wardrobe: two, three, five, or more coats are "normal." It seems that luxury consumption has become the hegemonic taste in post-Soviet society. As one respondent—a Moscow resident born in 1961—recalled: "Nowadays everybody wears fur coats, and, to stand out from the masses, you need not to wear one."

Notes

1. N. B. Lebina, "Meshchanstvo" and "Veshchizm," in *Entsiklopedia banal'nostei: Sovetskaia povsednevnost': Konturi, simvoli, znaki,* by N. B. Lebina (Saint Petersburg: Dmitry Bulanin, 2006), 231–34 and 485–86, respectively.

2. The term "little deal" is used by historians in opposition to the "big deal" (made by the Soviet state with the middle class in the 1930s). See V. Dunham, *In Stalin's Time: Middleclass Values in Soviet Fiction,* 2nd. ed. (Durham, N.C.: Duke University Press, 1990). See also James R. Millar, "The Little Deal: Brezhnev's Contribution to Acquisition Socialism," *Slavic Review* 44, no. 4 (1985): 694–706.

3. For a parallel discussion of this social group in East Germany, see G.-F. Budde, *Frauen der Intelligenz: Akademikerinnen in der DDR 1945 bis 1975* (Göttingen: Vandenhoeck und Ruprecht, 2003). On the term "ordinary Soviet person," see Iu. Gradskova, *Obychnaia sovetskaia zhenshchina: Obzor opisanii identichnosti* (Moscow: Sputnik, 1999); and Iu. Levada, ed., *Sovetskii prostoi chelovek* (Moscow: Intertsentr, 1993).

4. See A. Yurchak, *Everything Was Forever, Until It Was No More: The Last Soviet Generation* (Princeton, N.J.: Princeton University Press, 2005). On the classification of furs in the Soviet Union, see A. Besedin and S. Gontsov, *Tovarovedenie pushno-mekhovykh tovarov* (Moscow: Ekonomika, 1983).

5. See P. Bourdieu, *Distinction: A Social Critique of the Judgement of Taste* (London: Routledge and Kegan Paul, 1986); P. Bourdieu, "Die 'sowjetische' Variante und das

politische Kapital," in *Praktische Vernunft: Zur Theorie des Handelns,* by P. Bourdieu (Frankfurt am Main: Suhrkamp, 1998).

6. J. Baudrillard, *The Consumer Society: Myths and Structures* (London: Sage, 1998).

7. Such "thick descriptions" imply a "slipping out" from the mentalities and judgments of one's own culture and a "slipping into" the mentalities of another. They should aim to be, as far as possible, systematic, detailed, all-around descriptions of a culture without any preliminary prejudices, and written with the purpose of understanding a culture's own logic. See C. Geertz, *Dichte Beschreibung: Beiträge zum Verstehen kultureller Systeme* (Frankfurt am Main: Suhrkamp, 1983).

8. G. Rosenthal and W. Fischer-Rosenthal, "Analyse narrativ-biographischer Interviews," in *Qualitative Sozialforschung,* ed. U. Flick, E. von Kardorff, and I. Steinke (Reinbek bei Hamburg: Rowohlt Verlag, 2000), 456–68.

9. See, for example, S. Boym, *The Future of Nostalgia* (New York: Basic Books, 2001). On the "Sovietness" of post-Soviet clothing consumer culture, see A. Tikhomirova, "Sovetskoe v postsovetskom: Razmyshleniia o gibridnosti sovremennoi rossiiskoi kultury potrebleniia odezhdy," *Neprikosnovennyi zapas: Debaty o politike i kul'ture* 54 (2007), http://www.nlobooks.ru/rus/nz- online/619/620/ (accessed March 16, 2009).

10. Recent examples of post-Soviet *(n)ostalgia* include V. Todorovsky's film *Stiliagi,* 2008 (http://www.stilyagifilm.ru/); "Shirpotreb: Sovetskii kostjum, 1951–1966," exhibition organized in Moscow as part of the "Moda i stil' v fotografii-2009" festival (March 28–May 4, 2009), http://www.mdf.ru/exhibitions/today/shirpotreb_ms09; the media projects of L. Parfenov; and various nostalgic Internet communities, such as http://community.livejournal.com/1970_ru; http://community.livejournal.com/76_82; http://community.livejournal.com/soviet_life; http://community.livejournal.com/ru_vintage, etc.

11. "Mut zur Mode," *Brühl* 2 (1962): 24–25. One can trace the circulation of debates on the pages in *Brühl* and other specialist publications into the mainstream Soviet press and satirical magazines.

12. See, for example, A. Grigor'iants, "Iskusstvennoe volokno," *Pravda,* March 4, 1955, 4; and "V gostiakh u bol'shoi khimii," *Krokodil,* no. 16, June 10, 1958, 2. Propaganda campaigns for artificial furs were not limited to the Soviet press; feature films also served propaganda purposes. See, for example, *Neilon 100%,* directed by V. Basov (U.S.S.R.: Mosfilm, 1973).

13. *Zhurnal mod,* no. 4 (1955).

14. "Kombinirovannaia odezhda," *Zhurnal mod,* no. 3 (1960): 18.

15. On the classification of furs in the Soviet Union, see Besedin and Gontsov, *Tovarovedenie pushno-mekhovykh tovarov.*

16. L. Efremova, "Prishla zima," *Zhurnal mod,* no. 3 (1962): 6.

17. A. Donskaia, "Nashi modeli v Rio-de-Zhaneiro," *Zhurnal mod,* no. 4 (1962): 20–25.

18. "Leipziger Rauchwarenleute besuchen Pelzkonfektionsbetriebe in Moskau und Leningrad," *Brühl,* no. 1 (1961): 14–16.

19. "Mekhovaia promyshlennost'," in *Bol'shaia sovetskaia entsiklopediia,* 3rd ed. (1974), vol. 16.

20. Cited by G. Antonova, "Sovetskoe modelirovanie i promyshlennost'—Dlia naroda," *Zhurnal mod,* no. 3 (1977).

21. The connection drawn between furs and eroticism has a long tradition. See, for example, L. von Sacher-Masoch, *Venus im Pelz und andere Erzählungen,* ed. Helmut Strutzmann (Vienna: Edition Christian Brandstätter, 1995); J. Emberly, *The Cultural Politics of Fur* (Ithaca, N.Y.: Cornell University Press, 1997); C. Nadeau, *Fur Nation: From the Beaver to Brigitte Bardot* (London: Routledge, 2001).

22. For a definition of "import" see, for example, N. Lebina, "XX vek: Slovar' pov-sednevnosti," *Rodina,* no. 9 (2005): 95. The taste for imported clothes was one of the favorite targets of the satirical journal *Krokodil;* see, for example, B. Savkov, "A u Vas net tochno takikh zhe, no importnykh?" *Krokodil,* no. 16, June 16, 1973; and A. Iurov, "Pigmei iz podvorotny," *Krokodil,* no. 26, September 20, 1960.

23. A. Vasil'ev, *Russkaia moda: 150 let v fotografiiakh* (Moscow: Slovo, 2004).

24. On fox fur as an explicitly "feminine" fur see, for example, "Pal'to," *Zhurnal mod,* no. 4 (1967); "Pal'to elegantnogo stilia," *Zhurnal mod,* no. 4 (1972); "Vsegda modno," *Zhurnal mod,* no. 4 (1979).

25. For further discussion of etiquette and civilized behavior in Soviet consumer culture see, for example, C. Kelly, *Refining Russia: Advice Literature, Polite Culture, and Gender from Catherine to Yeltsin* (Oxford: Oxford University Press, 2001).

26. M. Edele, "Strange Young Men in Stalin's Moscow: The Birth and Life of the Stiliagi, 1945–1953," *Jahrbücher für Geschichte Osteuropas* 50 (2002): 37–61.

27. This was an institution founded in the late 1920s under conditions of rationing, with the purpose of supplying selected social groups. It survived until the collapse of the Soviet Union.

28. See, for example, "Etot vrednii, etot poleznyi skvozniak," *Krokodil,* no. 7 (1968): 2; B. Savel'ev, "Dushistye shubki," *Krokodil,* no. 2, January 1972, 2.

29. "Novoe pal'to," *Zhurnal mod,* no. 1 (1972): 13.

30. "Zimoi na ulitse," *Zhurnal mod,* no. 4 (1981).

31. Imported artificial fur coats were even sent illegally from the United States and then sold in the Soviet Union at double the price. For satirical comment on this practice, see, for instance, N. Labkovskii, "Podarki navynos," *Krokodil,* no. 6, February 29, 1960.

32. "1965—Das Jahr des Kanins," *Brühl,* no. 6 (1966): 6.

33. "Mekhovye tovary," in *Bol'shaia sovetskaia entsiklopediia,* vol. 16.

34. "Die Rolle der Produktion der Pelztierzucht im Rauchwarenexport der UdSSR," *Brühl,* no. 5 (1971): 6–7.

35. See, for example, E. Shukaev, "A interesno, siuda bol'shoi konkurs? Chetyre dublenki na odno mesto," *Krokodil,* no. 34, December 24, 1983, 7.

36. I. Kopytoff, "The Cultural Biography of Things: Commoditization as Process," in *The Social Life of Things,* ed. A. Appadurai (Cambridge, Eng.: Cambridge University Press, 1996), 64–95.

37. Inexpensive furs were in general a "shortage good" in the late U.S.S.R. and, as such, drew the attention of *Krokodil*'s satirists. See, for example, I. Skorobogatova, "Mekh—Da i tolko!" *Krokodil,* no. 4 (1988): 8–9.

38. A. Ledeneva, *Russia's Economy of Favours: Blat, Networking and Informal Exchange* (Cambridge, Eng.: Cambridge University Press, 1998); N. B. Lebina, "Blat," in *Entsiklopediia banal'nostei,* 65–67.

39. For a fuller treatment of this question of regular shopping tours to Moscow, and of provincial consumer culture in Brezhnev's time, see A. Tikhomirova, "V 280 kilometrakh ot Moskvy: Osobennosti mody i praktik potrebleniia odezhdy v sovetskoi provintsii (Iaroslavl', 1960–1980–e gody)," *Neprikosnovennyi zapas: Debaty o politike*

i kul'ture 37 (2004), http://www.nz-online.ru/print.phtml?aid=25011179 (accessed September 8, 2005). See also "Kolbasnyi poezd" in Lebina, "XX vek: Slovar' povsednevnosti," 98.

40. An "illegitimate" version of this practice was that of obtaining skins and then having fur clothes made "in the underground." In general this was less expensive than using an official atelier. But the sewing of fur garments by other methods was already unusual by the late Soviet period.

41. See, for example, L. Sluchevskii, "Sdelaite samy!" *Krokodil*, no. 3, January 30, 1965, 3; "Servisom napoval," *Krokodil*, no. 11 (1977): 3; A. Nikol'skii, "Prazdnichnyi siurpriz," *Krokodil*, no. 7 (1980): 10.

42. The distribution of fur clothes and fur caps sometimes featured in Soviet literature as a dramatic element in the story. In Voinovich's *Shapka*, Efim Rakhlin dies because he fails to get a fur cap when they are distributed. See V. Voinovich, *Shapka: Sbornik rasskazov* (Moskva: Eksmo, 2008).

43. "Berezka," in Lebina, "XX vek: Slovar' povsednevnosti," 100.

44. On "fur scandals" see also, for example, "Shuby-nevidimki," *Krokodil*, no. 24 (1972): 7; "Krokodil pomog," *Krokodil*, no. 35 (1973): 9.

45. For an example of a Soviet advice book on fur clothing, see A. Besedin and L. Lopasova, *Pokupateliu o mekhakh* (Moscow: Ekonomika, 1975).

46. El'sa Khagdal', "Umenie odevat'sia," *Zhurnal mod*, no. 3 (1958): 1 (supplement).

47. *Zhurnal mod*, no. 4 (1967).

48. L. Efremova, "Prishla zima," *Zhurnal mod*, no. 3 (1962): 6.

49. "V moroznuiu pogodu," *Zhurnal mod*, no. 4 (1980).

50. See, for example, A. Nikolaev, "Deshevo, no serdito," *Krokodil*, no. 14, May 15, 1972, 9; "A na dvore opiat' zima," *Krokodil*, no. 2 (1976): 3.

51. O. Gurova, "Bytovye veshchi v Sovetskoi Rossii, 1970–e gg.: Kollektivnyi proekt 'Tsennost' veshchei v sovetskoi i postsovetskoi Rossii" (2004), http://www.iriss .ru/display_epublication?id=000150072307 (accessed September 9, 2005).

52. K. Gerasimova and S. Chuikina, "Obshchestvo remonta," *Neprikosnovennyi zapas: Debaty o politike i kul'ture*, no. 34 (2004).

53. I. Tsepkina, "Esli u vas est' mekh," *Zhurnal mod*, no. 4 (1973), supplement; ibid.

54. J. Gronow, *Caviar with Champagne: Common Luxury and the Ideals of the Good Life in Stalin's Russia* (Oxford and New York: Berg, 2003).

55. On the appropriation of petit bourgeois good taste by Soviet official fashion discourse, see D. Bartlett, "Let Them Wear Beige: The Petit-Bourgeois World of Official Socialist Dress," *Fashion Theory* 8 (2004): 127–64.

56. See, for example, S. Oushakine, "Culture of Shortage and the Matter of Size: Practicing Consumption in Russia During the 1990s" (2002, unpublished paper); S. Oushakine, "The Quantity of Style: Imaginary Consumption in the New Russia," *Theory, Culture and Society* 17, no. 5 (2000).

57. Such topics have drawn the attention of researchers. See, for example, K. H. Partapuoli, "The Cultural Production of Luxury Goods in Russia: Fur as a Traditional and Modern Symbol of Russian Luxury," presentation at the Interdisciplinary Conference of Fashion and Dress Cultures, Copenhagen, October 26–28, 2005.

The Big Boar: the author's father with his three sons (*the one on the right is the author*), probably 1957

CHAPTER TWELVE

Nomenklatura with Smoking Guns: Hunting in Communist Hungary's Party-State Elite

György Péteri

> *Tibor Huszár:* Did you go hunting? Biszku was a passionate hunter.
> *Rezső Nyers:* No, I did not hunt. I did two sports—I swam in the morning or in the evening, and I played tennis.

Instead of going directly to the "realist" tale (i.e., to provide the reader with an "objectivist" representation and analysis of "what the sources reveal"), I would like to start in a "confessional" mode.[1] I have had personal experience with what I am reporting about in this chapter. The only correct way of describing this experience is to say that I used to be a native of the field observed: I was brought up in the 1950s and 1960s in a *nomenklatura* family in Budapest. After 1956 my father, István Péteri, ranked second—his title was deputy chief of department—at the Department of Administrative Affairs of the Central Committee of the Hungarian Socialist Workers' Party (MSZMP). In 1963 he was transferred to a national authority with the status of a government ministry: he worked until his retirement in 1983, as the first-ranking among three vice presidents of the Central Committee of People's Control (KNEB).[2] I lived in my parents' home during the first twenty-two years of my life, enjoying in some ways most of the privileges yielded by my father's position. These privileges included, among other things, considerably better-than-average housing; unlimited access to a state-owned car (from 1965 it was a black Mercedes 230 which, together with its chauffeur, Sándor Fábián, stood at my father's disposal even after working hours, with no limits as to mileage, weekdays, or time); access to the country's best resort areas at Lake Balaton and elsewhere; access to a well-equipped health care infrastructure (including the services of the National Central Hospital on Kútvölgyi Street); and access to opportunities for hunting in some of the country's absolutely finest wildlife areas. From the age of six until around seventeen (i.e., between 1957 and 1968), I regularly joined my father on his hunting excursions practically every weekend except for the summer months.[3] I have a great many memories from those times, and I believe that not to draw on them, or to ignore them while writing a paper on hunting among the elites of communist Hungary, would be dishonest and foolish.

Yet the reader of this paper should not be mistaken in her expectations: I do not intend to give an account of what I partook in or saw and heard, as is usual in the genre of memoirs. This is a scholarly paper based on empirical research, but I will allow my personal experience and knowledge to affect it with regard to facts considered, to questions asked, as well as with regard to the organization of my discussion. In this respect, however, it should also be noted that most of the archival documents and data I have managed to bring together for this paper relate to the "crème de la crème" among elite hunting circles: the "Egyetértés" (Concord) Hunting Club established by, and exclusively for, the top of the power elite, including members of the Communist Party's Political Bureau and Secretariat, members of the government (ministers and state secretaries), and the top leaders of other major institutions of state power (the Presidential Council of the People's Republic, the chairman of the Parliament, the attorney general, the chairman of the Supreme Court, and the president of the Hungarian National Bank).[4] While my father was invited on a number of occasions to Egyetértés (especially to collective hunts of small game such as hare and pheasant), he was not a member of this exclusive club: Egyetértés was one or two grades too high for his position. From the late 1950s and early 1960s he had his own club: the "May 1st Hunting Club," disposing of excellent territories in the Börzsöny Mountains in northeast Hungary, and shared by a membership of relatively high-ranking functionaries of the party-state.

The Place of Hunting Among the Pastimes of Communist Political Elites

"Did communist leaders go hunting?"—the reader raises her eyebrows incredulously. Indeed, the phenomenon requires some explanation on account of its seeming implausibility. After all, hunting in Hungary (and in most of the countries of communist Eastern Europe) was a recreational activity intimately associated, in the public imagination of the ancien régime as well as of the postwar communist era, with elite groups considered by communists to have been the most reactionary (landed) components of the former ruling classes (aristocrats and the "gentry"). The news might also come as a surprise because the leisure activities of Hungary's communist leaders in the postwar era received no publicity whatever at the time.[5] While newspaper readers in the 1920s would always know where and with whom the prime minister (Count István Bethlen) had been hunting and the number of deers or boars he had shot,[6] the only news to reach the broad Hungarian public about First Secretary János Kádár's recreational activities was a short communiqué, most often in the period from July through August, revealing that Comrade Kádár had commenced his annual, ordinary vacation.[7] Kádár himself had a rather ambivalent attitude toward publicity in this respect. On the one hand, he was proud of his achievements as a hunter: he had quite a few high-class, even gold-medal trophies, and he did not at all mind if they were included in exhibitions or professional publications.[8] On the other hand, he rejected the offer of a skillful game painter to produce a painting of a beautiful roe deer buck he shot in 1973. Kádár's arguments were as follows:

> As the hunter who shot the game is me, and as the whole matter concerns my person, I have to say in a straightforward manner that such a painting would make it very hard for me to continue hunting, the only leisure that gives me genuine recreation. Other considerations, connected with my official responsibilities [más—funkciómmal összefüggő—meggondolások], make the offer completely unacceptable for me.

Kádár begged for the painter's understanding and forgiveness.[9] To figure in the trophy lists of the National Directorate of Forestry or in the trophy exhibitions of the Museum of Agriculture was still compatible with the self-image of a semiprofessional hunter who, in his work contributing to the plan targets of agricultural exports, happened to shoot one or another game with an extraordinary trophy. A painting of his gold-medal buck, however, even without Kádár in the picture, would have easily been seen as a celebration of the might of the country's number-one political personality—thus, his hunting would have been pulled into the public domain and its meaning would have lost its integrity, and its status as an immaculately *private* leisure would have been compromised. Kádár enjoyed his power and seldom hesitated to wield it, but he was also keen on preventing the emergence of any "cult of the personality" around him which, in his eyes, was crucially dependent on the maintenance of a clear distinction between the private and public spheres of his activities.

But the veil hiding *nomenklatura* hunting cannot prevent us from establishing the fact that hunting was extremely popular among communist elites. For the year 1971, we have a detailed report on the activities in the Egyetértés Hunting Club.[10] In that year, the Political Bureau of the Central Committee of the Hungarian Socialist Workers' Party (the top of political power in communist Hungary) had fifteen members. Eight of these fifteen were members of Egyetértés and visited regularly the five estates belonging to the club (Egyetértés had exclusive access to Hungary's best hunting reserves: Gemenc, Telki, Gyulaj, Mezőföld, and Gödöllő). In the following tables I will present some of the main parameters of their use of the resources in Egyetértés. We'll take a look at the number of days they visited the estates of Egyetértés, the number of (small and big) game they shot, as well as some indicators of the extent to which they could use the infrastructure and resources of Egyetértés to the benefit of their relatives and other guests.

A comparison with national averages sets the accessibility and "efficiency" of hunting for this top elite into sharp contrast: according to calculations by

Top military leaders and leading apparatchiks of the Administrative Department of the Hungarian Socialist Workers' Party Central Committee, probably 1960 or 1961; the author's father is third from the left

Table 12.1. The amount of time devoted to hunting and the size of the game bag

Names	Number of days spent hunting	Number of big game shot	Number of small game shot
György Aczél	69	72	6
Antal Apró	14	33	0
Béla Biszku	38	38	201
Lajos Fehér	21	20	220
Jenő Fock	90	205	21
Sándor Gáspár	54	12	2,764
János Kádár	16	12	797
Károly Németh	40	57	1,366
Total	342	449	5,375
Average	43	56	672

The source for all three statistical tables in this chapter is MÉM Vadászati és Vadgazdálkodási Főosztály, "Jelentés az Állami Erdő- és Vadgazdaságok 1971, évi működéséről," Dr. Tóth Sándor főosztályvezető, Budapest, January 31, 1972 ("Report on the Operation of the National Farms of Forestry and Game Management in 1971," by Dr. Sándor Tóth, director of the Main Department of Hunting and Game Management of the Ministry of Agriculture and Food Industries—in the possession of Dr. Tóth).

the Hungarian National Association of Hunters (MAVOSZ) from 1979, the average recreational hunter in Hungary spent 26 days hunting annually and his bag carried no more than 3 pieces of big and 50 pieces of small game.[11] (For all the 60 members of the Egyetértés Club, the average number of hunting days was 24, but the average bag carried 29 pieces of big game and 247 pieces of small game in 1971.)

While members of Egyetértés spent altogether 1,452 hunting days[12] at the five estates, they also invited domestic guests (1,144 guest days), as well as guests from abroad (214 guest days). Our data allow us to show the extent to which families, friends, and colleagues of each individual Politburo member listed above could enjoy the resources of Egyetértés.

Among all the guests, the sons of eight club members (hunters themselves) can be identified. Besides the sons of Politburo members already listed in the above table, they are as follows: György Szénási, son of Attorney General Géza Szénási; Imre Cseterki, son of Lajos Cseterki, the secretary of the Presidential Council of the People's Republic; and Gábor Vallus, son of Pál Vallus, first vice president of the National Price Authority and president of MAVOSZ. Hungary's first lady, Mrs. Kádár, often went hunting too, and there are sporadic signs that even Mrs. Aczél and Mrs. Fehér took to a rifle every now and then.[13]

Table 12.2. Visits at the hunting reserves of Egyetértés
by family members and domestic guests

Hosting club member	Number of guest days by family members and domestic guests	Number of guest days by sons of club members*
György Aczél	178	0
Antal Apró	2	0
Béla Biszku	21	4 (György Biszku)
Lajos Fehér	4	11 (Lajos Fehér Jr.)
Jenő Fock	20	1·(Jenő Fock Jr.)
Sándor Gáspár	22	? (Gáspár János)
János Kádár	14	0
Károly Németh	19	14 (Károly Németh Jr.)
Total	280	30
Average	35	4

* The names of the sons of several Egyetértés members figure in the list of domestic guests, and
their visits are obviously not included in the number of guest days related in the lists to the club
members without identifying the visitor's name. This explains why, for example, in the case of Lajos
Fehér only four guest days are taken up for 1971, while his son, Lajos Fehér Jr., altogether spent
eleven hunting days at two estates (Mezőföld and Gödöllő) of Egyetértés.

Even though we lack the necessary data to compare the time and attention devoted to hunting with the time used for other leisure activities
(reading, going to concerts, tourism not related to hunting, playing tennis,
etc.), there can be no doubt about the relatively high importance of hunting.
On the average, the highest-ranking members of the Egyetértés Club (the
members of the Politburo) went hunting on 43 days of the year, which was
more than the official number of their paid vacation days.[14] Admittedly, this
average from 1971 conceals great variations from year to year as well as the
variations from member to member—it includes Prime Minister Fock's
90 days as well as Deputy Prime Minister (later Chairman of Parliament)
Antal Apró's 14 days. I still suspect that the average is not misleading, since
these days reflect only visits paid to the various reserves of Egyetértés—
some members of Egyetértés were also members of other clubs, and all
members of the club certainly received (and accepted) a considerable number of invitations to various corners of the country throughout the year.[15]
Therefore, in most of the cases, the data we have from Egyetértés should
be regarded as a very modest minimum estimate of the total days devoted
to hunting.

    Another indication of the importance of hunting for the party-state ap-
paratus elite is the considerable amount of time and attention they devoted

to policies of forestry and game management and, especially, to the affairs of Egyetértés and the management of its five reserves. Kádár's interest in hunting turned him into the most important single patron of such personalities as Count Zsigmond Széchenyi, already a passionate hunter and writer of travelogues and hunting stories in the interwar years, whose "expeditions" to Africa and India in the 1960s received crucial support from Kádár.[16] Kádár, together with György Aczél (the country's top politician reigning over cultural and academic life), promoted the publication of popularizing literature and nature (and hunting) films,[17] and their acceptance and consent was decisive in the (re)publication of such ancien régime classics on nature, wildlife, and hunting as those of Otto Herman, Kálmán Kittenberger, Herbert Nadler, and Zsigmond Széchenyi.[18] The importance attached to hunting is also well reflected in top politicians' (members of the Egyetértés Club) deep involvement in issues pertinent to the management of the club's estates. These state-owned (national) farms of forestry and game management were administered by the Department of Hunting and Game Management of the Ministry of Agriculture and Food Industries. The department had national responsibilities, but it was also directly responsible for controlling and coordinating hunting activities and game management on the reserves kept exclusively for Egyetértés. The director of this department was the "chief protocol hunter," who oversaw the organization and coordination of individual hunting visits to the estates, the reception and hunting provided to high foreign dignitaries (Leonid Brezhnev, for example, was a relatively frequent visitor to the reserves of Egyetértés), and, especially, the collective hunting events such as battues for boar and small game. Both directors in the 1960s and 1970s (István Dénes and Sándor Tóth) had to leave their position because some powerful personalities among the club members (especially Politburo members Béla Biszku and Károly Németh) were displeased with their activities. Dénes, responsible for protocol hunting ever since 1949, was fired because he wished to improve the economy of Egyetértés estates by allowing, at high prices, rich Western hunters into the reserves, and this had allegedly led to the corruption of the professional hunters and other employees at the estates who seemed to no longer pay enough attention to the needs of the "ordinary club members."[19] Dénes's place was taken over by Sándor Tóth, who was also a professional of forestry and game management. His rational ways of husbanding the resources of the Egyetértés estates, and the straightforward manner in which he reported about the current situation and the use of public resources by the club members, often made the top apparatchiks see red until they, indeed, got rid of him by promoting him to a higher position within the Ministry of Agriculture and Food Industries where he no

1980s, only 10,000 of a total of 30,000 registered hunters had rifles, and the official policy was that the number of rifle owners should not be increased. It was not without reason that hunters talked about "first-class citizens with a license to have a rifle, and second-class citizens with a license to have only a shotgun."[23] Sándor Tóth, too, confirmed that "those in possession of rifles had reason to regard themselves as high up socially; they were inside the circle."[24] Also, rifles (and rifle ammunition) were, of course, much more expensive than shotguns. (2) A hunting license was necessary too, and could be acquired only by going through an examination in "the theory and ethics of hunting." (3) Finally, but not less important, one had to be a member of a hunting club.

The third requirement was the hardest one to fulfill. After some growth from the late 1950s on—more in the number of clubs than in the number of club members—club membership had become by the end of the 1960s almost inaccessible. For young candidates, getting a membership proved to be harder than getting enrolled as a university student (which was really hard), as the president of MAVOSZ admitted in 1974. But the way in which the contemporary journalist understood this problem reveals what appears to have been a *social-hierarchical* impediment in the *commoners'* way of getting admitted to hunting clubs: "It is pretty hard nowadays to become a member of a hunting club [if one is] applying 'from the street.'"[25] Needless to say, it was not leading functionaries of the party-state who were applying "from the street." Established hunting clubs were hesitant to admit new members, and instead emphasized defending the interests (privileges) of their existing members. As another journalist noted, "One can but agree with the critical opinion that describes the hunting clubs as closed associations of the privileged—a person who wishes to become a member of a club has to wait very long before he would (if at all) get admitted."[26]

Nor was it easy to obtain membership through the establishment of new clubs. Legally, hunting clubs were regarded as associations, and as such their establishment was contingent not only upon the benevolence of the Ministry of Agriculture but also upon the permission of the Ministry of the Interior. The Department of Hunting and Game Management had to process (and most often reject) a steady stream of applications from groups who wished to establish hunting clubs and asked for the assignment of various hunting grounds.[27]

Membership, either by admittance to existing clubs or via establishing new clubs, was therefore in very short supply and, as in the case of other shortage goods, access to it tended to be distributed through transactions among and by the privileged and powerful. Word from the right kind of patron could make wonders happen—like in the case of Ferenc Varga, chairman of the successful agricultural cooperative "Óbuda," whose aspirations to become a member of a hunting club were rejected by the club. He then turned to János Kádár and asked for help. Appreciating Varga's merits as a successful cooperative leader,[28] Kádár intervened on his behalf and asked the president of MAVOSZ, Pál Vallus (himself a member of Egyetértés), to persuade the hunting club in question to admit Varga. In ten days' time Varga was a club member.[29]

The establishment of new hunting clubs was also dependent upon access to the proper networks. People in leading positions in my father's office (including my father) were all well taken care of, but other higher-ranking employees of KNEB (department chiefs and others) also got "contaminated" by the passion for hunting and mobilized their patrons to arrange for their own hunting club. They applied to the Ministry of Agriculture, asking for the assignment of a territory appropriate for big-game hunting. The application carried a list of nine suggested club members, only three of whom had not yet been the member of any hunting club. Most surprising to me among the latter three was to find my mother's name—this was obviously a tactical move, as both "new membership" and the presence of women improved the chances of a positive response.[30]

My father lent his support to the application by contacting directly the vice minister reigning over forestry and game management, László Földes (a member of Egyetértés).[31] The bid on behalf of KNEB was joined and supported by four top-level leaders of the Communist Party Committee of Fejér County.[32] This proved to be a powerful combination, and the ministry's Department of Hunting and Game Management did its best to oblige— the Székesfehérvár Nimród Hunting Club was operative from 1967 on. While his social standing was too low for a membership in Egyetértés, my father's status for Nimród soon proved too high. He left the club offended when other club members (some of them his employees at KNEB) had objections to securing him and my mother a separate room in the club's overcrowded cottage over the weekends in the season.[33]

Another case of success was when members of the Egyetértés Club managed to arrange for the establishment of two new hunting clubs, one to accommodate former Egyetértés members who retired or left their high positions for other reasons, and another to provide members' sons with proper hunting grounds. Carving out a part of the Telki Reserve (at Koldusszállás, close to the small provincial city of Tatabánya) in 1974, they established a separate club, Barátság (Friendship), for those members who for various reasons had lost the positions that originally made them eligible for membership in Egyetértés.[34] In a similar gesture, already in 1971, Egyetértés "donated" a

PRIVATE COLLECTION

**Stalking in a big-game area; the author's father
and mother and an unknown figure on
the left, probably 1957**

part of its territories (close to the city of Hatvan) on the basis of which adult
sons of the club's members got the unique privilege and chance to establish
their own club, the Young Nimrod Club (Nimród Ifjúsági Vadásztársaság).
Members of this new club included the sons of Béla Biszku, Lajos Cseterki,
Lajos Fehér (but also one of Lajos Fehér's daughters and son-in-law), Jenő
Fock, Károly Németh, Ferenc Szűcs, Pál Vallus (vice president of the Price
Authority, and president of MAVOSZ), Mihály Koller (general secretary
of MAVOSZ), and others.[35] János Kádár received an invitation from the
"Young Nimróds" to join them in partridge-shooting in Hatvan. In his let-
ter, club president Imre Cseterki, the son of Lajos Cseterki, emphasized:
"We, young hunters, have been with great love and devotion preparing for
this occasion. Considering especially all the efforts exerted by Comrade
Kádár in order to assist the establishment of our hunting club, we would
be most appreciative if you could accept our invitation."[36] Finally, a similar
solution was offered to interested wives of Egyetértés members: the idea
was enthusiastically promoted by Mrs. Lajos Fehér, and she was joined by
Mrs. Kádár too. Béla Csatári, first secretary of the party's Békés County organization, undertook to "organize" a proper piece of land for them, but the
project never reached implementation because the number of wives wishing
to become club members failed to reach the necessary minimum.[37]

All in all, the *nomenklatura* elite asserted their interests in the scramble for hunting grounds quite effectively through a whole series of hunting clubs possessed and controlled by them by the late 1960s: the high-up generals of the Ministry of Defense launched their own club, the "Máté Zalka" Hunting Club, upon the model of Egyetértés; the high officials of the council of the capital city, Budapest, had their hunting club; and so did the Ministry of the Interior (indeed, they had several clubs), the Attorney General's Office, the Ministry of Finance, the Ministry of Agriculture (and, within it, the Central Authority of State Farms), the National Council of Trade Unions, and the National Union of Food Industrial Workers; and there were a number of provincial clubs established and run by provincial council and party leaders.[38]

In its control over the distribution of hunting opportunities, of club memberships, and of hunting grounds, the party-state apparatus elite could to an increasing extent rely upon the National Association of Hungarian Hunters, MAVOSZ. Reading lists of the national and county-level leaders of MAVOSZ in the 1960s and 1970s is like reading lists of the *nomenklatura* of state socialist Hungary. Egyetértés was heavily represented among MAVOSZ's national board members and leading functionaries in the same way as, at the county level, MAVOSZ local organizations would include MSZMP county secretaries, presidents or vice presidents of the county council, and other dignitaries of the county's political and economic life. Regulations introduced in 1970 took away the professional supervision and control of game management and hunting from the administrations of county councils, and these responsibilities (and mandates) were transferred to the county organizations of MAVOSZ. The county organizations operated from 1968 with salaried secretaries (as a rule, a person appointed by and loyal to the local *nomenklatura* elite), and they had the right to "delegate" 25 percent of club members to newly established or dissolved and reestablished hunting clubs. As for the working of the new order, we know of cases where middle-level functionaries (county leaders, department chiefs, deputy chiefs of ministries, etc.) tried to execute takeovers. Through MAVOSZ and other authorities, they tried to forcefully dissolve certain hunting clubs which they wished to take into their possession. I am sure that, where the existing hunting clubs could not mobilize patrons powerful enough to counteract the bid, these actions could be successful. In a similar vein, MAVOSZ county organizations had the power to order old club members to undergo the examination for hunters introduced in 1964. Those who failed lost their rights and their club membership which, again, opened opportunities for MAVOSZ to nominate "good comrades to strengthen the club."[39] The county MAVOSZ organization (the provincial apparatchik elite of the party-state) also exercised full control over hunting when it came to invitations to gratis hunting (*térítésmentes meghívásos vadászat*) on the county's hunting areas. As Sándor Tóth explained it to me,

> this enabled the leaders of the county to utilize the gratis invitations towards building up their own networks and pleasing top functionaries of the country. This [system] meant, in practical terms, that good stags or bucks, or whatever game of interest were on offer by the county's hunting clubs for guests, were utilized by county leaders in their own name and they could thus act (and oblige) as generous hosts of top-ranking comrades [from Budapest].[40]

Multiple Club Memberships and Networks of Reciprocity

> If, for example, Antal Apró had been invited to hunt by a president of a county council or a county party secretary and if Apró was nicely treated and had a nice hunting experience, well, then that person from that county was invited to Egyetértés.[41]

Until 1964 (when Egyetértés was established and thorough legislation regulating hunting in the country was introduced), *nomenklatura* hunting took place to a great extent in a haphazard manner, at the will of central and local party-state bosses. The growing interest of *nomenklatura* circles in hunting from the late 1950s is clearly indicated in the archival documents. One manifestation of this was the higher frequency of serious accidents caused by "functionaries of various political and social organizations" who forced employees of various units of the national forestry and game management to allow them to hunt, even to lend them their weapons, although these functionaries had neither the necessary competence, nor the hunting license, nor a license to use the weapons.[42]

With the necessary legislation and other normative directives in place, and with the needs of top functionaries well taken care of by protocol hunting on the best reserves, the central authorities launched a campaign to discipline the lower (especially provincial) levels of the *nomenklatura* and confine their hunting to the legally prescribed frameworks. Significantly, one of the objectives of the campaign must have been to keep these lower strata of the apparatus class of the party-state away from the hunting grounds of Egyetértés—from the National Farms of Forestry and Game Management (NFGM). Vice Prime Minister and Politburo member Lajos Fehér's

"Strictly Secret!" circular to all presidents of county councils and municipal councils at the county level (including the council of the capital city, Budapest) is revealing in this respect:

> We have been informed that in several counties, council employees, mostly in leading positions, disregard the prevailing law and other binding norms of game management and hunting. In several cases they used their power to extort hunting opportunities from forestry farms and hunting clubs, even when on the territory in question the permitted contingent of shooting game had been fully exhausted and/or, within the frameworks of such a contingent, the hunting opportunities for small game and for trophy game had already been reserved ... [These uninvited guests], violating the law and the norms [of decent behavior], often fail to pay for catering and for other costs [which then have to be paid for out of the catering budgets of the units upon which the visits were imposed] ... This illegal hunting and the representation [catering] costs attendant to it are intolerable, they are not compatible with our employees' official duties, and they grossly violate socialist ethical norms [*a szocialista erkölcsöt*]. *The primary objective of the game management of national farms and national farms of forestry is to capture live game for export and breeding purposes, and to generate hard currency incomes by hunting organized for foreigners ... Therefore, this illegal hunting is not only immoral but it also causes serious economic losses.*[43]

Of course, besides export, breeding, and hunting by foreigners, game management on national farms also served the members and guests of the Egyetértés Club. But the problem addressed in Fehér's letter clearly shows the great interest in hunting exhibited by provincial party-state functionaries, as well as the resolution of the higher echelons of the political elite to preserve their monopoly rights over the best hunting grounds run by the NFGM.[44]

Under the legal frameworks, then, the only way of increasing the amount and variety of hunting opportunities at one's disposal was either by acquiring membership in several clubs or by establishing and developing informal networks among members of the various hunting clubs, extending invitations to one another on the basis of reciprocity.

Multiple memberships were formally not accepted but were tolerated. Sándor Tóth could identify fourteen such cases of multiple memberships among the members of Egyetértés.[45] Extending and receiving invitations probably had a greater contribution toward increasing hunting opportunities than multiple club memberships. An indication of the dimensions of such transactions is that the National Committee of Hunting Ethics of MAVOSZ felt it appropriate to spell out in detail the "Ethical Norms of Inviting Guest Hunters and Accepting Such Invitations" in 1974. The committee started its recommendations by encouraging this kind of hospitality among different hunting clubs, and it emphasized particularly the wisdom of exercising this "noble tradition" by inviting leading functionaries:

> Leaders of party and social organizations and state authorities are most welcome guests in hunting. Inviting them makes it possible for them to acquaint themselves with the inner life of our hunting clubs and their economic management: they can form an opinion of the work executed by our hunters, and their useful advice can be fruitfully utilized in our further work.[46]

It cannot be far from the truth to guess that the number and quality of invitations a hunter received increased and improved exponentially as a function of his social-hierarchical position. Also, between significantly different levels of the social-political hierarchy, the reciprocity of these transactions was probably skewed, to the benefit of those in higher positions—that is, those of higher standing could accept more invitations at the expense of issuing fewer ones, than those whose hierarchical position was lower.

True reciprocity tended to prevail among equals. When the initial phase of establishing hunting clubs by "lower-than-top" apparatchiks was over, invitations remained the main way of increasing the quantity and variation of hunting opportunities. The "1st May" Hunting Club in the Börzsöny Mountains, where my father was a member, had no small-game areas at all. My father's frequent excursions to small-game landscapes were made possible by the many invitations he received. I found photos among the documents he left after his death that were shot on small-game hunts he had been treated to, among others, by the "Máté Zalka" Hunting Club of the Ministry of Defense.

This club had probably the next best situation, after Egyetértés, when it came to the possession of large and excellent hunting grounds: thanks to the proliferation of military (missile) bases in the 1960s in northern as well as southwestern Hungary, civilians were banned from a considerable number of superb areas of big and small game over which the generals (top officials of the Ministry of Defense) successfully asserted exclusive hunting rights. Luckily for my father, during his time as a deputy department chief in the Central Committee apparatus, he established friendly relationships with a number of important members of the Máté Zalka Club: Ferenc Kaszás, Dezső

Trombitás, and Tibor Tarcsay (all generals, vice ministers, or group chiefs in the ministry after 1963–64) all used to be his colleagues in the Central Committee apparatus; he also had some working (and hunting) relations with the general Ferenc Szűcs (the head of military counterintelligence, a great enthusiast of hunting, and a central personality of Egyetértés) and with the minister of defense himself, Lajos Czinege.[47]

The Political and Moral Economy of Hunting: Meat, Hierarchies, and Social Distinction

Resources Appropriated

We have already seen that the annual game bag of elite clubs, such as Egyetértés or the Máté Zalka Club, was several times larger than that of the "average hunter" in Hungary. For this no club member had to pay more than a nominal annual membership fee and sometimes a cost-price for the catering. Let's look at the summary table of the game bag of Egyetértés for 1971 (table 12.3).

Considering the impressive size of the annual bag and the relatively large number of high-value trophies in it, the game bag itself represented an enormous economic value. Using the same prices for the game bag as the ones paid by foreign (Western) hunters—the only ones who had to pay anything like a market price for both the shooting and the services and infrastructure they used—we would come to shocking amounts. Relying on such prices as applied in 1964, the shooting fee for the eight gold-medal red deer stags alone would have cost half a million forints for the club members (the actual 1971 prices were probably much higher).[48] Once again,

Table 12.3. The 1971 game bag of Egyetértés

Red deer	Total	668
Red deer	Stags	253
Fallow deer	Total	77
Fallow deer	Bucks	38
Roe deer	Total	171
Roe deer	Bucks	126
Mouflon	Total	11
Mouflon	Rams	11
Boar	Total	839
Small game	Total	14,789

The chief of military intelligence, the minister of defense,
and the author's father pause in shooting small game,
probably 1960 or 1961

what Egyetértés's members shot on the domains of their own club is often significantly less than their individual annual game bag, due to the considerable amount of hunting they could do on invitations.

The second item that should be considered among the resources appropriated was the broad scale of services and the immense infrastructure that the hunter as consumer utilized. (1) One of the major advantages of the *nomenklatura* hunter in the competition for hunting opportunities was his state-owned but privately possessed car. Club members, like Prime Minister Jenő Fock, who visited the reserves of Egyetértés 90 or even 100 times a year could do so because they had at their unlimited disposal a car with a chauffeur who worked as their personal servant. The number of cars owned by private individuals in Hungary remained very low well into the 1970s, which makes *nomenklatura* privileges in this respect even more conspicuous.[49] Even the NFGM, serving the club, used a considerable amount of its resources to acquire and maintain special four-wheel-drive cars and horse-drawn carriages to be used in connection with hunting. (2) In general, the National Farms provided and took care of an infrastructure that served the *nomenklatura* hunters when they visited their reserves: there were a number of houses (often fine old manor houses) that served their comfort; there were personnel to cook for them[50] and clean the houses; there were professional hunters who were responsible locally for game management but who also acted as guides, advisers, and assistants for club members when they visited the various reserves; and on the occasions of battues, a whole army of beaters was recruited from the nearby villages for around fifty forints or a hare each day. (3) Members of Egyetértés received their ammunition gratis from the Department of Hunting and Game Management of the Ministry of Agriculture. Good-quality ammunition was manufactured specially for the protocol hunters of Egyetértés by the Hungarian Nitrokémia Works at Füzfő (otherwise, the ammunition, especially ammunition for shotguns, accessible for commoners had rather a bad reputation).[51] (4) Egyetértés had a unique situation (unlike other *nomenklatura* hunting clubs) in that the club lived in a symbiotic relationship with the NFGM. The National Farms operated as a fiscal organization financing their expenses (investments as well as current costs) out of grants in the state budget, and paying all their incomes into the same budget. It is little wonder that the National Farms prospered—their operation benefited the same top politicians who in effect decided upon the amount of public resources that were allotted to them every year. In 1963 the budget of the National Farms was 10 million forints; by the late 1960s it had grown to around 60–70 million forints; and by around 1985 it had increased to 350 million, channeled partly in investments into new luxury hunting houses built for the convenience of *nomenklatura* hunters.[52]

Besides the unique outing and hunting opportunities, the infrastructure, and the supplies of various services and ammunition to which the *nomenklatura* hunter had practically gratis access, we should also mention an almost vulgarly materialistic aspect: there was a great deal of meat to be brought home from hunting. There was a norm (called the *kompetencia*) according to which each hunter in Hungary could free of charge take home sixty kilograms of big game (one kilogram of big game could be replaced with one pheasant or a hare) every year. From each battue, Egyetértés members could take three pieces of small game or two kilograms of big game (battues were also organized in boar hunting). On individual hunts one could retain meat out of the game bag at the price the MAVAD would have given for it to the NFGM. This price was about half of the retail prices of comparable first-class pork or beef.[53] In other words, *nomenklatura* hunting yielded high-quality meat at low costs. In my family's meat consumption from the late 1950s on, game figured very high. I also remember that my father and his friends themselves produced sausages and salami of boar and deer for family consumption, which was extremely popular in our circles. Large demand of this sort is in evidence in the history of the Egyetértés Club too: the club used the services of the Szeged Salami Factory (where the well-known Pick Salami is produced) to process game and deliver, on the individual club members' orders, a variety of sausages and salamis at very lenient prices.[54]

Hierarchies and Social Distinction

No doubt hunting had been by tradition a gentlemen's sport in Hungary and, especially when it came to big game (red deer, fallow deer, roe deer, bear [for pre-1918 Hungary], and boar), it can even be said to have been a sport for the high nobility or aristocracy. The simple reason for this is that, from the early medieval era, hunting rights went hand in hand and were spatially coextensive with the ownership of lands, and the best and richest hunting grounds constituted parts of large estates that were mostly in the hands of aristocratic families until as late as 1945.[55] Hunting became a marker of social distinction which even affected the value and meaning of small-game hunting (i.e., hunting for hare, pheasant, partridge, bustard, waterfowl), where the accessibility of hunting areas was slightly more "democratic" than in the case of big game. The late nineteenth century and the interwar years saw the spread of recreational hunting among urban middle-class and even lower middle-class circles,[56] thanks to the possibilities of hiring communal areas in the "green belts" surrounding major cities (these areas were rented out in competitive auctions, and complaints over steeply rising prices during the interwar period indicate the growing popularity of hunting among social groups other than the traditional landed elites).[57] Nonetheless, the prevalent image of (big-game) hunting even after 1945 was that it was the exclusive pastime of the aristocracy.

Against this "stigmatizing" background it is understandable that the press of the communist era (as well as the propaganda of MAVOSZ) claimed repeatedly that the new socialist social order "democratized" hunting, making it accessible to those who, in the ancien régime, could only get close to hunting as beaters.[58] Besides "democratized hunting," another discursive avenue to cement the social reputation of hunting (and elite hunting) was the claim that hunting was a socioeconomically useful and ecologically important activity whose heroes, who exerted physical efforts for no remuneration using their free time, were the hunters themselves. Thanks to the regulations of the early 1960s reinforcing rational (scientific) wildlife management, elite hunters could pose as workers whose contribution was essential to maintaining and running a branch of the socialist economy that yielded substantial hard currency revenues through exports of meat and live game as well as by attracting hunting tourism from the West to Hungary. Also, hunters (and elite hunters) under state socialism partook in the transnational discourse that construed hunting as a crucial replacement for missing predators. Thus, it was argued, hunting was not only essential for maintaining the ecological balance within wildlife, but it also made a significant contribution toward securing the high quality of the game stocks by regularly "culling the herd," that is, selectively shooting low-quality individuals. To show that they shared the order applying to other hunting societies, Egyetértés every now and then made gestures to assert a strict regime of rationing in order to restrict the shooting of red deer and fallow bucks with high-class trophies, in order to leave these for rich Western visitors, and to concentrate instead on "substandard individuals" which, it was said, had to be prevented from playing a role in reproduction.[59]

By the mid-1960s, *nomenklatura* hunting had by and large been squeezed into the confines of "socialist legality," and apparatchiks of various descriptions were hunting with licensed weapons, on the basis of hunting licenses and as members of hunting clubs. In spite of regularly repeated assurances about the "democratic nature" of hunting under socialism, even the publicly accessible general social statistics of the hunters' "community" could reveal a strong bias in the distribution of hunting opportunities to the benefit of the general category of "professionals, intellectuals," or "white-collar employees" (where the *nomenklatura* was tucked away). In 1970 slightly more than 25 percent of all active earners belonged to the group of "managers and intellectuals" and "middle-level employees" (clerks, intellectuals).[60] Newspaper reports from press conferences granted by the officials of MAVOSZ regularly placed the share of "physical workers" in hunters' societies at around 50 percent.[61] In other words, the group of managers, professionals, and white-collar workers (and, if it had been possible to separate from among them, the *nomenklatura*) were strongly overrepresented in the membership of hunting clubs.

This skewed distribution of hunting opportunities was reinforced to the extreme by the already mentioned restrictions applying to the procurement and holding of weapons. Even as late as the 1980s, less than a third of socialist Hungary's hunters had the right to dispose of and use rifles—the rest had to content themselves with shotguns. Obviously, hunting with a rifle implied a world both quantitatively and qualitatively different from that of hunting with a shotgun. The rifle went hand in hand with big-game hunting in large expanses of mountain areas covered by forests; the shotgun, on the other hand, meant small-game hunting in rather restricted, flat, and agriculturally cultivated landscapes.[62]

The strong stratification of hunters' society was further enhanced by the highly unequal situation of different clubs in terms of the quality of their territories and the resources at their disposal. Elite clubs, like Egyetértés or the Máté Zalka Hunting Club, appropriated a great deal of public resources.

To begin with, the hunting grounds under their control were large and had the richest and highest-quality game populations in the country. Of the two named, however, Egyetértés was obviously the superior one. Trophy statistics make this quite obvious: in a period of six years (1970–75), Egyetértés members shot 71 stags of red deer and 60 bucks of fallow deer with gold-medal antlers. The Máté Zalka Hunting Club, although it disposed of much more extensive domains than Egyetértés, could "only" boast of 60 gold-medal antlers of red deer and 7 gold-medal antlers of fallow bucks, all shot in a period of 15 years.[63] The majority of the fallow deer population in the country had its habitat on two reserves (Gyulaj and Telki) belonging to Egyetértés.

Just as much as hunting remained an elite form of recreation, so did hierarchies prevail even within the top hunting clubs. In the generally privileged Egyetértés, special privileges were enjoyed by the most powerful Politburo members. János Kádár, Jenő Fock, Béla Biszku, and Lajos Fehér had their own favorite territories, hunting houses, and even favorite professional hunters over whose services they asserted priority claims. The Pilis area and its professional leader, Oszkár Dvorák, with the house at Hamvaskő, "belonged" to Lajos Fehér in the sense that if he wished to go out hunting there, then it was his house. The old hunting castle of Metternich at Gyarmatpuszta "belonged" to Béla Biszku and Jenő Fock. Between Christmas and three days after New Year's Eve, no one could challenge János Kádár's priority when it came to two areas of the Gemenc Reserve (Veránka and Upper Gemenc, taken care of by the professional hunters János Berek and István Parti).[64]

The Egyetértés Club was rather restrictive with invitations, and I agree with Sándor Tóth that this was so probably because "they did not wish to show outsiders how they were living and hunting, as they would not have liked to hear or read critical comments about their privileged situation." The few invitations that were issued, however, carefully targeted people who deserved an invitation for their good services to Egyetértés or who were on their way to top levels within the *nomenklatura:* "If a political leader from a county was invited to hunt, that was most often because the person in question was going to be promoted to a national top position (Kádár knew, of course, that they were going to appoint him)." That such an event was of great significance in the everyday life of the *nomenklatura* is clearly shown by the fact that secretaries of MSZMP county organizations went out of their way to prevent their lower-ranking employees from participating in Egyetértés hunts.[65]

Members of Egyetértés also signalized their status by retaining the services of several professional hunters from the ancien régime. Endre Nagy,

Ákos Szederjei, Oszkár Barát, István Parti, Kornél Böröcki, Géza Gosz-
tonyi, Antal Fuchs, Ferenc Stoflitz, Oszkár Dvorák, János Berek, and others were professional hunters (and/or sons of professional hunters) who
distinguished themselves in the service of pre-1945 large estates owned
by aristocratic families or the clergy. Many of these people had excellent
rapport with János Kádár, György Aczél, and other leading members of
Egyetértés.[66]

That hunting brought with it social status and distinction or, putting it
another way, that access to hunting required social status, was rather clear to
the rank and file too. They hardly bought the propaganda which maintained
that in hunting "social differences ceased to exist—all club members are but
hunters."[67] Indeed, we know of an occasion when they tried to cheat the
social order of hunting and establish a hunting club by faking the inclusion
of high *nomenklatura* personalities among their members.[68] The reaction of
the controlling authority is most revealing:

> I find it extremely remarkable that the hunting club in question was
> established under the circumstances described and I think MAVOSZ
> should not accept this. I find it quite impossible to believe that on
> July 19, comrades István Dobi and Ernő Mihályfi were present at the
> meeting in Vértesszöllős. The whole protocol is a flagrant abuse of
> their names. Comrade [Vice Minister Gyula] Balassa will contact
> Comrade Dobi in this matter ... It would not at all surprise me if
> the minutes would prove to be a vulgar fake. *It cannot be regarded as*
> *normal that Comrade István Dobi, who has at his disposal any of the na-*
> *tional reserves (which is only natural), would wish to "enter" the Sólyom*
> *Club of Vértesszöllős, where truck driver József Horváth is the chairman,*
> *and he would serve as "political officer," while the "master hunter" would be*
> *Comrade Ernő Mihályfi, one of the leaders of the Patriotic People's Front.*
> *Remarkable names, oddly misplaced [Elgondolkoztató nevek, különös beo-*
> *sztásban].* I cannot see it as probable that Comrades Dobi and Mihályfi
> are aware of these, for them, not too honorable appointments and the
> minutes. Or will it be the same István Csató, identified in the minutes
> as controller, who will control Comrade István Dobi?[69]

Department chief Dénes's horror over imagining Comrade Dobi as a member of the Sólyom Club where the chairman was a simple truck driver epitomizes a social world that was not only discriminating and exclusive against
the lower classes but also firmly placed hunting among the terrains of sociability (and forms of luxury consumption) demarcated for elite leisure.

Conclusion

My father was born and grew up in the interwar era. In his teenage years (the late 1930s and the war years) he started working in the Budapest textile industries and joined the Social Democratic youth organization and later the underground Communist Party. By then, it had become a tradition among Budapest socialist working-class youth to arrange much of their political and social life around hiking excursions to the hills and mountains to the northwest and northeast of the capital city. This kind of outing was practically the only accessible way for them to enjoy nature, to breathe fresh air, and to relax. The outings were also regarded as a useful conspiratorial practice in their efforts to escape the gaze of the political police (whose efficiency, however, was seriously undermined by the presence of numerous informers among its own ranks). This legacy of the past in the workers' movement certainly played some role in the upsurge of interest in hunting, especially after 1956. But hunting was more importantly one of the scarce opportunities for many of them to deploy the status and power they wielded in gaining *private* pleasure. In fact, opportunities for making one's high social status yield an "income" in terms of improved personal well-being were relatively restricted under the state socialist social order.[70] Normally, one could not amass a large private fortune and let it grow (in this respect, the opportunities to turn privileged access to *communal* infrastructure such as top-level rental housing into private fortunes came during the extensive privatization in the transition period after 1989). Forms of "conspicuous consumption" like the collection of rare coins, the private import of expensive Western furniture, and so on could easily become suspicious (since the salaries even of high functionaries were not lavishly high) and lead to scandals and even tragedies. Hunting, however, was a singularly appropriate hobby and form of leisure for which to develop and cultivate a "passion." With their exclusive hunting grounds in mostly uninhabited parts of the countryside, hunting clubs offered a benevolent refuge from the public eye. The general public could not know much about the particular circumstances attendant to the hunting of the apparatus class (or about the exceptional privileges enjoyed by them in terms of exclusive access to the best areas, the infrastructure and services extended to them by the state farms of forestry and wildlife management, etc.). The strict regulations of the first half of the 1960s were put in place in order, among other things, to enhance this privacy. Through disciplining and "normalizing" the hunting activities of the country's provincial and Budapest-based apparatchiks, Kádár managed to suppress the anarchic poaching that had been widespread among them during the late 1950s, and to secure optimal conditions to achieve a happy symbiosis between "socialist legality," rational forestry, and wildlife management, on the one hand, and the apparatus class's hunting interests, on the other.[71]

The communist takeover accomplished in Hungary in 1948 was not confined to political power. The socioeconomic transformation commencing during[72] and continuing right after the war yielded not only a political economy characterized by the maximal expansion of state ownership over the nation's wealth and productive infrastructure, but also resulted in a social order in which party-state apparatchiks could and did assert themselves as the new ruling class.[73] They owned the state and the state owned the country. As the owners of exclusive disposition rights over all the resources belonging to the state, they were the monopolists of the political sphere and, at the same time, the privileged proprietors and beneficiaries of the country's major infrastructures serving private comfort, pleasure, and leisure. Taking over all positions of political, economic, and administrative decision-making at local, regional, and national levels, concurrently and just as self-evidently they also settled in and took over the villas, houses, and summer and winter resorts of the old ruling classes.[74] Indeed, they took over not only the habitat but also the habits of their predecessors who constituted the main targets of their rhetoric of class hatred, especially in the early years of their power.[75] The solution to this seeming paradox lies partly in the political economy of the expropriation of the surplus value under state socialist conditions. The great bulk of this expropriation took the form of macroeconomic decisions of central planning affecting the division of annual national income between "consumption" and "accumulation." But part of the surplus value had to be used as dividends rewarding the party-state apparatus for its role and services in administering and maintaining the system. In an economy, however, where both market regulation and the accumulation of *private capital* were severely restricted, the appropriation of this part of the surplus value tended to happen *in natura* rather than in monetary form. Privileged access, at no or merely nominal prices, to health care with up-to-date medical technologies, to the finest recreational facilities (including the best hunting grounds, their personnel and complete infrastructure), to the highest-quality segments of communal housing, to a vast park of often luxurious cars, to the best secondary and higher education institutions for one's children, to the most sought-after opportunities for travel abroad, and so on—these were all forms of private appropriation of the social surplus. But they also had an instrumental as well as symbolic role in the social reproduction of status and class position. As we have seen, hunting, calculated at market prices, enabled its apparatchik practitioners to appropriate values several times their annual salaries. However, a membership in or regular invitations to the Egyetértés or other hunting clubs of the party-state apparatus elite also confirmed class affiliation and conferred social distinction.

Notes

The author is glad to acknowledge the inspiration he received from his conversations with Bruce W. Hevly over an early draft of this chapter. The epigraph for this chapter is from Tibor Huszár, *Beszélgetések Nyers Rezsővel* (*Conversations with Rezső Nyers*) (Budapest: Kossuth Kiadó, 2004), 277–78.

1. For the distinction between the realist and confessional genres, and other thoughtful distinctions pertinent to the various writing conventions and representational styles prevalent in ethnography (anthropology), see John Van Maanen, *Tales of the Field: On Writing Ethnography* (Chicago and London: University of Chicago Press, 1988).

2. KNEB (Központi Népi Ellenőrzési Bizottság) was the state audit authority with sweeping mandates and powers to control, from the point of view of law and national political objectives, the working of all sectors and all units operative in the country's economic and social life (all business operations irrespective of the form of ownership, and all other operations funded publicly). The KNEB had the same legal status as the Supreme Court or the Attorney General's Office. Its president had a rank (state secretary) next to minister, while his first deputy (my father) was ranked as a vice minister. They were appointed by the Presidential Council of the Hungarian People's Republic.

3. In the late spring and summer months of May–August we went fishing.

4. See Sándor Tóth, *A hírnév kötelez: Vadászat és vadgazdálkodás Magyarországon, 1945–1990* (*Obliging Reputation: Hunting and Wildlife Management in Hungary, 1945–1990*), 2nd enl. ed. (Budapest: Nimród Vadászújság, 2005), 126–27.

5. *Nomenklatura* hunting and its "achievements" were consistently kept away from the public eye. An episode typical of this is as follows: Egyetértés circulated among its members a satirical illustrated newsletter issued annually on the occasion of the club's end-of-the-year party. Its title was *Fácán Matyi* (the official satirical weekly magazine, the Hungarian counterpart of the Soviet *Krokodil*, was called *Ludas Matyi*). One of *Fácán Matyi*'s issues scornfully cites the wording of a news item carried by the tabloid daily *Esti Hírlap*: "20 fallow bucks were brought down during the October hunting season in Gyulaj, the famous reserve. Two native hunters have shot bucks with antlers weighing 4.37 and 4.46 kilograms, which are outstanding even among those winning gold medals. Indeed, they are not far off the world record trophies." On the illustration attached to the news (a drawing except for the heads, which are photos of the hunters), Politburo members Lajos Fehér and Béla Biszku are dancing *csárdás* in folk costumes and boots and a subtext says: "Two native hunters have shot beyond the world record" (*Fácán Matyi*, December 1970, 5). The text obviously referred to the fact that Fehér had twice shot fallow bucks with world record antlers in Gyulaj (see Bányai József, *Világrekord trófeák a Magyar Mezőgazdasági Múzeumban* [Budapest: Magyar Mezőgazdasági Múzeum, 1994]), and so did probably even Biszku, although he, unlike Fehér or Kádár, never donated his trophies to the Museum of Agriculture.

6. Ignác Romsics, *István Bethlen: A Great Conservative Statesman of Hungary, 1874–1946* (Highland Lakes, N.J.: Atlantic Research, 1995), 26.

7. I must admit that it was also publicly known about Kádár that he liked chess. But there was no publicity to his other favorite pastime: the very popular, lower-class card game in Hungary called *ulti*[*mo*]. On his private hunting excursions when he slept over at one of the reserves, he had with him a small and rather constant circle of people (the general Ferenc Szűcs, surgeon Zoltán Szabó, Kádár's bodyguard Ferenc Sebestyén, and Sándor Tóth, director of protocol hunting and head of the Department of Hunting and Game Management of the Ministry of Agriculture). As Sándor Tóth recollects, "In the evenings, after dinner, we had to work: *ulti* . . . Kádár was a very skillful card-player" (author's interview with Sándor Tóth, Budapest, June 25–26, 2004).

8. See Kádár's letters instructing officials of the National Directorate of Forestry as to which of his (and his wife's) trophies should be displayed; he was also careful to see to it that the visitors to the exhibition should not be able to see that they had several trophies from the same date: Kádár to Ernő Zsámbor, March 14, 1960; and G. Balassa to Kádár, December 21, 1960, Kádár János Titkárságának iratai, MOL M-KS-288, f. 47, cs. 730 őe. (papers of János Kádár's Secretariat, Hungarian National Archives).

9. Exchange of letters between Róbert Muray and János Kádár, May 23, 1973. Kádár János Titkárságának iratai, MOL M-KS-288, f. 47, cs. 756 őe.

10. MÉM Vadászati és Vadgazdálkodási Főosztály (Ministry of Agriculture and Food Industries Chief Department of Hunting and Game Management), "Jelentés az Állami Erdő- és Vadgazdaságok 1971, évi működéséről," Dr Tóth Sándor főosztályvezető, Budapest, January 31, 1972 ("Report on the Operation of the National Farms of Forestry and Game Management in 1971," by Dr. Sándor Tóth, director of the Main Department of Hunting and Game Management of the Ministry of Agriculture and Food Industries—in the possession of Dr. Tóth). This report was qualified "Strictly Confidential" after it was read by some members of the Egyetértés Club. As Tóth told me in the course of my interview with him, several Egyetértés members were immensely irritated by all of the personal details included in the eighteen pages and seven appendices of the report. I am most grateful to Sándor Tóth for having provided me with a copy of this important document.

11. R.J.I., "A férfiak sportja: Huszonnyolcezer puskás ember" ("The Sport of Men: Twenty-Eight Thousand Men with Guns"), *Magyar Hírlap*, November 16, 1979. All press materials quoted in this paper have been consulted in the excellent collection of newspaper clippings held by the Open Society Archives, Budapest.

12. A visit to Valkó (one of the starting points for hunters visiting the Gödöllő Reserve, some 40–50 kilometers northeast from the center of Budapest) right after working hours on a weekday afternoon was counted as a "hunting day." The Telki Reserve was even closer to Budapest (about 20–30 kilometers east)—83 of the 90 "hunting days" of Prime Minister Jenő Fock were spent there, and it is quite probable that most of the visits were such short late afternoon tours made without sleeping over.

13. This is quite apparent from the photos published in Tóth, *A hírnév kötelez*, as well as from MÉM Vadászati és Vadgazdálkodási Főosztály, "Jelentés az Állami Erdő," where Mrs. Kádár and Mrs. Aczél are identified in the Egyetértés's annual game bag as hunters who shot three stags and seven boars (Mrs. Kádár) plus one stag (Mrs. Aczél). See also the trophy lists of the Egyetértés Club for 1970–75: *Trófea Bemutató—Az Erdő- és Vadgazdaságok területén 1970: Évi bőgés idején elejtett szarvas- és dámbikák trófeáiról*, printed by the Erdészeti Műszaki és Szervezési Iroda, Budapest, in 120 copies—(same for 1970, 1971, 1972, 1973, 1974, 1975).

14. János Kádár had probably the longest vacation, which, according to a source of mine from the mid-1960s was six weeks, that is, 42 days total (or 36 working days). See the "Top Secret!" medical report on the state of health and suggestions for diet and lifestyle for János Kádár by the Central National Hospital of Kútvölgyi Street, signed by hospital director Imre Fenyvesi and Kádár's personal doctor of internal medicine, Imre Gergely: Kádár János Titkárságának iratai, MOL M-KS-288, f. 47, cs. 735 őe.

15. For a few examples of such invitations coming in to János Kádár, see Kádár János Titkárságának iratai, MOL M-KS-288, f. 47, cs. 724 őe. (István Szabó's and Zoltán Szabó's letter to Kádár); and 756 őe. (István Gergely's letter to Kádár).

16. For some of Kádár's contacts with Count Széchenyi and his widow, see Kádár János Titkárságának iratai, MOL M-KS-288, f. 47, cs. 733 őe. and 762 őe.

17. Kádár personally intervened at various points of time to assist the projects of István Homoki-Nagy, a director of feature films with animal casts, with a great deal of footage in areas with the richest wildlife in the country (like Gemenc or the Hortobágy), and with plenty of episodes with hunting. For some of Kádár's contacts with Homoki-Nagy, see Kádár János Titkárságának iratai, MOL M-KS-288, f. 47, cs. 739 őe.

18. For a bibliography of hunting-related literature published in Hungary, see György Vuray, Gábor Fodor Rácz, and Zoltán Szabó, eds., *A magyar vadászirodalom képeskönyve: Vadászat és horgászat az irodalomban és a képzőművészetben* (Budapest: Mezőgazda Kiadó, 2000). The "rehabilitation" of Kittenberger, Nadler, and Széchenyi, "auf Kádárs Wunsch" (according to Kádár's wish), is acknowledged by (Count) Philipp Meran, *Wenn die Wolken weiterziehen: Ein Leben für die Jagd* (Graz and Stuttgart: Leopold Stocker Verlag, 1992), 48.

19. For Dénes's case, see his letter to János Kádár, November 16, 1963, as well as the latter's exchanges with Károly Németh and Béla Biszku, all in Kádár János Titkárságának iratai, MOL M-KS-288, f. 47, cs. 734 őe.

20. Author's interview with Sándor Tóth, Budapest, June 25–26, 2004.

21. MÉM Vadászati és Vadgazdálkodási Főosztály, "Jelentés az Állami Erdő," 9.

22. Author's telephone interview with Sándor Tóth, October 31, 2005.

23. Imre Szász, *Ez elment vadászni . . .* (Budapest: Szépirodalmi Könyvkiadó, 1984), 84. (The title of this book—a documentary report about hunting in the Hungarian countryside—is untranslatable: it is a passage from a children's rhyme. If translated literally it can be rendered as "This [one] has gone to hunt . . .").

24. Author's interview with Sándor Tóth, Budapest, June 25–26, 2004. A revealing document in this respect is the letter of István Dénes, head of the Department of Hunting and Game Management of the National Directorate of Forestry, to Police Captain Szabó of the Gödöllő Police District. The Police Department was inclined to reject the application of Antal Fuchs Jr. for licenses both for shotgun and for hunting rifle. The motivation was Fuchs's bad ("class-alien") social background: he came from a family of professional hunters of the old regime—his father, Antal Fuchs Sr., served on Count Tamás Eszterházy's estate as chief hunter. Dénes emphasized that nothing incriminating could be found in Fuchs's records and that the young Fuchs was among the professionals of game management who enjoyed a high reputation. István Dénes to Police Captain Szabó, September 9, 1959, copy, documents of the Ministry of Agriculture, Hungarian National Archives, MOL XIX-K-13–a 174, d. 1959, 58–1/486/ 1959. Antal Fuchs Jr. worked at the Gödöllő Reserve, which was one of the "protocol

areas" even before 1964, when Egyetértés was formally established. For a short biography of Antal Fuchs Sr., see Antal Fuchs Jr., "Id. Fuchs Antal, 1883–1968," in *Száz év, száz vadász* (*One Hundred Years, One Hundred Hunters*), ed. Sándor Békés (Budapest: Millenniumi Vadászati Bizottság, 2001), 86, which confirms that, after 1956, Fuchs Sr. again enjoyed full recognition for his professional competence.

25. "Milliók—Kedvtelésből" ("Millions, for the Fun of It"), *Figyelő,* November 27, 1974.

26. F.B., "Nyitott kapuk?" ("Open Doors?"), *Szabad Föld,* December 8, 1974.

27. A couple of examples: "Vadászterület iránti kérelem," MOL XIX-K-13–a, 247 d. 8501/1962; Miskolci Városi Tanács VB. Elnökhelyettese ír földművelésügyi miniszternek, vt. alakítása és vadászterület kérése, MOL XIX-K-13–a, 137, d. 1958, 25–1/246/1958; A Homokvasút és Kerületi Hányóüzem MSZMP alapszervezete, Dorog, levele Kádár János et.nak vadászterület elvételének sérelmezése, MOL XIX-K-13–a, 174, d. 1959, 58–1/138/1959. All these documents (applications and complaint regarding hunting grounds) are in the papers of the Ministry of Agriculture at the Hungarian National Archives.

28. I happen to know that Varga had a good reputation and also a certain popularity because of his cooperative's semiprivate services, on often very advantageous terms, for many high officials of the party-state (these services were connected with building, renovating dachas, taking care of gardens, etc.).

29. For the related exchanges of letters from October 1985, Kádár János Titkárságának iratai, MOL M-KS-288, f. 47, cs. 774 őe.

30. The share of women among the officially registered hunters of communist Hungary never reached 1 percent. In 1974 only 80 of about 25,000 hunters were women (József Simányi, "Évente több mint tízmillió lövés: Beszélgetés dr. Koller Mihállyal, a MAVOSZ főtitkárával" ["More Than Ten Million Shots Annually: Conversation with Dr. Mihály Koller"], *Magyar Hírlap,* July 21, 1975).

31. By the time this application was filed, my mother had gone through two major operations with slipped disks and she was not at all fit for the physical exercises attendant to hunting. The whole documentation of the case from 1964 can be found in "NEB 'Béke' Vt. részére a Vérteskozmai 806–os vadászterület bérbeadása," MOL XIX-K-13–a, 324, d. 14, t. 12589/1964, Országos Erdészeti Főigazgatóság (National Directorate of Forestry, which was a division of the Ministry of Agriculture).

32. Ödön Fáczányi, *Egy hajdani vadásztársaság: A Székesfehérvári (Csákvári) Nimród vadásztársaság története 1967–1997* (*A Hunting Club of the Past: The History of the Nimrod Hunting Club in Székesfehérvár [Csákvár], 1967–1997*) (Budapest: Nimród Alapítvány, n.d.), 23.

33. Interview with László Fekete-Győr in Fáczányi, *Egy hajdani,* 102.

34. Author's interview with Sándor Tóth, Budapest, June 25–26, 2004.

35. There were altogether twenty-five "Young Nimrods," including the sons and daughters of Egyetértés members as well as their invited friends and student comrades (author's interview with Sándor Tóth, Budapest, June 25–26, 2004). It is disturbing to see the rather cynical manner in which Mihály Koller, general secretary of MAVOSZ, presented to the press the establishment of the Young Nimrod Club (carefully leaving out who the members were): "We [MAVOSZ] believe it is extremely important to rejuvenate the membership of hunting clubs and, especially, [to make good use of] the educational effects of the communities of hunting clubs upon the youth . . . Even a separate club has been established for young people in the neighborhood of Hatvan

under the name Young Nimrod. They work with great enthusiasm, they hunt and they husband [their resources]" (Jenő Csalló, "Vadgazdálkodás és vadászat" ["Wildlife Management and Hunting"], *Magyar Hírlap*, February 7, 1972).

36. Imre Cseterki's letters to János Kádár, September 26 and October 5, 1972, Kádár János Titkárságának iratai, MOL M-KS-288, f. 47, cs. 774 őe. As I said, the "Young Nimrods" could launch their club only thanks to the fact that Egyetértés accepted the transfer to them of one of their finest small-game areas in the Hatvan region (originally belonging to the Gödöllő estate). In the name of "socialist legal-ity," the transfer went through the council of Pest County—Pest County took into its posssession the territory from the Gödöllő National Farm of Forestry and Game Management; but the county had been given to understand that Comrade Kádár and other comrades wished this piece of land to be let out for the Nimrod Youth Hunting Club. The loss suffered by Egyetértés was immediately "compensated" by qualifying the Soponya estate as a national farm of game management, thus establish-ing exclusive access to the area for the Egyetértés Club. Soponya is about a hundred kilometers southwest of Budapest and is arguably the most superb small-game land in the country; it is also where, at the age of fourteen, I shot my first and only game, a hare and a pheasant.

37. Author's interview with Sándor Tóth, Budapest, June 25–26, 2004.

38. Ibid.

39. See Szász, *Ez elment vadászni*, 91–92.

40. Author's interview with Sándor Tóth, Budapest, June 25–26, 2004.

41. Ibid.

42. Letter of Pál Ágoston, head of main department, Attorney General's Office, to the National Directorate of Forestry, December 31, 1960, "Vadászati balesetek megelőzésére irányuló intézkedések megtétele" ("The implementation of measures to prevent hunting accidents"), papers of the Ministry of Agriculture, Hungarian National Archives, MOL XIX-K-13-a 228, d. 117–1/7/1961. See, also here, the response of István Dénes, head of the Department of Hunting and Game Manage-ment, January 11, 1961, which tells about high-level intervention in the matter (strict instructions to stop the anarchistic hunting by functionaries issued to the provincial party organizations by the Central Committee secretary György Marosán).

43. The circular, dated April 3, 1964, is printed in its entirety in Sándor Tóth, *A hírnév kötelez: Vadászat és vadgazdálkodás Magyarországon, 1945–1990*, 1st ed. (Bu-dapest: Nimród Alapítvány, 1998), 67–68 (my emphasis). This circular was preceded by a similar circular to all directors of the National Farms of Forestry by the vice minister of agriculture and leader of the National Forestry Directorate, Gyula Balassa, on January 10, 1964. Its subject matter was "Stopping irregular hunting"—published in Sándor Tóth's just-quoted book, on page 66. It is very probable that similar circu-lars were sent from the Central Committee apparatus to the county and lower-level MSZMP organizations.

44. The campaign may have been successful with regard to maintaining the "integrity"of the hunting grounds of Egyetértés. What it could achieve beyond that is highly questionable: a sociological survey made in the first half of the 1980s revealed that the local and national *nomenklatura* regularly extorted various "favors" (*szíves-ség*) from the chairmen of agricultural cooperatives—one of these favors was the arrangement of hunting excursions for them. See Árpád Pünkösti, *Az elithez tartozni: A téeszelnökök kapcsolatrendszere (Belonging to the Elite: The Networks of Chairmen of*

Agricultural Cooperatives) (Budapest: Tömegkommunikációs Kutatóközpont, 1986), 62 and 66–67. The book was qualified as "Belső kiadvány" (internal publication), which meant that it was not publicly accessible.

45. Author's interview with Sándor Tóth, Budapest, June 25–26, 2004.

46. The document, dated Budapest, February 25, 1974, is reproduced in Tóth, *A hírnév kötelez*, 1998, 168–69.

47. I am in the possession of a postcard from Defense Minister Lajos Czinege which he sent to my father on October 29, 1961, from Prague, Czechoslovakia. The photo shows the "Imperial" Sanatorium of Karlovy Vary from the foot of a towering statue on the top of which an impressive mountain buck is standing—the circle drawn by Czinege's blue pen around the buck on the photo (as if the sight of the gun were already resting on the buck . . .) carried more than half of the message between two comrades who had already shared a great deal of hunting experience.

48. The price information is from Tóth, *A hírnév kötelez* (2005), 246–50; the data for the game bag are from MÉM Vadászati és Vadgazdálkodási Főosztály, "Jelentés az Állami Erdő."

49. There were 3 passenger cars per 1,000 inhabitants in Hungary in 1960, and 23 in 1970—the same data for Britain are 108 and 215, and for Austria 57 and 161, respectively: György Péteri, "Streetcars of Desire: Cars and Automobilism in Communist Hungary (1958–70)," *Social History* 34, no. 1 (February 2009), 3, 5. In 1970 only 6 out of 100 households in Hungary owned cars (Ignác Romsics, *Magyarország története a XX. században* [*The History of Hungary in the 20th Century*] [Budapest: Osiris Kiadó, 1999], 479).

50. As Tóth recollected during my interview with him, in 1969 all the cooks of the National Farms were sent to the famous Gundel Restaurant in Budapest to learn the art of cooking and serving, but when high-ranking foreign guests were hosted, the NFGM relied on the services of the Gundel and Taverna restaurants and their personnel themselves.

51. Author's interview with Sándor Tóth, Budapest, June 25–26, 2004.

52. Detailed budget data for 1971 can be found in MÉM Vadászati és Vadgazdálkodási Főosztály, "Jelentés az Állami Erdő." The total for the mid-1980s is from the author's interview with Sándor Tóth, Budapest, June 25–26, 2004.

53. Author's interview with Sándor Tóth, Budapest, June 25–26, 2004. We should also keep in mind that first-class pork or beef was not always available in retail shops during the 1960s and 1970s. In 1960 the per capita meat consumption in Hungary was 49.1 kilograms, and by 1970 it had grown to 60.4 kilograms—see Romsics, *Magyarország története a XX. században*, 479.

54. Author's interview with Sándor Tóth, Budapest, June 25–26, 2004.

55. For a useful historical overview of hunting in Hungary, from the beginnings to the state socialist era, see Pál Csőre, *A magyar vadászat története* (*A History of Hungarian Hunting*) (Budapest: Mezőgazda Kiadó, 1994).

56. This is interestingly documented in the private footage of György Pető, a young Jewish businessman of interwar Szeged—see the art documentary film of Péter Forgács, *Free Fall* (1996).

57. An instructive discussion of these tendencies can be found in an anonymous note made for Zoltán (Tildy), the president of the National Bureau of Nature Conservation (Országos Természetvédelmi Hivatal) in 1967. The author of the note undertook to discuss the question of why small-game populations declined so conspicu-

ously in the postwar era, in comparison to the interwar years (clearly indicated in the annual game bags of the early 1930s: around 2.2 million small game, as opposed to around 800,000 in the mid-1960s). The writer of the note offered to explain the phenomenon as a consequence of the changing social composition of the hunters' community and the increasingly utilitarian attitudes among them. The note, lacking title, date, and author, addressed to "Kedves Zoltán!" (Dear Zoltán!), is an attachment to Kálmán Tolnay's letter to "Mrs. Comrade Fock" (quite probably Prime Minister Fock's wife, who worked within forestry and game management, under Vice Minister Gyula Balassa), September 29, 1967, papers of the Ministry of Agriculture, Hungarian National Archives, MOL XIX-K-9-aj 28, d. 8, t. 1967. Tolnay had been asked to give his opinion about the note, which he now returned. Tolnay was, until sometime in the mid-1960s, the director of the Gödöllő Reserve; before 1956 he was an officer in Rákosi's much-dreaded State Security Authority; in the mid-1960s he became the director of the penitentiary in Dunaújváros. He was also the author of some popular cookbooks specializing in game.

58. Jenő Csalló, "Vadászok és vadászat" ("Hunters and Hunting"), *Magyar Hírlap*, January 8, 1973.

59. Revealingly, when the restrictions were ignored because a hunter of high standing wished to get a better trophy than what he had permission for, it was the professional hunter accompanying him who got penalized. See János Zoltán, *Legenda és valóság: Az Egyetértés és a Zalka Máté Vadásztársaság története* (*Myth and Reality: The History of the Egyetértés and Máté Zalka Hunting Clubs*) (Budapest[?]: Dénes Natur Műhely, 1996), 57.

60. See Tibor Valuch, "Changes in the Structure and Lifestyle of the Hungarian Society in the Second Half of the XXth Century," in *Social History of Hungary from the Reform Era to the End of the Twentieth Century*, by Gábor Gyáni, György Kövér, and Tibor Valuch (Boulder, Colo.: Social Science Monographs, 2004), 585.

61. Ferenc Baktai, "Nimródék kétmillió dollárja" ("The Two Million Dollars of the Nimróds"), *Népszava*, February 24, 1965; Csalló, "Vadászok és vadászat"; "Nem kedvtelés csupán—Gazdálkodás" ("Not Only Pastime—An Economic Activity"), *Pestmegyei Hírlap*, January 12, 1975; Simányi, "Évente több mint tízmillió loves."

62. Shotguns were, however, used for hunting boar with special ammunition called "pearl bullets" (a single lead "pellet" fitting in size the diameter of the bore of the gun, called "*gyöngygolyó*" in Hungarian). These bullets were often homemade and could only be used with a particular kind of shotgun (the whole bore had to be of the same diameter). These guns worked only at short range (not more than thirty to forty meters) and with low precision. *Gyöngygolyós* hunting had a low status (a shotgun with such bullets was "the poor hunter's rifle"); the ammunition could only be used in boar hunting, in battues, where one had the chance to shoot at close range.

63. *Trófea Bemutató*, for 1970–75; and János Zoltán, *Legenda és valóság*, 75.

64. Author's interview with Sándor Tóth, Budapest, June 25–26, 2004.

65. Ibid.

66. Ferenc Stoflitz, leader of the Telki Reserve, who worked, before 1945, on the estates of Count Tisza, received a high-level decoration upon his retirement in 1966. Kádár also asked Károly Németh (chairman of the club, at the time first secretary of the Budapest Party Committee of the Hungarian Socialist Workers' Party) to see to it that Stoflitz received invitations from Egyetértés to collective hunts (Kádár János Titkárságának iratai, MOL M-KS-288, f. 47, cs. 739 őe). In 1958 Kádár and his wife

gave Stoflitz a rifle as thanks for Stoflitz's "diligent efforts on behalf of our pastime" (Kádár János Titkárságának iratai, MOL M-KS-288, f. 47, cs. 720 őe.). According to Sándor Tóth, Stoflitz was Mrs. Kádár's favorite guide on her hunting excursions.

67. Baktai, "Nimródék kétmillió dollárja."

68. It was the case of the Sólyom (Falcon) Hunting Club in Vértesszöllős. In the minutes of their July 19, 1959, meeting (where the club was declared to be established), they included the names of István Dobi (president of the People's Republic) and Ernő Mihályfi (general secretary of the Patriotic People's Front) in the list of members. Indeed, they even "appointed" Dobi to be the "political officer" (*politikai felelős*) of the club, while Mihályfi got the honorable role of "master hunter" (*vadászmester*). The MAVOSZ apparently accepted the new club, but the Department of Hunting and Game Management of the Ministry of Agriculture put an end to their career in the bud. István Dénes's letter to MAVOSZ, September 5, 1959, copy, Archives of the Ministry of Agriculture, MOL XIX-K-13-a 174, d. 1959, 58-1/487/1959.

69. István Dénes's letter to MAVOSZ, September 5, 1959 (italics added).

70. This no doubt created tensions among the ranks of the apparatus class which reached the agenda of the highest political decision-making bodies. For example, the Central Committee Secretariat of the Hungarian Socialist Workers' Party at its meeting on March 25, 1968, discussed a detailed "Report Concerning the Social Status, Economic and Social Situation, and Moral Acknowledgment of Full-Time Political Functionaries." The report, as well as the minutes of the meeting, is in the Hungarian National Archives, MOL M-KS-288 f. 7, cs. 299 őe.

71. Thanks to this symbiosis, little Hungary became by the 1960s and 1970s a most attractive place for Western European hunting tourism. Hungarian wildlife management earned an international reputation manifest, among other ways, in the fact that the World Exhibition of Hunting in 1971 was located in Budapest.

72. See Jan Gross's important essay "War as Revolution" in *The Establishment of Communist Regimes in Eastern Europe, 1944–1949,* ed. Norman Naimark and Leonid Gibianskii (Boulder, Colo.: Westview, 1997), 17–40.

73. Part of the inspiration for the short discussion below is from George Konrád and Ivan Szelényi, *The Intellectuals on the Road to Class Power* (New York: Harcourt Brace Jovanovich, 1979); and Iván Szelényi, *Új osztály, állam, politika* (*New Class, State, Politics*) (Budapest: Európa Kiadó, 1990).

74. A revealing document of the early phases of this expropriation of the old ruling classes by the emerging new one is the memoirs of Klára Szakasits, the daughter of Árpád Szakasits, leader of the Hungarian Social Democratic Party and one of the leaders of the Hungarian Workers' Party (after the merger of Communists and Social Democrats). On the one hand, this is an account in which the author talks about how upset she had been when she saw on a former neighbor a piece of her clothing from her apartment that had been abandoned in the late stage of the war. On the other hand, Mrs. Szakasits also tells her reader in great detail how she, thanks to the high positions of her father and of her husband, who was also a leading leftist Social Democrat, was offered and accepted in 1945 a large villa in one of the best areas of the Buda hills and was shown to a huge storehouse of "ownerless goods" (furniture, carpets, paintings, etc.) from which she could properly furnish her new house. Both the house and the furniture and other articles belonged to the former ruling classes of Hungary (among them high officials in public administration who had fled from the country as it was occupied by the Soviet Red Army, as well as Jewish victims of

the Holocaust and Arrow Cross rule from among the capitalist middle classes). Significantly, all these "ownerless goods" were disposed of by a governmental agency (Elhagyott Javak Kormánybiztossága) jointly controlled and run by the Communist and the Social Democratic parties. See Schifferné Klára Szakasits, *Fent és lent 1945–1950* (*Up and Down 1945–1950*) (Budapest: Magvető Könyvkiadó, 1985), 63–76.

75. Looking beyond hunting and the boundaries of Hungary, an interesting case in point is the career of the dacha during the Soviet era, as discussed in Stephen Lowell's superb book *Summerfolk: A History of the Dacha, 1710–2000* (Ithaca, N.Y., and London: Cornell University Press, 2003), 118.

CONTRIBUTORS

Paulina Bren teaches in the Department of History at Vassar College and is the author of many essays on postwar socialism. Her book *The Greengrocer and His TV: The Culture of Communism After the 1968 Prague Spring* was published by Cornell University Press in 2010. She is currently working on a coedited volume with Mary Neuburger entitled *Consuming Communism: Cultures of Consumption in Postwar Eastern Europe.* Her next research project is on the Bat'a Shoe Works.

David Crowley is a historian with an interest in Eastern Europe who teaches at the Royal College of Art in London. He is the author of various books, including *Warsaw* (2003) and two volumes coedited with Susan Reid. He was consultant curator of "Cold War Modern: Design 1945–1970," an exhibition at the Victoria and Albert Museum in London in 2008 (and coauthor of the accompanying book). He is currently writing a book on the intertwined histories of photography and communism.

Jukka Gronow is a professor of sociology at Uppsala University, Sweden, with an interest in the social and cultural history of the Soviet Union. His publications include *The Sociology of Taste* (1997), *Ordinary Consumption* (2000, coedited with Alan Warde), and *Caviar with Champagne: Common Luxury and the Ideals of the Good Life in Stalin's Russia* (2003). He is currently writing, with Sergey Zhuravlev, a book on the history of Soviet fashion.

Katherine Lebow has held positions at the University of Virginia and the College of Charleston. She is currently a lecturer in European history at Newcastle University, where she is completing a book on the social history of Nowa Huta. Her recent and forthcoming publications include coauthorship of "Forum on Everyday Life: Six Historians in Search of *Alltagsgeschichte,*" in the journal *Aspasia* (2009), and "'We Are Building a Common Home': Destruction, Reconstruction, and the Moral Economy of Citizenship in Postwar Poland," in *Histories of the Aftermath: Postwar Europe in Comparative Perspective,* edited by Frank Biess and Bob Moeller (July 2010). Her current research focuses on Polish International Brigade volunteers in the Spanish civil war.

Josie McLellan is a senior lecturer in modern European history at the University of Bristol. She works on the social and cultural history of East German communism and is currently completing a book entitled *Love in the Time of Communism: Intimacy and Sexuality in the GDR*. Her other publications include *Antifascism and Memory in East Germany* (2004) and articles on nudism and nude photography in the *Journal of Modern History* and *Past and Present*.

Ina Merkel is a professor of European ethnography at Philipps University, Marburg. She has published widely on the culture of East Germany, and her books include *Die Geschichte der Konsumkultur in der DDR* (1999), *Wir sind doch nicht die Meckerecke der Nation* (2000), and *Das kollektiv bin ich* (with Franziska Becker and Simone Tippach-Schneider, 2000). She contributed an essay on the changing meanings of consumption in East Germany to *The Making of the Consumer: Knowledge, Power and Identity in the Modern World*, edited by Frank Trentmann (2006).

Scott Moranda is an assistant professor of history at the State University of New York at Cortland. He received his Ph.D. in 2005 from the University of Wisconsin–Madison and is currently revising a manuscript on tourism and environmentalism in East Germany. His research and teaching interests include consumerism and tourism during the Cold War, as well as global environmental history.

Mary Neuburger received her Ph.D. in history from the University of Washington and is an associate professor in the Department of History at the University of Texas at Austin, where she has taught since 1997. She is the author of *The Orient Within: Muslim Minorities and the Negotiation of Nationhood in Modern Bulgaria* (2004). She is currently working on two book projects, a monograph entitled *Inhaling Modernity: Tobacco Consumption, Commerce and Production in Bulgaria 1856–1989* and a volume coedited with Paulina Bren entitled *Consuming Communism: Cultures of Consumption in Postwar Eastern Europe*.

György Péteri has been a professor of contemporary European history at the Norwegian University of Science and Technology since 1994. He is a graduate of the Karl Marx University of Economics in Budapest, where he also completed his doctorate. He was an affiliate scholar at the Department of Economic History of Uppsala University in Sweden (1980–94). His writings cover the economic history of early socialist regimes, the monetary and financial history of the interwar era, the history of intellectual and cultural life under state socialism, and the sociocultural history of communist elites. His books include *Academia and State Socialism* (1998) and *Global Monetary Regime and National Central Banking* (2002), and he is the editor of *Academia in Upheaval* (with Michael David-Fox, 2000), *Muddling Through in the Long 1960s* (with János M. Rainer, 2005), and *Nylon Curtain* (2006).

Susan E. Reid is Professor of Russian Visual Culture at the University of Sheffield. She has published widely on Soviet art and visual culture, gender, home culture, and consumption, with a focus on the 1950s and 1960s. She is the coeditor with Melanie Ilič and Lynne Attwood of *Women in the Khrushchev Era* (2004), with Polly Blakesley of *Russian Art and the West* (2007), and with David Crowley of *Style and Socialism: Modernity and Material Culture in Post-War Eastern Europe* (2000) and *Socialist Spaces: Sites of Everyday Life in the Eastern Bloc* (2002). She is currently completing a monograph on homemaking, taste, and consumption in standard apartments constructed in the Khrushchev-era Soviet Union.

Kristin Roth-Ey is a lecturer in modern Russian history at the School of Slavonic and East European Studies, University College London. She completed her Ph.D. at Princeton University in 2003. Her first book is a study of the mass culture industries in the postwar Soviet Union entitled *Soviet Culture in the Media Age* (Cornell University Press, 2010).

Anna Tikhomirova is currently finishing her Ph.D. thesis on socialist fashion and the consumption of clothing in the Soviet Union and East Germany between the 1960s and 1980s at the University of Bielefeld. She has published articles on the consumption of clothing from East Germany by Soviet women from the 1960s to the 1980s; on Soviet children's clothing in the 1980s; on clothing culture in the Soviet province of Yaroslavl between the 1960s and 1980s; and on the "Sovietness" of post-Soviet dress. Tikhomirova is currently working on a book provisionally entitled *Russkij Berlin—Deutsches Moskau: Porträts: Vergleich, Beziehungen, Verflechtungen.*

Narcis Tulbure is a doctoral candidate in social anthropology at the University of Pittsburgh. His thesis analyzes the changing notions of money and value in Romania in the period of post-socialist transformation. With an educational background in finance, history, and anthropology, Tulbure has researched the organization of work and leisure during and after the period of socialism in Romania, the production and consumption of alcohol in the "second economy," and the contemporary meanings attached to money in Eastern Europe. Tulbure is currently a lecturer at the Bucharest Academy of Economic Studies.

Larissa Zakharova earned her Ph.D. in history and civilizations from the École des Hautes Études en Sciences Sociales in Paris in 2006 with her thesis "Clothing Soviet: Fashion Under Khrushchev: Transfers, Production, Consumption." She is the author of several articles on Soviet fashion and the Thaw. From 2002 to 2005 she was a lecturer in Soviet history at the Institut des Langues et Civilisations Orientales in Paris, and in 2008 at the Russian State University of Humanities in Moscow.